PRESIDENTIAL PRIMARIES

PRESIDENTIAL PRIMARIES
Road to the White House _____

JAMES W. DAVIS

Contributions in Political Science, Number 41

GREENWOOD PRESS
WESTPORT, CONNECTICUT • LONDON, ENGLAND

Library of Congress Cataloging in Publication Data

Davis, James W   1920-
    Presidential primaries.

    (Contributions in political science ; no. 41
ISSN 0147-1066)
    Bibliography: p.
    Includes index.
    1. Primaries—United States. 2. Presidents—
United States—Election. I. Title. II. Series.
JK522.D3 1980   329'.0223'0973   79-54062
ISBN 0-313-22057-3

Library of Congress Catalog Card Number: 79-54062
ISBN: 0-313-22057-3
ISSN: 0147-1066

First published in 1980

Greenwood Press
A division of Congressional Information Service, Inc.
51 Riverside Avenue, Westport, Connecticut 06880

Printed in the United States of America

10 9 8 7 6 5 4 3 2 1

Contents_____

Tables

Figures

Preface

The first edition of this study, which appeared more than a decade ago, pointed to several new trends in presidential nominating politics: new candidate strategies turning presidential primaries into the dominant force in selecting nominees; the "early-bird" candidacy, formerly considered too risky, becoming distinctly advantageous for enabling the candidate to become better known and helping him gain the inside track to the nomination; the growing influence of polls and network television in singling out the front-runner and winnowing out weak candidates; the displacement of state party leaders and organizations by the presidential candidate's personal campaign organization; and the transformation of the national nominating convention into a ratifying body endorsing the popular favorite of the primaries.

Since 1968, the ever changing U.S. political landscape has shifted almost as much as a Pacific beach. The number of presidential primary states has more than doubled (from fifteen to thirty-three), the percentage of national convention delegates selected in the primary states has jumped from less than one-half to more than three-quarters of all delegates, and the number of pledged delegates has risen proportionately. The spread of the Oregon all-candidate blanket ballot to approximately half the primary states has made it almost impossible for a presidential candidate to remain unannounced and still be considered seriously for the nomination. Congress has authorized federal matching subsidies up to $5 million for each presidential candidate who qualifies by raising a total of $100,000 ($5,000 in each of twenty states in sums of $250 or less) and has further stipulated, in the 1974 Federal Election Campaign Act, that individual campaign contributions must not exceed $1,000, thus eliminating the possibility of a few "fat cats" bankrolling a presidential candidate's entire nominating campaign; Congress has also imposed spending ceilings on mass media expenditures in each primary state to give less financially advantaged candidates a fair chance. Finally, the first-round "open" caucus states, such as Iowa, have begun to attract the same type of national media attention that has made the New Hampshire, Florida, and Wisconsin primaries such important political battle-grounds.

This second edition strives to provide the reader with a comprehensive update of the presidential nominating process in light of the rapid pro-liferation of primaries, the recent precedent-shattering congressional legislation on primary and general election campaign finance, and Demo-cratic party reforms of the convention delegate selection process spawned by the strife-ridden 1968 Democratic convention in Chicago.

An added feature of this new edition is a special chapter on "Polls and Primaries" by James R. Beniger, Princeton University. Shortly before the 1976 primary season, Beniger's article in the *Public Opinion Quarterly* on the dynamics of polls and primaries attracted a national audience. Beniger has generously agreed to incorporate data from the 1976 primaries and other new material into a new chapter 5, and for this I am deeply indebted to him.

Detailed information on state primary laws, especially those statutes approved since the 1976 election, has been made available by Ms. Elaine Kamarck, Executive Director, Compliance Review Commission, Demo-cratic National Committee, Miss Josephine Good, Republican National Committee, and Ms. Carol F. Casey, Congressional Research Service, Library of Congress. Collection of the recent primary election data would not have been possible without the solicitous assistance of secretaries of state and their staffs in the presidential primary states. Ms. Judith L. Corley, Federal Election Commission, has been most helpful in providing up-to-date information on presidential primary campaign finances. *The Congressional Quarterly* has also aided the author in tracking down hard-to-find election data on obscure candidates.

Over the years the author has received frequent encouragement from Professor Austin Ranney, American Enterprise Institute, and has relied heavily on his exhaustive research on presidential primaries. A debt of special gratitude is also owed to Professor Charles H. Backstrom, Uni-versity of Minnesota, whose unfailing counsel has helped the author avoid numerous pitfalls in analyzing the complicated presidential primary system. Professor Steven L. Schier, Wittenberg University, has also offered a number of valuable suggestions to aid the reader in under-standing the intricacies of the presidential nominating process.

One of the most rewarding aspects of my quarter-century involvement in presidential primary politics has been the periodic interaction with members of the national press on the primary campaign trail. No one is more aware of each presidential candidate's strength of character and flaws than members of the traveling press.

Finally, the author wishes to express his personal appreciation to Mrs. Patricia Houtchens and Mrs. Helen Peterson for their tireless assistance in the mechanical preparation of the manuscript, to Dr. James Sabin, Marian Schwartz, and Lynn Taylor for their editorial guidance, and to Western Washington University's Bureau of Faculty Research for underwriting travel costs to observe at first hand presidential primary campaigns in several states. Accountability for any errors of fact or interpretation that may exist, however, rests with the author alone.

PRESIDENTIAL PRIMARIES

The Emerging Influence of _____1
Presidential Primary Politics

The time was 3:00 A.M. in the lobby of the Kanawha Hotel in Charleston, West Virginia. The date was May 11, 1960. Senator John F. Kennedy of Massachusetts had just thanked the happy, milling throng of West Virginians for their support in pushing him to an uphill victory in the Mountaineer State presidential primary against Minnesota's Senator Hubert H. Humphrey.

As the young Bostonian departed the hotel for his plane and another round of presidential primary campaigning in Maryland, the defeated Senator Humphrey was bidding a tearful farewell to his workers at his own state headquarters, also in Charleston. Earlier in the evening, Humphrey had announced to the press and television cameras his withdrawal from the presidential nominating race. Humphrey had become another victim of the survival-of-the-fittest warfare that now characterizes presidential nominating campaigns in the United States.

Kennedy's smashing victory in the West Virginia Democratic presidential primary was not just another election. More than anything else, the 1960 West Virginia primary established Kennedy as the popular favorite and opened the road to the Democratic presidential nomination at the Los Angeles convention and ultimately to a brief and tragic occupancy of the White House. In the hills of West Virginia, an overwhelmingly Protestant state with only 6 percent of the voters listed as Roman Catholic, Senator Kennedy had laid to rest the religious issue that had been haunting him throughout his pre-convention campaign. Kennedy had proved to the skeptical, uncommitted, big-city Democratic leaders—a power bloc which at that time still heavily influenced the choice of party nominee—that he was the type of vote-getting candidate needed to sweep the party to victory in November.

Presidential nominating campaigns would never be the same again. Indeed, what happened in the 1960 presidential primary duels between Kennedy and Humphrey—the all-out drive to win a single state primary, marked by repeated personal visits to the state, town-to-town campaigning, countless bean feeds and ox roasts, evening receptions, and widespread use of TV and radio advertising—marked a breakthrough in presidential nominating politics.

Growing Importance of Primaries

Since World War II a gradual transformation in the process of nominating presidential candidates has been taking place in the United States. Presidential primary elections have now become the crucial factor in capturing the nomination of the out-of-power party. Within the past decade the number of states using the primary has doubled from fifteen to 33 and there are indications that this figure may be even higher by the beginning of the 1980 primary season. According to the 1970 census, total population of states using some form of presidential primary exceeds 167 million, or more than double the population of presidential primary states in 1968. (See Table 1.1.) The 1980 census figures are expected to show an even higher percentage of the nation's population in the primary states.

The percentage of national convention delegates chosen in the primaries jumped from less than 38 percent in 1968, to 60 percent in 1972, and rose to more than 72 percent before the 1976 nominating race opened. The remaining 28 percent of the convention delegates are selected through a multi-tiered system of party caucuses and conventions. (See Table 1.2.)

In less than two decades the formerly dominant power of caucus-convention delegate states has declined to a relatively minor influence at the national convention. Most of the 17 caucus-convention states are now found in the thinly populated West Central, Southwest, and Great Basin states. All twelve of the largest states—California, New York, Pennsylvania, Texas, Illinois, Ohio, Michigan, New Jersey, Florida, Massachusetts, Indiana and North Carolina—now use presidential primaries. In 1976 these twelve states had a delegate total of 1,745 in the Democratic party, more than 58 percent of the national convention vote. Within the GOP the total number of delegates from these states, however, totaled only 48 percent of the GOP convention, chiefly because the present GOP delegate apportionment formula favors the smaller, less populous states. Table 1.1 shows the twelve big primary states having a combined electoral vote of 285, fifteen more than the majority needed to elect a president.

With this kind of concentrated political firepower presidential contenders naturally focus major attention on these "battleground" states in both the nominating and general elections campaigns. Indeed, with almost four-fifths (in 1980) of all national convention delegates up for grabs in the primary states, presidential contenders must of necessity

TABLE 1.1
POPULATION AND ELECTORAL COLLEGE VOTES OF
PRESIDENTIAL PRIMARY STATES, 1970 CENSUS

State	Population	National Ranking	Electoral Vote
California	19,953,134	1	45
New York	18,190,740	2	41
Pennsylvania	11,793,909	3	27
Texas	11,196,730	4	26
Illinois	11,113,976	5	26
Ohio	10,652,017	6	25
Michigan	8,875,083	7	21
New Jersey	7,168,164	8	17
Florida	6,789,443	9	17
Massachusetts	5,689,170	10	14
Indiana	5,193,669	11	13
North Carolina	5,082,059	12	13
Georgia	4,589,575	15	12
Wisconsin	4,417,933	16	11
Tennessee	3,924,164	17	10
Maryland	3,922,399	18	10
Louisiana	3,643,180	20	10
Alabama	3,444,165	21	9
Kentucky	3,219,311	23	9
Connecticut	3,032,217	24	8
Kansas	2,249,071	28	7
Oregon	2,091,835	31	6
Arkansas	1,923,295	32	6
West Virginia	1,744,237	34	6
Nebraska	1,483,791	35	5
New Mexico	1,016,000	38	4
Rhode Island	949,723	39	4
New Hampshire	737,681	41	4
Idaho	713,008	42	4
Montana	694,409	43	4
South Dakota	666,257	44	4
Nevada	488,738	47	3
Vermont	444,732	48	3
	167,450,635		424

Source: The World Almanac and Book of Facts, 1978 edition: copyright ©, Newspaper Enterprise Association, New York, New York, 1977, pp. 188 and 191; and U.S. Congress, Senate, *Nomination and Election of the President and Vice President of the United States Including the Manner of Selecting Delegates to National Political Conventions,* compiled under the direction of Francis R. Valeo, Secretary of the Senate, for the U.S. Senate Library (Washington, D.C.: Government Printing Office, 1976), pp. 402-03.

TABLE 1.2
NUMBER OF DELEGATES CHOSEN OR BOUND BY
PRESIDENTIAL PRIMARIES, 1968-80

Democratic party	1968	1972	1976	1980
Number of primary states	17	23	29	33
Number of votes cast by delegates chosen or bound by primaries	983	1,862	2,183	2,700
Percent of all votes cast by delegates chosen or bound by primaries	37.5	60.5	72.6	81.3
Republican party				
Number of primary states	16	22	28*	32*
Number of votes cast by delegates chosen or bound by primaries	458	710	1,533	1,507
Percent of all votes cast by delegates chosen or bound by primaries	34.3	52.7	67.9	75.6

Source: Congressional Quarterly Weekly Report XXXIV, January 31, 1976, pp. 225-42; *XXVII,* August 4, 1979, p. 1612.
*Does not include Vermont, which held a non-binding presidential preference poll but chose all delegates by caucus convention.

contest for these large blocs of delegates—unless they wish to bank all their hopes on a deadlocked convention and pray they can become the convention's compromise choice.

Transformation of the Nominating Process

Two all-but-forgotten presidential candidates, Harold E. Stassen in 1948 and Estes Kefauver in 1952 and 1956, were the first to conclude that if they were ever to reach the White House they would have to follow the primary route. Probably this was the only avenue open to Stassen in the Republican party and Kefauver in the Democratic party, since they both lacked the needed delegate support from party chieftains in the then thirty-five caucus-convention states and those states with advisory primaries. By taking their candidacies directly to the people in the primary states, Stassen and Kefauver established the precedent that all leading presidential contenders in the out-of-power party since have emulated, namely, that the presidential primary route is the road to the White House.

The campaign tactics of Stassen and Kefauver also suggested that the hazard of the "early bird" candidacy, of being the marked man, was not necessarily a handicap. Conventional wisdom had held that the early front-runner became fair game to every favorite son and dark horse candidate anxious to create a convention stalemate. With a convention deadlock, such a candidate might then become the compromise nominee or a vice-presidential running mate, or pry some special post-election concessions from the nominee. In this age of mass communications, however, the early announced candidate finds it much easier to become visible and identified by the average voter. The rise of presidential primaries, public opinion polls, and network television now enable the front-runner to capitalize on his popularity to enhance his position as the leading contender for the nomination. George McGovern formally announced for the presidency in January 1971, almost eighteen months before the 1972 Democratic convention, and Jimmy Carter declared his 1976 candidacy in December 1974, nineteen months before the 1976 New York City convention. Generally, this early start helps the candidate get airborne in the primaries. Developing a winning image early on helps attract financial support for a contender. Considering the high start-up costs of presidential primary campaigning, the importance of looking like a winner early in the game should not be underestimated. Midway in the 1976 primary season Senator Frank Church (D, Ida.), one of Carter's rivals for the Democratic nomination, sought to portray Jimmy Carter's front-runner position in the darkest terms. "He's trying to lead a wagon train through a series of mountain passes," said the Idaho senator, "and there's a different candidate waiting to ambush him at each one."[1] But in real life it was the favorite sons, regional candidates, and the late entrants, such as Senator Church, who could do nothing more than resort to sporadic, ineffective guerrilla attacks against the front-running Carter.

In the past two decades candidates in the losing party have begun campaigning in the out-of-power party shortly after the presidential election. Presidential campaigning has become a year-in, year-out activity, with no off season. For the Democrats, the newly established midterm convention in 1974 heightened the growing interest in the presidential nominating process. Although this mini-convention was held more than a year before the opening of the 1976 primary season, all of the major candidates—announced and unannounced—were on hand to greet the delegates and make an early pitch for their support. With Democratic President Jimmy Carter in the White House two years later, however, the 1978 Democratic midterm conference in Memphis, Tennessee, lost some of its utility as a showcase for presidential aspirants because incumbent presidents do not relish the thought of building up the political stock of potential intraparty competitors. Even so, Senator Edward M. "Ted" Kennedy nearly stole the show from Carter with a rousing speech in favor of national health insurance at one of the conference panels. The

Republicans do not hold midterm conferences, but in the meantime, as the out-of-power party until 1980, and perhaps longer, the GOP can be expected to devise new ways of publicizing its early starting candidates and of maintaining pressure on the Democrats during the period between elections—at least until they recapture the presidency. There can be little doubt that we are now seeing the gradual emergence of another American political phenomenon: the continuous four-year presidential nominating campaign.

It is hardly an exaggeration to say that the candidates themselves have also turned the presidential primaries into a form of "plebiscitary" democracy. Front-running candidates, such as General Dwight D. Eisenhower, John F. Kennedy, Richard Nixon and outsider candidates George McGovern and Jimmy Carter, have all used hard-won victories in the primaries to persuade their rivals and the uncommitted delegates that they are the top choice of rank-and-file voters. This transmutation of the presidential primary into a gigantic popularity contest is a far cry from the original plan of the Progressives to take the convention decision making out of the hands of political bosses and put it into the hands of the people, acting through their popularly elected delegates. Ironically, this transformation of the primary system into a mass popularity contest was originally made possible by the generally conservative-oriented, anti-party leaders in the years immediately following the 1912 Bull Moose Party revolt. These opponents of the presidential primary successfully watered down the delegate pledge to an "advisory mandate" in several big states in order to reserve the power of making the presidential nomination for themselves. But since the 1950s, party leaders have stood by helplessly as they have watched their power to select presidential nominees gradually be whittled away by the emergence of preferential primaries, "beauty contests" among the leading candidates, and the rapid growth of mandatory primaries, in which more and more delegates run pledged to specific candidates. No longer can the party insiders' hand-picked choice, a favorite son, or a "dark horse" expect to receive the nomination. These marginal candidates have been swept aside by candidates who have demonstrated their vote-getting strength and personal popularity in the primaries.

Over the past three decades, it seems clear, the presidential selection machinery gradually has been transformed from a closed, "insider" system to a popular, "outsider" selection process. In other words, the old-fashioned national convention in which the party's most mature, experienced and respected leaders pick the "best-qualified" candidate, with due consideration to all factions and interest groups, has been displaced by a national convention dominated by popularly elected and mandated delegates chosen in thirty-three state presidential primaries.

Instead of nominating choices being negotiated by state party leaders in "smoke-filled rooms" and then endorsed on the convention floor by leader-controlled state delegations, rank-and-file voters in the primary states now ignore the party leader preferences and instruct their delegates to vote for the popular national favorites, as determined in the primaries. With rare exceptions, the prospective nominee in each of the major parties is now clearly identified by the voters in the primary states and national media several weeks before the delegates flock to the convention city.

Since 1956, all presidential nominees in the out-of-power party, with the possible exception of Senator Barry Goldwater in 1964, have by virtue of victories in key primaries won nomination on the first ballot. Presidential candidates of the out-of-power party must face the stark reality that there is no longer any "safe" course, such as the unannounced candidacy and "waiting game" strategy of yesteryear, to winning the nomination. They must contest for delegates in the primaries to prove their national popularity or risk political oblivion. The same dynamic forces operating on candidates in the out-of-power party foreshadow the strong possibility of more intraparty challenges to first-term incumbents. More will be said about incumbent challenges in Chapter 7.

Primaries Assume Major Function of National Conventions

Officially, presidential nominees of the two major parties are still nominated by delegates to national party conventions, just as they have been for more than 140 years. But over the past three decades presidential primaries have, in effect, taken over the latent functions of convention balloting. In the traditional national nominating convention, multiple ballots served the function of informing delegates about the relative delegate strength of the various contenders and of pointing to the likely nominee. In recent years, however, this balloting or informing function has, in fact, been usurped by the presidential primaries.[2] Unlike the typical four-day national conventions, presidential primaries are held over four months. Winning a single primary is not sufficient to sweep the nomination. Instead, candidates can acquire only a percentage of delegates in each state. Building a majority of delegates to win the nomination is a slow, incremental process. Delegates chosen over the 105-day period from the New Hampshire to California primary are much less susceptible to the bandwagon psychology that in the past sometimes enabled a "favorite son" or "dark horse" candidate to stampede the convention. Primaries offer far more latitude and opportunity for convention delegates and the general public to assess the "presidential" qualities of the candidates. If the primary returns do not point to a clear-cut winner, the delegates always have the standby option to use the convention as a "brokering" agency for arriving at a compromise choice. But in point of fact the national convention over the past two decades has declined from a decision-making body into a ceremonial institution which merely serves as a plebiscitary mechanism to legitimatize the popular favorite. The convention then automatically transmutes itself into a coronation to anoint the party nominee. Within a single generation presidential primaries have, in effect, transformed the national convention from a deliberative body into a ratifying assembly. The convention decision has become, in one observer's words, "a symbolic culmination of a process that began much earlier and whose decisive stages occurred long before."[3] More will be said about this phenomenon later.

Powerful Impact of Television

The television revolution has also spread to the presidential primaries. Over the past two decades presidential contenders and their managers have all concluded that presidential nominating races simply cannot be conducted successfully without using the national media, especially television, to communicate with voters in the primary states. Before the 1976 campaign season opened, Gerald Rafshoon, Jimmy Carter's media advisor, summed the situation up this way: "The media is an extension of the campaign." One campaign manager has gone even further: "The media is the campaign."[4] Richard Rubin, a perceptive observer of contemporary political parties, has noted,

The development of television, for example, has provided lesser-known challengers, shunned by established party leaders, with a quick and effective way to gain recognition among the party's mass electorate. And as a result, the rapid development of modern communications techniques together with the decline of patronage-supported organizational workers have shattered the near monopoly over campaign resources once maintained by local machines in primary competition.[5]

To win over the national media's opinion makers and become better known has therefore become the top priority of presidential aspirants. As Chris Arterton has put it, "Name recognition has become a critical ingredient in the calculus of electability."[6]

The rapid growth of primaries in the past decade has also complicated the presidential contenders' task of trying to reach large numbers of voters in the primary states. The only way this can be done is to rely almost exclusively upon the national media. Consequently, campaign operatives develop media strategies to build candidate visibility and needed press coverage. As Arterton has observed, "Campaigners take the view that the press corps constitutes an alternative electorate within which they must campaign simultaneously with their efforts to gather votes."[7] Moreover, federal limitations on campaign spending (for the first time in 1976) made it more imperative than ever that the candidate turn to the national and local media as early as possible to reach—without cost to the candidate's treasury—the voting public and uncommitted delegates.

This frantic concern to obtain early media coverage is understandable because of the overwhelming attention given to the winners and losers in the early primaries and caucuses. Candidates know they must build a quick record of success or risk political oblivion. The 1976 nominating campaign in the out-of-power Democratic party provides ample documentation for the crucial importance of early media coverage.

Before the primary season officially opened in January 1976, the only rank ordering of candidates in the Democratic party available to the general public was a Gallup Poll, conducted in October 1975. As shown in Table 1.3, at this early stage, the 1976 Democratic race was wide open. As it turned out, three of the six top Democratic contenders on this preference list and Senator Edward M. Kennedy did not even enter the 1976 presidential sweepstakes at all. Notably missing from this list is the name of Jimmy Carter, then still a political unknown. Generally, during this pre-primary period all of the candidates, announced or unannounced, are in a holding pattern, since they cannot hope to do much to improve their standings in the opinion polls—or the delegate count—until the January caucuses and the early primaries. Public opinion polls, as a matter of fact, are of little utility until the electorates in the

TABLE 1.3

DEMOCRATIC PRESIDENTIAL PREFERENCE POLL,
OCTOBER 1975

Candidate	Preference Percentage
Humphrey	23
Wallace	19
Jackson	11
McGovern	9
Muskie	9
Shriver	8
All others	9
No opinion	12

Source: Gallup Opinion Index, no. 125 (November-December 1975): 38-39.

primary states begin passing judgment on the various contenders. But the candidates and their handlers are busy putting their campaign organizations together and cultivating the national press corps and the local media in the key primary and caucus-convention states. New Hampshire becomes a Mecca for presidential candidates. Ranking forty-first in population, New Hampshire offers candidates one of the last opportunities in the United States to practice "retail politics," the one-on-one, personal contact between the presidential candidate and the individual voter at the local town hall, drug store, small shoe factory, or even citizen's living room. In the twelve-month period from December 1974 to December 1975, for example, Jimmy Carter visited this New England state fourteen times. Representative Morris Udall, the first to make a bid for New Hampshire votes, made sixteen trips to the state between August 1974 and December 1975. The early caucus-convention states also attract most of the announced candidates; Jimmy Carter in his 1976 drive for the presidency spent a total of seventeen days campaigning in Iowa, the first state to hold precinct caucuses. In the meantime, the national media are developing their rating systems on the presidential contenders. Like bookmakers, the national press quote the odds on candidates as 8 to 1, 20 to 1, 50 to 1, and so on; or they may categorize the candidates in gridiron terms, such as "varsity," "junior varsity," or "taxi squad," or some similar rating system. During this long waiting period before the first caucuses and primaries, the national media become the chief handicappers of candidates. This process of separating the serious contenders from the marginal candidates—described as "the invisible primary" by Arthur Hadley—has only recently begun to attract the attention it deserves.[8] Clearly, the national media have more influence than anybody else in determining which aspirants emerge at the beginning of the presidential election year as "the generally recognized major contenders."

Television, with its insatiable demand for exciting and confrontational news, thrives on presidential nominating politics. Primary campaigns have become a great media story because they have a built-in plot, a cast of exciting characters, and a winner and loser. In the minds of television network executives, presidential primaries have become a new form of political Olympics. Throughout the fifteen-week primary season the networks frequently devote upwards to one-third of their evening newscasts to presidential candidates and their primary campaigns.[9] Indeed, coverage throughout the primaries frequently exceeds the general election coverage because there are so many primaries and candidates to follow and the intraparty competition is so intense. All three networks interrupt their late evening entertainment programs to broadcast the election returns of the key primaries. Election headquarters are often established in the biggest city or the state capital as well as the network headquarters in New York City. Just as in the general election, the networks' leading news commentators—Walter Cronkite, John Chancellor, David Brinkley, and Frank Reynolds—analyze the primary returns. After each primary the commentators determine the standing of the major candidates, tabulate their delegates, and label them as front-runners or also-rans. Judgments by the electronic journalists significantly affect candidates' chances in future primaries. Keech and Matthews, among others, have pointed out that the national media make vital judgments on the rank-order standing of candidates. "If the mass communications media do not pay attention to a person he has no chance of becoming president. . . . The media's picture of the world matters more than the reality."[10]

All three networks, using key precinct voting data and electronic computers, also attempt to predict the state primary winner long before all the returns are in. With more than thirty state primaries to cover, the networks put their reputations on the line virtually every Tuesday night from late February to early June in projecting the "winner" soon after the polls close. Indeed, so anxious was CBS to "scoop" its network rivals in the 1964 California Republican primary that the network announced its projected "winner" thirty-eight minutes before some of the polls closed in northern California! This "call" was made with only 2 percent of the returns on the tally board. Regarding the intense network competition, there was more than an element of truth in one TV executive's comment on the 1964 California primary: "As far as we're concerned this thing isn't between Goldwater and Rockefeller, it's between CBS and NBC."[11] This heavy network coverage, in turn, generates further public interest in the presidential selection process.

Presidential nominating contests also continue to receive heavy coverage from the wire services, the daily press, and the mass-circulation magazines. Presidential candidates dominate front-page coverage for weeks before the primary season opens, and this coverage continues through the national conventions and the general election campaign. As one commentator has noted, "the early caucuses and primaries are seen as the first 'hard news' stories of the presidential race, a perception which almost guarantees an inflated value placed on the results of these events."[12] Twice during a key nine-week period of the 1976 primaries the new Democratic front-runner, Jimmy Carter, made the covers of both *Time* and *Newsweek*. President Ford and Governor Ronald Reagan matched Carter cover-for-cover and page-for-page during most of this period. Indeed, Reagan, a former Hollywood star, frequently outdistanced the president and Carter in the publicity generated.

As soon as the primary season begins to heat up, several dozen network reporters, camera crews, and reporters from the wire services and the

country's leading newspapers begin barnstorming with the major candidates on their chartered jets. The national press corps have also become
an integral part of the primary campaign in another unanticipated way:
it is the airfare chargebacks (one and one-half first-class fare rate) assessed
each media representative that defray most of the cost of the candidate's
chartered airplanes.

Though less prominent than television coverage, the continued heavy
impact of radio news coverage during the primaries should not be ignored
either. Over 300 million radios are now in use in the United States, carry-
ing hourly newscasts about the candidates' round robin contests in the
primaries.

Over the years the mass media have served a variety of functions in
presidential nominating races: publicizing and furnishing commentary
on the leading candidates, ranking the various candidates' chances of
winning the nomination as well as analyzing the outcome of the primary
races, and keeping a boxscore on each candidate's delegate count. Contrast this flood of news and public interest with the limited impact that
daily and small weekly newspapers had on nominations in years past.
Before the advent of radio and television, presidential candidates did
not campaign personally in the primaries, preferring instead the "front
porch" type of campaign popularized by William McKinley shortly
before the turn of the century.

As late as 1932, Governor Franklin D. Roosevelt conducted a traditional front porch nominating campaign. Throughout the spring of 1932
he handled his New York state business at the capitol in Albany and
then returned to his Hyde Park estate to receive delegations from the
various states. His opponent, President Hoover, remained at the White
House trying valiantly, but ineffectively, to pull the country out of the
Great Depression and occasionally meeting state GOP delegations in the
weeks before the GOP convention. Traditionally, presidential challengers
maintained this same low profile before the convention. Since the bulk of
the delegates were selected in the caucus-convention states, and because
the candidate did not want to appear to be blatantly seeking the office
and hustling delegates, the presidential candidates relied heavily on their
"drummers"—fieldmen who traveled from state to state—to round up
delegates and reach "understandings" with state party leaders. While the
candidates' staffers were out recruiting delegates, the small Washington
press corps remained camped in the nation's capital until convention
time and then relaxed during the balance of the humid summer before
they joined the candidate's (or the president's) whistle-stop campaign
special in the fall. Life moved at a much slower pace. There was no morning
press conference for the television cameramen to shoot footage for the

evening newscast; no radio news spot items every hour on the hour; no media entourage searching for a special "scoop" or human interest story. Newspaper publishers, ever watchful of their profit ledgers, would have taken a dim view of heavy travel expense accounts from reporters when all the news could be picked up from the wire service. The leading news magazines, *Time* and *Newsweek,* did not even exist, and their predecessors did not engage in frantic search for hot copy. Under the formerly dominant caucus-convention nominating system the candidate's survival did not depend upon his exposure in the mass media, and newspaper editors did not feel that their professional reputation rested upon filling the front page with the latest events from the primary front.

New Political Barometers: The Opinion Polls

Public opinion polls, still in their infancy when World War II began, have become sensitive political barometers in presidential nominating races. Except for a brief loss of confidence after the polls incorrectly predicted that Governor Thomas E. Dewey would defeat President Harry S Truman in the 1948 general election, the polls have become a pervasive force in the selection of presidential candidates. Party leaders and convention delegates watch the nationally circulated polls with hawk-like vigilance. Since the national convention delegates in many caucus-convention states still rely on their own impressions or those of their party leaders in selecting the nominee, the polls serve as an important source of political information. Long before convention time the polls single out the front-runner or show nip-and-tuck races between the leading contenders and expose the poor vote-getters. Failure to run well in the polls is fatal to a candidate.[13]

In the age of primaries, private polls can be as valuable to a presidential candidate as a campaign manager. Senator John F. Kennedy first popularized the use of private polls in the primaries. His pollster, Louis Harris, made a political reputation for both his client and himself during the 1960 Democratic primaries. Since then, leading presidential candidates in both parties have regularly used pollsters to sift out the key issues and map campaign strategy. In the final 1964 California primary round, for example, Senator Goldwater's private pollster, Thomas W. Benham, of Opinion Research Corporation, found that Republican voters were most concerned about foreign policy, especially Cuba and South Vietnam. Consequently, Goldwater hit these issues hardest in his successful California campaign against Governor Nelson Rockefeller. This carefully conceived strategy was mapped long before the earlier Oregon primary and was kept intact despite Goldwater's loss to Rockefeller in that state.

Four years later, former Vice President Nixon hired his own polling organization for the primary campaign. The pollster, according to Nixon's managers, was asked to find the issues most appealing to the electorate.[14]

Polls can be taken long in advance and used to "program" the candidate's primary campaign. Another function of a survey expert, according to Patrick H. Caddell, Jimmy Carter's favorite pollster, is to assess accurately a candidate's "potential," especially if he starts low in the polls. For longshot candidates like Jimmy Carter and George McGovern, the ability to assess this potential is a vital necessity. In 1972, for example, Senator McGovern relied heavily on Caddell, then only twenty-two years old, to help him chart the pre-convention drive that carried him from obscurity to the Democratic nomination. But Caddell subsequently discovered that he had joined a losing cause when McGovern lost 49 out of 50 states in the November election. Less than three years later, Caddell signed up with another Democratic outsider candidate, Jimmy Carter. As the only experienced national campaigner in Carter's inner circle, Caddell exercised a major influence on Carter's campaign strategy. Caddell's early polling, for example, showed that Carter could expect a strong support from black voters, a crucial factor in Carter's winning strategy. Hamilton Jordan, Carter's campaign manager and later a top White House advisor, has given Caddell much of the credit for Carter's upset victory over Wallace in Florida. "I doubt we would have won Florida without Pat," said Mr. Jordan. The young pollster, according to Jordan, not only reinforced their own tactical calculations with his accurate data but also showed them where to concentrate their resources in the primary that destroyed Wallace as a serious rival for the 1976 nomination. In some primary states Caddell's sophisticated polling operation was conducted on virtually a daily basis to help Carter maximize his campaign time and resources. As Caddell himself observed, "Day to day life and death decisions for a candidate are really made on where you can put his time, resources, and money effectively and not waste them."[15]

Presidential contenders, it seems fairly clear, have come to depend far more on private polling organizations than on the widely circulated public polls, such as the Gallup and Harris polls. Indeed, it is highly unlikely that a presidential candidate will ever venture into future primary campaigns again without a trusted private pollster at his side.

Delegates and the general electorate rely on public opinion polls to see how a specific candidate is running against his intraparty rivals as well as leading contenders (or an incumbent president) in the opposition party. Although the polls chart the general progress in the nominating campaign, they do not tell the candidate or the public how many delegates he has. This is not necessary, since his own delegate counters can furnish him with this vital information. But the polls do show his popular standing relative to his intraparty rivals. The Gallup polls cited in Table 1.4, for example, reflect Jimmy Carter's steady rise in nationwide popularity during the 1976 pre-convention race.

TABLE 1.4
JIMMY CARTER'S GALLUP POLL RATINGS,
NOVEMBER 1975 TO JUNE 1976

1975	1976					
November	*January*	*February 27*	*March 16*	*April 3*	*May 24*	*June*
2%	4%	12%	27%	30%	35%	53%

Source: Gallup Opinion Index, no. 133 (August 1976): 6-7.

Because the Gallup (and Harris) polls have come to be considered reliable barometers of candidate popularity, all presidential contenders make it one of their key pre-convention objectives to gain the top spot in the poll ratings. If the candidate is doing well in the polls, it is a foregone conclusion that he is doing well in the primaries. If, conversely, the candidate cannot break out of the "also-ran" category in the Gallup polls after the first few weeks of the primary season, his candidacy is destined to fail. In early April 1976, for example, Senator Henry Jackson, who had been traveling for three years on the political circuit trying to move into a front-running spot in the Gallup poll, suffered the acute embarrassment of dropping to fifth place (7 percent) behind California Governor Edmund G. "Jerry" Brown (9 percent), who had entered the race only two weeks earlier. Mr. Brown also ran well ahead of Representative Morris Udall (4 percent) and former Senator Fred Harris (1 percent), both of whom had been campaigning hard for more than a full year. These low poll ratings told in simple numbers midway in the primary season that Jackson, Udall and Harris were for all practical purposes finished insofar as winning the 1976 nomination was concerned.

Nationalization of American Politics

There is still another aspect of the nominating process that cannot be ignored. Politics are becoming "nationalized," that is, there has been a fairly steady extension of the two-party system into traditionally one-party states since the end of World War II. Austin Ranney, basing a statistical study exclusively on state office elections—that is, for governor, house of representatives, state senate, and a combined tabulation of all three offices—lists twenty-three states as competitively two-party states. His study covered elections between 1962 and 1973.[16]

This steady trend toward a two-party structure, in turn, has weakened sectional influence. The "solid South" has vanished for the Democrats in presidential races; the GOP has captured almost as many states in the South as the Democrats since 1948. Democrats, on the other hand, have won the governorships in the traditional GOP strongholds of Maine, North Dakota and Nebraska. South Dakota, the third most Republican state in the country (according to Ranney's calculation), had in 1972 a Democratic governor and two Democratic U.S. Senators. Throughout the country, shifts in voting strength have created the possibility of periodic change of party in the White House. Between 1933 and 1961, three presidents—Roosevelt, Truman and Eisenhower—held office for the equivalent of seven four-year terms. Since then, five presidents— Kennedy, Johnson, Nixon, Ford and Carter—have been in office for the equivalent of just over four four-year terms. Also, presidential politics have become highly competitive. Between 1948 and 1976 each major party has won four presidential elections. No wonder the competition for the presidential nomination within each party has intensified. Under these circumstances it requires no crystal ball to predict that with 33 states now using presidential primaries, White House aspirants will follow this route as they try to lock up the nomination before convention time with outstanding vote-getting performances in the primaries.

The nationalization of presidential competition does not mean, at least not yet, the development of strong national party organizations. To be sure, the Democratic National Committee has decreed proportional representation for the election of national convention delegates and has endeavored to shorten the delegate selection process from about six months to three months (a period known as the "window"), and the Democratic National Convention has banned winner-take-all primaries. But these actions have not shifted the power structure within the party significantly. Equally important, the Republican party has been disinclined to strengthen its national organization. Except for basic guidelines, the Republican National Committee has traditionally maintained a hands-off policy on all but the most essential aspects of the national convention delegate selection process. Nearly all important decisions are left to state parties or state law. Indeed, under long-standing GOP party rules no major changes in the delegate selection process (or any other aspect of national-state-party relationships) can be made except by the Republican National Convention—an institution controlled by the state parties.

Declining Influence of State Parties

Veteran party observers are generally agreed that the extension of presidential primaries has contributed further to the "decomposition" of state parties. Gerald Pomper, speaking of the declining influence of the state parties at national conventions, has noted, "The state party as a distinct organization is not accorded a legitimate role. It does not choose the delegates, it cannot operate as a unified delegation on the convention floor and, indeed, it has almost no ability to bargain over the presidential nomination at all."[17] Once a state legislature adopts a presidential primary, the party organizations become little more than administrators of the national convention delegate selection process, especially within the Democratic party. Thus, in primary states using proportional representation, delegates are usually chosen by the parties only *after* the primary results have mandated how they will vote.

As primaries continue to displace congressional district and state party conventions in selecting national convention delegates, the state parties may become the ghost towns of American politics. With state parties no longer serving as bargaining agents beween its supporters in the electorate and its elected officials, the business of nominating presidents may come to be viewed purely as the decisions of "a collectivity of individuals."[18] Under this doctrine, delegates owe their allegiance to the voters, not the party. Party interference with judgments of the voting public in the primaries is viewed as undemocratic interference with the nominating process. After all, under the prevailing democratic ethos of our society it is the vote of the individual citizen that counts. The extension of mandatory primaries, which require delegates to vote in accordance with the verdict of the primary election, and the determination to make each vote count through proportional representation, however, has a plebiscitary tone. By forcing state parties out to the presidential nominating process, the parties will no longer be able to hold nominees accountable, if elected. This ominous trend, unless further expansion of the presidential primary movement is halted, will push us further down the path toward a new form of plebiscitary democracy. With this potential threat in mind, an underlying theme of this study will be a renewed defense of the existing "mixed" system of mandatory and advisory presidential primaries and caucus-conventions for choosing the party nominees for president of the United States.

Emergence of Personal Campaign Organizations

The declining influence of traditional party groupings—state party leaders, county chairpersons, and delegation power blocs—in presidential nominating races has been hastened by the fact that the prime means whereby most voters derive their information about candidates are the mass media. This, in turn, has led to the emergence of self-sufficient, nationwide candidate organizations called into being by a nominating process that requires presidential hopefuls to mount long, far-flung campaigns. The Kennedy for President, President Richard Nixon's Committee to Re-elect the President (CREEP), the Carter for President and the President Ford committees are the best known examples of huge, personalized campaign organizations. As noted by one veteran party watcher, "The modern candidate organization is an arsenal replete with all the skills and weapons of modern political combat: speechwriters, advance men, pollsters, public relations specialists, media consultants, fund raisers, computerized voter lists and experts in targeting a general staff with lieutenants in every state."[19] In less than a generation these entrepreneurial candidate organizations have drastically altered the strategic environment in which presidential nominees are selected.

As a result of the new sophisticated political technology—polls, computerized mailings, telephone banks and TV advertising—and new campaign finance legislation, presidential candidate dependence on state and local party organizations for electoral success has been reduced to nearly zero. Even when state parties cast aside their traditional neutrality during the primary race to support a specific presidential candidate, the pervasive reach of television has eliminated candidate dependence upon the party to serve as an intermediary between the voter and the candidate. The parties' role has in effect been taken over by candidate organizations. Moreover, candidate organizations are far more efficient than most present-day state and local party organizations. In 1972, for example, George McGovern's personal campaign organization recruited a virtual army of door-to-door canvassers, totaling almost 50,000 persons in California. Four years later, scores of Georgians—the "Peanut Brigade"— traveled to New Hampshire to ring doorbells for Jimmy Carter, while several hundred Michiganians went to Florida to campaign door to door for home state President Gerald Ford.

Polling data, obtained by hired professionals, provides the presidential candidate and his managers with information on the electorate far more accurate than that available from local leaders. Computerized, targeted mailing lists and direct mail solicitation enable presidential candidates to raise large amounts of cash independently of the party. For example, the Washington, D.C.-based conservative direct mail expert, Richard A. Viguerie, who has raised huge sums of money for George Wallace, Philip M. Crane, and John Connally, is reputed to control a mailing list of 4 million political conservatives.

Since late 1974, matching federal grants to candidates in the presidential primaries have fostered far greater candidate self-sufficiency than ever before. Already the new federal campaign subsidies have meant a major shift of money, the most vital resource in politics, from political parties to presidential candidates. With more than one-third of their campaign money now furnished by Uncle Sam, White House aspirants can pour these federal subsidies into their own personal campaign organizations. Candidates are thus in a position to appeal directly to the voters and special constituencies via the mass media, especially in the primary states, without ever bothering to make political alliances with governors or local party organizations. It is illustrative that in the 1976 Democratic nominating race Jimmy Carter, relying almost exclusively on his own personal organization, did not have the endorsement of a single governor in the early phases of his campaign. On the last day of the primaries (June 6)— one month before the national convention—Carter had only six gubernatorial endorsements.[20]

Independent candidate organizations also seem to blend in well with the growing independent voting preferences of the U.S. electorate. Only one of every five or six voters was classified an independent in the 1950s, but today a 33 to 40 percent are independent.[21] With candidate-directed campaign organizations drumming up popular support and with such a large independent voter constituency, who needs a political party?

The rise of multifaceted candidate organizations is a direct consequence of a transformation in the presidential nominating process that makes it necessary for a candidate to win a majority of the primaries, capture "open" precinct caucuses and rank high in the polls if he expects to win the nomination. When presidential nominees were selected by a congressional caucus and by national conventions dominated by state and local party "bosses," an independent, self-sufficient campaign organization was not needed or required. But, as Jeane Kirkpatrick recently observed, "our own history and that of other democracies suggests that the emergence of powerful candidate organizations is a necessary institutional by-product of popular participation in the nominating process."[22] In the past two decades the operation of powerful candidates' organizations interacting with the presidential primaries, nationwide television and the printed media, and national opinion polls have become integral parts of the presidential nominating process.

As the kick-off dates for starting a White House drive keep being pushed inexorably further and further ahead of the New Hampshire presidential primary and the early state precinct caucuses—by late March 1979, Representative Philip Crane of Illinois, the first announced GOP candidate for the 1980 nomination, had visited New Hampshire twenty times and Senator Robert Dole, an unannounced candidate, had made fifteen visits—the emergence of special campaign committees will continue to proliferate.

POLITICAL ACTION COMMITTEES

The latest campaign invention for the unannounced presidential candidate is the Political Action Committee (PAC). Almost unnoticed, PACs have suddenly mushroomed into a major force in presidential nominating politics during the pre-primary phase. Formed ostensibly to promote the fortunes of party office seekers around the country, the committees have become a convenient way for undeclared presidential aspirants to circumvent federal campaign finance laws during the early "testing of the political waters" stage of their candidacies. Presidential GOP hopeful Senator Bob Dole's special committee, Campaign America, for example, paid for eight of his trips to New Hampshire in 1978. Another GOP presidential aspirant, George Bush, used another such group, Fund for Limited Government, to pay for $40,203 in air travel during 1978, while he checked out his presidential prospects. Ronald Reagan's Committee for the Republic helped the defeated 1976 GOP contender build up a mailing list of more than 300,000 contributors and maintain a regular campaign staff of twenty-six full-timers throughout most of 1978, preparatory to another try for the GOP nomination in 1980.

There's nothing illegal about these committees. A by-product of stringent reporting requirements of the 1974 Federal Election Campaign Act, PACs "allow presidential hopefuls to do what presidential hopefuls have always done without breaking the law."[23] Political action committees have been set up by virtually all leading aspirants for the 1980 GOP presidential nomination to avoid coming into conflict with the Federal Election Commission, which administers the 1974 law. The newly developed committees skirt the law in two ways. First, they avoid low contribution limits. Individual contributors are normally limited to giving $1,000 to a candidate, but individuals can give $5,000 to a "multi-candidate political action comittee." Second, the committees enable presidential hopefuls to raise and spend substantial amounts of money without counting it against their maximum presidential primary spending limits—which are expected to be about $16.8 million in 1980. These spending ceilings apply to every candidate who accepts federal matching funds, which most are expected to do.

Budgets of these political action committees rival those of traditional special interest lobbies. Ronald Reagan's Committee for the Republic operated in 1978 with a budget of $2.5 million, a sum larger than the political arms of the AFL-CIO, the American Medical Association, the anti-gun-control lobby, or the United Auto Workers.

Technically, the Dole, Bush, and Reagan groups—and similar organizations keeping alive the presidential hopes of John B. Connally and former President Gerald Ford—were established to aid Republican campaign efforts across the land. But few party watchers seriously believed that this was their main purpose, and with good reason. Less than 6 percent of the $202,000 the Dole group raised went directly to state or local candidates in the 1978 campaign. Only 11 percent of the $230,000 the Bush group collected went to GOP candidates. Most of the money was used for committee overhead and the presidential contender's travel, especially in the primary states. Of the $2.5 million Reagan's Committee for the Republic spent in 1978, $1.9 million went for operating expenses; John Connally's Citizens Forum spent $498,305 of its $632,812 budget on operating expenses.

Political action committee money enabled former California Governor Reagan to visit eighty-six cities in twenty-six states during 1978, and former Texas Governor Connally, while an unannounced candidate, visited 167 cities in thirty states during the same period. At each stop, the candidate could smilingly claim to be helping Republican office seekers and face the local television and news reporters asking their favorite question: "Are you going to be a candidate for president in 1980?"

As shadow presidential committees, the extra-legal committees provide all the regular campaign services, including advance men, fund raisers, political advisors and accountants. "They look like presidential campaign committees, they act like them, but they aren't," explains Herbert Alexander, one of the nation's best known experts on campaign finance. "They're deceptive. But all of the candidates need them if they're going to test the waters. There is really no other way to do it."[24]

As the 1980 presidential primary season approached, the political action committees began closing up shop as each contender announced his formal candidacy. Meanwhile, the committees will have fulfilled their real, not ostensible, purpose of collecting campaign "seed" money, providing a good test run for the pre-primary campaign organizations, and furnishing travel money and visibility for the unannounced candidates as they prepare for an all-out drive for the presidency. Unless outlawed by the Federal Election Commission in the future, political action committees can be expected to become a standard feature of almost every early pre-convention presidential drive, whether the candidate is a Republican or a Democrat.

PRESIDENTIAL "EXPLORATORY COMMITTEES"

Another early step in a presidential nominating campaign—again encouraged by the Federal Election Campaign Act of 1974—is the formation of an "exploratory committee." Presidential aspirants who, for tactical or financial reasons, do not want to make an early official announcement of their candidacies have discovered that the formation of an exploratory committee can serve as a convenient intermediate step in their White House quest. Thus, on February 22, 1979, Senator Robert

Dole of Kansas, the GOP vice-presidential nominee in 1976, formed an exploratory committee to start raising and spending funds for a possible bid for the 1980 GOP presidential nomination. By filing the necessary papers with the Federal Election Commission, Dole and other unannounced candidates have used exploratory committees to test the waters for a presidential campaign without officially committing themselves. If the potential contender concludes after a thorough reconnaissance around the country that his or her prospects are dim, the candidate can gracefully withdraw without serious loss of face.

More importantly, formation of an exploratory committee enables the candidate to qualify for federal matching funds (up to $5 million) for the presidential primaries, if he or she can first raise $100,000 in contributions—$5,000 in each of twenty states in amounts no larger than $250. Since no federal matching money is released to candidates until January 1 of the presidential year, the exploratory committee's fund-raising activities enable a candidate to launch his official race at full speed instead of wasting precious weeks and months gearing up to raise the necessary qualifying funds for Uncle Sam's matching dollars.

Formation of an exploratory committee also provides another contrived media event to generate further publicity for an unannounced candidate. Supporters of Ronald Reagan, the pre-season front-runner for the 1980 GOP nomination, proudly announced the establishment of an exploratory committee in early March 1979, while the former movie star remained at his ranch near Pacific Palisades, California. Before an audience of at least 100 reporters, a bevy of network cameras, and a host of GOP faithful in the nation's capital, Senator Paul Laxalt, his 1976 campaign director, declared, "Not since General Eisenhower's election almost thirty years ago has there been such a perfect 'fit' between man and the public mood as there is today with Governor Reagan and the American people."[25]

Senator Laxalt, in establishing the Reagan for President Committee, furnished reporters with a twenty-three page list of adherents, which included the names of four former cabinet members who had served under Presidents Nixon and Ford, five U.S. senators, 22 representatives, and a host of other prominent supporters of his former opponent, then President Ford. But Reagan, always the master of public relations, did not announce his candidacy formally. Instead, reporters at the media ceremony in the Eisenhower Lounge of the Republican National Committee building were handed a "Dear Paul" letter in which Reagan consented to formation of the committee but emphasized that he was not yet ready to make a personal declaration of candidacy. The former California governor stated modestly that he would await the findings of the committee's explorations "with great interest."[26]

Unlike several other GOP contenders, Reagan also had persuasive financial reasons for postponing his official announcement. Formation of an exploratory committee instead of an official campaign organization enabled the Californian to continue marketing his lucrative radio commentary show without violating the Federal Communications Commission's equal time rules. Once in the fray he would have to give up this profitable enterprise and probably his syndicated newspaper column, his major sources of income since retirement from Hollywood and the California governorship. However, the Federal Election Commission deemed him a candidate since he approved the formation of the committee.

The announcement of the Reagan for President Committee, followed quickly by the opening of a national campaign headquarters in Los Angeles, was also intended by Reagan's handlers to emphasize the nationwide strength of their candidate. If this show of force did not discourage other candidates from seeking the 1980 Republican nomination, Reagan's strategists hoped that the establishment of the quasi-official committee would at least convince other Republicans of the futility of backing his rivals.

Presidential political action and exploratory committees, spawned by the 1974 Federal Election Campaign Act, are of course merely transparent devices to delay the formal opening of presidential nominating drives. In nearly every respect, committees serve presidential candidates in the same capacity as official committees. As unofficial campaign arms, they help the restless presidential contenders mount their presidential primary drives long before the filing dates yet allow the unannounced candidates to keep their options open. In the years ahead, formation of exploratory as well as political action committees in the early pre-primary period will probably become standard operating procedure for candidates of the out-of-power party.

White House incumbents have also come to realize the distinct advantages of forming an ''exploratory'' reelection committee before officially announcing their renomination plans. In early March 1979, President Carter authorized the formation of an exploratory campaign committee to raise money for his reelection and to begin the task of building a Carter organization around the country.[27] Establishment of a reelection committee, even earlier than President Ford did in 1975, was expected to help Carter's campaign handlers regularize the political operations that had already been going forward, using White House and the Democratic National Committee staff and the national committee's budget. Formation of a campaign committee was also thought to diminish the risk of complaints and political sniping that funds other than those specifically committed to the campaign would be used improperly. Carter's early formation of an unofficial committee was triggered, in part, by President Ford's unfortunate experience four years earlier. Many political insiders believe that one of Mr. Ford's major electoral mistakes in 1976 was not getting going early enough. Most party professionals now feel that with thirty-plus state primary campaigns and the serious threat of intraparty competitors lurking on all sides, an incumbent president rarely can start too early. Gone forever are the days when a White House incumbent could relax in getting reelection campaign underway until the final six months before the national convention.

In the chapters that follow, our goal will be to describe and explain how in the past thirty years, by utilizing their own national campaign organizations, sophisticated political technology, their ratings in the opinion polls, and the heavy publicity generated by national media, presidential candidates have short-circuited the political parties and made presidential primaries *the* road to the White House.

Notes

1. New York *Times,* May 11, 1976.

2. Eugene B. McGregor, "The Uncertainty Principle and National Nominating Convention" (Paper delivered at the American Political Science Association annual meeting, Chicago, Illinois, September 1-4, 1976), p. 34.

3. Donald R. Matthews, "Presidential Nominations: Process and Outcome," in *Choosing the President,* ed. James David Barber (Englewood Cliffs, N.J.: Prentice-Hall, 1974), p. 39.

4. F. Christopher Arterton, "Campaign Organizations Face the Mass Media in the 1976 Presidential Nominating Process" (Paper delivered at the American Political Science Association annual meeting, Washington, D. C., September 1-4, 1977).

5. Richard L. Rubin, *Party Dynamics: The Democratic Coalition and the Politics of Change* (New York: Oxford University Press, 1976), p. 153.

6. Arterton, "Campaign Organizations," p.6.

7. Ibid.

8. See Arthur T. Hadley, *The Invisible Primary* (Englewood Cliffs, N.J.: Prentice-Hall, 1976).

9. Network television coverage of presidential primaries has increased in recent campaigns. According to Richard L. Rubin, CBS News covered six primaries in 1968; four years later the network covered seventeen primaries. In 1976 the number covered by CBS News rose to twenty-nine. His source of information was Warren J. Mitofsky, Director of the CBS News Election and Survey Unit. See Richard L. Rubin, "Presidential Primaries: Continuities, Dimensions of Change, and Political Implications" (Paper presented at the American Political Science Association annual meeting, Washington, D. C., September 1-4, 1977), p. 41, fn. 25.

10. William Keech and Donald R. Matthews, *The Party Choice* (Washington, D. C.: Brookings Institution, 1976), pp. 9-10.

11. "The Battle to Call a Winner," *Business Week* (June 6, 1964): 24.

12. F. Christopher Arterton, "Campaign Organizations Confront the Media Environment," in *Race for the Presidency,* ed. James David Barber (Englewood Cliffs, N.J.: Prentice-Hall, 1978), p. 21.

13. Bad poll ratings can knock candidates out early in the race. The first GOP candidate to drop out of the 1980 nominating campaign, Senator Lowell P. Weicker (R, Conn.), announced in mid-May 1979 that he was pulling out due to his low poll ratings. A privately conducted survey by his pollster showed Weicker running third in his home state of Connecticut behind former President Gerald R. Ford and Ronald Reagan. The poll gave Ford 23.6 percent, Reagan 20.6 percent and Weicker 13.9. "Those are the numbers," Weicker told the news conference. "You can't buck against them." Associated Press dispatch, *Bellingham* (Washington) *Herald,* May 17, 1979.

14. See Joe McGinnis, *The Selling of the President* (New York: Trident, 1969).

15. Charles Mohr, New York *Times,* August 1, 1976.

16. Austin Ranney, "Parties in State Politics," in *Politics in the American States,* ed. Herbert Jacob and Kenneth N. Vines, 3rd ed. (Boston: Little, Brown, 1976), pp. 60-63.

17. Gerald M. Pomper, "New Rules and New Games in the National Conventions" (Paper delivered at the American Political Science Association annual meeting, Washington, D. C., September 1-4, 1977), p. 31.

18. Ibid.

19. Jeane J. Kirkpatrick, "Dismantling the Parties: Reflections on the Role of Policy in the Process of Party Decomposition" (Paper delivered at the American Political Science Association annual meeting, Washington, D. C., September 1-4, 1977), p. 20.

20. Gary R. Oren, "Candidate Style and Voter Alignment in 1976," in *Emerging Coalitions in American Politics,* ed. Seymour Martin Lipset (San Francisco: Institute for Contemporary Studies, 1978), p. 147.

21. Norman H. Nie, Sidney Verba, and John R. Petrocik, *The Changing American Voter* (Cambridge; Harvard University Press, 1976), pp. 83-84.

22. Jeane J. Kirkpatrick, "Dismantling the Parties," p. 21.

23. Bill Peterson, Washington *Post,* February 3, 1979.

24. Ibid.

25. Seattle *Post-Intelligencer,* March 11, 1979.

26. New York *Times,* March 8, 1979.

27. Ibid., March 4, 1979.

Nominations—American Style _____ 2

Nineteenth-century political boss William Marcy Tweed once observed, "I don't care who does the electing just so I can do the nominating." This sage observation underscores the basic political fact of life that nominations are the most decisive stage in the entire process of presidential selection. Put simply, the presidential nominating process narrows the alternatives from a theoretical potential candidate pool of the millions who meet the constitutional requirements for the office to only two candidates, one Republican and one Democrat, with a realistic chance of winning the White House. Donald R. Matthews has also noted, "The nominating decision is one of the major determinants of who wins in November."[1] Indeed, because electoral decisions usually take on greater importance in nominating decision making than calculations on probable performance in the White House, the presidential nominating process has as much effect, if not more, as the presidential election itself in shaping the future direction of the country. The choice of Franklin Delano Roosevelt over Alfred E. Smith in the 1932 Democratic race, the Republicans' preference for Dwight D. Eisenhower over Senator Robert A. Taft in the 1952 GOP contest, the selection of John F. Kennedy over fellow Democrats Adlai E. Stevenson and Lyndon Johnson in 1960, and the Democrats' choice of Jimmy Carter over Morris Udall and California Governor Edmund G. "Jerry" Brown in the 1976 Democratic race are all cases in point. Also, it is sometimes forgotten that getting nominated may be a bigger hurdle toward winning the presidency than the general election itself. In 1952, for example, Dwight D. Eisenhower experienced far more difficulty in capturing the GOP nomination from his intraparty rival, Senator Taft, than in defeating his Democratic opponent, Governor Stevenson, in the general election. (Eisenhower led Taft 595 to 500 votes on the first ballot at the GOP convention before several delegations quickly shifted to Ike, giving him a clear-cut majority before the first ballot roll call tally was officially announced.) For these reasons, the nominating system occupies a central role in the U.S. party system.

The U.S. presidential nominating process is unique among Western political systems. Indeed, the presidential nominating procedure permits a degree of popular control and mass participation not found elsewhere in the Free World, except Canada. This "openness" in the nominating process has been accomplished in the twentieth century chiefly by the introduction of the presidential primary, a modified form of direct primary. Earlier, the presidential nominating machinery had been strongly influenced by the forces of frontier democracy, with its demand for wider suffrage, and by the rise of the national nominating convention, which displaced the tightly controlled Congressional Caucus. Prior to 1824, the Congressional Caucus—in effect, the legislative branch—handpicked presidential candidates without any rank-and-file party participation.

Leadership Selection in Other Western Democracies

That rank-and-file voters should have a voice in the selection of a national party leader seems bizarre to a foreign observer. In European democracies, there is a clear distinction between the nominating and electing processes. To be sure, the final choice of national leaders is left to the people but not the preliminary decision about which candidates are to be considered and which are to be ignored. Leaders are selected entirely through internal party machinery. Generally, they are chosen by the members of parliament or by the party executive. Members of the national party conference are then given the privilege of ratifying the choice of the party's inner circle. The leader of the British Parliamentary Labour party, for example, is chosen by the party's members in the House of Commons. But the choice of the potential prime minister has already been narrowed down by demonstrated leadership in the cabinet or while serving in the opposition party's "shadow" cabinet (members who will be given cabinet rank if their party wins the next general election). Let's take a closer look at this leadership selection process in several Western democracies.

GREAT BRITAIN

The British leadership selection process, as Hugh Heclo has noted, is an "apprenticeship" system.[2] Party chieftains must climb up the parliamentary ladder, step by step, serving first in secondary cabinet posts before advancing to the front bench. Prime Minister Margaret Thatcher served as a member of Parliament (MP) for sixteen years (1959-75) before taking over the Conservative Party reins—and another four years before moving into 10 Downing Street in May 1979. Sir Winston Churchill, long regarded as a party maverick, was an MP for thirty-eight years (1902-40) before being called by the Conservatives to head the party and assume the prime ministership during Britain's darkest hour in 1940. Former Prime Minister James Callaghan served thirty-one years in Parliament (1945-76) before moving into the leadership of the Labour Party. Sir Harold Wilson, former leader of the party, was a member of the House of Commons for eighteen years before taking over his party's stewardship. Leadership selection within the Labour and Conservative parties was different formerly, but within the past fifteen years the process has become quite similar.

The Parliamentary Labour Party (PLP) selects its leader by what is known as an "exhaustive ballot." Used at all levels within the party, the process is actually a form of proportional representation (the single transferable vote if more than one ballot is held). Each member of Parliament has one vote to cast for the leader. If more than two candidates are running and no one receives a majority on the first ballot, the candidate with the fewest votes is dropped from the list, and each MP votes again. Thus, those who voted for the least popular candidate on the first ballot have a chance to vote again for a more popular candidate (they transfer their vote). The leadership selection process continues until one candidate has an absolute majority. As one British writer has noted, "One often praised feature of this system is that it tends to promote the chances of those who are acceptable to a wide range of the electorate (he wins who gains many 'transferred' votes) against the chances of candidates who, though they have a large band of devoted followers, cannot win votes from anyone else."[3] The exhaustive ballot system is generally thought to help "moderate" candidates against "extremists," thus promoting unity within the broad, diverse membership of the Labour party and giving all candidates and groups a reason to reconcile their differences.

Following former Prime Minister Clement R. Attlee's resignation as Labour party leader after thirty years at the helm in December 1955, Hugh Gaitskell, former chancellor of the exchequer in the second Attlee government (1950-51) and party treasurer, clearly outdistanced his two rivals, Herbert Morrison, the party's deputy leader who was sixty-eight, and Aneurin Bevan, fiery spokesman for the party's dissident left wing. With strong backing from front bench MPs and the trade union chieftains, Gaitskell polled 157 votes to Bevan's seventy and Morrison's forty among the party's House of Commons members.[4] The same story was repeated in 1963, following Gaitskell's sudden death. Three parliamentary contenders sought the top post: Harold Wilson, the Labour shadow foreign secretary; George Brown, deputy party leader; and James Callaghan, the shadow chancellor of the exchequer. (The shadow cabinet member serves as the opposition party spokesperson for the portfolio he or she holds in the House of Commons.) On the first ballot Wilson, who had openly opposed Gaitskell's party direction in 1960, polled 115 votes, Brown eighty-eight, and Callaghan forty-four. In the second, or run-off ballot, Wilson defeated Brown 144 to 103. Wilson held the Labour Party leadership post until he resigned unexpectedly in March 1976. He served as prime minister for eight years (1964-70 and 1974-76), the longest term of service in the twentieth century, if Churchill's wartime coalition is excluded. Wilson's successor, Foreign Secretary James Callaghan, long-time member of the Labour Party inner circle, was chosen as new leader—and prime minister—over Michael Foot, secretary of the state for employment and champion of the party's left wing, on the third ballot, 176 to 137.[5] Technically, the vote was only to confer the leadership of the Labour party on Mr. Callaghan as Wilson's successor. But since Mr. Wilson resigned as prime minister midway through the Labour Party government's five-year term of office, Mr. Callaghan's succession as party leader automatically elevated him to prime minister.

The race to pick Wilson's successor had been a six-man contest. On the first ballot Mr. Foot led with ninety votes, trailed by Mr. Callaghan, the odds-on favorite with eighty-four. The two front-runners were followed by Roy Jenkins, the home secretary, with fifty-six; Anthony Wedgewood-Benn, the energy secretary, with thirty-seven; Denis Healey, the chancellor of the exchequer, with thirty; and Anthony Crosland, environmental secretary, with seventeen. Under party rules Mr. Crosland was promptly eliminated because he finished last. Shortly after the first-round vote was announced Mr. Wedgewood-Benn, another favorite of the left, dropped out and announced his support for Mr. Foot. Mr. Jenkins, leader of the right wing of the party, also withdrew, but without announcing his preference. On the second ballot, among the 315 Labour Party members of Parliament eligible to vote, Callaghan collected 141 votes while his chief rival, Mr. Foot, captured 133 and Mr. Healey drew only thirty-eight; three members abstained. With party rules requiring Mr. Healy, the low vote-getter, to step aside, the Labour MPs then chose Callaghan in the final run-off.

Since February 1965, the British Conservative party also has chosen its leaders by a vote of its parliamentary members. Prior to this change, however, former Conservative leaders, such as Winston Churchill and Harold Macmillan, were selected by the "customary processes," that is, informal agreement among a closed inner circle of Tories. Backbenchers in the House of Commons were never allowed to vote directly on his selection. Indeed, until the recent overhaul of the Conservative party election machinery, the precise method of leadership selection among the Tories had been one of the most jealously guarded secrets in the British Commonwealth.

Edward Heath, the first Conservative leader to be chosen by the new party leadership selection machinery, outpointed his chief rival, Reginauld Maulding, and party maverick Enoch Powell by a plurality margin on the first ballot. Before the run-off second ballot, Maulding withdrew and conceded the leadership post to Heath without a fight. Heath, who served as prime minister in 1970-74, held the Conservative leadership position until February 1975.

After his third loss in four election campaigns against the Labour Party, however, Heath was ousted in a new balloting for the party leadership by Mrs. Margaret Thatcher, formerly secretary of state for education. Mrs. Thatcher on the first ballot collected 130 votes to 119 for Heath, with sixteen votes going to a minor candidate and eleven members not voting.[6]

Under the Conservatives' new rules calling for a leader to run annually for reelection by the party's MPs, Mrs. Thatcher would have had to lead Mr. Heath by a majority of 139 votes—and a margin of 15 percent (forty-two votes)—to win the leadership outright on the first ballot. According to party rules, second-round balloting requires only a simple majority.[7] Despite a phalanx of four male opponents, including the popular William Whitelaw, former minister in Ulster and ex-Commons leader, Mrs. Thatcher nevertheless confounded her opponents and the elaborate party rules by sweeping them all aside on the second ballot. She captured 149 votes, ten more than a majority. The first woman to lead a British political party, Mrs. Thatcher originally commenced her bid for power as an outside challenger to the hierarchy of a party whose tradition has little place for outsiders. In early May 1979, Mrs. Thatcher became Britain's first woman prime minister when she ousted Labourite James "Sunny Jim" Callaghan from office.

Unlike the U.S. presidential primary system, contesting for party leadership in Great Britain more closely resembles the selection of a leadership post in the state legislature. To win office, British prime ministers do not have to participate in thirty-three state primaries, travel thousands of miles on the campaign trail, shake countless hands, consume an endless number of hurried meals, drink several hundred cups of coffee, hold dozens of press conferences and endure an almost continuous string of sixteen-to-eighteen-hour campaign days and nights for the five-month period of the primary season. The Labour Party's low-key leadership selection campaign has been described, and perhaps slightly understated, by one American reporter as follows: "Each candidate has a manager, who confines his efforts to telephone calls and earnest little chats in the Commons tea room."[8]

It is noteworthy that British party leaders, unlike their American counterparts, remain at their posts from one election to the next, win or lose, unless forced to step down by their colleagues or illness causes their resignation. Thus, in recent years Harold Wilson served as leader of the Labour Party for thirteen years and Heath ten years for the Conservatives.

In contrasting British and American leadership selection, Heclo has commented, "The British system is usually considered conducive to stability of party leadership, while the United States with its constitutionally required quadrennial elections is subject to greater fluctuations."[9] Neither the British nor the American system appears entirely satisfactory, but the critics have yet to persuade the defenders of the existing leadership selection process on both sides of the Atlantic that a more suitable alternative is available.

WEST GERMANY

On the Continent, leadership selection has followed much the same pattern as found in Great Britian. In West Germany, Konrad Adenauer assumed control of the Christian Democratic Union (CDU) and was installed as Chancellor shortly after World War II, even before the CDU had even formally elected a leader or set up a national organization.[10] As chancellor and party chairman, Adenauer ruled the CDU with an iron hand throughout most of his fourteen years' tenure. But when it came time to name a successor, the CDU party leaders overruled his objection to Vice Chancellor-Economics Minister Dr. Ludwig Erhard and chose him as Adenauer's successor. The showdown with the aging chancellor came in mid-April 1963, when the fifty-six-man executive committee of the CDU and its Bavarian affiliate, the Christian Social Union (CSU), met privately. At this closed meeting they agreed to recommend to its party representatives in Parliament that Dr. Erhard be nominated for the chancellorship. In the months preceding this most important party meeting in thirteen years, the CDU-CSU leaders decided that the party's fortunes would be improved by Adenauer's early retirement. Following the executive committee's action, the CDU-CSU deputies caucused behind closed doors; in a secret ballot, they voted 159 to forty-seven, with nineteen abstentions, for Erhard. Only Chancellor Adenauer and one of his associates, according to one of the participants, openly contested the choice of Dr. Erhard.[11] In 1966 the CDU-CSU leadership, dissatisfied with Erhard's performance, turned to Kurt Kiesinger to replace the ailing chancellor. Kiesinger lost the chancellorship to Willy Brandt, the Social Democratic party (SPD) Mayor of Berlin, in 1969. Faced with further parliamentary member defections to the opposition, after five deputies jumped ship, Kiesinger finally stepped down in 1972. Rainer Barzel was chosen to take over the CDU-CSU parliamentary reins.

Since purging the old party leadership left over from the 1960s, the CDU-CSU seemed unable to find a new chieftain or group of leaders able to exert clear-cut dominance over party affairs in the Adenauer-Erhard tradition. Barzel, the party's unsuccessful candidate against Social Democratic Chancellor Willy Brandt in 1972, soon fell into political eclipse. In May 1975, Helmut Kohl, minister president or governor of the state of Rhineland-Palatinate, was picked by the CDU executive board as its candidate in an unsuccessful run against Chancellor Helmut Schmidt in the 1976 general election.

Three years later, the Christian Democratic Union (CDU) and its smaller Bavarian sister party, the Christian Social Union (CSU), headed by Franz Josef Strauss, minister president of Bavaria, nominated Strauss to oppose Chancellor Helmut Schmidt in the 1980 federal elections. Passed over three times previously for the top leadership post by the CDU-CSU parliamentary caucus, Strauss defeated Ernst Albrecht, minister president of Lower Saxony and personal choice of Helmut Kohl, the outgoing chairman of the Christian Democratic Union, by a vote of 135 to 102.[12] Despite the grim predictions from some CDU party members that the right-wing Bavarian's nomination would cost the coalition the chancellorship in 1980, the CDU-CSU members of the Bundestag (parliament) selected the controversial Strauss, who served as defense minister in the government of Chancellor Konrad Adenauer but resigned in the furor created by a 1962 police raid on the news office of the popular news magazine *Der Speigel.* Strauss became finance minister in 1966, serving three years until the CDU-CSU was turned out of office in 1969.

In the rival Social Democratic Party (SPD), leadership control has long been concentrated in the party executive. More than half a century ago, Robert Michels, in his classic study of oligarchical rule among European political parties, commented on the SPD chieftains' tight-reined control of the party organizations.[13] In 1961, the selection of Willy Brandt, the Social Democratic party's new candidate to oppose Chancellor Adenauer, underscored once again the tight control of the party by its leaders. It was a poorly kept secret that as early as March 1960, the party executive had settled on Brandt as the candidate for the chancellorship. The party king-makers were seeking a replacement for Erich Ollenauer, a colorless Clement R. Attlee-type of standard-bearer, who had led the party down the road of defeat three times, in 1949, 1953 and 1957. After the executive committee agreed upon Brandt, his candidacy was ratified by the parliamentary deputies. Only then was Brandt's name put forward for final approval at the November 1960 Hanover party congress.[14] A winner of the Nobel Peace Prize, Brandt served as chancellor for five years (1969-74) until forced out of his leadership post after discovery that an East German spy had been working as one of his top staff aides for several years. The SPD party executives then turned to Helmut

Schmidt, deputy party chairman and finance minister, to take over the chancellorship.

CANADA

The only Western parliamentary democracy that permits a degree of rank-and-file participation in leadership selection is Canada. That the Canadian parties have not persisted in following entirely the leadership selection methods of their British forebears may be attributed in part to the influence of U.S. nominating procedures. But the trend in Canada toward greater rank-and-file participation in choosing the prime minister and party leader is a comparatively recent phenomenon. From the passage of the British North American Act of 1867—Canada's self-governing charter—until the end of World War I, Dominion party leaders were selected by an elite circle of party politicians, chiefly the parliamentary caucus and a handful of defeated or prospective candidates. But since 1919, the two major parties, the Liberals and Conservatives, have adopted the larger, more representative leadership convention or conference. These national party conventions, unlike those in the United States, are not held quadrennially, but generally meet only when a vacancy occurs in the national party leadership by death or resignation.[15] Thus, since 1919, the Liberals and Conservatives have held a combined total of only eleven conventions. Of these, the Liberals have convened only four, in 1919, 1948, 1958 and 1968. The Conservatives, more reluctant than the Liberals to broaden rank-and-file participation, held their first national convention in 1927.

The Canadian national leadership conventions are only slightly less flamboyant and boisterous than their U.S. counterparts. Much of the same terminology and format has been adopted. Like the U.S. convention, there is a keynote speaker. The platform-making task is also undertaken before the delegates (usually 1,400 or more, chosen in the parliamentary constituencies) settle down to the serious business of choosing their leader.

Unlike the U.S. conventions, the rival contenders in Canada each address the convention briefly before the balloting; usually a twenty-minute time limit is imposed. These prenominating speeches can "make or break" a candidate's chances; and a poor performance will most surely eliminate a contender from serious consideration. The delegates then vote by secret ballot individually (not orally on a roll call by state delegations as in the United States); a simple majority is sufficient for election. Both the Liberals and the Conservative party—technically, the Progressive-Conservative Party—have a rule that if three or more candidates run and no one receives a majority, the low man is automatically eliminated after each ballot.[16]

The all-time record for tenure established by Liberal Prime Minister W. L. MacKenzie King (1924-48) made it unnecessary for more than a quarter century to call a Liberal national convention. Liberal leader Lester Pearson, who moved into the prime ministership in 1963, was chosen to head his party at the 1958 convention, following the retirement of former Prime Minister Louis St. Laurent. Pearson defeated former Minister of Health (and later Minister of External Affairs) Paul Martin, 1,074 votes to 305. When Mr. Pearson retired in 1968, the Liberal leadership convention, held in Ottawa, selected Minister of Justice Pierre Eliot Trudeau to step into the prime ministership. Trudeau defeated Mr. Robert Winters (a former Pearson cabinet member) on the fourth ballot.

John G. Diefenbaker, the first Progressive-Conservative prime minister (1957-63) since the 1920s, was chosen to head his party at the December 1956 national party conclave. This convention had been made necessary a few months earlier by the retirement of Progressive-Conservative leader George Drew. Diefenbaker's victory—774 votes of 1,285 cast—came on his third attempt for the top party post. In 1967, the Progressive-Conservative leadership convention, dissatisfied with Diefenbaker, ousted the aging party chieftain and replaced him with Mr. Robert Stanfield, premier of the Nova Scotia provincial government.

The 1967 Progressive Conservative leadership convention in Toronto, as Hugh Heclo has commented, "marked the first time in Canadian history that a party leader's position was taken from him not by his parliamentary colleagues but by an extra-parliamentary institution."[17] Stanfield, in three national elections, failed to dislodge Premier Trudeau from office. Upon Stanfield's retirement in early 1976, the Progressive-Conservative leadership convention chose Joseph Clark, a thirty-six-year old MP from Alberta and a Stanfield protege. The youngest Tory leader ever named, Clark narrowly defeated Claude Wagner, a Quebec MP, by sixty-five votes on the fourth ballot. Wagner had formerly served as attorney general in the Quebec Liberal government before switching to the Conservatives. In picking Clark, a young standard-bearer who had served in the Canadian House of Commons only two years, the Tory convention delegates displayed the same pragmatic flexibility of some U.S. conventions that have turned to new fresh party leaders, for instance, John F. Kennedy and Jimmy Carter, because they appear to have the label "winner" stamped after their names. The Progressive Conservatives made a successful choice. Clark captured the prime ministership on his first try in May 1979, ending sixteen years of Liberal control of the national government.

As mentioned earlier, the idea of creating a special body, the national leadership convention, to choose the party leader is a fairly recent importation from the United States. But this does not mean that the party professionals of both major parties in Canada have always been enchanted with this political import. One leading Canadian observer commented some years ago:

It is probably an accurate statement that neither Liberals nor Conservatives have accepted wholeheartedly and with genuine conviction the system of choosing a national leader by the convention system. Most people believe in its efficacy as a vote-getter and rouser of enthusiasm; but this belief is tinged with a definite lack of confidence in the reliability of the convention's judgment of men and measures.[18]

Nevertheless, this same commentator conceded that the practice of choosing national party chieftains—or provincial leaders—is not likely to be repudiated. To argue for a return to restricted choice by the party inner circle would be interpreted as undemocratic and thus politically imprudent. According to Dawson and Ward,

The practice of making selections by the convention method is not likely to be repudiated in the foreseeable future; for to do so would be to show open preference for a restricted method of choice rather than based on the representative and (so it is universally believed) the democratic principle. No party will willingly expose itself to the reproach that it is afraid to trust the judgment of its own representative convention.[19]

Still, the national and provincial party leaders have succeeded in keeping their hands on the political throttle. There is a decided tendency in both parties to provide generously for the official section of the party, the members of the federal and provincial cabinets and legislatures, at all national conventions. The Liberals, for example, at their 1968 convention not only named their 130 members of Parliament as delegates ex officio, but gave the same status to 128 candidates defeated in the previous federal election, no matter how few votes they may have received; also 161 Legislative Assembly members from the provincial legislatures served as delegates.[20] Consequently, these party leaders, by virtue of their experience, prestige, familiarity with the issues and candidates, and other factors, can usually exercise a great influence over, if not actually dominate, the convention.

Neither of the major parties, apparently, has considered the possibility of apportioning delegates on the basis of party vote in previous national elections, though the heavy representation of dominion and provincial legislators at the national conventions has accomplished this to a limited degree. Nor has there been a serious demand in Canada for legal regulation of the nominating process, such as occurred in the United States when the direct primary was introduced at the turn of the twentieth century.

It can be seen then that this process of leadership selection outside the United States, except in Canada, has been largely impervious to the wishes of the rank-and-file member. Only after the party leader has been chosen by his parliamentary colleagues are the voters allowed to express their preference in the general election. Indeed, the party elite would consider it unthinkable to place the nominating process in the hands of the voters. But in the United States rank-and-file party members and voters over the years have been permitted, indeed, demanded, to participate in growing numbers in the presidential nominating process through presidential primaries and the caucus-convention structure. But to understand how this dual selection system works, it is first necessary to explain the emergence of the direct primary.

What Is a Primary?

The dichotomy between nominating and electing candidates in this country has been blurred in almost all of the states by the adoption of the direct primary election system whereby the voters, instead of the party leaders, have been given the right, first by custom and then by statute, of voting on candidates for public office to run in the general election. Under the primary system the voters participate directly in the nominating process, in contrast to their former method of acting through a multi-tiered party convention system several steps removed from the electorate.

The presidential primary, which is a form of the direct primary, cannot be characterized merely as an offshoot of the direct primary system. For one thing, the direct primary provided for a full-fledged intraparty election to be held in individual states to choose a single candidate from each party to run for public office in the general election. The presidential primary system is more like a round robin elimination contest among the various contenders. No one state presidential primary election is conclusive as in the case of a state direct primary election. But final-round presidential primaries may become "sudden-death" contests in which the losers are removed, in effect, from further serious contention.

Generally, direct primary elections have a degree of finality not found in a presidential primary election. In the North, for example, the winning candidate is automatically selected in the direct primary, even though he wins by only a plurality (less than a majority), and goes on the ballot in the general election. But in the Deep South, a predominantly one-party Democratic area where there are usually a number of candidates competing for the same office (the Alabama Democratic gubernatorial primary, for example, may have a half dozen or more candidates entered), it is necessary to have a second or run-off primary, unless one candidate captures a majority of votes in the first primary. (Only infrequently does one candidate emerge victorious in the first primary. The late Mrs. Lurleen Wallace, first wife of Governor George Wallace, did it in 1970 when she ran to succeed her husband, who was then constitutionally ineligible to seek a second consecutive term.) The run-off primary thus assures that the winner will receive an absolute majority, not merely a plurality. Until the recent emergence of a Republican party opposition in many parts of the South, winning the Democratic run-off primary has been tantamount to election.

In the case of the presidential primary, even after the thirty-three spring contests have been held, the party nominee still has not been chosen officially. The party's national nominating convention reserves this prerogative for itself. In short, presidential primary elections are only one phase of the nominating process, not the final act of choice. However, it will be argued throughout this book that presidential primary victories in contested elections usually will be the decisive factor in determining the presidential nomination for the party not occupying the White House. In eleven out of twelve contested nominations in both parties since 1956 the winner of the primaries has become the party nominee. Presidential primaries also appear to have become a significant factor affecting the outcome of the nomination in the party whose leader sits in the White House. President Lyndon Johnson's withdrawal from his renomination race in 1968 shortly before an impending defeat in the Wisconsin primary and President Gerald Ford's close-call victory over his Republican challenger Ronald Reagan in the 1976 primaries (Ford bested Reagan in sixteen out of twenty-six contests) immediately come to mind.

How did the complicated presidential nominating procedure in the United States all come about? Let's make a short historical review of the process.

Evolution of U.S. Nominating Procedures

In the early years of the Republic the Congressional Caucus, an oligarchical group of congressional leaders, agreed upon their choice of presidential candidates. Jefferson, Madison and Monroe were all chosen under this system. But the Congressional Caucus broke down in 1824 under the heavy pressure of intraparty factional rivalries in what was at that time essentially a one-party system. (Four candidates sought the presidency that year: John Quincy Adams, the victor, Andrew Jackson, Henry Clay and W. H. Crawford.) The growing sectionalism in the country, especially the challenges of Jacksonian frontier democracy, was also undermining the old nominating system. "King Caucus" also smacked too much of the aristocratic privilege associated with the defunct Federalist party.

After brief experimentation with the use of state legislatures and state party conventions to nominate Jackson and John Quincy Adams in 1828, a new political mechanism, the national party convention, was adopted in the 1830s to fill the gap caused by the demise of the Congressional Caucus.

Used first by an obscure minor party, the Anti-Masons, the national nominating convention answered the popular demands for greater voice in choosing presidential candidates. The national nominating convention was well suited for the young nation because (1) it was representative in character; (2) it divorced presidential nominations from congressional control and added to the prestige and independence of the president; (3) it provided for a broad-based formulation of a party program; (4) it concentrated the party's strength behind a single presidential ticket; and (5) it reconciled personal rivalries and group or sectional interests.[21] By the mid-1840s the national convention had reached full maturity. ·

Similarly, on the state and county level, by mid-century the convention system had displaced the legislative caucus in selecting candidates for public office. The multi-tiered convention system was considered to reflect the "popular will" because delegates to these conclaves had been chosen by the party membership at the precinct and county level.

The convention system remained the dominant method of nominating party candidates until about 1910.[22] But, like its predecessor, the legislative caucus, the party convention came to be regarded as an instrument of control by the state and big city party leaders. The rapid growth of industry and finance after the Civil War had made domination of state and city governments a valuable prize for seekers of special privilege. Those who wished to pull the strings in government worked through the party convention system because it was the vital link in the governing process. Small wonder, then, that Boss Tweed and others were determined to manage nominations; without the power to choose candidates for office, the bosses would be thwarted in spinning their web of control. Political critics and outnumbered minority faction leaders, however, began protesting that the political rings were manipulating the state nominating conventions and that the delegates attending these conventions and those chosen to represent the state at the national nominating convention were often unsavory characters affiliated with monied interests and the underworld.[23] Complaints were also made about the use of "snap" primaries, strong-arm squads, and high-handed presiding officers at party conventions.

By the end of the nineteenth century, the reformers' charges against the party bosses and the vested interests who worked hand in glove with them reverberated throughout the land. It was this rising discontent among the middle class—small businessmen, professionals and independent farmers—that spawned the Progressive movement. From this protest movement was to emerge the direct primary system and the first major reform of the national nominating convention in almost a century—the presidential primary.

If, the Progressives asked, the direct primary could be used to take power away from the vested interests controlling nominations for state and local office, why couldn't this system be applied to presidential nominations as well? Indeed, some of these reformers believed that the national party convention eventually should merely ratify the choice for president made in the state presidential primaries held throughout the United States. But the tide of reform ebbed long before this goal of nationwide system of presidential primaries could be achieved.

History of the Presidential Primary

There are four distinct periods in the history of presidential primaries:

1. The early period (1905-16), during which over half the states experimented with this new form of presidential nomination;
2. The ebbtide period (1917-45), during which eight states repealed their presidential primary laws and presidential candidates largely ignored primary campaigning;
3. The period of reawakened interest in primaries (1948-68), during which front-running and outsider candidates, such as Harold Stassen and Estes Kefauver, sought to use their vote-getting and popularity in the primaries as a springboard to the nomination;
4. The "great leap forward" period (1968-76), which saw the number of primary states double from fifteen to twenty-nine. During this period the percentage of delegates selected in presidential primary states jumped from 37 percent in 1968 to almost 72 percent in 1976 (see Table 2.1). Since 1976 four more states—Connecticut, Kansas, Louisiana and New Mexico—have been added to the presidential primary list.

The reformers used two approaches, or some combination of the two, to bring nominations under popular control. They passed laws which provided for either the direct election of delegates to the national conventions (and, in some cases, for instruction to the delegates as to the popular preference for president), or a presidential preference primary

TABLE 2.1
NUMBER OF STATES HOLDING PRESIDENTIAL PRIMARIES AND PERCENT OF CONVENTION DELEGATES FROM PRIMARY STATES, 1912-76

	Democratic		Republican	
	Number of Primaries	*Percent of Delegates*	*Number of Primaries*	*Percent of Delegates*
1912	12	32.9	13	41.7
1916	20	53.5	20	58.9
1920	16	44.6	20	57.8
1924	14	35.5	17	45.3
1928	17	42.2	16	44.9
1932	16	40.0	14	37.7
1936	14	36.5	12	37.5
1940	13	35.8	13	38.8
1944	14	36.7	13	38.7
1948	14	36.3	12	36.0
1952	15	38.7	13	39.0
1956	19	42.7	19	44.8
1960	16	38.3	15	38.6
1964	17	45.7	17	45.6
1968	15	40.2	15	38.1
1972	22	65.3	21	56.8
1976	30	76.0	30	71.0

Source: F. Christopher Arterton, "Campaign Organizations Confront the Media-Political Environment," in *Race for the Presidency*, ed. James David Barber, copyright 1978 by the American Assembly, Columbia University, p. 7. Reprinted by permission of Prentice-Hall, Inc., Englewood Cliffs, New Jersey.

only, or some combination of the two. The term "presidential primary" is applied to all these laws, most of which were originally passed during the golden age of the Progressive movement during the first fifteen years of the twentieth century.[24]

EARLY PERIOD (1901-16)

Florida claims to be the first state to have enacted a presidential primary law. A 1901 statute gave state or local party officials the option to hold a primary election to choose any party nominee, including delegates to the Democratic national convention. But to Wisconsin and its most illustrious son, Robert M. LaFollette, Sr., belongs much of the credit for pioneering the movement to secure more popular control over the selection of presidential candidates. After a frustrating experience at the 1904 Republican national convention, in which the Stalwart Republican delegations were seated instead of his own Progressive Republican delegation, LaFollette and the Progressive-dominated Wisconsin legislature decided that the only democratic way to select national convention delegates was to let the rank-and-file voter do it in a presidential primary. As LaFollette proclaimed at the time, "No longer . . . will there stand between the voter and the official a political machine with a complicated system of caucuses and conventions, by the manipulation of which it thwarts the will of the voter and rules of official conduct."[25] The 1905 Wisconsin law provided for the direct election of delegates to the national party conventions but said nothing about delegate preference for presidential candidates.

Pennsylvania took the first step toward a presidential primary in 1906, with a law providing that each delegate to the national convention could have printed beside his name on the official ballot the name of the presidential candidate he would support at the convention. But in 1908 no member of either party saw fit to exercise this option.

Oregon is usually given credit for adopting the first presidential preference primary, which enabled voters to express their preference for a specific presidential candidate. The preferential primary—popularly called the "beauty contest"—gives the voter an opportunity to register a vote for his favorite candidate, separate and apart from the vote for convention delegates. In 1910, the preference primary idea was put before the voters as an initiative measure.[26] Oregon voters approved this preference primary law, which still remains on the statute books in modified form. The law provided for both popular choice of presidential candidates— a preference primary—and the election of delegates legally pledged to support the winner of the preference primary.

By the spring of 1912, as the campaign forces of Republican President William Howard Taft and former President Theodore Roosevelt girded for the all-out nomination battle, twelve states had primary laws providing for direct election of delegates, a preference vote or both. Three more states had optional primaries giving state party committees the option of permitting the voters to elect convention delegates.

Following the wild Republican convention of 1912, amidst Roosevelt charges that Taft had "stolen" the nomination, it was freely predicted that the presidential primary idea would sweep the country. Among the leading planks of Roosevelt's Progressive Bull Moose party platform of 1912 was a recommendation for a nationwide presidential primary. President Woodrow Wilson, in his first message to Congress in 1913, called for a national presidential primary law. But this suggestion had low priority on his legislative agenda and was soon pushed aside by more pressing domestic legislation and mounting international crises in

Europe and Mexico. The rejection of the popular choice for Republican nomination in 1912 also left a bad taste in the mouths of many Progressive voters throughout the country. Disillusionment with the primary system began setting in.

Still, between 1912 and 1916 the Progressive-inspired reforms continued to spread. Nine states—Indiana, Iowa, Michigan, Montana, Minnesota, New Hampshire, North Dakota, Vermont and West Virginia—adopted some form of presidential primary. The Texas legislature also passed a presidential primary law, but it was declared unconstitutional by the state supreme court. In several of the primary states, however, the anti-primary forces sought to defeat or undermine the operation of the Presidential primary. In Michigan, the conservative Republican legislature blocked immediate implementation of the March 1912 law so that it could not be used until 1916. Governor Chase Osborn called a second special session of the legislature but was unsuccessful in his efforts to get the state senate, dominated by the Taft forces, to amend the statute to give it immediate effect. Not only did the state senate refuse to do this, but it also eliminated the provision for the direct election of national convention delegates.[27] This shrewd maneuver kept a majority of the Michigan Republican delegation safely in the hands of the Taft faction and badly hurt the Roosevelt drive.

Similarly, the original Maryland presidential primary bill of 1912 provided for a preference vote and the direct election of delegates to the convention. Although the law as passed contained a preference primary clause, it gave the state convention sole authority to select national delegates under a "county unit" plan that discriminated against the under-represented metropolitan counties.[28] Also, the law allowed the state convention to decide whether it wanted an instructed delegation pledged to support the winner of the preference primary or an uninstructed delegation.

By 1916, presidential primary laws had been passed in twenty-five states—those dominated by the Progressive forces. But the uneventful 1916 pre-convention race among the out-of-power Republicans, still weakened by the deep schism between the Old Guard and the Progressives, did little to spur expansion of the presidential primary and the other Progressive reforms, such as the initiative, referendum and recall, that had failed to measure up to the extravagant claims of their proponents. Then, too, the gathering war clouds dimmed enthusiasm for further crusades. After World War I the presidential primary movement fell into marked decline.

EBBTIDE OF THE PRESIDENTIAL PRIMARY MOVEMENT (1917-45)

Between 1917 and 1949, only one state, Alabama, adopted a presidential primary law. Passed in 1924, the Alabama statute reportedly was pushed through the legislature to give Senator Oscar W. Underwood, Alabama's favorite son, the power to name his own delegates to the Democratic national convention.[29] Eight of the twenty-five states with presidential primary legislation abandoned these laws by 1935. Primary laws were repealed in Iowa (1917), Minnesota (1917), Vermont (1921), Montana (1923), North Carolina (1927), Indiana (1929), Michigan (1931) and North Dakota (1935). In addition to opposition from party leaders, there were several reasons for the repeal of these laws: first, the high cost per capita of conducting presidential primary elections, especially if they were not held simultaneously with state primary elections; second, leading candidates frequently ignored the presidential primaries; and, third, low voter participation. A typical explanation of why some of these states wished to repeal their laws is contained in the 1932 report of the North Dakota governmental survey commission:

In the last Republican preference primary in this state (1928) neither of the candidates whose names appeared on the ballot for the nomination to the presidential candidacy had the support of any considerable number of the Republican voters. So far as expressing the preference of the Republican voters of the state was concerned, the election was a farce which cost the taxpayers of the state $135,635.[30]

The decline of interest in the presidential primary could also be attributed to the relative lack of concern for reform during the "roaring twenties" and the preoccupation with domestic economic and social problems created by the Great Depression during the early 1930s. Political reform also remained on the shelf during World War II.

The waning influence of the presidential primary was mirrored also in the behavior of the candidates. With the exception of the 1920 three-way Republican race among General Leonard E. Wood, Senator Hiram Johnson of California, and Illinois Governor Frank O. Lowden, presidential candidates for the next two decades generally downgraded the use of primaries in their nominating campaigns. In 1924, New York Governor Alfred E. Smith, a leading Democratic contender, did not enter a single primary. His principal opponent, William G. McAdoo, filed in several, but only in Ohio was there a contest, against a favorite son. Smith, making his second try four years later and apparently cognizant of the need for wider popular support, switched his pre-convention strategy and allowed his name to appear on the primary ballot in seven states. Republican front-runner Herbert Hoover permitted his name to be entered in eight Republican primaries. But he, like Smith, did not campaign personally in a single state. In 1932, Governor Franklin D. Roosevelt of New York skillfully exploited the use of his name in eleven primaries, but at no time did he leave Albany or Hyde Park to hit the campaign trail.

Presidential primary campaigning did not make national news again until Wendell Willkie's debacle in the 1944 Wisconsin primary. In seeking the GOP nomination for the second time, he chose to make his performance in the Wisconsin primary the acid test of his ability to win renomination. News of his staggering defeat—he failed to win a single delegate and finished last in a four-way preference contest—flashed across the country. Since that fateful spring election, there has been a marked revival of interest in presidential primaries.

REAWAKENED INTEREST (1948-68)

To defeated presidential primary campaigner Harold E. Stassen, former governor of Minnesota, goes much of the honor for the renewed interest in primaries. Viewed as an upstart candidate by many old-line Republican leaders, Stassen used the early presidential primary contests in 1948 as his chief weapon to challenge the GOP Old Guard in his surprising, though ultimately unsuccessful, drive for the nomination. Stassen upset Dewey in Wisconsin and Nebraska and bested Dewey with write-ins in the Pennsylvania primary. He might have captured the top prize had he not pushed his luck too far by dueling rival contender Senator Robert A. Taft of Ohio in his home state. Not only was Stassen's drive slowed by his failure to win more than nine delegates in Ohio, after he had already defeated Taft and Dewey in Nebraska, but his Ohio foray also took away valuable campaign time from the decisive primary battle against Governor Thomas E. Dewey in Oregon. Dewey, with his back to the wall after his earlier defeats in the primaries, spent three solid weeks campaigning in Oregon. His heavy investment paid off. He halted Stassen's drive by narrowly winning the Oregon primary. Dewey then went on to win renomination on the third ballot. Stassen had needed an Oregon triumph to sustain his momentum. Though he failed, Stassen demonstrated that by upsetting the leading contenders in the primaries a hard-hitting outsider candidate could attract nationwide attention and force party leaders to take serious note of his candidacy.

With the revived interest in presidential primary campaigning, three states that had repealed their presidential primary laws between 1916 and 1928—Minnesota, Indiana and Montana—passed new primary laws. When Minnesota's new law was enacted in 1949, the Twin Cities' press reported that the early date in March had been selected by pro-Stassen legislative leaders to give Stassen's second try for the presidency in 1952 an early send-off.[31] The new Indiana law was passed in 1953 at the behest of newly elected Republican Governor George N. Craig, an ardent Eisenhower supporter who had been steamrollered by the ruling Taft faction at the 1952 state convention. Similarly, Montana's new presidential primary law was passed in 1953 as a result of the efforts of pro-Eisenhower

Republicans, a number of whom had suffered from the cavalier treatment of the controlling Taft majority at the 1952 GOP state convention.

Voter participation in presidential primaries increased sharply from 4.8 million in 1948 to 12.7 million in 1952. The hotly fought Eisenhower-Taft race in the 1952 Republican primaries was undoubtedly a major reason for the rekindled voter interest, as it was for the sudden, marked resurgence in presidential primary legislation.

After Minnesota, Indiana and Montana all approved new presidential primary laws for a second time, it appeared that the old Progressive demand for more direct voter participation in presidential nominations might be catching on again. In the spring of 1953, the Nevada legislature passed a presidential primary law patterned after the California statute. But it was repealed in 1955 without ever having been put to a test.[32]

The history of the Alaskan presidential preference primary was almost as abbreviated. Passed by the territorial legislature in April 1955, the primary was used only in the 1956 election and then was repealed in 1959. No law specifically repealed the primary, but the first session of the new Alaskan state legislature in 1959 changed the date of the state primary from April to August, past the date when the national party conventions would have nominated presidential candidates. The repeal of the Minnesota and Montana presidential primary laws, also in 1959, signaled a halt to the movement for another decade. In 1965, the Maryland state legislature also repealed its presidential preference primary law, which had been in effect since 1912.[33] Few tears were shed by the political leadership of either party in the Free State when it was repealed, for those leaders had long wanted to be able to send uninstructed or favorite-son delegations to their national convention.

THE "GREAT LEAP FORWARD" (1969-76)

The presidential primary tide changed again after the divisive 1968 Democratic convention. Maryland decided for a third time in 1969 to adopt a presidential primary law. Between 1969 and 1971, six other states joined the presidential primary club. Indeed, the 1972 presidential primary season turned out to be the busiest since the high tide of the Progressive era before World War I. In all, twenty-three states and the District of Columbia held primaries. Almost two-thirds of the delegates (2,015 of 3,103) of the out-party Democratic nominating race were chosen in states using some form of presidential primary.

Why the sudden boom in presidential primary legislation? It would be difficult to pinpoint all the reasons, but the flurry of presidential primary activity appeared to be, in part, a response to protests by Senator Eugene McCarthy's supporters within the Democratic party against organization leaders' domination of the delegate selection process.

This tension was a contributing factor leading to the strife-torn 1968 Chicago convention. More important, the subsequent Democratic McGovern-Fraser Commission's proposed party reforms on the delegate selection process triggered action on primary legislation in several states, especially in closed caucus states where handpicked delegates were most common. Figures showed, however, that relatively few states with open caucuses abandoned their caucus-convention method of electing delegates. Three heavily-Democratic states (Maryland, New Mexico and Rhode Island) passed presidential primary legislation in 1969 before the McGovern-Fraser party reform commission guidelines had reached final draft. While the McGovern-Fraser Commission was officially neutral on the question of primaries, four more states—Arkansas, Michigan, North Carolina and Tennessee—adopted primaries after the McGovern-Fraser guidelines had been incorporated into the "call" of the 1972 convention. On-the-scene observers generally agreed that the three Southern states shifted to presidential primaries in an effort to comply with the national party directives without upsetting the state party's traditional ways of handling party business. With national party rules in a state of flux, the three Southern states were afraid that failure to shift to a primary system would make them more vulnerable to credentials challenges at the next convention.

Members of the McGovern-Fraser Commission did not anticipate the rapid proliferation of primaries after 1968, but once the wheels of reform were set in motion it was impossible to predict when the spread of primaries would halt. Historically, a surge in presidential primary legislation has usually occurred as a result of divisive conventions, the four major cases being after the 1912 and 1952 GOP and the 1968 and 1972 Democratic conventions.

As a result of the revived primary movement, almost 22 million voters turned out in the 1972 Democratic and Republican primaries, almost double the 12 million in 1968.[34] Of this number approximately 16 million participated in the Democratic primaries. (Republican turnout in their primaries in both years was much lighter, 4.5 million in 1968 and 6.2 million in 1972, because the nominee, Richard M. Nixon, had only token opposition.) That twice as many Democrats voted in 1972 as in 1968 can be attributed chiefly to two factors: first, more states held primaries in 1972; and, second, more states had competitive races in 1972 than four years earlier. For example, the number of voters in the Florida Democratic primary increased from 512,357 in 1968 to 1,264,554 in 1972; in Pennsylvania the number jumped from 597,089 to 1,374,839.

Another factor that heightened interest in the presidential primaries in 1968 and 1972 was the spread of the Oregon blanket ballot "all-candidate" primary to nine states. Under the "Oregon Plan," the secretary of state is authorized to put on the primary ballot the names of all presidential candidates "generally advocated or recognized as candidates in the national news media throughout the United States." Since candidates know that their names will appear on the ballots in these states—unless the candidate publicly declares that he is not a presidential candidate— the Oregon all-candidate primary usually guarantees a lively contest among the various contenders, and this helps bring out the voters.

The late flurry of presidential primary legislation in 1975 also could be attributed in part to the Watergate scandal, which produced further demands for more open, direct government. In a few states party leaders preferred to let voters make decisions in primaries rather than compete with "new politics" activists in caucuses. Some states also passed primary laws in order to attract publicity for the state and to capture additional political tourist dollars, such as New Hampshire has done for more than two decades.

By 1976 seven more states—Georgia, Idaho, Kentucky, Montana, Nevada, Texas and Vermont—had adopted presidential primary laws. The twenty-nine primaries in 1976 was an increase of fourteen over 1968. Only one state, New Mexico, has repealed its primary law since 1972. Democratic and Republican turnout in 1976 in the twenty-nine state primaries and District of Columbia reached an all-time high of 26 million— approximately 29 million if all the unavailable vote figures for district delegates in Alabama, New York and Texas were tabulated.[35] More than 16 million voters turned out in the 1976 Democratic primaries, a slight increase over 1972. The Republican voter turnout of approximately 10.3 million, almost double the 1972 GOP figures, reflected the intense Ford-Reagan rivalry for the GOP nomination. Still, the overall turnout in the recent presidential primaries has never exceeded one-third of the general election turnout. More will be said about voter turnout in Chapter 6.

Future Directions

What does the future hold for presidential primaries? Even before the 1976 presidential primary season opened, Democratic National Chairman Robert Strauss appointed a special party commission, headed by the Michigan State Democratic Chairman Morley Winograd, to make a comprehensive study of presidential primaries. Before the Winograd task force, officially known as the Commission on Presidential Nomination and Party Structure, began its deliberations, however, the 1976 Democratic National Convention passed the following resolution:

Resolved further that this convention, recognizing the responsibility of our National Party to provide for our presidential nominating process, urges the U. S. Congress to refrain from intervening in these party affairs unless and until the National Party requests legislative assistance and in no case should Congress legislate in any manner which is in derogation of the right of a National Party to mandate its own affairs.[36]

Subsequently, the Democratic National Committee also asked Democratic leaders on Capitol Hill to defer further consideration of various national and regional primary bills until after the Winograd Commission completed its work. The Winograd Commission Report, which did not appear until 1978, came out "strongly opposed to proposals for a national primary." Instead, the Democratic task force adopted a safe, middle course of endorsing, with some improvements, the present "mixed" system of presidential primaries and caucus-conventions. According to the final report, "Both systems have inherent strengths and weaknesses, and the question of which system is better for use in particular states is a decision best made by the state party and not by the direction of the National Party."[37] The Winograd Commission concluded, "The best course is to work within the existing system to establish improved standards for primary and caucus systems that will ensure that those delegate selection processes contribute to the values of openness, full participation and party building with which the Party has been concerned."[38]

Unlike the Democrats, the Republican party has not taken an official stand on a national primary or expressed its preference for one nominating system (primaries) over the other (caucus-convention). Republicans traditionally have believed presidential primary and caucus details should be determined by the individual states. Inasmuch as the Democrats control both houses of Congress by sizable majorities—nearly two to one in the House of Representatives—it can be expected that no official floor action will be taken on national or regional primary bills until Democratic House Speaker Thomas P. "Tip" O'Neil and Senate Democratic Majority Leader Robert Byrd flash the green light.

Because the methods through which states select delegates to presidential nominating conventions are being recognized increasingly as critically affecting decision making and convention choice, we will examine in the next chapter the bewildering variety of presidential primary laws used in the thirty-three states and the District of Columbia. Also, we will take a few moments to explain the delegate selection machinery in the seventeen states that continue to use the caucus-convention system.

Notes

1. Donald R. Matthews, "Presidential Nominations: Process and Outcomes," in *Choosing the President,* ed. James David Barber (Englewood Cliffs, N.J.: Prentice-Hall, 1974), p. 36.

2. Hugh Heclo, "Presidential and Prime Ministerial Selection," in *Perspectives on Presidential Selection,* ed. Donald R. Matthews (Washington, D.C.: Brookings Institution, 1973), p. 28.

3. H. M. Drucker, "Leadership Selection in the Labour Party," *Parliamentary Affairs* 29 (Autumn 1976): 378-79.

4. R. T. McKenzie, *British Political Parties,* 2nd ed. (New York: Praeger, 1963), p. 601.

5. Drucker, "Leadership Selection," pp. 388-92.

6. New York *Times,* February 12, 1975.

7. Should no candidate receive a majority then, the Conservatives require a third ballot be held two days later. It is limited to the top three contenders, with members indicating their first and second choices. If no one collects a majority of first-choice votes, the third candidate drops out, and his or her second choices are distributed among the top two to decide the winner. Ibid.

8. Robert B. Semple, Jr., Ibid., March 26, 1976.

9. Heclo, "Presidential and Prime Ministerial Selection," p. 21.

10. Arnold J. Heidenheimer, *The Governments of Germany* (New York: Thomas Y. Crowell, 1961), p. 64.

11. *Christian Science Monitor,* April 25, 1963.

12. New York *Times,* July 4, 1979.

13. Robert Michels, *Political Parties: A Sociological Study of the Oligarchical Tendencies of Modern Democracy,* trans. Eden and Cedar Paul (New York: Free Press, 1949), *passim.*

14. Terence Prittie, "The Western German Election," *The Atlantic Monthly* 208 (August 1961): 64.

15. Since 1966, however, the Liberals' biennial national party meeting has been empowered, if necessary, to call a national leadership convention (which it has never done) should the delegates deem it necessary to review the party leadership. In 1969, the Progressive Conservatives amended their constitution to enable periodic review of the leadership by party convention. John C. Courtney, *The Selection of National Party Leaders in Canada* (Hamden, Conn.: Shoe String Press, 1973), pp. 99-104. Following Pierre Eliot Trudeau's decision to step down as leader of the opposition Liberal party in November 1979, party officials agreed to hold its next national leadership convention in Winnepeg, Manitoba, in late March 1980.

16. The low-man-out rule, which appears to reinforce the strong position of the early leader, was first applied in the 1967 and 1968 leadership conventions, although both parties had used a variation of it in earlier conventions. It is noteworthy that the leader on the first ballot has always been elected to the party leadership. Carl Baar and Ellen Baar, "Party and Convention Organization and Leadership Selection in Canada and the United States," in *Perspectives on Presidential Selection,* ed. Matthews, pp. 66-67.

17. Heclo, "Presidential and Prime Ministerial Selection," p. 64.

18. Robert MacGregor Dawson, *The Government of Canada* (Toronto: University of Toronto Press, 1948), p. 555.

19. Robert MacGregor Dawson, *The Government of Canada,* 5th ed., rev. Norman Ward (Toronto: University of Toronto Press, 1970), pp. 463-64.

20. Courtney, *Selection of National Party Leaders in Canada,* pp. 122-23; see also D. V. Smiley, "The National Party Leadership Convention in Canada: A Preliminary Analysis," *Canadian Journal of Political Science* 1 (December 1968): 373-97.

21. Eugene H. Roseboom, *A History of Presidential Elections* (New York: Macmillan, 1957), p. 373.

22. V. O. Key, Jr., *Politics, Parties, and Pressure Groups,* 5th ed. (New York: Thomas Y. Crowell, 1964), p. 373.

23. Though the following chronicle may not be typical of boss control during this

period, the late Professor E. M. Sait relates the following story about the delegate list of the Cook County (Chicago, Illinois) convention of 1896, as originally reported by R. M. Easley. "Among the 723 delegates, seventeen had been tried for homicide, forty-six had served terms in the penitentiary for homicide or other felonies, eighty-four were identified by detectives as having criminal records. Considerably over a third of the delegates were saloon-keepers; two kept houses of ill-fame; several kept gambling resorts." Howard R. Penniman, *Sait's American Parties and Elections,* 5th ed. (New York: Appleton-Century-Crofts, 1952), p. 283. There were also eleven former pugilists and fifteen former policemen, some of whom had backgrounds not dissimilar to those of the other convention delegates described above. Ibid.

24. The authoritative work on the early period of the presidential primary is Louise Overacker, *The Presidential Primary* (New York: Macmillan, 1926), p. 308.

25. Quoted by Austin Ranney, *Curing the Mischiefs of Faction* (Berkeley: University of California Press, 1975), p. 124.

26. Albert Pike, "Jonathan Bourne, Jr.—Progressive" (Ph.D. diss., University of Oregon, 1957), p. 135.

27. Overacker, *The Presidential Primary,* p. 17.

28. Ibid., p. 16.

29. Ibid.

30. North Dakota, *Public Documents,* vol. 3 (Bismarck, N.D.: Secretary of State, 1932), p. 3437.

31. Minneapolis *Morning Tribune,* April 12, 1949.

32. *A Study of the Presidential Primary,* Nevada Legislative Council Bureau Bulletin, no. 32 (Carson City, Nev.: NLCB, 1958), pp. 9-12.

33. *Acts* of 1965, Chapter 784.

34. See tables for 1968 and 1972 presidential primaries in Appendix.

35. Ibid.

36. Quoted in "Openness, Participation and Party Building: Reforms for a Stronger Democratic Party," *Report of the Commission on Presidential Nomination and Party Structure* (Washington, D. C.: Democratic National Committee, 1978), pp. 31-32.

37. Ibid., p. 30.

38. Ibid., p. 36.

Rules of the Game:————————3
Primary Laws and
Caucus-Convention Systems

Throughout the twentieth century both major parties have used a mixed nominating system to send delegates to the national conventions. The term "mixed system" refers to the optional, dual-tracked method involving both presidential primaries and the caucus-convention system used in the fifty states to select national convention delegates. (Table 3.1 lists separately the presidential primary and caucus-convention states.) As explained earlier, the United States is the only Western country to use a type of popular election in a majority of states to select delegates to attend an equally unique nominating body—the national convention.

Prior to 1900, presidential candidates were nominated by national convention delegates chosen exclusively through a "closed" caucus-convention system. With the rise of the presidential primary movement early in the twentieth century, however, legislatures in two dozen states gave rank-and-file voters a direct voice in the selection of national convention delegates. After World War I, the presidential primary movement ebbed. In 1935, only fifteen states used this form of direct popular participation in the presidential nominating process, and thirty-five states used the traditional caucus-convention system. But there was a major revival of primaries in the late 1960s and early 1970s. By 1976, the spread of presidential primaries to twenty-nine states resulted in the formation of almost twenty-nine varieties of primaries.[1] With thirty-three primaries scheduled for 1980, the variety of primaries may soon approach the number popularized by a famous food company. In this chapter our main task will be to analyze and classify the various types of primaries. Our attention will then shift briefly to an examination of the caucus-convention system used in the remaining seventeen states.

TABLE 3.1
PRESIDENTIAL PRIMARY AND CAUCUS-CONVENTION STATES, 1980

Presidential Primary		
Alabama	Louisiana	Ohio
Arkansas[a]	Maryland	Oregon
California	Massachusetts	Pennsylvania
Connecticut	Michigan	Puerto Rico
District of Columbia	Montana	Rhode Island
Florida	Nebraska	South Dakota
Georgia	Nevada	Tennessee
Idaho	New Hampshire	Texas
Illinois	New Jersey	Vermont
Indiana	New Mexico	West Virginia
Kansas	New York	Wisconsin
Kentucky	North Carolina	

Caucus-Convention		
Alaska	Maine	South Carolina[b]
Arizona	Minnesota	Utah
Colorado	Mississippi	Virginia
Delaware	Missouri	Washington
Hawaii	North Dakota	Wyoming
Iowa	Oklahoma	

a. Arkansas primary is for Democrats only.

b. The Republican Party of South Carolina will hold a party-sponsored presidential preference primary on March 8, 1980. The South Carolina Democratic Party will continue to use the caucus-convention system.

Types of Primaries

Despite their wide variation in form, state presidential primary laws can be divided into two general types: presidential preference votes, such as between Eisenhower and Taft, McGovern and Humphrey, Ford and Reagan, or Carter and Udall—the so-called ''beauty contest'' or popularity poll; and direct election of delegates to the national convention. However, because several of the states use various combinations of the two forms, there are actually four basic categories of primaries. Table 3.2 lists all of the presidential primary states and the types of primaries used by Democrats and Republicans in each state.

DELEGATE SELECTION ONLY

In four states—Alabama, New York, Ohio, Texas, and formerly South Dakota—the names of presidential candidates do not appear separately on the ballot. Voters cast ballots only for national convention delegate candidates who either have listed their presidential preference, run individually with no designation of presidential preference, or are designated simply as a slate pledged to a specified presidential candidate or identified by the name of the chairman of an uncommitted group, with no listing of individual delegate candidates on the ballot. Until recently, the state of New York held a delegate primary in which all district delegates ran unpledged. Under this "blind" ballot the party organization-selected candidates for delegate invariably won the election. In 1972, however, Senator George McGovern's reform-minded challengers entered full slates of unpledged candidates in nearly all congressional districts and won 263 of the 278 delegates in the Empire State Democratic primary. Shortly before the 1976 New York presidential primary, the state legislature repealed the confusing unpledged feature of the state law and permitted a pledged delegate requirement.[2] In Ohio, 75 percent of the delegates are chosen in congressional districts. Each delegate candidate must file with his declaration of candidacy a statement, signed by him, in which he shall state his first and second choices for presidential nominee of his party. In South Dakota delegate candidates have run on slates at the district level and at large, showing presidential preference or uncommitted status, but in 1980, South Dakota, for the first time will add a presidential preference primary to the ballot. The one-time-only Texas presidential primary, passed in May 1975 and valid for the 1976 election only, was written to self-destruct after the delegate selection process had been completed.[3] Unlike most states, Democratic delegates in Texas are elected from state senate districts and apportioned by a formula giving equal weight to population and the vote for Democratic candidates in the last two presidential elections.

BINDING PRESIDENTIAL PREFERENCE

Only the Republican party continues to use the straight binding presidential preference primary (the Democrats require that all binding preferences be based on proportionality). In 1980 the Republicans will use the binding (winner-take-all) primary in the following states: California, District of Columbia, Florida, Georgia, Indiana, Maryland, Ohio, Texas, Vermont, and Wisconsin. The results of the presidential preference primary bind district delegates to the winner of the preference primary in each congressional district and at-large delegates to the statewide winner.

TABLE 3.2

PRESIDENTIAL PRIMARY STATES AND TYPES OF PRIMARIES TO BE USED IN 1980

State	Date	Filing Deadline	Type of Primary	Declaration of Candidacy; Nominating Petition; Petition to Party
Alabama	March 11	January 14 (R) 15 (D)	Proportional	Petition filed by state chair between January 1-15, 1980.
Arkansas	May 27	April 1	Proportional (D)	Candidates file fee or petition with state committee of political party between March 11, 1980 and April 1, 1980.
California	June 3	March 21	P (D) WTA* (R)	Unselected candidates must file nomination papers with secretary of state.
Connecticut	March 25	February 8	Proportional	Petition filed with secretary of state by January 25, 1980. Candidate's written consent is required.
District of Columbia	May 6	March 7	P (D) WTA (R)	Petition filed with board of election by March 7, 1980. Candidate's signature required.
Florida	March 11	January 22	P (D) WTA (R)	Unselected candidates must submit written request.
Georgia	March 11	February 10	P (D) WTA (R)	Unselected candidates must submit written request by January 10-15, 1980.
Idaho	May 27	April 28	Proportional	Unselected candidates may file a nominating petition with secretary of state by April 27.
Illinois	March 18	December 31	AD	Candidates file petition with 3,000-5,000 signatures of party electors with State Board of Elections by December 24-31, 1979.

Signatures Required	Filing Fee	Placement of Names on Ballot of Recognized Candidates by Secretary of State	Withdrawal of Candidates
500 registered voters in the state or 50 in each district. At discretion of state party.	$100 (R)		State party chair notifies candidates who have 10 days to withdraw.
1% of registered party voters (R). Also 1,000 voters whichever is less.		Secretary of state places nationally recognized candidates on ballot by February 1, 1980.	File affidavit for withdrawal with secretary of state by March 31, 1980.
1% of the total number of enrolled party members.		Nationally recognized candidates are selected by secretary of state by January 25, 1980.	Candidates not nominated by petition may withdraw by February 12, 1980.
		Nationally recognized candidates are selected by secretary of state by January 8, 1980.	File affidavit for withdrawal with Department of State by January 22, 1980.
		Nationally recognized candidates selected by secretary of state by February 1, 1980.	Candidate files affidavit for withdrawal with secretary of state by February 20, 1980.
1% of votes cast in state for president at last election.		Nationally recognized candidates are selected by secretary of state by March 28, 1980.	

TABLE 3.2 (continued)

State	Date	Filing Deadline	Type of Primary	Declaration of Candidacy; Nominating Petition; Petition to Party
Indiana	May 6	March 7	P (D) WTA (R)	Candidates file petition with secretary of state between February 6 and March 7, 1980.
Kansas	April 1	February 12	Proportional	Petitions must be filed with secretary of state by February 12, 1980.
Kentucky	May 27	April 2	Proportional	Unselected candidates must file petition and fee with secretary of state by April 2.
Louisiana	April 5	February 29	Proportional	Candidate files petition with secretary of state or qualifies in two or more other states by February 25-29, 1980.
Maryland	May 13	March 3	P (D) WTA (R)	Candidates must file petition with State Administrative Board of Elections by February 19, 1980. Candidate's written consent required.
Massachusetts	March 4	January 4	Proportional	Candidate files petition or state chair of candidate's party submits candidate's name to secretary of state by January 4, 1980.
Michigan	May 20	March 21	Proportional	Candidate files petition or state Central Committee submits candidate's name by March 21, 1980.
Montana	June 3	March 15	P (D) A (R)	Candidate files petition with secretary of state by March 15, 1980.
Nebraska	May 13	March 14	P (D) AD (R)	Unselected candidates must file petition with secretary of state by March 14, 1980.
Nevada	May 27	April 25	Proportional	Unselected candidates must file petition with secretary of state by April 25, 1980.

Signatures Required	Filing Fee	Placement of Names on Ballot of Recognized Candidates by Secretary of State	Withdrawal of Candidates
500 registered voters in each congressional district.			Candidate must notify secretary of state by March 7, 1980.
Signed by 1,000 voters of same political party.	$100		
Signed by 5,000 registered voters of same political party.	$250 which shall be refunded if candidate receives 3% of the vote.	State Board of Elections will nominate all nationally recognized candidates by April 2, 1980.	
5,000 registered voters.			
Signed by 400 registered voters.	None	Nationally recognized candidates are selected by secretary of state by March 3, 1980.	Declaration of non-candidacy in the state, rather than nationally, is required.
2,500 registered voters.	$10	Nationally recognized candidates are selected by secretary of state by January 4, 1980.	Candidate must file affidavit with secretary of state by January 11, 1980.
0.5% of total vote cast for party's candidate in last election.		Nationally recognized candidates are selected by secretary of state by March 7, 1980.	Candidate must notify secretary of state by March 21, 1980.
1,000 qualified electors from each congressional district.			Candidate files affidavit with secretary of state by April 14, 1980.
Signed by 100 electors in each congressional district.		Nationally recognized candidates are selected by secretary of state by March 14, 1980.	Candidate files affidavit with secretary of state.
Signed by at least 5% of total votes cast for all candidates for Congress in last election.		Nationally recognized candidates are selected by secretary of state by April 25, 1980.	

TABLE 3.2 (continued)

State	Date	Filing Deadline	Type of Primary	Declaration of Candidacy; Nominating Petition; Petition to Party
New Hampshire	February 26	December 28	Proportional	Candidates file fee and petition with secretary of state by December 14-18, 1979.
New Jersey	June 3	April 24	P (D) AD (R)	Candidates file petition with secretary of state by April 24, 1980.
New Mexico	June 3	April 3	Proportional	Unselected candidates must file petitions with secretary of state by April 3, 1980.
New York	March 25		P(D) WTA(R)	
North Carolina	May 6	February 5	Proportional	Unselected candidates must file petitions with secretary of state by February 5.
Ohio	June 3	March 20	P (D) WTA (R)	Candidate forms steering committee to file slate of delegates. Candidate files petition with secretary of state for at-large delegates or with County Board of Elections by March 20, 1980.
Oregon	May 20	March 11	Proportional	Unselected candidates must file a petition with secretary of state between September 13, 1979 and March 11, 1980.
Pennsylvania	April 22	February 12	P (D) AD (R)	Petitions must be filed with secretary of the commonwealth by February 12, 1980.
Puerto Rico	Feb. 17 (R) March 16 (D)	January 14	WTA (R) P (D)	

Signatures Required	Filing Fee	Placement of Names on Ballot of Recognized Candidates by Secretary of State	Withdrawal of Candidates
Signed by at least 500 qualified voters of each congressional district.	$500		Candidate may withdraw within 10 days after being notified that his name is going to be placed on the ballot.
1,000 voters.			Candidate must write secretary of state by April 30, 1980.
2% of total presidential vote cast in each district in last election.		Nationally recognized candidates are chosen by secretary of state by March 5, 1980.	Candidate must notify secretary of state.
10,000 registered voters.		The State Board of Elections shall select all presidential candidates eligible to receive payments from the Presidential Match-Payment Account of February 25, 1980.	
1,000-3,000 registered party voters for at-large delegates and 150-300 for congressional district positions.			Candidate notifies person with whom he originally filed by March 30, 1980.
1,000 registered voters in each congressional district.		Nationally recognized candidates are selected by secretary of state.	Candidate files reasons made under oath with secretary of state 67 days prior to primary.
Signed by 100 registered party members in each of 10 counties.			Candidates may withdraw by filing written notice with secretary of the commonwealth by February 19, 1980.

TABLE 3.2 (continued)

State	Date	Filing Deadline	Type of Primary	Declaration of Candidacy; Nominating Petition; Petition to Party
Rhode Island	June 3	February 28	Proportional	Unselected candidate files petition or state party chair submits candidate's name to secretary of state by February 28, 1980.
South Dakota	June 3	April 1	P (D) SP (R)	Unselected candidate files writ of mandamus against State Board of Elections. A hearing must be held within five days.
Tennessee	May 6	March 4	Proportional	Unselected candidates file petition with state election committee by March 4, 1980.
Texas**	May 3	February 4	SP (R)	Candidates must file an application and a petition with secretary of executive committee by February 4, 1980.
Vermont	March 4	February 12	A (D) WTA (R)	Candidates file petitions with secretary of state by February 12, 1980.
West Virginia	June 3	March 29	AD	Candidates must file fee with secretary of state between February 25 and March 29, 1980.
Wisconsin	April 1	March 4	P (D) SP	Unselected candidates may file petitions with secretary of state by March 4, 1980.

Sources: Democratic National Committee; Republican National Committee; U.S. Congress, Senate, *Nomination and Election of the President and Vice President of the United States Including the Manner of Selecting Delegates to National Political Conventions*, compiled under the direction of Francis R. Valeo, Secretary of the Senate, for the U.S. Senate Library (Washington, D.C.: Government Printing Office, 1976), pp. 180-84; Carol F. Casey, Government Division, Congressional Research Service, The Library of Congress.

Signatures Required	Filing Fee	Placement of Names on Ballot of Recognized Candidates by Secretary of State	Withdrawal of Candidates
1,000 qualified voters.		Nationally recognized candidates are selected by secretary of state by February 20, 1980.	Files affidavit with secretary of state by May 4, 1980.
		Recognized candidates or persons filed with Federal Election Commission are selected by state board by April 1, 1980.	Candidate files withdrawal with secretary of state by April 1, 1980.
Petition must be signed by 2,500 registered voters.		Nationally recognized candidates are selected by secretary of state by March 4, 1980.	Candidate files affidavit with secretary of state by March 21, 1980.
5,000 registered voters.			Candidate files request with secretary of state by March 13, 1980.
Petition must be signed by 200 registered voters.	$1,000		Candidate must write secretary of state within 10 days of notification.
	$2,000		
1,000 to 1,500 qualified voters from each congressional district.		Nationally recognized candidates are selected by secretary of state by February 8, 1980.	May file an affidavit of withdrawal by February 29, 1980.

Note:
*   Types of primaries
A   Advisory
AD   Advisory with delegates on the ballot
P   Proportional
SP   State party decision
WTA Winner take all ("loophole" primary)
**   Texas State Democratic Executive Committee will decide
      in March 1980 whether to hold a presidential primary on May 3.

National convention delegates may be elected in the primary (District of Columbia, Maryland, Ohio, and South Dakota), by state convention (Indiana and Vermont), or through other procedures outlined in state party rules (California, Florida, Georgia, and Wisconsin).

In the California Republican primary, which retains the winner-take-all principle, the voter may mark a single box at the top of the delegate slate column headed by, say, "Candidates preferring Ronald Reagan." This mark on the ballot, in effect, represents a combined voter preference for Reagan and a vote for a full statewide delegate slate pledged to him. Thus, Reagan's victory over President Ford in the 1976 California Republican presidential primary netted him all 167 delegates under the "winner-take-all" law. Four years earlier, the 1972 Democratic National Convention, after a bitter credentials fight over the apportionment of delegates under California's "winner-take-all" primary, went on record as opposing this feature of the California law, used also in Rhode Island, Oregon and South Dakota. One of the recommendations of the Democratic National Committee's second reform task force, the Mikulski Commission, was to ban "winner-take-all" primaries.[4] Subsequently approved by the Democratic National Committee, this recommendation (Rule 11) became one of the new 1976 delegate selection rules. However, it was partially vitiated by a later national party ruling that permitted a so-called loophole primary at the congressional district level. This aberrant party rule is discussed later in the chapter. Although national convention directives do not supersede state primary laws, the Democratic-controlled California legislature scrapped the winner-take-all primary for the Democratic party and substituted proportional representation at the congressional district level.

ADVISORY PRESIDENTIAL PREFERENCE WITH SEPARATE
ELECTION OF NATIONAL CONVENTION DELEGATES

In Nebraska, New Jersey, Pennsylvania, and South Dakota for Republicans only; in Vermont for Democrats only; and in Illinois and West Virginia for both parties, one of the oldest and most popular forms of presidential primary is used. Voters mark their ballots twice: once to indicate their choice for president and once to indicate a choice of delegate candidates identified on the primary ballot as pledged, or, in New Hampshire, as "favorable to" a presidential candidate or "undesignated." In Illinois and West Virginia voters can express a preference choice for president and also choose district delegates who may be pledged or unpledged. Because the advisory preference primary was not binding on the elected delegates, presidential candidates in the past sometimes avoided these states, in which case no preference primary was held. With increasing competition for delegates and popular interest in the primaries, however, these states can usually expect a contest in their advisory preference primary. Vermont uses a non-binding preference primary, with delegates chosen through a separate caucus selection system which is completed at the state convention.

PROPORTIONAL REPRESENTATION—PRESIDENTIAL PREFERENCE

Some form of proportional representation is used in twenty-seven states. In 1980 the following states will use proportional representation in both parties: Alabama, Connecticut, Idaho, Kansas, Kentucky, Louisiana, Massachusetts, Michigan, Nevada, New Hampshire, New Mexico, North Carolina, Oregon, and Tennessee.

Proportional representation will be used in 1980 by the Democrats only in these states: Arkansas, California, District of Columbia, Florida, Georgia, Indiana, Maryland, Montana, Nebraska, New Jersey, Ohio, Pennsylvania, South Dakota, and Wisconsin. Allocation of national convention delegates to presidential candidates is based on the proportion of the preference vote each presidential candidate receives, either in a congressional district or on a statewide basis (see Table 3.2). Under 1976 rules, 80 percent of Idaho's delegates were allocated proportionately to each presidential candidate receiving at least 5 percent of the vote; in Kentucky, delegates were allocated proportionately only to the four presidential candidates receiving the highest number of votes, provided that each received at least 15 percent of the total votes cast. In Michigan and Nevada, delegates were allocated proportionately to each presidential candidate receiving at least 5 percent of the total vote. In California, the District of Columbia, Florida, Rhode Island and Wisconsin, delegates were allocated proportionately to each presidential candidate receiving at least 15 percent of the total vote. In Massachusetts, North Carolina and Oregon, the specific proportional allocation was determined by the state party.[5] In Oregon national convention delegates were not elected on primary day but subsequently chosen by district conventions.

According to the Democratic party ground rules drawn up before the 1976 primary season, future convention delegates must "be chosen in a manner which fairly reflects the division of preferences expressed by those who participate in the presidential nominating process."[6] Presidential preferential primaries are permitted for advisory purposes only, unless delegates are allocated to presidential candidates in proportion to the votes such candidate received, provided the candidate received at least 15 percent of the vote. Under Democratic rules, at least 75 percent of the delegates in every primary state have to be selected in units no larger than a congressional district. Under the 1980 Democratic proportional representation rules, delegates are allocated to presidential candidates in proportion to their popular vote in the primary, but in no case can the threshold for qualifying as a district delegate be higher than 25 percent of the vote in the district. In the caucus-convention states, delegates to the Democratic national convention are allocated in proportion to the support each candidate wins at the caucus, county convention, and district convention levels. The 1980 Democratic rules establish a flexible threshold for determining when a presidential candidate is guaranteed at least one delegate under proportional representation. In caucus states party officials may set a threshold no lower than 15 percent nor higher than 20 percent of the vote. Republican party rules do not prohibit the use of the winner-take-all rule in either presidential primary or the caucus-convention states. More will be said about the role of caucus-convention states below.

Special Categories

In discussing the various types of presidential primaries several new terms have been added to the nomenclature in recent years: "loophole" primaries, winner-take-all primaries and crossover primaries. To avoid misunderstanding a brief explanation of each term is in order.

LOOPHOLE PRIMARIES

Democratic party rules for 1976, as explained above, permitted broad exception to the proportional representation requirement—the "loophole" primary. For the list of states using this form of presidential primary, see Table 3.3. The loophole referred to the rule that permitted a presidential candidate in the primary to sweep all delegates on a "winner-take-all" basis at the congressional level. Thus, if a congressional district had five delegates and a candidate ran a full five-member slate that finished one through five, he won all five delegates. If a candidate repeated this performance in other congressional districts, he captured all of the district delegates. Under this loophole, a presidential candidate could theoretically sweep all of the delegates from the congressional districts within a state by a plurality (less than a majority) margin and not have to share district delegates proportionately, as is done in the other Democratic primary states. By virtue of the winner-take-all principle, the candidate would also collect the bulk of the statewide at-large delegates, too. More than half the 1976 convention delegates were chosen under this legalized loophole in the Democratic party rules. Despite support for the loophole primary by the Carter forces, the 1976 Democratic National Convention nevertheless voted to ban all loophole winner-take-all primaries in the future. But the Democrats have no assurance that the legislatures of the loophole states will cooperate and repeal the winner-take-all

TABLE 3.3
1976 PRESIDENTIAL PRIMARIES

Loophole	Proportional Representation (statewide)	Proportional Representation (by congressional district)	Advisory Preference only
California (R)	North Carolina	Massachusetts	Vermont
Florida (R)	Michigan	Florida (D)	
New Hampshire	Idaho	Indiana (D)	
Illinois	Kentucky (R)	Oregon	
New York	Nevada	California (D)	
Pennsylvania	Montana (D)	Wisconsin (D)	
Texas	Rhode Island	Kentucky (D)	
Georgia	South Dakota		
Nebraska	Arkansas		
West Virginia	District of		
Maryland (R)	Columbia (D)		
New Jersey	Tennessee		
Alabama			
Ohio			
Wisconsin (R)			
Indiana (R)			
Montana (R)			
District of			
Columbia (R)			

provision for the 1980 race. In the event that some legislatures refuse to do away with loophole primaries, the 1980 Democratic National Committee will require that delegates be selected by party caucuses and divided proportionately according to the popular vote.[7]

Democratic party rules for 1980 also ban single-member district primaries, that is, electoral districts in which only one national convention delegate is elected. Single-member district primaries are, of course, a subtle evasion of the loophole primary ban.

WINNER-TAKE-ALL PRIMARIES

As the term indicates, the victor in this type of primary wins all of the delegates in a congressional district or even the entire state. Because the Republicans at the national level have not outlawed winner-take-all primaries, challenger Ronald Reagan was able to win shut-out victories over President Ford in the 1976 California, Georgia, Montana and Texas primaries. Without these winner-take-all victories, Reagan probably would have been knocked out of the race larger than congressional districts. In other words, each presidential candidate can put up a slate of delegates pledged to him in areas no before the end of the primary season. In California, as mentioned earlier, Reagan swept all 167 delegates, even though President Ford collected 34 percent of the popular vote. Under a proportional representation system Ford would have been entitled to approximately fifty-seven delegates. During an early phase of the 1976 California primary campaign, a Ford supporter in the California legislature suggested that the GOP adopt the same proportional representation rules used by the Democrats. But this proposal met thunderous opposition from Reaganite Republicans who accused the Ford partisans of attempting to "change the rules in the middle of the game."[8] The 1976 Republican National Convention, even though controlled by President Ford's supporters, took no action to ban this form of primary from their delegate-selection process. In 1980 the Republicans, as indicated earlier, will hold winner-take-all primaries in nine states and the District of Columbia.

CROSSOVER PRIMARIES

Another complicating factor in the already highly complex primary system is that fifteen states in 1976 permitted voters to cross party lines and cast ballots for candidates of the opposite party.[9] Heretofore, crossover voting had been confined to "open" primary states (Wisconsin and Michigan) whose voters were not asked their party affiliation.[10] In crossover primary states voters are required to register but no party affiliation is indicated. The primary laws in crossover states contain no means for keeping Democrats from voting in Republican primaries or vice versa. In 1976, President Ford supporters complained that crossover voters cost them the Indiana primary and hurt their delegate count in several other states, especially Texas.

CLOSED PRIMARY

The other major form of presidential primary is the "closed" primary. In a closed primary system, participation is limited to party members. Fourteen states used closed presidential primaries in 1976.[11] In each state every voter is required to register as a Republican, Democrat, Independent or member of a third party. On primary election day, only a voter registered as a member of a party is eligible to vote in the party's primary, though in New Hampshire registered Independents can vote in whichever primary they choose. During a period of from nine to thirty-eight days before the primary a voter may change his or her party registration. But on primary election day the voter in the closed primary must vote a straight party ticket or his ballot will be invalidated. Primaries also vary in other ways.

ACCESS TO BALLOT

Until the early 1960s, presidential candidates could pick and choose the primaries they wished to enter; indeed, this was one of the major complaints made against the primary system.

In states—Alabama, Arkansas, Illinois, Indiana, Kansas, Louisiana, Montana, New Hampshire, New Jersey, Pennsylvania, Rhode Island, Texas, Vermont, and West Virginia, and the District of Columbia—the presidential candidate or his supporters still can exercise his discretion on entering or avoiding the primary. To obtain a place on the ballot he must take the initiative by filing a petition signed by a specific number of voters in the state. But in the remaining primary states neither the candidate nor his supporters possess the discretion to enter or stay out of the primary.

In eleven states—California, Connecticut, Idaho, Maryland, Massachusetts, Michigan, Nebraska, Nevada, Oregon, Rhode Island, and Tennnessee—the secretary of state places the names of all "generally advocated and nationally recognized presidential candidates" on the ballot.

In seven states—Florida, Georgia, Kentucky, New Mexico, North Carolina, South Dakota, and Wisconsin—a special nominating committee determines which presidential candidate will be listed on the ballot.

In three states—Massachusetts, Michigan, and Rhode Island—the state party may also nominate presidential candidates.

BINDING NATURE OF THE PRIMARY

The extent to which delegates are bound by the state presidential preference primary or by delegate pledges can, of course, affect delegate voting patterns at the national convention. The binding mandate on the delegate, however, varies from state to state.[12]

One ballot. In seventeen states—Alabama (D), Arkansas (D), District of Columbia, Indiana, Kansas, Kentucky, Louisiana, Maryland (D), Massachusetts, Montana (D), Nebraska (D), New Mexico, New York, North Carolina, Pennsylvania (D), Rhode Island (D), South Dakota (D), Vermont (R), and West Virginia—delegates are bound for only one ballot.

Two ballots. Michigan and Nevada delegates are bound for two ballots. National convention delegates from Florida, Georgia, Maryland (R), Nebraska (R), and Oregon are bound for two ballots, unless the candidate receives less than 35 percent of the votes needed for nomination on the first ballot. Tennessee delegates are bound for two ballots, unless the candidate receives less than 20 percent of the vote on the second ballot. For California (R), delegates are released after the first ballot if the candidate receives fewer than 10 percent of the votes required for nomination.

Three ballots. Texas delegates are bound for three ballots, unless the candidate receives less than 20 percent of the vote on the second ballot.

All ballots. In Connecticut, New Hampshire, and Rhode Island (R) delegates are bound until released. Wisconsin's delegates are bound until the candidate receives less than one-third of the total convention vote. The extent to which a primary is binding upon delegates beyond the first ballot, however, may not be as important as it appears for several reasons. First, neither party's national convention enforces state laws binding delegates. Second, within the Democratic party the right of a presidential candidate to approve national convention delegates identified with his candidacy ensures that delegates supporting him will remain loyal regardless of the state law governing a delegate's pledge. Third, for the past six conventions over the past two decades neither party has needed to go beyond the first ballot to find a nominee.

Not bound. National convention delegates are not legally bound by the results of the presidential preference primary or by their stated presidential preference in Idaho, Illinois, Montana (R), New Jersey, Ohio, Pennsylvania (R), or Vermont.

Far more important than the binding nature of the primary law on the convention outcome is the type of primary plan used: proportional, "winner-take-all," or districted. In the past few years the trend nationwide has been toward proportional primaries, especially within the Democratic party. But in 1972 this was less true; hence the differential impact of the type of primary used could be studied more extensively. Lengle and Shafer, in "replaying" the three major types of primaries, found that the same voting patterns would have brought a different distribution of delegate strength under each set of rules (see Table 3.4).[13]

Thus, in theory, Humphrey and Wallace would have done better under any of the three delegate plans, if they had been used consistently in all fifteen pre-California primaries, and McGovern would have been worse off. But in the real world of varied delegate selection plans McGovern fared best. Clearly, McGovern's adaptive strategy of tailoring his campaign to the type of primary plan used in a state, e.g., districted plan in Wisconsin and winner-take-all in Massachusetts, paid the maximum dividends.

TABLE 3.4
**DIFFERENTIAL IMPACT OF TYPE OF PRIMARY USED ON
ELECTORAL OUTCOME IN FIFTEEN PRE-CALIFORNIA
DEMOCRATIC PRIMARIES, 1972**

Candidate	Winner-Take-All	Proportional	Districted	Actual
Humphrey	446	314	324	284
Wallace	379	350	367	291
McGovern	249	319	343	401.5
Muskie	48	82	52	56.5
Others	0	27	6	59

Source: James I. Lengle and Byron Shafer, "Primary Rules, Political Power, and Social Change," *American Political Science Review* 70 (March 1976): 25-40.

If the 1976 primaries in both parties were replayed in a slightly different manner than Lengle and Shafer's 1972 study, the results would be similar in the Democratic party but not in the GOP.

In the fourteen Democratic states using proportional representation in 1976, Jimmy Carter was, according to a recent study by Jerome S. Burstein and Larry N. Gerston, overrepresented by an average of 5.1 percent. In Republican proportional primary states, President Ford was overrepresented by 2.1 percent. Translated into convention delegates, Carter gained forty-six additional delegates through proportional representation while Ford gained only one. In the loophole primary states both candidates scored additional gains. In eleven Democratic states using loophole primaries with aggregate statewide results, Carter was overrepresented by an average of 10.5 percent. Compared with a pure proportionality model, Carter gained ninety-five additional delegates through the loophole method, chiefly due to victories in the Texas and Ohio primaries. In the ten Republican loophole states, Burstein and Gerston calculated that President Ford was overrepresented by 5.8 percent. Ford picked up thirty delegates through the loophole method, chiefly because he scored well in states with big delegations, such as Illinois, New Jersey and Ohio.[14]

In the two winner-take-all Republicans primaries (Democratic party rules have banned winner-take-all primaries after 1976) President Ford had, at best, mixed success. In Wisconsin Ford was overrepresented by 45 percent (twenty delegates), but he was underrepresented in California by 34 percent (fifty-seven delegates). Combined, the totals showed that Ford received thirty-seven delegates less than he would have obtained under a pure proportionality model.

When all three types of primary states were totaled, Democratic nominee Jimmy Carter received an extra 141 delegates, while GOP nominee Ford lost six. It is ironic, as Burstein and Gerston point out, that in light of numerous Democratic delegate selection reforms over the past decade, Carter gained a free "bonus" of 141 delegates—almost the equivalent of an extra Ohio delegation—under the reformed rules in the primary states, whereas the delegate total of Gerald Ford, the GOP nominee, more accurately reflected true proportional representation, even though the Republican party has made only nominal changes in its national delegate selection process during this period.[15]

Caucus-Convention System

Among the remaining seventeen states sending delegates to the national convention, thirteen use the traditional three- four-tier caucus-convention system. To many citizens, the caucus-convention system remains a mystery, chiefly because they have never been involved in the political process. But the system, which dates back to the time of President Andrew Jackson, and even earlier, is not that complex. The operation of the caucus-convention system, though it may vary from state to state, begins in January, February, or the early spring with precinct caucuses or some other type of local mass meeting open to all voters. No national convention delegates, it should be noted, are elected at the precinct meetings.

As a first step, the caucuses elect delegates to county conventions. At the county level a smaller group of delegates is then elected to congressional district conventions; these same delegates usually also go to state conventions. The time frame for the caucus-convention system is similar, though slightly longer than the primary season—the final state conventions are sometimes not held until late July. As political insiders have long known, the key phase of the caucus-convention delegate selection process takes place at the precinct level, because it is the persons elected from this level who eventually decide who will attend the congressional district conventions, which pick 75 percent of the state's delegates to the national convention.

The congressional district conventions elect a minimum of two delegates to the national conventions. (The Democratic party allocates between two and seven delegates, based upon a combined formula of Electoral College representation and the size of the party's presidential vote in the past three elections.) The Democratic party in the caucus-convention states sets aside 25 percent of their delegates to be chosen at large by the state party conventions; within the Republican party the number of at-large delegates may run as high as 50 percent and even higher in some small states carried by the GOP presidential candidate in the last election. This arrangement enables state parties to select governors, U.S. senators, congressmen, state party chairpersons and other high party officials to serve as national convention delegates without competing for delegate seats against party members at the district convention.[16] Although the remaining three states—Hawaii, Arizona and Delaware—are all listed officially as caucus-convention states, they hold what are known as "firehouse primaries." In these states party members attend local mass meetings (often at a fire hall, school or other type of public building), vote on their presidential choice, and send delegates to congressional district conventions, which pick national convention delegates committed to specific presidential candidates.

Between 1968 and 1976, the number of caucus-convention states declined from thirty-four to twenty-one states. The proportion of convention delegates elected in the caucus-convention states (plus the territories) has, of course, similarly dwindled. In 1968 caucus-convention state delegates within the Democratic party comprised more than half (approximately 60 percent) of the convention membership. By 1976, the percentage of delegates selected under the caucus-convention system declined to less than 28 percent (732 delegates) in the Democratic party. Within the Republican party the number continues to be slightly higher because in a number of Southern states the GOP, unlike the Democrats, uses the caucus-convention system rather than primaries to pick delegates. Since 1968, only one state, New Mexico, dropped its presidential primary in favor of the caucus-convention system, but the New Mexico Legislature has again approved a new primary law for 1980. In 1976, the twenty-five states with the largest delegations to the Democratic national convention included only six caucus-convention states; of the twenty-six states (including the District of Columbia) with the smallest delegations, fifteen were caucus-convention states. Within the GOP the twenty-five states with the largest delegations to the Republican national convention included only seven caucus-convention states; the twenty-six states (including the District of Columbia) with the smallest delegations included sixteen caucus-convention states.

In 1976 approximately 750,000 Democrats participated in caucuses or mass meetings to select delegates in twenty-one states and four territories. The turnout ranged from 600 for county mass meetings in Wyoming to an estimated 120,000 for a party-operated delegation selection primary in Louisiana.[17] In Iowa's first-in-the-nation precinct caucuses, approximately 7.8 percent of registered Democrats (38,000 of 497,790) turned out statewide for the caucuses.[18]

Normally, the "definitive outcome" of the precinct caucuses is not confirmed for several weeks, until the precinct delegates elected to the county and congressional district conventions choose national convention delegates pledged or identified as supporters of a particular presidential candidate. This "time lag" in registering caucus results may explain, in part, why caucus-convention states have failed to command the media attention of primaries.[19] But greater interest in the caucuses by both the candidates and the national media occurred in 1976 for several reasons.

First, the national media focused their corps of network cameras and reporters on heretofore neglected "early bird" caucuses of five states— Iowa, Maine, Mississippi, Oklahoma and Alaska—which commenced their delegate selection process before the first-in-the-nation primary in New Hampshire.

Impatient for the biggest primary season ever to open, the national media in 1976 spotlighted their attention especially on the Iowa caucuses, 2,500 neighborhood meetings held in mid-January, as the rival Democratic presidential contenders sought to gain the early inside track in the nominating race before New Hampshire.[20] For the first time in history, pre-primary caucuses in a handful of states became recognized in 1976 as the first nationwide tests of political strength for the wide open field of Democratic presidential contenders. Second, the new Democratic party rules allocating delegates proportionately to presidential candidates who received at least 15 percent of the vote at the precinct-county-congressional district levels convinced all the presidential contenders that they had a chance to capture a share of the early caucus delegates and thereby attract nationwide media attention to their candidacy. Third, the new stipulation in the Democratic party rules requiring all caucus participants to declare their presidential preference or uncommitted status at the initial caucus meeting made for a wide open race. With these new rules the national media and delegates in other states could pinpoint support for each contender much more readily. Also, it became almost impossible for some presidential aspirants to claim a groundswell of delegate support from large blocs of uncommitted delegates when in fact they did not have it, because many prospective delegates, especially in the Democratic party, had already announced their preference by caucus time. In a word, the new "open" caucus system removed much of the backroom, behind-the-scenes manipulation that formerly characterized the delegate selection process in these caucus-convention states. As Leon Epstein recently observed, "The more open method character of the [caucus-convention] method, particularly under post-1968 Democratic rules, means that its import is not so radically different from that of the primaries as it was when there were stronger state party leaders."[21]

Because the more open participatory delegate selection process, spawned by the McGovern-Fraser and Mikulski reform commissions, has destroyed centralized delegation control by long-time party leaders, one observer reminds us "nomination politics requires the accumulation of delegates by candidate organizations through marshalling disparate support of various types of party voters and activists in an open competition for delegates in each state.''[22] Consequently, presidential contenders in both major parties have become more aware than ever that delegates chosen in the caucus-convention states count as one vote each, just as in the primary states. Delegate-hunting expeditions in the caucus-convention states are, however, extremely time-consuming, ''nickel-and-dime'' operations. But in a tight nominating race presidential contenders cannot afford to ignore the numerous small batches of delegates to be picked up in states such as Iowa, Missouri, Minnesota, Virginia and Washington. In 1976, Jimmy Carter collected over 500 delegates (70 percent of those elected by caucus-convention) from these states on his way to the nomination—and the presidency. Likewise, President Gerald Ford captured 277 delegates (43 percent) from the caucus-convention states to help produce his razor-thin 117-delegate margin over Ronald Reagan at the GOP convention in Kansas City.

Defeats in the early precinct caucus contests, it might also be noted, may sometimes be almost as devastating as defeats in the early primaries. In 1976, Texas Senator Lloyd Bentsen, an early challenger in the 1976 Democratic race, quietly dropped out of contention—despite an expenditure of $2 million in testing the political waters—after two disastrous setbacks in the Oklahoma and Mississippi precinct caucuses. As a Southerner, Bentsen's inability to run well in the early precinct caucus contests in his own region, especially his lowly 2 percent showing in Mississippi, quickly flattened his candidacy.[23]

In view of the high network media coverage given to Jimmy Carter's plurality victory in the 1976 Iowa first-in-the-nation precinct caucuses, it can be anticipated that Republican—and Democratic—challengers will all be lavishing suitor-like attention on the Iowa first-round precinct caucuses in 1980 and the years beyond. Iowa, in the minds of some candidate managers, has now replaced New Hampshire as the first important way station on the road to the presidential nomination. In any case, the caucus-convention states have taken on a new importance in the delegate selection process, even though the number of states using this time-honored system of picking national convention delegates has declined by over 50 percent in the past twelve years.

In summary, the dual-tracked presidential nominating process used in the United States is without doubt the most convoluted, time-consuming and expensive system for selecting national leaders extant in the Western world. It begins in January in snow-swept Iowa and continues on through thirty-three state primaries, the District of Columbia, Puerto Rico, and sixteen other caucus-convention states without interruption until shortly before national convention time in early July or August.

The spread of presidential primaries to more than thirty states and the

Democratic party's numerous rule changes in the delegate selection process—notably, the widespread adoption of proportional representation for both the primaries and the caucus-conventions—has produced a new strategic environment within which presidential candidates compete for the grand prize. Spillover from Democratic party reforms has also affected the Republican party's delegate selection process, especially in the states using proportional representation primaries. Let us, therefore, turn our attention to how presidential contenders in both parties have operated within this mixed system of primaries and caucus-conventions to formulate winning strategies.

Notes

1. For the most comprehensive study of the 1976 delegate selection process in all fifty states and the territories, see *Nomination and Election of the President of the United States* (Washington, D. C.: Government Printing Office, 1976). Compiled under the direction of the Secretary of the Senate, this informative document is issued quadrennially before each presidential election. Data in this chapter are derived chiefly from this source.

2. New York *Times,* March 12, 1976. The law applied only to the Democratic primary vote and to the 1976 primary only. In 1980, the only names on the New York Democratic ballot will be those of presidential candidates, a change from four years earlier. Unlike the 1976 "loophole" or winner-take-all primary law, the new law provides that Democratic delegates from each congressional district will be apportioned to match the presidential candidate's percentage of the district popular vote. Republicans in the Empire State will continue to use a winner-take-all delegate primary in 1980; no preference primary will be held. See *New York Times,* November 8, 1979. Source of information on 1980 GOP primary is Republican National Committee, Washington, D.C.

3. See *Congressional Quarterly Weekly Report XXXIV* (January 31, 1976): 233-34; Washington *Post,* February 27, 1975.

4. "Democrats All," mimeographed (Washington, D. C.: Democratic National Committee, 1973), p. 18.

5. For a convenient summary of primary laws in effect in 1976, see "Rules and Rigors of Year's Record Primaries," *Congressional Quarterly Weekly Report XXXIV* (January 31, 1976): 229-42.

6. "Democrats All," p. 18.

7. The Democratic National Committee's Compliance Review Commission (CRC), set up to review the 1980 delegate selection process in all fifty states and the territories, has recently made a few exceptions to the loophole ban. The CRC, for example, granted an exemption for the 1980 Illinois district winner-take-all primary. This was done after the Democratic legislative leaders in Springfield sought to establish a proportional primary in Illinois and their efforts were blocked by a coalition of Republicans and downstate Democrats. Although Democratic party rules now require proportional representation in delegate selection, the CRC has also approved two cases in which a candidate could win all the delegates in a district—if a candidate received at least 85 percent of the vote or if a candidate was at least fifty percentage points ahead of the runner-up, who received no more than 15 percent of the vote. "Democrats Struggle With Interpreting Rules," *Congressional Quarterly Weekly Report XXXVII* (September 15, 1979): 2006.

8. For details, see Los Angeles *Times,* June 6, 1976.

9. Crossover primary states: Arkansas, Alabama, Georgia, Idaho, Illinois, Indiana, Michigan, Montana, New Jersey, Ohio, Rhode Island, Tennessee, Texas, Vermont and

10. The Michigan and Wisconsin "open primaries" are in conflict with national Democratic party rules limiting participation in the delegate selection process to Democrats only. In 1976 the Democratic National Committee granted exemptions for these two state primaries. Thus far, however, the national party has made it clear that no exemptions will be granted for the 1980 primaries. If the Michigan and Wisconsin legislators do not "close" their primaries for 1980, Democrats in both states could be forced to elect their delegates in caucuses, instead of primaries. See "Presidential Primaries Reach Record Level," *Congressional Quarterly Weekly Report XXXVII* (August 4, 1979): 1614.

11. The closed primary states in 1976 were California, the District of Columbia, Florida, Kentucky, Maryland, Massachusetts, Nebraska, Nevada, New Hampshire, New York, North Carolina, Oregon, Pennsylvania, South Dakota and West Virginia.

12. *Nomination and Election of the President and Vice President of the United States,* pp. 177-78.

13. See James I. Lengle and Byron Shafer, "Primary Rules, Political Power, and Social Change," *American Political Science Review* 70 (March 1976): 25-40.

14. See Jerome S. Burstein and Larry N. Gerston, "Representation Theory and Presidential Primaries: An Examination of the 1976 Nominations" (Paper delivered at the annual meeting of the Midwest Political Science Association, Chicago, Illinois, April 19-21, 1979), p. 12.

15. Ibid., p. 15.

16. The Democratic party's recent rules review task force—the Winograd Commission—recommended in 1978 the expansion of each state delegation by 10 percent to accommodate state party and elected officials. These "automatic" delegates are to be elected by either a state party convention or previously-selected national convention delegates with special consideration given to Democratic governors, U.S. senators and representatives, and state party chairmen. Adopted by the Democratic National Committee in June 1978, the new rules also stipulate that the "automatic" delegates must reflect for one ballot the presidential preferences of the national convention delegates chosen earlier in caucuses and presidential primaries. Inclusion of these additional delegates will make the 1980 Democratic National Convention the largest in the party's history—3,331 delegate votes, 323 more than 1976. See "Presidential Primaries Reach Record Level," *Congressional Quarterly Weekly Report XXXVII* (August 4, 1979): 1609-10.

17. See "Caucuses: Light Turnout Many, Many Uncommitted," *Congressional Quarterly Weekly Report XXXV* (July 10, 1976): 1809-11.

18. Steven L. Schier, "The 1976 Iowa Democratic Presidential Caucus/Convention Process: Explaining Participation and Candidate Support" (Paper delivered at the Midwest Political Science Association Meeting, April 19-21, 1979, Chicago, Illinois).

19. For an excellent comparison of caucuses and primaries, see Thomas R. Marshall, "Caucuses vs. Primaries: How Much Do Delegate Selection Institutions Really Matter?" (Paper delivered at the 1977 annual meeting of the American Political Science Association, Washington, D. C., September 1-4, 1977).

20. The Iowa story is best told by Schier, "The 1976 Iowa Democratic Presidential Caucus/Convention Process."

21. Leon D. Epstein, "Political Science and Presidential Nominations," *Political Science Quarterly* 93 (Summer 1978): 187.

22. Schier, "The 1976 Iowa Democratic Presidential Caucus/Convention Process."

23. "Oklahoma Defeat Reduces Bentsen to Favorite Son," *Congressional Quarterly Weekly Report XXX* (February 14, 1976): 322.

The Winning Formula_____4

Over the past three decades several lessons have emerged from the presidential primary campaigning that are instructive about a process which, more than anything else, transforms a candidate for the highest office in the land into the party nominee. In this chapter we will endeavor to explain and summarize the strategies of winning (and losing) candidates in the primaries.

Importance of an Early Start

In recent years the successful party nominee for president has invariably developed a long-range campaign plan long before his formal announcement of candidacy. Clearly, the opening phase of a presidential nominating campaign in a fifty-state constituency of 220 million citizens no longer can be postponed until the final months before the convention. The task of collecting a majority of national convention delegates has become too complicated, especially with thirty-three presidential primary races. Over the past two decades the country has seen the gradual emergence of the continuous four-year presidential nominating campaign—a campaign which quietly begins for contenders in the losing party soon after the ballots have been counted in the last presidential election. Candidates do not, of course, for tactical and other reasons immediately hold a press conference to announce their candidacy. But some of the early aspirants, especially leading senators and former vice presidents, begin traveling the Lincoln Day and Jefferson-Jackson dinner circuit to help raise money for the state party organization—and to become acquainted with prospective delegates and potential campaign contributors. Statesman-like utterances on the major domestic and international issues are heard with greater frequency. Foreign tours, with stop-offs in London, Paris, the Kremlin and, with luck, Peking, are *de rigueur* for future White House contenders. Correspondents of the national media begin paying increasing attention to the prospective contenders. GOP Senate Minority Leader Howard Baker, an unannounced but highly touted contender for the 1980 Republican nomination, provides a recent example of the continuous presidential nominating campaign. While appearing at one of several Tennessee GOP receptions and press interviews in late August 1977, Baker was asked if this tour was the opening round of his quest for the GOP nomination in 1980. Baker responded, "I have no presidential campaign." Guffaws from the press corps prompted him to amend the answer to, "Right now there is no presidential campaign."[1] Baker's reply was not unlike that of other recent White House aspirants who, for a variety of political reasons, have wished to hold off a formal announcement. But the candidate must start early. For each successful nominee of the out-of-power party in the past four national elections the centerpiece of the nominating plan has been an intensive early bird presidential primary campaign to capture delegates and build psychological momentum.

The kick-off of John F. Kennedy's spectacular drive for the 1960 Democratic nomination actually took place at the 1956 Democratic convention in Chicago. Kennedy and his Massachusetts advisors decided at the eleventh hour that the smart strategy for making a determined run for the presidency in the 1960 election would be to conduct a trial run by offering his name as a vice-presidential candidate at the 1956 Democratic conclave. This was not an empty gesture. Democratic nominee Adlai Stevenson, throwing tradition to the winds, had decided to allow the convention delegates to choose his vice-presidential running-mate, instead of traditionally making the selection himself. Even before the balloting started, it seemed obvious to many convention watchers that Senator Estes Kefauver of Tennessee, Stevenson's chief adversary in the primaries, was the delegates' sentimental favorite. Kefauver won the vice-presidential nomination, but not until after Kennedy had given him a hard race. During the second ballot Kennedy at one point reached 647.5 votes—only thirty-nine votes short of a majority—but last-minute shifts to Kefauver in several delegations finally put the Tennessee senator over the top.[2] Even in defeat, Kennedy proved to be a popular new face in the party. By failing to win the vice-presidential nomination, Kennedy also avoided being directly tarnished with the "loser" label after the Stevenson-Kefauver ticket went down in flames in the 1956 general election against President Eisenhower.

Soon after the second Democratic presidential defeat in a row, Kennedy wasted no time in laying plans for an all-out assault on the presidency in 1960. Normally, during the first two years after the out-of-power party fails to regain the White House a political vacuum exists within its ranks.

Demoralized from defeat and uncertain about its leadership, the out-of-power party slowly starts casting about for a prospective nominee to make the next try for the White House. Kennedy and his advisors, however, saw this political doldrum period as a golden opportunity to build future support. Kennedy, a war hero, Pulitzer Prize-winning author and member of a famous family, accepted numerous speaking invitations to Democratic fund-raising dinners and other party events throughout the land. During this era it was still customary for candidates to disavow presidential ambition early in the pre-primary period. Kennedy was no different than many of his predecessors when, on several public occasions in 1957, he denied interest in the nomination. At the Women's National Press Club in April 1957, he stated that he was "not a candidate" for either the presidency or vice presidency. "Nor do I expect to be nominated for either job," he added.[3] Although he faced re-election to the U. S. Senate in 1958, Kennedy campaigned extensively for other Democratic senatorial, congressional and gubernatorial candidates, winning friends and building up future political IOUs. When Kennedy demolished his 1958 senatorial opponent by more than 800,000 votes, the national media soon began focusing more and more attention on the attractive young Massachusetts senator. Meanwhile, his administrative assistant, Theodore Sorenson, continued building his needed political files on important state party leaders and potential delegates. (Most delegates during this period were chosen by the caucus-convention system, and many prospective delegates could be identified easily early in the selection process; only sixteen states used presidential primaries, and most of them had advisory, not mandatory, delegate voting instructions.) By the time Kennedy formally announced for the Democratic presidential nomination, on January 4, 1960, he and Sorenson had laid the groundwork for a well-organized campaign: seven primary and several key caucus-convention states.

Looking back, Kennedy had merely taken a page out of Franklin Delano Roosevelt's campaign book for his 1932 drive for the White House. FDR's brilliant campaign manager, James A. Farley, had devoted most of the previous two years to visiting and corresponding with prospective delegates across the land, paving the way for Roosevelt's fourth ballot nomination at the 1932 Chicago convention. To be sure, Kennedy did not face one Gibraltar-sized obstacle that Roosevelt encountered—the Democratic two-thirds rule (repealed in 1936), which required a two-thirds majority of all delegates to win the nomination. Nevertheless, he had to overcome the formidable handicaps of youth (he was only forty-three years old), his Roman Catholicism (then regarded as a serious barrier to the nomination), and his yet-to-be-demonstrated vote-getting ability. Much of the credit for Kennedy's successful drive for the nomination and the presidency can be attributed to his early, well-organized start, especially in the primary states.

Since then, other successful candidates in the out-of-power party have used the same format of a continuous four-year nominating campaign: Senator Barry Goldwater in 1964, former Vice President Richard Nixon in 1968, Senator George McGovern in 1972, and former Georgia Governor Jimmy Carter in 1976.

Senator Goldwater, a token opponent to Vice President Richard Nixon at the 1960 GOP national convention (he collected only eleven votes), began laying plans to run for the 1964 GOP presidential nomination soon after Kennedy narrowly defeated Nixon in November 1960. As chairman of the Senate Republican Campaign Committee, Goldwater happily accepted numerous speaking engagements nationwide, especially at GOP fund-raisers during the 1962 off-year election campaign. Although he did not formally enter the 1964 GOP sweepstakes until January of that year, Goldwater had developed the nucleus of an effective grass-roots campaign organization, particularly in the caucus-convention states (two-thirds of the delegates were still chosen in these states), during his numerous forays around the political circuit. Goldwater's early start, far ahead of all his intraparty rivals, coupled with his excellent organizational campaign planning, especially in the caucus-convention states, enabled him to win a one-sided, first-round victory at the 1964 Republican convention.

Following Goldwater's disastrous loss to President Johnson in 1964, former Vice President Nixon quietly began laying the foundation for another White House try in 1968. During the 1966 off-year elections, Nixon traveled more than 30,000 miles, speaking on behalf of more than eighty-two candidates—and building up a large number of political due bills, cashable in 1968. By the fall of 1967 Nixon had lined up veteran campaign supporters in most of the key primary states. So effective was Nixon's early campaign start that he successfully preempted most of those party leaders and thereby thwarted Michigan Governor George Romney, his chief competitor, from building an organizational network in the primary states. Romney, frustrated by Nixon's undercover work in these states and handicapped by weak ratings in the opinion polls, suddenly bowed out of the 1968 race ten days before the first primary in New Hampshire.[4]

Senator George McGovern's long, arduous bid for the 1972 Democratic nomination really began shortly after Robert Kennedy's assassination in June 1968. At the riot-torn 1968 Democratic convention in Chicago, McGovern served as a presidential stand-in candidate (he collected 126 votes) for the leaderless Kennedy supporters. Though his brief 1968 presidential bid failed, McGovern nevertheless established the grass-roots political contacts and fund-raising base needed to mount a drive for the 1972 Democratic nomination. Formally announcing his presidential candidacy in January 1971—eighteen months before the 1972 convention—McGovern concentrated on building up a cadre of dedicated supporters in both the primary and caucus-convention states long before his chief rivals, Senators Muskie, Humphrey and Jackson and New York Mayor John Lindsay, realized what was happening.[5] During the early stages of the race Muskie and Humphrey appeared, on paper at least, to be more formidable contenders than McGovern. Throughout the three-year pre-primary period the Gallup polls showed Senators Edward M. Kennedy, Humphrey and Muskie far in the lead as presidential choices of Democratic voters. But unlike McGovern, they failed to recognize soon enough the vital importance of building up organizational support at the grass-roots level long before the primary season opens. Humphrey especially was hurt by his late entry in the 1972 presidential sweepstakes. The "Happy Warrior" did not enter the race formally until January 10, 1972, nor seriously "make a frontal assault on the nomination" until shortly before that date. Later, Muskie and Humphrey also discovered that ideologically oriented, activist candidates, such as McGovern, sometimes possess a special advantage over middle-of-the-road candidates in low-turnout primaries; they can mobilize their supporters to go to the polls while the moderates' would-be backers stay home waiting until the November general election to vote. But then it is too late.

Jimmy Carter, an obscure, lame duck Georgia governor who in two short years after stepping down from office became president of the United States, borrowed extensively from the McGovern nominating game plan, most notably the importance of starting early. Freed from his gubernatorial responsibilities in 1975 by a constitutional limit of one term, Carter was able to devote more than 260 days of solid campaigning for the presidency throughout the country while most of his rivals were preoccupied with official duties in Washington. Carter's early bird campaign helped him win the vital, first-round precinct caucuses in Iowa and the lead-off New Hampshire primary. Overnight Carter became a national figure. Although less than one-quarter of the 3,000 Democratic delegates were chosen during the first three months of 1976, Carter and his managers shrewdly concluded that the major political confrontations would take place during this early period. "It was a 'high-risk' approach," explained Hamilton Jordan, Carter's campaign manager, "but we expected that even though there were relatively few delegates at stake during this period, there would still be a high level of attention, which, if we could do well, will not only provide us with psychological momentum but also eliminate some of the other candidates."[6]

Reflecting on the history of recent successful presidential nominating campaigns, it seems beyond question that future "how to win a presidential nomination" campaign handbooks will include a chapter on the basic requirement that the presidential contender mount an early, if not continuous, four-year nominating campaign.

Merely to start early, however, is no magic formula for winning the nomination. Senator Edmund Muskie launched his 1972 nominating drive at least a year before the Miami Beach convention, but he failed miserably. One of the main causes of Muskie's ill-fated drive was his managers' attempt to organize his campaign from the top downward, that is, by relying on big-name endorsements from U.S. senators, former governors, elder statesmen, and so on, instead of building from the bottom up in the primary states. Only in retrospect did Muskie recognize his failure to develop his campaign at the grass-roots level. Lack of sound organizational groundwork led to early round defeats in Florida, Wisconsin, Pennsylvania and Massachusetts, losses from which Muskie never recovered. This topic will be discussed further below.

Crucial Early Media Impact

With the gradual decline of political parties in the United States, the role of the mass media in the electoral process has steadily expanded. No wonder political candidates, whose ultimate goal is the White House, focus on the mass media to build name recognition—a basic ingredient of a successful campaign. To move into the front-runner spot, presidential campaign managers in the out-of-power party stay up until the wee hours devising methods to capture television network and national press media coverage early in the nominating race. With twenty-nine primaries in 1976, candidate managers faced the complicated task of reaching huge numbers of voters with only limited funds. The only possible way that candidate organizations could hope to establish contact with the mass voting public was "to load onto the media the costs of voter communication through the adoption of explicit strategies for dominating news coverage."[7]

Jimmy Carter recognized this crucial factor long before intraparty rivals in his drive for the 1976 Democratic nomination. By capturing a plurality victory in the Iowa precinct caucuses—the first test in the 1976 race—Carter gained priceless national media exposure. Carter's much misunderstood Iowa "victory" was actually less than a smashing triumph. The largest bloc of caucus support, 38.5 percent, went to uncommitted delegates. Carter received only 29.1 percent of the precinct caucus vote. Senator Birch Bayh, who came in second among the active contenders, received 13 percent, followed by Fred Harris, 10 percent, Udall, 6 percent, and Sargent Shriver, who fell badly off the pace, with 3.3 percent. But to hear the national television and press reports from Iowa the sideline observer might have concluded that Carter had won the greatest victory since Wellington defeated Napoleon at Waterloo. CBS correspondent Roger Mudd reported:

With 88 percent of Iowa's 2,500 caucuses in, no amount of bad mouthing by others can lessen the importance of Jimmy Carter's finish. He was the clear winner in this psychologically crucial test. With thirteen projected national convention delegates, almost 28 percent of the total, Carter has opened ground between himself and the rest of the so-called pack.[8]

Almost overnight, his recognition factor among rank-and-file voters skyrocketed. Carter's first-place finish in Iowa had made him a national celebrity. The next week's issue of *Time* and *Newsweek* devoted 726 lines to his candidacy; Udall, Harris, Bayh, Jackson and Shriver were given but thirty lines apiece. Then, too, Carter received special post-election coverage on the networks' morning "Today" show-type programs, and the CBS, NBC, and ABC evening half-hour news programs showered him with five times as much coverage as each of his major rivals. As a bonus, the printed media gave him approximately four times as many column inches as his opponents. Carter's media coverage also served to publicize cost-free the "new face" image he sought to project across the country.[9]

Carter's newly acquired national stature also helped him, as planned, to win a narrow victory in the first-in-the-nation New Hampshire primary. Long before the candidates began moving through New Hampshire's hills and mills, Carter had concluded that New Hampshire would, at least in 1976, exert a critical power over presidential aspirations of the half dozen entrants. Although this small New England state sent only seventeen of 3,008 delegates (0.6 percent) to the 1976 Democratic National Convention, New Hampshire, by virtue of its huge media influence, probably had more to say about who the out-of-party nominee would be than any other state. Carter's New Hampshire victory produced an instant publicity bonanza. Declared NBC's Tom Pettit, "So Carter emerges from New Hampshire as the man to beat."[10] According to *Newsweek,* "On the Democratic side, former Georgia Governor Jimmy Carter was the unqualified winner, with 30 percent of the vote in a crowded field."[11] Carter's face adorned the covers of both *Time* and *Newsweek.* On the inside pages he received 2,630 lines. Second-place finisher Morris Udall got only 96 lines. In fact, all of Carter's major opponents—Udall, Harris, Shriver and Bayh—received a combined total of only 300 lines.[12] Ironically, less than 5,000 votes separated Carter from second-place finisher Udall in the New Hampshire primary; further-more, the four Democratic liberal candidates, Udall, Bayh and Harris, and Shriver, received a combined total of almost 60 percent of the Democratic vote to Carter's 30 percent. But this fact was conveniently ignored by the national news media, which were interested only in telling listeners and readers about the victorious candidate, Jimmy Carter. In primary elections, as in all elections, winning is everything. More than any of his rivals, Carter and his campaign managers recognized that the New Hampshire primary has become, in columnist David Broder's words, "the most heavily promoted media event of our outrageously theatrical presidential nominating system."[13]

The enormously amplified effect of the New Hampshire presidential primary has now been clearly documented through an in-depth study of network television newscasts during the 1976 presidential nominating campaign. Michael J. Robinson and Karen A. McPherson, monitoring the three national television network shows from November 24, 1975, to April 9, 1976, counted 337 stories about primary races in the first eight states to hold primaries. Almost one-third of the stories—100 to be exact—were devoted to New Hampshire.[14] In a seventy-day period before the New Hampshire primary, approximately 54 percent of the campaign news on television and 34 percent of the campaign stories in the news-papers were mostly or entirely devoted to New Hampshire (see Table 4.1).

Robinson and McPherson found that New Hampshire, which gave Carter his first primary victory, cast a total of 82,381 Democratic votes, and on the day following the election generated 2,100 seconds of total news time on the three television networks, 700 news seconds per net-work. New York, won by Senator Henry Jackson a month later, cast 3,746,414 Democratic votes, but on the following day received only 560 seconds on the three network newscasts, or fewer than 190 news seconds per network. Proportionately speaking, New Hampshire received 170 times as much network news time per Democratic vote as did New York. Uniformly, the three network news shows, all of which originate in New York City, downplayed the Empire State primary in favor of the small first-in-the-nation New England primary, even though New York State's population is forty times larger than New Hampshire.

Viewed from the standpoint of convention delegates, New Hampshire got 2.6 TV stories for each of the 38 delegates it elected to the two national conventions. The next two most publicized states, Massachusetts and Florida, together selected more than seven times as many delegates as New Hampshire, but received no more television exposure than the small New England state. In contrast, the ten non-primary states that started the delegate-selection process before the New Hampshire primary picked twelve times as many delegates but received far fewer stories combined than New Hampshire did alone.

TABLE 4.1

**PERCENT OF ATTENTION GIVEN TO EACH STATE BY
NETWORK TELEVISION (1972, 1976) AND DAILY
NEWSPAPERS (1976), DELEGATE SELECTION STORIES ONLY**

State	1976 TV	1976 Print	1972 TV
Alabama			
Alaska		0.5	
Arizona			1.3
Arkansas			
California	2.2	1.8	
Colorado			
Connecticut			
Delaware			
District of Columbia		0.9	
Florida	7.5	10.4	25.7
Georgia			
Hawaii			
Idaho			
Illinois	1.6	4.1	2.6
Indiana			
Iowa	5.9	6.6	3.3
Kansas			
Kentucky		0.2	
Louisiana			
Maine	0.5	0.7	
Maryland		0.2	1.3
Massachusetts	17.3	8.8	2.0
Michigan			1.3
Minnesota	0.5	0.5	
Mississippi	1.1	2.5	
Missouri			
Montana			
Nebraska			
Nevada			
New Hampshire	53.5	34.3	46.1
New Jersey		0.2	
New Mexico			
New York		9.8	
North Carolina	0.5	0.2	
North Dakota			
Ohio	0.5	5.2	
Oklahoma	2.2	2.0	
Oregon			2.0
Pennsylvania	1.1	0.9	4.6

TABLE 4.1 (continued)

State	1976 TV	1976 Print	1972 TV
Rhode Island			
South Carolina		0.2	
South Dakota			
Tennessee		0.2	
Texas		0.7	
Utah			
Vermont		1.1	
Virginia			
Washington			
West Virginia	1.6	0.9	2.0
Wisconsin	1.6	1.1	5.3
Wyoming			
Puerto Rico		0.2	
Virgin Islands			
No state	0.5	2.0	2.0
Multiple states	1.6	3.6	
Total number	185	441	155

Source: Michael Robinson and Karen McPherson, "The Early Presidential Campaign in the American News Media: Images That Matter in Television News," Washington, D. C., Catholic University, 1977, mimeo.

Note: Percentages for 1976 cover the seventy days from November 24, 1975, to April 9, 1976.

Another survey, conducted by Robinson and McPherson, which included both the three television networks and three newspapers (New York *Times*, Washington *Post* and Columbus [Ohio] *Dispatch*) showed that between November 24, 1975, and April 9, 1976, all fifty states received a total of 616 news stories on the national convention delegate selection process. Of this number New Hampshire alone received 250 news stories—41 percent of the total. The second most closely covered state, Massachusetts, received seventy-one stories, only 28 percent of the New Hampshire total.

All ten non-primary states that held their caucuses before the New Hampshire primary received a total of seventy-seven news stories. New Hampshire, alone, received more than three times as many, despite the fact that these ten states had been apportioned more than 500 delegates (both parties) to the nominating conventions, more than twelve times as many as New Hampshire. Veteran party watchers in 1976 suggested that these opening round precinct caucuses might be stealing headlines away from New Hampshire. But the Robinson-McPherson data show that these ten states combined received only one-fifth the number of news stories devoted to New Hampshire.

On the basis of their media analysis, Robinson and McPherson concluded, "recent history leads us to believe that winning New Hampshire and one of the two big communications states (Massachusetts and Florida) is tantamount to winning the nomination."[15] This view, while appealing at first glance, overstates New Hampshire's influence, although it is true, as New Hampshire citizens remind us, that ever since Dwight Eisenhower's primary victory in 1952, no one has been elected president of the United States who has not won its primary. But the record also shows that several New Hampshire primary victors in the out-of-power party have not won the nomination: Senator Estes Kefauver (D, Tenn.), 1956; former Senator Henry Cabot Lodge (R, Mass.), 1964; Senator Edmund Muskie (D, Maine), 1972. Still, it is beyond dispute that New Hampshire exerts a disproportionately heavy influence on the presidential nominating process, probably greater indeed than the influence of the primaries in our two most populous states, California and New York. Columnist David Broder, paraphrasing Sir Winston Churchill's famous statement, has aptly described the enormous influence of the New Hampshire primary, "aspiring presidents will continue to believe that nowhere else can so much be gained from so few."[16]

Carter's other attention-getting activities—his anti-Washington posture, his peanut farmer background, and his "born again" Baptist religion—produced extraordinary one-sided press coverage in the early primaries. As a leading authority on political television has reported:

In the critical period between the New Hampshire and Pennsylvania primaries he received 43 percent of the network evening news given the Democratic contenders, 59 percent of the space in *Time* and *Newsweek,* and 46 percent of the newspaper coverage. Jackson and Udall were the next most covered candidates, but they received nowhere near the attention of Carter. Each ended up with less than 20 percent of newspaper and television coverage, less than 15 percent of *Time*'s and *Newsweek*'s. Wallace got even less coverage, averaging just over 10 percent of that given to the Democratic candidates. Harris, Bayh, and Shriver received only passing attention in the news.[17]

This type of "winner-take-all" journalism helped Carter's public recognition increase fourfold, rising from 20 percent to over 80 percent; no other active candidate's recognition so much as doubled or, excepting George Wallace, reached as high as 50 percent.

As all political experts know, "the dynamic element in an election campaign is rising or declining (or stagnating) political support."[18] The exaggerated media coverage was a major factor in generating Carter's bandwagon momentum during the early stages of the primary season. Political momentum is not easily defined, but it's the one essential factor that all candidates are looking for. Probably no one is a better authority on momentum than the perennial 1976 primary loser, Representative Morris Udall. "Never underestimate the importance of momentum in these presidential elections," Udall said. "We all said we weren't going to let New Hampshire do it to us again, and New Hampshire did do it. We all said the Iowa caucus wasn't that important, and the press made it that important. . . . Once that avalanche starts down the ski slope, get out of the way."[19] In another interview Udall described Carter's media influence this way: "If I had to sum up the reason for Carter's success, I would do it in one word—'momentum,' " he said. "It's the scoreboard psychology—who's ahead, who's behind. . . . Only a handful of votes separated us, but Carter got the magazine covers, the TV interview, the headlines."[20] A leading authority on parties has summed up momentum dynamics this way:

When this "momentum" is combined with the proportionality or "fair reflection" rules, which guarantees the early front runner sizable blocs of delegates from later primaries even in states where he finishes only second or third in the preferential polls, it makes the fast start almost irresistible.[21]

Carter's surprising popularity and media coverage in the early caucus-convention and primary states also helped him enormously in pushing up his rating in the public opinion polls. Ten months before the 1976 Democratic National Convention Carter's name was not even listed among the viable presidential candidates in the Gallup poll standings, except to note that he was among ten candidates who received support from less than three percent of the respondents. Presidential primaries are the major vehicle to gaining leadership in national public opinion.

If presidential contenders wish to take full advantage of the primary season to mobilize public opinion, they must catapult out of the starting blocks during the first half dozen primaries. This is because public opinion remains highly volatile for only the first few weeks of the primary season while most candidates' faces are new and their positions unknown to the general public. Voters—and the national media—begin to choose up sides soon after the Iowa caucuses and the New Hampshire primary. The early round primaries, notably New Hampshire and Wisconsin, have had by far the greater impact on national opinion than later primaries, even in much larger states. New Hampshire, according to James R. Beniger, has been worth an average of 8.4 points on the Gallup poll over the past forty years.[22] Unlike a horse race, the first quarter of the presidential primary sweepstakes is likely to be far more important than the second half, because the front-runner can move ahead so swiftly that other lagging candidates will drop out of the race entirely rather than attempt a comeback in the last half mile. In 1976 Jimmy Carter gambled that the momentum generated by his early victories would carry him through the later primaries, even though he won only six of the last sixteen match-ups. As one of Carter's aides readily conceded in a post-convention interview, "We organized only three states in depth—Iowa, Florida, and New Hampshire."[23] It is noteworthy that during the early phase of the nominating race, Jimmy Carter's rating in the Gallup poll leaped from 4 percent in the January 23-26, 1976, poll to 29 percent in the March 19-23 poll. Recent nominating history shows that late starters can entertain little hope of catching up with the front-runner who capitalizes on his early primary victories to pyramid his standing in the opinion polls.

Other Democratic candidates in 1976, especially Senator Henry "Scoop" Jackson, who had been in hot pursuit of the presidency for more than four years, tried and failed to win the kind of media coverage that could get their campaigns rolling. Even though Jackson won two early big state primaries, Massachusetts and New York, and led Carter in the overall primary vote before the Pennsylvania primary by approximately 1.9 million to 1.6 million votes, he was unable to score a breakthrough on the national media after the first wave of primaries. Morris Udall, another early starter, finished second in both Iowa and New Hampshire, but the Arizonan received precious little media attention for his efforts. Speaking of his own plight, Udall complained, "The people want winners and losers, and if you make 27 points in a football game and I make 26, you're called a winner and I'm called a loser."[24] Nor did Udall's photo finish losses to Carter in Wisconsin and Michigan enhance his media coverage, except to acquire the label "Second-place Mo." It does not take much imagination to guess how the level of network television coverage would have changed if either candidate had swept the primaries won by Carter. The mass media have no time for losers.

Carter was not, of course, the first candidate in recent years to concentrate on winning heavy media coverage early in the pre-convention race. Before his 1960 race, John F. Kennedy never passed up an opportunity to capitalize on his famous family name, his war record, or his Pulitzer Prize credentials to advance his candidacy in the national media. In Kennedy's case, the national news magazines, the mass-circulation pictorial weeklies, *Life* and *Look,* and even the Hollywood screen magazines repeatedly put Kennedy on their front covers, a priceless publicity coup at no cost to the candidate. Until the emergence of Carter as a new national political figure sixteen years later, no presidential contender had come close to matching the media coverage that JFK generated in his day. Carter's heavy media coverage was in some respects even more noteworthy because Carter was a virtual unknown on the national scene and because he started out competing against almost a dozen Democratic rivals in the early primaries.

In the years ahead it can be expected that most presidential contenders, especially in the out-of-power party, will pattern their pre-convention plans to win media attention on the Kennedy-Carter model.

Need for Grass-Roots Organization

In recent years no presidential contender has won the nomination without first setting up an effective campaign organization in at least half of the presidential primary states and in a sizable number of caucus-convention states.

John F. Kennedy, in his successful 1960 drive for the Democratic nomination, laid the needed organizational structure at least two years before the opening primary in New Hampshire. Kennedy, using his home base in Massachusetts, relied on old political friends to set up his campaign organization in the uncontested New Hampshire primary. But in far-off Wisconsin Kennedy could no longer depend on his close neighbor ties. Instead, he counted heavily on his famous family, several close friends, and Wisconsin Lieutenant Governor (later Governor) Patrick Lucey to carry the Kennedy colors in the Dairyland State. In Ohio, Kennedy used a combination of alliances with the Cuyahoga County (Cleveland) Democratic leaders and a threatened entry in the Ohio primary to force Governor Michael DiSalle, who wanted to run as a favorite son, to join the Kennedy forces.[25] Kennedy also used similar bare-knuckled tactics in Maryland to induce Maryland Governor Millard Tawes, who wanted to head an uninstructed delegation, to help Kennedy win this border state primary. Although he did not enter the California primary, Kennedy's hard-nosed organizational efforts persuaded the California favorite son, Attorney General Edmund G. "Pat" Brown (Governor Jerry Brown's father), to share one-third of his delegation with the Massachusetts senator at the convention. In the caucus-convention states, some of Kennedy's most notable successes occurred in the Mountain States, where Denver lawyer Byron "Whizzer" White, former All-American football player and Rhodes scholar, rustled more than a score of delegates away from the Lyndon Johnson forces, who were thought to be in solid control of those states.[26] Consequently, it was more than coincidence that White was asked by President Kennedy to serve as deputy attorney general in the new administration and subsequently was appointed to the U. S. Supreme Court.

Senator George McGovern's long-shot strategy for the 1972 Democratic nomination was based heavily on early organizational planning. Soon after his formal announcement of his presidential candidacy in January 1971, McGovern began putting his campaign agents into the key early primary states of New Hampshire, Wisconsin and Massachusetts. McGovern's first primary victory in Wisconsin, the fourth primary on the calendar, has been attributed in large part to the year-long organizational efforts by McGovern's twenty-five-year-old campaign director, Gene Pokorny, who recruited 10,000 volunteer workers for the Wisconsin campaign.[27] Similar grass-roots organizations were set up in more than a dozen other primary and caucus-convention states. Thus, although McGovern was listed as the choice for president by only 5 percent of the Democratic voters in the early 1972 Gallup polls, he could confidently push ahead with his nominating campaign, because he had a solid corps of youthful volunteers, attracted by his anti-Vietnam War views, willing to campaign for him no matter how great the odds. McGovern's early grass-roots organization gradually helped attract more young supporters. By the time he reached the showdown battle in California against Senator Hubert Humphrey, McGovern had almost 50,000 volunteers ringing doorbells for him in the West Coast primary. Humphrey's small band of partisans was no match for McGovern in California or at the Democratic National Convention, which picked McGovern on the first ballot.

Four years later, Jimmy Carter borrowed a chapter from the earlier nominating plans of John F. Kennedy and George McGovern to mount his successful 1976 drive for the Democratic nomination. Shortly before Senator McGovern's disastrous defeat in his 1972 presidential bid, Governor Jimmy Carter of Georgia asked his executive secretary, Hamilton Jordan, to draft a memorandum on what it would involve to become president. Among Jordan's suggestions was the proposal for Carter to plant an agent on the Democratic National Committee in Washington to learn national politics from the inside. Carter went one step further. In early 1973 he volunteered his own services as a national campaign coordinator to Democratic National Chairman Robert Strauss. As chairman of Campaign 1974, Carter visited forty states, became acquainted with congressional candidates and incumbents in many of the 435 congressional districts across the land and met with hundreds of state and party officials. While Carter was in the field, Jordan served as Carter's in-house representative at the national party headquarters, collecting and storing huge quantities of political information for future use. Carter, in his own words, has described his early campaign planning:

Our strategy was simple: a total effort all over the nation. After leaving office as governor during the first months alone, I visited more than half the states, some of them several times. Each visit was carefully planned—by my small Atlanta staff and a local volunteer in each community—to be included during the week's trip. Our purposes during this early stage of the campaign were: to become known among those who have a continuing interest in politics and government to recruit supporters and to raise campaign funds; and to obtain maximum news coverage for myself and my stand on many local and national issues. The most important of all was for me to learn this nation—what it is, and what it ought to be.[28]

Throughout all of his forays in the primary and caucus-convention states Carter always ate and stayed in the homes of his newly recruited volunteers, getting better acquainted with his supporters and building lasting bonds of loyalty. As an ex-governor and part-time peanut farmer, Carter had the large blocs of neded free time in 1975 to build up his organizational network more than a half year ahead of his chief rivals, Henry Jackson, Morris Udall, Birch Bayh and George Wallace. Former Oklahoma Senator Fred Harris also pursued the same type of highly personalized, early bird campaign schedule as Carter, but Harris's far left position on the major issues failed to attract a substantial following.

Decisiveness of Early Fund Raising

In the presidential nomination sweepstakes the dollars raised early in the quiet pre-primary period have become a prime determinant of who runs where and how well. The ability to raise money early for matching federal subsidies suddenly has also become a major criterion—at least in the eyes of the national press corps—for measuring the viability of a presidential candidacy. Although no federal matching funds can be released under the new law to the candidate until January first of the presidential election year, members of the national press concluded early in the 1976 pre-primary period that the ability to raise $100,000— $5,000 each in twenty states in denominations of $250 or less—was an important "qualification" of a serious contender for the presidency.

One of the early drop-outs in the 1976 Democratic race, Terry Sanford, former governor of North Carolina, discovered that members of the national press refused to take his candidacy seriously until he met the twenty-state matching fund requirement of the 1974 Federal Election Campaign Act. Sanford's staff and those of several other candidates were told specifically by some media representatives in mid-summer 1975, according to one source, that they would not be given coverage for the 1976 race until they qualified for federal subsidies.[29] Several campaign managers complained to reporters, and Mr. Sanford objected publicly to viewing subsidy qualification as a "license to practice."[30] Nevertheless, the national press largely ignored Sanford and the other candidates until they qualified for Uncle Sam's dollars.

At this juncture, there does not seem to be much doubt that the ability to raise the necessary matching money will become a national media benchmark for measuring presidential candidate qualifications in future nominating races. And the national press, as it seeks to sift out and analyze the serious and weak contenders in the early pre-primary period, may have a point. Raising money in twenty states instead of three or four necessitates an entirely different organizational structure, stretching thin resources of an outsider candidate to the limit. Unless a candidate can demonstrate some organizational and financial support in a score of states early in the game, he or she will not obtain serious consideration. Ability to generate campaign funds cannot be equated precisely with grass-roots political strength, but a candidate who cannot find minimum financial backing and the supporters to raise it in twenty states will not stand much chance of winning in a thirty-three-state primary nominating system.

Although the money-raising ground rules changed in 1976 (the new Federal Election Campaign Act imposed strict limits, $1,000 per year, on the size of individual contributions) money continued to dictate major strategic decisions of the presidential contenders, especially those of the out-of-power party.

Jimmy Carter, the 1976 Democratic nominee, raised more than $900,000 in 1975, about half from his home state of Georgia.[31] This early money enabled Carter to mount an ambitious campaign in both the primary and caucus-convention states. When the first federal subsidies became available in January 1976, Mr. Carter collected more than $500,000 on the basis of matching private contributions, a big assist for what was still a relatively low-budget campaign.

To develop the needed momentum in pre-primary fund raising, a candidate must also be able to attract a top-notch fund-raiser. Jimmy Carter persuaded Morris Dees, the direct mail fund-raising wizard of George McGovern's 1972 campaign, to join his campaign in November 1975. From that time forward, Dees redoubled Carter's money-raising efforts, though not so much by direct mail as conventional methods— cocktail parties, campaign breakfasts, local telethons and rock concerts. Thus, throughout the early phase of the primary campaign Carter had a steady stream of dollars flowing into his treasury. With careful budgeting and only modest salaries for his staff, Carter stretched his campaign dollars further than any of his campaign rivals. As a result of this penny pinching, Carter avoided the financial trauma that suddenly hit Senator Jackson when he discovered his $6 million campaign treasure chest empty after his loss in the Pennsylvania primary.[32] Jackson, with no immediate hope of replenishing his funds, had no alternative but to pull out of the race.

Carter's relatively modest fund-raising efforts in the early stages of the 1976 pre-primary period, according to campaign finance experts inside and outside Mr. Carter's campaigns, helped protect him from a money blitz by intraparty rivals.

Some political experts believe that if the new campaign funding law had not existed, Carter's candidacy might have been suffocated by rivals with connections to big spenders. The new law, with its $1,000 ceiling on individual contributions, is of enormous benefit to a new candidate who is unknown nationally and who lacks access to the big givers within the party.

Failure to raise adequate funds in the months prior to the 1976 pre-primary period was fatal to several candidates. For example, Senator Birch Bayh of Indiana, heavily in debt (he had raised less than $350,000 in 1975), was forced to abandon his campaign after only two primaries, despite the fact that he had a strong political base in New York, a big delegate, pro-labor state where he was expected to run well.

Also, former Senator Fred R. Harris of Oklahoma, who had assured his supporters after poor showings in New Hampshire and Massachusetts that he would continue to conduct his campaign no matter what the odds, took another look at his campaign checkbook after the Massachusetts primary and decided to let his campaign lie dormant for two months, hoping to raise enough money to return to active competition in the late April Pennsylvania primary. But the needed funds never materialized, and Harris's campaign quietly faded away in May.

In previous years other successful presidential contenders from the out-of-power party have also identified, attracted or possessed the needed campaign funds early in the game.

John F. Kennedy, a wealthy candidate, never lacked access to large amounts of campaign capital. One of his chief financial sources was his father, Joseph P. Kennedy, a multimillionaire investor who had accumulated a fortune by wisely selling "short" before the economic crash in October 1929. Nor should it be forgotten that Kennedy campaigned in an era when nondisclosure of primary funding sources was the rule of the day. To refute charges that his father had picked up the huge campaign tab, Kennedy invited a St. Louis *Post Dispatch* reporter to inspect his primary expenditures.[33] The record showed that five Kennedy-for-President committees, including one in his homestate of Massachusetts, contributed more than $500,000 to his nominating drive. Most of the remainder of the $1 million pre-convention campaign bill was picked up by Kennedy and other members of the family. Equally important from a campaign planning standpoint, Kennedy knew at any point in the campaign that he could always draw huge sums, if needed, from the family fortune. Most presidential contenders, of course, do not have the luxury of this kind of financial cushion.

Senator Barry Goldwater, the 1964 GOP nominee, also never suffered from serious financial privation during his successful drive for the nomination. Although himself a millionaire, Goldwater's financial support came chiefly from his right-wing ideological supporters in California and other Sun Belt states. Goldwater's California supporters, for example, raised $1 million, half his presidential primary bill, in California alone. So successful were these California partisans that they contributed $150,000 to the national Goldwater headquarters, an almost unheard of development at that time in presidential nominating finances.[34]

Four years later, former Vice President Richard M. Nixon's financial planner, Maurice Stans, raised a huge war chest for the primary campaign long before the 1968 primary season opened. Most of these funds, however, were not expended until the general election campaign because once Nixon's chief rival, Governor George Romney of Michigan, dropped out of the race, Nixon did not have to make a major outlay of campaign funds in the primaries to win the nomination.

Senator George McGovern, the 1972 Democratic nominee, demonstrated that it was possible for an unknown candidate to come from out of nowhere to win the nomination—if he had adequate campaign funds to underwrite the drive. In the early phase of his 1972 primary drive McGovern depended heavily on small direct-mail contributions from old mailing lists compiled in 1970 to collect money for election and reelection of United States senators opposed to the Vietnam War. Without this steady flow of direct-mail contributions before McGovern's breakthrough primary victory in Wisconsin, it seems doubtful that McGovern could have developed the momentum that carried him to seven straight primary triumphs in the final two weeks of the primary season. Senator McGovern also was acutely aware that his giant-killer triumphs in the early primaries earned valuable prime time on the television network news programs and front-page coverage in the national press—another key ingredient in a victorious nominating campaign.

Early fund raising has not been confined exclusively to out-party challengers. The chairman of the 1976 Carter-Mondale Presidential committee, Evan S. Dobelle, reemphasized the importance of early fund raising in April 1979, when he announced that his committee had collected enough money in twenty states for President Carter to become eligible for federal matching funds in 1980. Even though U. S. Treasury funds generated by the federal income tax check-off are not paid out until January first of the presidential election year, Dobelle explained, "your objective is to try to raise as much money as you can before the primaries or caucuses so you don't have to spend your political time trying to raise funds in February or March" of the convention year.[35]

To reach the $16.8 million limit on 1980 primary expenditures set by the Federal Election Committee, the Carter-Mondale chairman indicated that his group would attempt to raise $9 million, preferably before 1980, and rely on federal matching funds for the balance of the needed campaign money. In contrast, President Ford's committee for the 1976 campaign raised only $1.7 million in 1975, less than his GOP challenger, Ronald Reagan, the former California governor.

Ideally, presidential contenders should not be distracted by fundraising chores during the primary season. But it seems unlikely that most aspirants will be able to fill their coffers sufficiently to qualify for the maximum subsidy from Uncle Sam before the opening gun is sounded for the primaries—or, for that matter, anytime before the curtain comes down in the final round California primary. Nevertheless, serious presidential contenders realize that they must endeavor to raise as much campaign money as possible before the primary season to avoid the major distraction of searching for funds during the heat of the springtime campaign.

Pluralities not Majorities

American voters are prone to think of electoral victories in terms of majorities, not pluralities (more votes than any opponent but less than a majority). But in presidential primary politics, especially within the Democratic party, plurality victories have become an important stepping stone to the nomination. Undoubtedly this thought crossed Senator Henry Jackson's mind in his memorable statement, upon winning a plurality victory in the 1976 New York primary, "We won a smashing victory but not a majority." Alas, Jackson failed to win any more primary victories, majority or plurality, in his fruitless quest for the presidency.

Jimmy Carter, like his predecessor George McGovern in 1972, built much of his nominating strategy around winning plurality victories in the primaries. Running in a multi-candidate field—the Democrats had eleven candidates in the starting gates when the 1976 primary season opened—Jimmy Carter and his aides reasoned that winning an absolute majority (50.1 percent) of the primary vote in most states might well be an impossible task. Consequently, they willingly settled for second best—pluralities—in a number of states. Carter, the middle-of-the-road Democrat, benefited especially in the early primaries from the fact that the votes for the liberal Democratic contenders—Harris, Bayh, Shapp and Shriver—were split four ways, whereas Carter preempted most of the centrist Democratic vote for himself. How crucial this divided vote was to Carter's early nominating strategy can be adduced from his narrow victories in three key states. Had the votes that went to Bayh, Harris, Shapp, or Shriver been shifted to Udall, the Arizonan would have defeated Carter in New Hampshire, Wisconsin and Michigan—and the story of the 1976 Democratic nomination might have had a different ending. Carter's New Hampshire primary victory, as noted earlier, captured the nation's headlines, but it was achieved with only 28.4 percent of the popular vote, a bare plurality. Two weeks later, Carter's "decisive" victory over George Wallace in Florida, the primary triumph that lifted Carter from a regional candidate to national status, was achieved with 34.5 percent of the popular vote. (This low winning percentage resulted from a three-way split of the vote among Carter, Wallace and Jackson.) Likewise, Carter's breakthrough victory in Pennsylvania, the triumph that opened the road to nomination, was achieved with only 37 percent of the popular vote.

All in all, Carter's seventeen primary victories netted him 39 percent of the Democratic primary vote, far less than a majority (see Table 4.2). In only eight of his seventeen primary triumphs—North Carolina, Georgia, Indiana, Arkansas, Kentucky, Tennessee, New Jersey and Ohio—did Carter register an absolute majority of the popular vote. In most of the Southern primaries (in five of which he won absolute majorities), Carter profited especially from the proportional division of delegates; his top-heavy popular majorities netted most of the delegates in these states.

Carter also capitalized on an old political rule-of-thumb: electoral systems of any kind tend to exaggerate the share of seats captured by the leading faction.[36] In several of the largest states, for example, Carter received large bonuses: in Texas (112 rather than sixty-two delegates, under strict proportional division); Michigan (sixty-nine instead of fifty-eight); and Ohio (126 rather than seventy-nine). Pennsylvania and New York yielded a fair share to the Georgian. Only in Illinois, where the preference poll he led was unrelated to the selection of delegates, was Carter shortchanged on delegates.

Conversely, Carter's rivals lost votes under the existing Democratic party rules that they would have won under strict proportional representation had it been applied statewide with no minimum quotas. Jackson, Udall and Wallace together, it has been calculated, would have garnered a third of the delegates in the early primaries instead of the quarter they actually collected.[37]

In two instances early in the 1976 primary race the Democratic proportionality rule helped Carter immensely. Although he lost two big primary states (Massachusetts and New York) to Jackson, he nevertheless received his proportionate share of delegates. If a plurality winner-take-

TABLE 4.2
JIMMY CARTER'S 1976 PRIMARY CAMPAIGN RECORD

State (Primary Date)	Votes for Carter	Delegate Vote	Percentage of Vote	Place
New Hampshire (February 24)	23,373	17	28.4	1
Massachusetts (March 2)	101,948	104	13.9	4
Vermont (March 2)	16,335	11	42.2	1
Florida (March 9)	448,844	81	34.5	1
Illinois (March 16)	630,915	169	48.1	1
North Carolina (March 23)	324,437	61	53.6	1
Wisconsin (April 6)	271,220	68	36.6	1
Pennsylvania (April 27)	511,905	178	37.0	1
District of Columbia (May 4)	9,759	17	39.7	1
Georgia (May 4)	419,272	50	83.4	1
Indiana (May 4)	417,463	75	68.0	1
Nebraska (May 11)	65,833	23	37.6	2
Maryland (May 18)	219,404	53	37.1	2
Michigan (May 18)	307,559	133	43.4	1
Arkansas (May 25)	314,306	26	62.6	1
Idaho (May 25)	8,818	16	11.9	2
Kentucky (May 25)	181,690	46	59.4	1
Nevada (May 25)	17,567	11	23.3	2
Oregon (May 25)	115,310	34	26.7	2
Tennessee (May 25)	259,243	46	77.6	1

TABLE 4.2 (continued)

State (Primary Date)	Votes for Carter	Delegate Vote	Percentage of Vote	Place
Montana (June 1)	26,329	17	24.6	2
Rhode Island (June 1)	18,237	22	30.2	2
South Dakota (June 1)	24,186	17	41.2	1
California (June 8)	697,092	279	20.5	2
New Jersey (June 8)	210,655	108	58.4	1
Ohio (June 8)	593,130	152	52.3	1
Total	6,227,809	1,814	39.0	

Source: Congressional Quarterly Weekly Report XXXIV (July 24, 1976): 1987; *Nomination and Election of the President and Vice President of the United States Including the Manner of Selecting Delegates to National Political Conventions* (Washington, D. C.: Government Printing Office, 1976), p. 404. Also, see Appendix A.

Note: These do not include delegate-selection primaries in New York, Texas or Alabama.

all system had prevailed statewide in these two states, Jackson would have swept all 378 delegates, and he would have come up to the crucial Pennsylvania primary leading Carter by approximately 140 delegates.[38] Moreover, Jackson would have been labeled the front-runner, and he would not have had to carry the heavy burden of appearing to be but a stand-in candidate for a reluctant Hubert Humphrey. Under such circumstances the Carter nomination drive might well have been stalled. But this hypothetical set of circumstances never came to pass, and Carter was of course able to lock up the nomination on the first ballot.

Four years earlier, McGovern's handling of the multi-candidate primaries was also a masterful job. The South Dakota senator and his campaign staff recognized that it was necessary to win only a plurality—not a majority—of delegates to capture dominant or total control of at least half a dozen state delegations. McGovern's troops, for example, captured all four winner-take-all primaries, California, Oregon, Rhode Island and South Dakota. This strategy netted him a tidy 344 delegates. If the delegates in the first three of these states (McGovern was unopposed in his home state of South Dakota) had been apportioned on the basis of the percentage of votes cast in the primary, McGovern would have received only 171 delegates, slightly less than half the original number. Wisconsin was almost as profitable. His victories in seven of nine

TABLE 4.3
SENATOR McGOVERN'S 1972 PRIMARY CAMPAIGN RECORD

State	Number of Delegates	% of Vote for McGovern	% of Convention Delegates Vote for McGovern	Place
New Hampshire	18	37.0	60.0	2
Florida	81	6.2	2.5	6
Wisconsin	67	29.6	80.6	1
Massachusetts	102	52.7	100.0	1
Pennsylvania	182	20.4	27.0	3
Ohio	153	39.3	43.8	2
Nebraska	24	40.7	70.8	1
Maryland	53	21.9	11.3	3
Michigan	132	26.8	28.8	2
Oregon	34	50.3	100.0	1
Rhode Island	22	41.0	100.0	1
California	271	44.3	100.0	1
New Mexico	18	33.0	55.0	1
South Dakota	17	100.0	100.0	1
New Jersey	109	*	82.0	1
New York	278	*	94.0	1

Source: Congressional Quarterly Weekly Report XXX (July 8, 1972): 1655.
*No preferential primaries held in these states.

congressional districts netted him 80.6 percent of the state delegation, even though he received only 29.6 percent of the popular vote statewide. Only in Florida and Maryland, primaries carried by George Wallace, did McGovern receive fewer votes than his percentage of the primary vote. Overall, McGovern's record of plurality victories as shown in Table 4.3 served as an excellent working model for Jimmy Carter four years later.

Staff Expertise on Primary Laws

Before the recent proliferation of presidential primaries and the Democratic party reforms, a detailed understanding of presidential primary laws and caucus-convention ground rules was less critical to presidential contenders. But the fate of the nominee now hinges on his popularity with the delegates chosen in the thirty-three presidential primary states. No candidate or his staff, for example, can afford to overlook filing deadlines, such as George Wallace's inexperienced managers did in the 1972 California primary. This careless oversight automatically excluded Wallace from competing directly for a winner-take-all package of 271 convention delegates in this West Coast primary, and, since California law does not permit write-ins, Wallace was completely denied any opportunity to prove his popularity with California voters. Failure to beat the California filing deadline—the Wallacites were concentrating that week on the Florida primary—slowed down the Wallace bandwagon and prevented him from developing the heavy campaign momentum that his primary victories in Florida and Michigan should have generated. Even if the near-fatal assassination attempt had not put him out of the 1972 campaign after the Maryland primary, it seems doubtful that he could have overtaken George McGovern in the delegate race without a winner-take-all victory in California, but failure to get on the California ballot was an egregious organizational blunder from which the Wallace forces never fully recovered.

Another essential item in a campaign handbook is that candidate managers fully understand the filing procedures of all thirty-three state primary laws. Again, the failure of Governor Wallace's managers to understand the complicated filing procedures cost him delegates in several states. In Pennsylvania, for example, Wallace's supporters entered him on the presidential preferential ballot but failed to file pledged delegate candidates who would stand for him in several congressional district races. Wallace finished comfortably ahead in districts which should have netted him sixteen delegates, but since they contained only two pledged Wallacites, the Alabama governor lost fourteen of these sixteen to other candidates (Humphrey, Muskie and especially McGovern).[39] Understanding the rules is especially important for such complicated laws as the Ohio statute, designed originally by organizational politicians to discourage all out-of-state entrants. It is estimated to take at least six to eight weeks full-time by a candidate's organizers to obtain all of the needed petition signatures for delegate candidates within each district, plus statements from each delegate candidate indicating his or her first and second choices for nomination as president.

Complex petition procedures can also cause endless legal headaches to a candidate. In 1976, for example, Congressman Morris Udall was denied a spot on the ballot of the early May Indiana primary because he was shy fifteen signatures in one congressional district. Even an appeal to the U. S. Supreme Court failed to win Udall a place on the Hoosier ballot. Udall's lawyers argued that the Indiana requirement "gives the voters in only one congressional district an absolute veto power over the nomination of a presidential candidate."[40] The court declined without dissent and without comment to expedite his case before the May 4th primary.

Calendar deadlines dictate candidate strategy, especially in the presidential primaries. The entire delegate selection process begins much earlier than the public realizes in both the primary and caucus-convention states.

In 1976, for example, ten caucus-convention states had held their precinct caucuses before the New Hampshire first-round primary in late February. By the time of the Wisconsin primary (April 6th)—the seventh primary of the 1976 season—the delegate selection process had started (at least precinct caucuses had been held and presidential candidate and national convention delegate filing deadlines had passed) in more than forty states.

Decisive breakthroughs in the primary campaign are unpredictable, but recent history shows that the candidate who understands the intricacies of the primary calendar deadlines and rules will be better prepared to capitalize on the "breaks" of the campaign. In 1976, for example, Jimmy Carter scored his decisive knockout punch against Senator Jackson in Pennsylvania, the eighth primary of the twenty-nine-primary campaign. By April 28th, the day after the Pennsylvania primary, Carter had barely won more than one-third of the 1,505 delegates needed for the nomination. But with seven challengers beaten into submission, he and his campaign aides knew that delegates pledged to those candidates would fall into their laps like ripe apples once the defeated candidates withdrew.

Although Carter was to lose ten of the remaining twenty-one primaries, most of them to Senator Frank Church and California Governor Edmund C. "Jerry" Brown, Jr., the Georgian and his staff had concluded early in the race that under the new Democratic proportionality rule used in fourteen states (which required that all candidates receiving 15 percent of the primary vote be given their proportionate share of the delegates), a candidate did not need to run well everywhere; any respectable showing in the primary would net a fair share of the delegates, even with second-, third-, or fourth-place finishes in those states adhering to proportional representation. Carter was also fortunate that every significant primary loss he suffered was invariably offset by a win on the same day in another state: Massachusetts by Vermont; New York by Wisconsin; Maryland by Michigan; Oregon by Kentucky; Idaho by Tennessee; Rhode Island by South Dakota; and California and New Jersey by Ohio.

In the loophole primary states Carter, of course, competed on a winner-take-all basis at the congressional district level. But he modified his strategy in Illinois, a loophole primary state and the stronghold of the late Mayor Richard J. Daley of Chicago, by targeting his campaign in specific districts. Carter and his staff reasoned that he would have an excellent chance of picking up small batches of delegates in the downstate and suburban areas. Thus, in the Illinois primary Carter was able to rustle fifty-five delegates—one-third of the state delegation—away from Mayor Daley's statewide ticket without a direct confrontation with Daley's forces in Chicago.

Like Senator McGovern and his campaign aides in the 1972 primaries,

Carter's team understood the new party rules and their impact on the delegate selection process far better than any of his Democratic challengers. Carter's rich delegate harvest and subsequent nomination could be attributed in considerable part to this shrewd understanding of the nominating process in its entirety. No wonder political insiders have long considered understanding the rules to be more than half of the game.

High-Risk Strategy

Presidential nominations in the out-of-power party usually go to a candidate who is willing to gamble and risk his political future on a bold course of action.

John F. Kennedy, in 1960, made a calculated gamble by invading the Wisconsin primary, a state thought to be sewn up by next-door neighbor Senator Hubert H. Humphrey of Minnesota. By defeating Humphrey on his own turf, Kennedy captured national headlines and clearly established himself as the Democratic front-runner. Kennedy, a Roman Catholic, also boldly entered West Virginia's primary, a state whose population was 94 percent Protestant. Again, he defeated Humphrey. More than anything else these two Kennedy triumphs opened the door to the nomination because it persuaded big state Democratic leaders, especially Mayor Richard J. Daley of Chicago and Governor David Lawrence of Pennsylvania, and many uncommitted delegates that Kennedy had the winning credentials the Democrats needed to recapture the White House.

In 1972 George McGovern, a long-shot presidential candidate, decided to challenge the then Democratic front-runner, Senator Edmund Muskie, in the New Hampshire primary. A fellow New Englander from Maine, Muskie was considered unbeatable in New Hampshire. Though McGovern did not win the New Hampshire primary, he surprised party watchers, capturing 37 percent of the vote to Muskie's 46 percent. In McGovern's case, the cynic might say it is the appearance of winning rather than what is won that is important, especially to a little-known candidate seeking a glimmer of national recognition. Muskie's failure, on the other hand, to win at least a clear majority of a next-door primary was viewed as a sign of weakness by national reporters. McGovern's strong showing in Muskie's own backyard also helped generate financial and organizational support that eventually carried McGovern to the nomination.

Four years later, Jimmy Carter adopted the same type of high-risk strategy popularized by John F. Kennedy. Carter's "run-everywhere" strategy of contesting all the primaries was indeed far more audacious than Kennedy's battle plan, which included only seven. And, in light of Senator Edmund Muskie's ill-fated attempt to enter all primaries in 1972, when there were only twenty-three instead of twenty-nine primaries,

Carter's intrepid plan to take on all comers everywhere appeared to border on political suicide. Among most political professionals the sheer task of campaigning in all twenty-nine primaries, except West Virginia, was thought to be beyond the physical endurance, to say nothing of the financial resources, of any candidate, except a Kennedy or a Rockefeller. Carter's big gamble was not limited to ambitious campaign planning.

Unlike his intraparty rivals, Carter was willing to plunge heavily into debt to deliver a knockout punch to his opponents. Carter's "good old boy" ties with two leading Atlanta banks enabled him to engage in heavy (and successful) deficit financing during a decisive period in the primary campaign. Between March and late May 1976, Carter and two of his chief rivals, Representative Morris Udall and Senator Henry Jackson, were in desperate financial straits because the Supreme Court had overturned part of the 1974 Federal Election Campaign Act, which led to a two-month suspension of federal matching subsidies.[41] Faced with this severe financial crisis, Carter borrowed over $1 million, mostly unsecured (except for the anticipated Federal Election Commission money) from two Atlanta banks, Fulton National Bank and Citizens & Southern. Thus, while Carter's major rivals were starved for campaign funds during the two-month federal dollar drought, the former Georgia governor "was tapping what looked like an unending, and unsecured pipeline of Southern cash."[42] As a result, Carter was able to outspend Senator Jackson $459,653 to $167,149 in the critical Pennsylvania primary and elsewhere. In addition to the bank loans, Carter's campaign managers also had the benefit of what amounted to short-term unsecured loans of almost $1 million from Southern supporters—chiefly from the advertising agency of Gerald Rafshoon, Carter's media advisor. Rafshoon and the other Southern vendors agreed not to demand quick payments for services rendered in order to help their favorite local candidate make good. In other words, Carter had an almost $2 million advantage over his closest competitors, Jackson and Udall, while they were going broke during the crucial middle phase of the nominating campaign. Senator Jackson and his finance director, facing the same cash shortfall before the Pennsylvania primary, borrowed only $42,700. "Bankers and our finance people were very skittish about the bankability of FEC due money, whether it could be used for collateral," said Jackson's campaign manager, Robert J. Keefe.[43] Representative Udall, hard-pressed for cash, borrowed $70,000 on his own signature, but that was it. "We had no easy access to real money markets," said John Gabusi, director of Udall's campaign. "We didn't have bankers, and we just couldn't get loans like that. And we had no deal like the Rafshoon thing—nobody would give us credit."[44] Carter's gamble, as we know, paid off. His victory in Pennsylvania knocked Jackson out of the race and cleared the path for Carter's first-ballot

nomination. By the time Udall and the other surviving candidates had
some ready cash in late May (from the renewed federal matching subsidies) it was too late to stop the front-running Carter. If the Federal
Election Commission had not been reconstituted (for several weeks it
was touch and go as President Ford and Democratic congressional leaders
haggled over the membership selection process) and if Jimmy Carter had
not won the nomination, the two Atlanta banks might have had to write
off most of their $1 million in loans to Carter as "bad loans," and Gerald
Rafshoon might have had to ask Carter to auction off his peanut ware-
house business to pay for his political advertising bills. Such are the
"might have beens" and the luck of the cards in presidential politics.
Without his audacious primary campaign tactics, which entailed both
high risk and the possibility of rich rewards, President Carter might now
be residing as a private citizen in Plains, Georgia.

In assessing the Carter campaign plan, his pollster Patrick Caddell
summarized it best. "Skill and luck—they're both key parts of the political
process. And in 1976 we had the best of both."[45] Carter, like several of
his predecessors, recognized that for an outsider candidate, such as a
former one-term Georgia governor, there is no safe, easy course to the
White House. Carter's high-risk primary campaign plan in 1976 will
undoubtedly remain the model that future outsider candidates will turn
to whenever they begin charting their pre-convention drives.

Unwillingness to take the big gamble in the presidential sweepstakes is
of course the opposite side of the high-risk coin. No candidate in recent
years paid a higher price for pursuing the "play-it-safe" strategy than
Senator Henry Jackson in 1976. In retrospect, Jackson's manager,
Robert J. Keefe, conceded at a post-election seminar that Jackson's
decision to skip the New Hampshire preferential primary was probably
the most critical strategic error any Democratic contender made in the
nomination fight.[46] Fearful of a first-round loss, Jackson and his advisors decided to concentrate heavily on the Massachusetts primary
during the early phase of the pre-convention jousting. "The problem
with New Hampshire was how to keep from finishing poorly," another
staff member said. "There were only two ways to do that. One was to
win, the other not to run. Not running was a considerably lower risk."[47]
Unfortunately, Jackson's low-risk stategy boomeranged.

By staying out of the New Hampshire "beauty contest" primary,
Jackson allowed Jimmy Carter to become the sole moderate-conservative
candidate against the four left-of-center contenders, Udall, Bayh, Shriver
and Harris. As explained earlier, Carter captured less than 30 percent of
the popular vote, but he won New Hampshire because the four liberals
split most of the remaining 70 percent of the Democratic vote four ways.
Carter's 4,663 vote margin over Udall made him an instantaneous front-

runner and triggered a publicity bonanza in the national media that left his rivals, especially Jackson, traumatized.

Had Jackson entered the New Hampshire preferential primary, he might not have won. But, at worst, he probably would have split the moderate-conservative vote with Carter and thrown the victory to Udall. In that event, Keefe argued, Udall, Jackson, and Carter would each have won one victory in the first three important primaries (with Jackson winning in Massachusetts and Carter, Florida), and the Democratic race might have gone down to the wire, instead of being an early Carter triumph.[48] In short, Jackson's extreme caution permitted Jimmy Carter to make the decisive, early breakthrough that he needed to put his candidacy beyond reach of Jackson, Udall and the two strong late entries, Senator Frank Church and Governor Edmund G. "Jerry" Brown, Jr.

Morris Udall was another victim of the play-it-safe strategy in the 1976 Wisconsin primary, a traditional proving ground of candidates. Udall lost the Wisconsin primary by less than 7,000 votes after first being projected the winner by two television networks. His loss of the Dairyland State primary has been attributed by several observers to his unwillingness to borrow $50,000 in the final days before the primary to mount a major television and direct-mail advertising campaign. Since Udall himself viewed Wisconsin as the linchpin in his strategy to halt Jimmy Carter's nominating drive, it was necessary that he go all out for the win. But because he was financially strapped due to the Federal Election Commission's cut off of all federal matching funds (see above), Udall was unwilling to plunge heavily into debt to stop Carter. The Arizonan has given his own version as to why he refused to borrow money for the telecast blitz and to send out 100,000 political flyers to Wisconsin rural voters.

Those flyers might have made the difference. I don't know. . . . I told my wife and I have told myself. I've seen candidates grubbing around for ten years and being harassed by creditors, seeing your campaign managers prosecuted and all kinds of shady things going on and I simply don't want to be President bad enough to be paying off debts the rest of my life.[49]

In retrospect, Udall's failure to ignite the type of bandwagon support needed to capture the nomination—Udall's highest rating in the Gallup Polls was five percent—suggests that a win or loss in Wisconsin was not determinant of his ultimate inability to win the nomination. But his unwillingness to borrow money to play for the big stakes in Wisconsin cost him dearly.

Within the Carter camp there was little disagreement that Udall's failure in Wisconsin to mount an expensive television advertising campaign was fatal. "That had to be the difference," Hamilton Jordan, Carter's manager, conceded in an interview a couple of weeks later. "A weekend of television has to be good for 5,000 or more votes easily. It had to make the difference. That's how they lost it. That's how we won."[50]

These two scenarios are, of course, all twenty-twenty hindsight, but they illustrate once again the fateful cost paid by presidential aspirants who shy away from a high-risk strategy. Recent history shows that the convention nominee of the out-party candidate has usually been the candidate who was willing to risk big stakes in the primaries. John F. Kennedy's nominating race in 1960 and Jimmy Carter's performance in the 1976 primaries are the best examples.

Notes

1. Adam Clymer, New York *Times,* September 3, 1977.

2. Richard C. Bain and Judith H. Parris, *Convention Decisions and Voting Records,* 2nd ed. (Washington, D. C.: Brookings Institution, 1973), pp. 297-98.

3. New York *Times,* April 3, 1957.

4. Theodore H. White, *The Making of the President, 1968* (New York: Atheneum, 1969), pp. 127-37; Lewis Chester, Godfrey Hodgson, and Bruce Page, *An American Melodrama: The Presidential Campaign of 1968* (New York: Viking Press, 1969), pp. 381-93.

5. Theodore H. White, *The Making of the President, 1972* (New York: Atheneum, 1973), pp. 42-43.

6. James T. Wooten, New York *Times,* June 10, 1976.

7. F. Christopher Arterton, "Campaign Organizations Confront the Media Environment," in *Race for the Presidency,* ed. James David Barber (Englewood Cliffs, N.J.: Prentice-Hall, 1978), p. 6.

8. CBS News, January 19, 1976, as cited by Thomas E. Patterson, "Press Coverage and Candidate Success in Presidential Primaries: The Democratic Race" (Paper delivered at American Political Science Association annual meeting, Washington, D. C., September 1-4, 1977).

9. Ibid. Carter's rising visibility resulting from his strong performance in the early round primaries and precinct caucuses was quickly reflected in the New York *Times*/CBS poll. In late March 1976, the proportion of respondents who recognized and had an opinion of Carter jumped from 24 percent to 54 percent in six weeks. New York *Times,* March 29, 1976.

10. NBC Evening News, February 25, 1976, as cited by Patterson, "Press Coverage and Candidate Success," p. 6. Carter gained heavier than usual election night television coverage in New Hampshire because the Ford-Reagan contest was too close to call for the networks. Rather than err in predicting a GOP winner, the network producers concentrated their coverage on the Democratic candidates, especially Jimmy Carter.

11. *Newsweek,* March 8, 1976.

12. Patterson, "Press Coverage and Candidate Success," p. 6.

13. David Broder, Washington *Post,* February 24, 1977.

14. Michael J. Robinson and Karen A. McPherson, "Television News and the Presidential Nominating Process: The Case of Spring, 1976," mimeographed (Washington, D. C.: Department of Politics, Catholic University, 1977).

15. Ibid.

16. Washington *Post,* April 17, 1976.

17. Patterson, "Press Coverage and Candidate Success," p. 3.

18. Arterton, "Campaign Organizations Confront the Media Environment," p. 19.

19. Washington *Post,* April 17, 1976.

20. James Wieghart, New York *Daily News,* July 12, 1976.

21. Austin Ranney, *The Federalization of Presidential Primaries* (Washington, D. C.: American Enterprise Institute, 1978), pp. 29-30.

22. James R. Beniger, "The Legacy of Carter and Reagan: Political Reality Overtakes the Myth of the Presidential Primaries," *Intellectual Magazine* (February 1977): 237.

23. "People Don't Know Who I Am," *Time* 108 (August 2, 1976): 14.

24. Washington *Post,* April 17, 1976.

25. William H. Hessler, "How Kennedy Took Ohio," *The Reporter* 22 (March 3, 1960): 21.

26. Theodore H. White, *The Making of the President, 1960* (New York: Atheneum, 1961), p. 143.

27. White, *The Making of the President, 1972,* pp. 96-107.

28. Jimmy Carter, *Why Not the Best?* (Nashville: Broadman Press, 1975), pp. 141-42.

29. Arterton, "Campaign Organizations Confront the Media Environment," pp. 14-15.

30. New York *Times,* July 13, 1975.

31. Ibid., November 18, 1976.

32. Seattle *Post Intelligencer,* April 30, 1976.

33. St. Louis *Post Dispatch,* August 7, 1960.

34. Herbert E. Alexander, *Financing the 1964 Election* (Princeton, N.J.: Citizens Research Foundation, 1966), pp. 20-21.

35. New York *Times,* April 4, 1979.

36. Douglas Rae, *The Political Consequences of Electoral Laws* (New Haven: Yale University Press, 1967), chap. 5.

37. Gerald M. Pomper, "New Rules and New Games in the National Conventions" (Paper delivered at American Political Science Association annual meeting, Washington, D. C., September 1-4, 1977), p. 18.

38. Ibid. Jackson also received a last-minute bad break in New York when the state legislature changed the "blind" ballot primary three weeks before the election. Under the old law only the name of the uncommitted prospective delegation was listed on the ballot. Under the new statute the delegate could run pledged to a specific presidential candidate. Jackson, who had built strong ties with many New York City organizational Democrats and expected to capitalize on his organizational advantage under the blind ballot, suddenly found many previously unpledged delegates running pledged to Carter, Udall, Wallace and so forth. Jackson had planned to use his well-financed organization to educate the voters on which uncommitted delegate slates supported him in each congressional district. But this plan now had to be modified. New York *Times,* March 12, 1976.

39. James I. Lengle and Byron Shafer, "Primary Rules, Political Power, and Social Change," *American Political Science Review* 70 (March 1976): 29-30, n 8.

40. New York *Times,* April 20, 1976.

41. The Supreme Court ruled that the Federal Election Commission, consisting of three members appointed by Congress and three members selected by the president, was an unconstitutional hybrid of legislative and executive powers. New York *Times,* January 31, 1976.

42. Richard Reeves and Barry M. Hager, "The Good Old Boy Network," *New Republic* 177 (September 10, 1977): 6. *See also* Herbert E. Alexander, *Financing the 1976 Election* (Washington, D. C.: Congressional Quarterly Press, 1979), pp. 240-44.

43. Ibid., p. 7.

44. Ibid.; see also New York *Times,* April 29, 1979.

45. Martin Schram, *Running for President* (New York: Pocket Books, 1976), inside cover.

46. David Broder, Washington *Post,* December 27, 1978. Instead, Jackson chose an uneasy compromise of avoiding the "beauty contest" portion of the New Hampshire primary while filing a slate of delegates in the separate delegate races within the two congressional districts. Thus, Jackson did not risk a direct confrontation with other Democratic contenders, but if his delegates had won some of the seventeen delegate spots, he could claim a partial victory. Ibid., December 20, 1975.

47. New York *Times,* February 29, 1976.

48. Washington *Post,* December 27, 1978.

49. Ibid., April 17, 1976.

50. Schram, *Running for President,* pp. 138-39; for a more detailed account of Udall's financial problems in Wisconsin, see Jules Witcover, *Marathon* (New York: Viking Press, 1977), pp. 278-88.

Polls and Primaries _____ 5

James R. Beniger
Princeton University

Who wins the Democratic and Republican party nominations to run for president of the United States? Is it the candidate who ranks highest in national opinion polls, the candidate who makes the best showing in state primary elections, or are both factors—national polls and state primaries—important in winning the nomination? What are the dynamics of interaction between these two factors in influencing the choice of party conventions?

These questions motivated this author's earlier study of polls, primaries and the presidential nomination, published just before the 1976 state primary season in the *Public Opinion Quarterly*.[1] That article, intended as a recapitulation of the past model of presidential nomination campaigns, provided a historian's answer: "The candidate who stands highest in national opinion has the best chance of winning both the state primaries and the presidential nomination. Success in the primaries can change national opinion somewhat, but it is much more likely that early standing in the polls will influence primary outcomes."[2]

Much the same conclusion has been reached by other political analysts of the presidential nomination process. In a Brookings Institution study published about the same time, for example, Keech and Matthews state,

The search for a consensus candidate often produces a leader whom the press, the polls and party leaders recognize as the unofficial nominee before the first primaries; and such candidates usually survive with their advantages intact. Rarely are the primaries instrumental in developing candidates who go on to win nomination.[3]

Fortunately, given the events of the ensuing 1976 presidential campaign, my own conclusion was preceded by a caveat: "The general model may be breaking down in favor of . . . an increased role for state primary elections."⁴ This caveat was prompted by the successful nomination campaign of George McGovern, a relative unknown at the start of the 1972 primary season who at that time stood sixth among Democratic candidates with 3 percent of his party's support.

Jimmy Carter's even more meteoric success in the 1976 campaign lends further support to the suspicion that the historical model of presidential nomination campaigns has broken down in favor of an increased role for state primary elections. Carter began the 1976 primary season with 4 percent of his party's support (ranking seventh among candidates aspiring to the nomination). Three months later, after eight victories in the first ten primaries, the former Georgia governor had risen to top position in the poll of Democrats with 40 percent support, eleven points ahead of the longtime leader Hubert Humphrey. Carter's subsequent loss of seven primaries, including five west of the Mississippi—Nebraska, Idaho, Montana, Nevada and Oregon—to two late-entry candidates, Senator Frank Church of Idaho and California Governor Edmund G. "Jerry" Brown, slowed down his bandwagon. As a result, Carter's Gallup rating dipped to 36 percent. But his smashing victory in the last-round Ohio primary, coupled with an uninterrupted string of victories in the Southern states—Texas, Tennessee, Kentucky and Arkansas—in May pushed his stock in the final pre-convention Gallup poll to 53 percent, the highest figure ever achieved by a non-incumbent Democratic contender in the Gallup standings (see Table 5.1).

Given these successes of two dark-horse candidates, McGovern and Carter, in the past two nomination campaigns, it is all the more essential to reexamine the historical model, especially the dynamics of interaction between national opinion polls and state primary elections. This question, crucial to both nominating politics and public opinion research, can be better answered now, thanks to the ever-increasing body of data on national polls and state primaries. National polls first appeared in the 1936 presidential nomination campaign and now constitute a sample of eleven elections, twenty-two major party elections and almost 100 declared and undeclared candidates.

Before considering the question of polls and primaries in determining nominations, however, it is useful first to answer an even more basic question, one which speaks directly to the success of the party nominating system as a democratic process: Do presidential nominations go to the candidates most preferred by party voters? This has indeed been the case in twenty of twenty-one nominations for which Gallup polls are available.⁵ Only once, with Adlai Stevenson in 1952, was the nominee not the most popular candidate among party voters in the final pre-convention poll; Stevenson finished a distant third (with 12 percent) behind Estes Kefauver (45 percent) and Alben Barkley (18 percent). In

TABLE 5.1
DEMOCRATIC VOTER PREFERENCES AMONG CANDIDATES FOR DEMOCRATIC NOMINATION
JANUARY-JUNE 1976
(PERCENT)

Candidate	January 2-5	January 23-26	February 27-March 1	March 10-13	March 19-23	March 26-29	April 9-12	April 23-26	April 30-May 3	May 21-24	June 11-14
Birch Bayh	4	3	3	—	—	—	—	—	—	—	—
Lloyd Bentsen	*	1	—	—	—	—	—	—	—	—	—
Edmund Brown, Jr.	—	—	—	—	—	9	6	9	6	15	15
Robert Byrd	—	2	1	—	—	—	—	—	—	—	—
Jimmy Carter	4	4	12	26	29	29	28	29	40	36	53
Frank Church	—	1	1	—	—	3	2	2	3	4	3
Fred Harris	—	1	1	—	—	1	*	—	—	—	—
Hubert Humphrey	19	17	18	27	30	30	31	33	29	28	13
Henry Jackson	7	5	5	15	10	7	8	7	4	—	—
Terry Sanford	1	*	—	—	—	—	—	—	—	—	—
Milton Shapp	1	*	1	1	—	—	—	—	—	—	—
Sargent Shriver	2	3	1	3	2	—	—	—	—	—	—
Morris Udall	2	2	3	4	4	4	5	4	4	5	5
George Wallace	15	18	14	15	17	13	13	12	9	9	7
Others	40	40	31	1	1	1	1	*	*	*	*
Undecided	5	4	9	5	6	3	7	4	5	3	4

Source: Gallup Opinion Poll Index, no. 133 (American Institute of Public Opinion, Princeton, N.J., August 1976): 6-7.

*Less than 1 percent.

**Some column totals may exceed 100 percent due to rounding of percentages.

Note: For the first three surveys of the year—January 2-5, 23-26, and February 27-March 1—the names of Senator Edward Kennedy as well as other prominent Democrats who had been mentioned as possible nominees but who had not formally announced their candidacies were included. Beginning in March, only those men who were formally in the race for the nomination and Senator Hubert Humphrey were included on the list of names handed respondents.

the 1964 Republican race, nominee Barry Goldwater tied with Richard Nixon (at 22 percent) in the final pre-convention poll; they finished in a virtual dead heat with two other candidates, Henry Cabot Lodge (21 percent) and William Scranton (20 percent). In a third case, the 1972 Democratic race, nominee McGovern trailed both Humphrey and George Wallace until the month of the convention; the final pre-convention poll produced no statistically significant differences between McGovern at 30 percent, Humphrey at 27 percent and Wallace at 25 percent.

These three exceptions or near-exceptions, nominees Stevenson (in 1952), Goldwater and McGovern, rank among the period's five weakest candidates (along with Alfred M. Landon and Stevenson in 1956), as measured by percentage of popular vote in the presidential election. This suggests that conventions have been prudent in abiding by the preferences of their own party's voters.

Strong Position of Pre-Primary Poll Leader

Convention choices usually have been foreshadowed early by Gallup preference polls, often in the first poll of the campaign, taken up to three years before the conventions. In thirteen of twenty-one campaigns the most popular candidate in this first poll went on to receive the nomination (see Table 5.2). Even excluding the six cases in which incumbent presidents won renomination, the first poll predicted the nominee 47 percent of the time (seven of fifteen cases).

As shown in Table 5.2, both the midterm November elections and the early state primaries have produced temporary leaders who quickly fell from favor in the polls (for instance, George Romney after the elections of November 1966; Henry Cabot Lodge after the New Hampshire primary in 1964). Nevertheless, as the conventions draw nearer, national public opinion—as reflected in the polls—has tended to shift to the eventual nominees. This raises the question of whether the party nominating process is truly democratic, that is, whether it expresses the choice of party voters, or whether their opinion swings (in a "bandwagon" effect) to what increasingly looks like the inevitable convention choice.

An examination of the 226 Gallup preference polls that were followed by a subsequent poll (that is, excluding the twenty-one final polls) suggests that such polls do not generate bandwagon movements. In 107 cases the leading candidate rose in the next poll, in ninety-seven he fell, and in twenty-two his percentage of support among party voters remained the same. Nor were the increases comparatively larger than the declines: the mean change was an increase of .17 percentage point. There are no significant time trends, either for the forty-year period or over the course of the campaigns.

TABLE 5.2
MOST POPULAR CANDIDATES AMONG PARTY VOTERS, AS MEASURED BY LAST GALLUP PREFERENCE POLL, AT CRUCIAL POINTS IN PRESIDENTIAL NOMINATION CAMPAIGNS

Election Year and Party	First Poll of Campaign	First Poll after Midterm November Elections	First Poll after First Major Primary	Final Poll of Campaign	Nominee
1936 D*	—	—	—	—	ROOSEVELT
R	Landon	Landon	Landon	Landon	Landon
1940 D	ROOSEVELT	ROOSEVELT	ROOSEVELT	ROOSEVELT	ROOSEVELT
R	(Dewey)	(Dewey)	(Dewey)	Willkie	Willkie
1944 D	ROOSEVELT	ROOSEVELT	ROOSEVELT	ROOSEVELT	ROOSEVELT
R	Dewey	Dewey	Dewey	Dewey	Dewey
1948 D	TRUMAN	TRUMAN	TRUMAN	TRUMAN	TRUMAN
R	Dewey	Dewey	(Stassen)	Dewey	Dewey
1952 D	(TRUMAN)	(Eisenhower)	(Kefauver)	(Kefauver)	Stevenson
R	Eisenhower	Eisenhower	Eisenhower	Eisenhower	Eisenhower
1956 D	Stevenson	Stevenson	Stevenson	Stevenson	Stevenson
R	EISENHOWER	EISENHOWER	EISENHOWER	EISENHOWER	EISENHOWER
1960 D	(Kefauver)	(Stevenson)	J. Kennedy	J. Kennedy	J. Kennedy
R	Nixon	Nixon	Nixon	Nixon	Nixon
1964 D	JOHNSON	JOHNSON	—	JOHNSON	JOHNSON
R	(Nixon)	(Rockefeller)	(Lodge)	Goldwater and Nixon (tie)	Goldwater
1968 D	(R. Kennedy)	(R. Kennedy)	(R. Kennedy)	Humphrey	Humphrey
R	Nixon	(Romney)	Nixon	Nixon	Nixon
1972 D	(Muskie)	(Muskie)	(Humphrey)	McGovern	McGovern
R	NIXON	NIXON	—	NIXON	NIXON
1976 D	(E. Kennedy)	(E. Kennedy)	(Humphrey)	Carter	Carter
R	(Agnew)	FORD	FORD	FORD	FORD
% Predict nominee (all races)	62% (13/21)	62% (13/21)	63% (12/19)	95% (20/21)	
% Predict nominee (presidents excluded)	47% (7/15)	43% (6/14)	50% (7/14)	93% (13/14)	

Source: The Gallup Poll, Public Opinion 1935-1971, Volumes 1-3, New York, Random House, 1972; *The Gallup Opinion Index,* various numbers, Princeton, N.J., Gallup International, 1971-1976.

*The index of *The Gallup Poll, Public Opinion 1935-1971* does not list any Democratic voter preference polls on President Franklin Roosevelt's renomination in 1936.

Note: Presidents in capital letters, unsuccessful candidates in parentheses.

Historical Model: Pre-Primary Polls Usually Determine Nominee

From this evidence emerges the historical model of nomination campaigns. The conventions almost always have nominated the candidate with the greatest support among party voters; this candidate more likely than not will lead even the earliest preference polls, taken several years before the convention; the leader in the polls is gradually more likely to receive the nomination, even though there is unlikely to be much bandwagon movement in his direction.

Of the twenty-one cases, one-third constitute deviations from this general historical model of nomination campaigns. These seven cases include four "eleventh-hour" changes, campaigns in which a relative latecomer (Wendell Willkie in 1940, Estes Kefauver in 1952, Hubert Humphrey in 1968 and Carter in 1976) managed to beat out the favorite in the final preference polls,[6] and three "genuine horseraces," campaigns in which the popular lead changed several times among several candidates (Democrats in 1960 and 1972; Republicans in 1964).[7] Because one such case has occurred in each of the past five presidential election years, there is some evidence that the general historical model, accurate for earlier campaigns, may no longer hold. As noted four years ago in my original study, "the hypothesized breakdown of the traditionally sober nomination process merits continued attention in the years ahead."[8]

One special aspect of the general historical model, the role of state primaries in the presidential nominating process, is of particular interest here. The model would seem to suggest that there is little part for the primaries to play because the eventual nominee emerges, more often than not, in the first poll of the campaign, taken several years before the primary season. The leader in the polls is gradually more likely to receive nomination down to convention eve, when that likelihood has been a virtual certainty. Except for Carter's 1976 campaign, eleventh-hour changes do not argue for the importance of state primary elections: neither Willkie nor Humphrey won a single state primary, and Kefauver—although he won twelve of fourteen primaries (mostly uncontested)—lost the nomination to Adlai Stevenson.

On the other hand, in the past two presidential elections, McGovern and Carter, relatively unknown at the beginning of the election year, used the system of state primary elections to gain their party's nomination. In four earlier campaigns (Thomas Dewey in 1948, Dwight Eisenhower in 1952, John Kennedy in 1960 and Barry Goldwater in 1964) state primaries also seemed to play a major part in influencing national opinion and eventual party nominations.

In considering these possible exceptions to the view, as suggested by the general historical model, that state primaries play a relatively minor

TABLE 5.3
**REPUBLICAN VOTER PREFERENCES AMONG CANDIDATES
FOR THE REPUBLICAN NOMINATION, FEBRUARY-JUNE 1948
(GALLUP POLL)
(PERCENT)**

Candidate	February	March	April	May	June
Dewey	38	34	29	24	33
Stassen	15	15	31	37	26
MacArthur	14	19	16	12	11
Vandenberg	6	13	10	13	13
Taft	15	12	9	8	10
Warren	5	3	2	2	2
Martin	1	1	1	1	1
Others or no opinion	6	3	2	3	4

Source: Public Opinion Quarterly 12 (Fall 1948): 562.

role, at least compared to the national opinion polls, in determining major party nominations, it is important to distinguish the achievements of McGovern and Carter from those of the earlier candidates. To read the dynamics of the McGovern and Carter campaigns back into those of Dewey, Eisenhower, Kennedy and Goldwater is to miss one of the most significant developments in American politics in recent years, that state primary elections, long thought to play an independent role in the presidential nominating process, finally have become important in determining both national opinion, as measured by the public opinion polls, and major party nominations.

The Dewey and Eisenhower cases are examples of "staved-off challenges," campaigns in which the early favorite lost and then regained the lead in election-year polls.[9] Dewey lost the lead to Harold Stassen in two polls in April 1948, after Stassen's early victories in the Wisconsin and Nebraska primaries, but regained the lead in late May, after the candidates split four contested primaries: Dewey won in New Jersey and Oregon, Stassen in Pennsylvania and West Virginia (see Table 5.3). Eisenhower staved off a challenge from Robert Taft between January and March 1952, when Taft pulled ahead by a single percentage point, with an Eisenhower victory in New Hampshire and a strong second write-in campaign (behind Stassen) in Minnesota (see Table 5.4).

These two "staved-off challenges" do not necessarily suggest that state primary elections played decisive roles, however. Both Dewey and Eisen-

TABLE 5.4

**REPUBLICAN VOTER PREFERENCES AMONG CANDIDATES
FOR THE REPUBLICAN NOMINATION, MARCH-JULY 1952
(GALLUP POLL)
(PERCENT)**

Candidate	March 2	April 9	May 2	June 4	July 2
Eisenhower	33	37	44	43	46
Taft	34	34	33	36	35
MacArthur	14	12	10	9	10
Warren	6	—	—	—	—
Stassen	6	—	—	—	—
Others and uncommitted	7	17	13	12	9

Source: Gallup Opinion Index, 125 (American Institute of Public Opinion, Princeton, N.J., November-December 1975): 54.

hower topped the first poll of their respective campaigns (Eisenhower, however, led both parties in all Gallup polls in 1951). Both candidates led public opinion in a majority of polls (Dewey in fifteen of seventeen, Eisenhower in thirteen of fourteen, with one tie). Both led throughout most of their campaigns, both were ahead by a significant margin in the final polls, and both secured the nomination. For all these reasons, the two "staved-off challenges" in the past forty years of U.S. presidential campaigns are not significant deviations from the relatively minor role predicted by the general historical model for state primary elections.

Among the "genuine horseraces," the 1960 Democratic campaign that culminated in the nomination of John Kennedy still seems to many the best evidence that state primaries played an independent role in the presidential nominating process prior to McGovern's campaign in 1972. In the late 1950s, the top spot in the preference polls of Democratic voters did switch five times between Adlai Stevenson and Kennedy before the latter gained it for the last time in January 1960. By the start of the 1960 primary season, however, Kennedy was already the clear choice of Democratic voters, eleven points ahead of Stevenson, the party's leader for almost a decade. At the time of the Wisconsin and West Virginia primaries, which drew national media attention, Kennedy was preferred by a national plurality of 39 percent. Hubert Humphrey, his major opponent in those two primaries, ranked fourth among Democratic candidates with only 7 percent (see Table 5.5). As might have been expected from the general

TABLE 5.5
DEMOCRATIC VOTER PREFERENCES AMONG CANDIDATES FOR THE DEMOCRATIC PRESIDENTIAL NOMINATION, MARCH-JULY 1960 (GALLUP POLL) (PERCENT)

Candidate	Before New Hampshire Primary March	After Wisconsin Primary April	Before Oregon Primary May	After West Virginia and Oregon Primaries June	Final Survey
Kennedy	34	39	41	42	41
Stevenson	23	21	21	24	25
Johnson	15	11	11	14	16
Symington	6	6	7	8	7
Humphrey	5	7	—	—	—
Others	9	8	16	5	4
No opinion	8	8	4	7	7

Sources: Gallup Opinion Index, no. 125 (November-December 1975): 42; American Institute of Public Opinion, Princeton, New Jersey.

historical model, Kennedy won both primaries by margins in excess of 80,000 votes; over the primary season, he ran actively in seven states—and carried all seven by comfortable margins. Despite this record, however, Kennedy gained only seven points in the Gallup poll during the entire nomination campaign, mainly because he already had widespread support among party voters. Again, Kennedy's campaign did not involve state primaries in a way significantly different from that predicted by the general historical model.

In the 1964 Republican race, which culminated in Goldwater's nomination, the poll lead went from Richard Nixon to Nelson Rockefeller to Goldwater to Nixon to Henry Cabot Lodge before Goldwater and Nixon finally tied in the last pre-convention poll (see Table 5.6). As indicated, this is one of the three "genuine horseraces" in American politics over the past forty years. State primaries did not significantly alter Goldwater's support as already established in the pre-primary polls, however. Although Goldwater won five of the eleven primaries he entered (while Lodge won three, Rockefeller two, and Scranton one), Goldwater gained only a single percentage point in the polls over the primary season and virtually tied with Lodge and Scranton in the pre-convention poll.

TABLE 5.6

**REPUBLICAN VOTER PREFERENCES AMONG CANDIDATES FOR THE
REPUBLICAN NOMINATION, FEBRUARY-JULY 1964
(GALLUP POLL)
(PERCENT)**

Candidate	Before Primaries February	Before New Hampshire Primary March	After New Hampshire Primary April	Before Oregon Primary Mid-May	After Oregon Primary Late May	After California Primary June	Late June	July 14
Goldwater	20	17	14	15	16	21	22	22
Rockefeller	16	13	6	7	17	10	8	6
Lodge	12	16	42	36	28	26	19	21
Nixon	31	34	26	27	29	25	22	22
Scranton	7	5	4	5	4	9	18	20
Romney	5	6	4	4	2	5	—	—
Others or no preference	9	9	4	6	4	4	11	9

Sources: Gallup Opinion Index, no. 125 (November-December 1975): 52; American Institute of
Public Opinion, Princeton, New Jersey.

Not until McGovern's 1972 campaign did a presidential candidate first
manage to use state primary elections as a vehicle to overcome initial low
standing in the public opinion polls. On the eve of the New Hampshire
primary, according to the Gallup poll, McGovern ranked fifth among
Democratic voters, with only 6 percent naming him as their choice for
president. Less than four months later, after winning ten primaries,
McGovern entered the Democratic convention as the top choice of party
voters, with 30 percent support compared to 27 percent for Humphrey
and 25 percent for George Wallace (see Table 5.7). Never before had a
candidate used the primaries to climb from obscurity to become the first
preference of his party's voters—and then secure the party nomination.
Four years later, Jimmy Carter became the first candidate to owe the
presidency to the state primary system.

With the unprecedented achievements of McGovern and Carter, the
presidential primary system, a uniquely American institution, had finally
emerged as the single most decisive phase of the party nominating process. These developments, among the most significant events in the history
of American politics, demand a more rigorous quantitative analysis of
the dynamics of interaction among national opinion polls, state primary
elections and the Democratic and Republican nominations.

TABLE 5.7
**DEMOCRATIC VOTER PREFERENCES AMONG CANDIDATES
FOR THE DEMOCRATIC NOMINATION, JANUARY-JULY 1972
(GALLUP POLL)
(PERCENT)**

Candidate	January	Before New Hampshire Primary	Before Wisconsin Primary	After Wisconsin Primary	July 10
McGovern	3	6	5	17	30
Humphrey	17	31	31	30	27
Muskie	32	23	22	17	6
Wallace	—	15	17	19	25
Jackson	2	3	5	4	3
McCarthy	5	5	4	3	2
Lindsay	5	7	5	—	—
Chisholm	2	2	4	5	3
Yorty	2	—	*	—	—
Hartke	1	1	*	—	—
Mills	—	2	1	1	2
Kennedy	27	—	—	—	—
Others and no preference	4	5	5	4	4**

Source: Gallup Opinion Index, no. 125 (American Institute of Public Opinion, Princeton, N.J., November-December 1975): 42.

*Less than 1 percent.
**Some column totals may exceed 100 percent due to rounding of percentages.

Quantitative Data on Dynamics of Polls and Primaries

The analysis here will be based on the 247 nationwide Gallup opinion polls, conducted during the period 1936-76, which measure preferences for candidates among voters of the same party. These "Presidential Preference Lists," as Gallup calls them, present a situation analogous to a national party primary, with those surveyed asked to choose from a list of possible candidates from their own party their personal preference for the nomination. The Presidential Preference List (here referred to simply as "preference poll") includes all candidates who have formally announced their candidacy, plus persons receiving 3 percent or more of the nominations submitted to Gallup by "political analysts, newspaper editors, television commentators and voters themselves."[10] Excluded from the analysis are only those presidential campaign polls demanding a choice between just two contenders for a party nomination (what Gallup calls a "Showdown Test"), polls opposing two or three candidates of

TABLE 5.8
GALLUP PARTY PREFERENCE POLLS AND STATE
PRESIDENTIAL PRIMARIES, BY ELECTION YEAR AND PARTY

Election Year and Party		Polls	Primaries
1936	D	0*	13
	R	5	11
1940	D	4	8
	R	16	10
1944	D	4	9
	R	10	9
1948	D	10	8
	R	17	9
1952	D	10	14
	R	14	13
1956	D	14	17
	R	3	15
1960	D	18	15
	R	16	11
1964	D	1	13
	R	23	14
1968	D	5	14
	R	18	10
1972	D	12	21
	R	2	14
1976	D	21	30
	R	24	28
Totals	D	99	162
	R	148	144
Total		247	306

Source: The Gallup Poll, Public Opinion 1935-1972, Volumes 1-3, New York, Random House, 1972; *The Gallup Opinion Index,* various numbers, Princeton, N. J., Gallup International, 1971-1976.

*The index of *The Gallup Poll, Public Opinion 1935-1971,* does not list any Democratic voter preference polls on Franklin Roosevelt's renomination in 1936.

rival parties ("Trial Heats"), and post-convention polls on the actual nominees ("Test Elections").

Also used in the analysis will be results of 306 state primary elections held during the same period, which in some way involved candidates by name (in any combination of preference vote or delegate election). This includes elections with only a single "favorite son" but excludes elections in which the outcome was not associated with candidates by name (as in elections of delegates-at-large, uninstructed delegates, and so on). The 247 polls and 306 primaries, which, according to the sources,[11] constitute

TABLE 5.9

MEAN PERCENTAGE CHANGES IN NEXT GALLUP PREFERENCE POLL, CONDUCTED AFTER STATE PRIMARY, BY WINNING AND LOSING PRIMARY CANDIDATES AND PARTY, 1936-76

Primary Outcome and Party	Number of Primaries	Number of Candidates	Mean Change in Next Poll
Winner			
Democratic	115	115	+ 3.76
Republican	102	102	+ 0.51
Total	217	217	+ 2.23
Loser			
Democratic	86	267	− 0.01
Republican	77	164	− 0.59
Total	163	431	− 0.23
All candidates			
Democratic	115	382	+ 1.12
Republican	102	266	− 0.17
Total	217	648	+ 0.59

Source: The Gallup Poll, Public Opinion 1935-1971, Volumes 1-3, New York, Random House, 1972; *The Gallup Opinion Index,* various numbers, Princeton, N. J., Gallup International, 1971-1976.

an exhaustive list, are distributed by election year and party as shown in Table 5.8.

Because of the relative paucity of data, the complex dynamics of polls and primaries will be reduced to three simple questions of causal inference: (1) Do the outcomes of individual state primaries cause immediate changes in national preferences among the party electorates? (2) Is a candidate's overall primary performance related to an aggregate change in his standing in national opinion during the same period? (3) Does national opinion, as measured and publicized by the preference polls, affect a candidate's fortunes in the state primary season? These three questions are now addressed here in turn.

Do the outcomes of individual state primaries cause immediate changes in national party preferences? The available data suggest that this is indeed the case, even though the effect on national opinion of a candidate's primary showing varies considerably by whether he wins or loses, his party, and the timing of the primary. As seen in Table 5.9, a total of 217 primaries can be assessed as intervening between two preference polls; the winners of these primaries gained a mean 2.23 percentage points in the latter poll (an amount unchanged by the 1976 campaign). By contrast, the 431 losers (second place or lower) in the same primaries

TABLE 5.10

RANK OF STATE PRIMARIES, BY MEAN PERCENTAGE CHANGES IN NEXT GALLUP PREFERENCE POLL CONDUCTED AFTER THE PRIMARY, FOR PRIMARY WINNERS AND LOSERS, 1936-76

	Winners					**Losers**		
Rank	Primary	Number of Candidates	Mean Change in Next Poll		Rank	Primary	Number of Candidates	Mean Change in Next Poll
1	New Hampshire	10	+7.10		1	Wisconsin	32	−2.54
2	Wisconsin	18	+4.28		2	Illinois	26	−1.96
3	Nebraska	15	+4.26		3	Maryland	9	−1.33
4	Pennsylvania	16	+3.13		4	Pennsylvania	53	−1.04
5	Florida	8	+2.87		5	New Hampshire	25	−0.64
6	Illinois	16	+2.75		6	Nebraska	32	+0.15
7	Oregon	16	+2.50		7	Massachusetts	33	+0.21
8	Ohio	9	+1.56		8	Oregon	40	+0.23
9	California	13	+1.15		9	New Jersey	22	+0.50
10	New Jersey	12	+0.92		10	Ohio	12	+0.75
11	Maryland	6	+0.83		11	California	12	+1.33
12	South Dakota	11	+0.82		12	Florida	18	+1.33
13	Massachusetts	11	+0.18		13	Indiana	7	+2.29
14	Indiana	7	−0.57		14	West Virginia	4	+3.50
15	West Virginia	9	−2.34		15	South Dakota	10	+3.70

Source: The Gallup Poll, Public Opinion 1935-1971, Volumes 1-3, New York, Random House, 1972; *The Gallup Opinion Index,* various numbers, Princeton, N. J., Gallup International, 1971-1976.

Note: Although a total of thirty-three states held at least one primary election that qualified for the data set, the fifteen states listed here account for over 90 percent of all cases. These are the same fifteen states that Davis lists as the "presidential primary states" (James W. Davis, *Presidential Primaries: Road to the White House* [New York: Thomas Y. Crowell, 1967], pp. 38-39). The strategy here is to include only these fifteen states in analyses by states but to use data from all thirty-three states in other analyses. The other eighteen states, with the number of their primaries that qualified for the data set in parentheses, are Alabama (4), Alaska (2), Arkansas (2), District of Columbia (6), Georgia (2), Idaho (2), Kentucky (2), Michigan (4), Minnesota (4), Montana (4), Nevada (2), New Mexico (1), New York (1), North Carolina (4), Rhode Island (4), Tennessee (4), Texas (3) and Vermont (2); the total number of primaries in the data set is 306.

fell a mean .23 percentage point in the next poll (up from .50 through the 1972 campaign). Democratic party winners gained substantially more than the winners of Republican primaries (3.76 versus .51, a margin which has widened from that of 3.36 versus .93 through the 1972 campaign) and lost slightly less than the Republican losers (.01 versus .59, a relationship which has reversed from that of .58 versus .42, respectively, through the previous campaign).

Little more than the direction of these mean percentage changes can be given much credence, of course, because the data are complicated by countless extraneous factors. In all cases, however, the direction of change is consistent: as a general rule success or failure in a state primary election does translate into a corresponding change in national voter preferences for the candidates. If it is also safe to conclude on the basis of these data that winning has a greater positive effect than losing has a negative effect, it may be because many elections have several losers and the small losses of support for each of these losers combine in a much larger gain in support for the winner.

Primaries in several particular states traditionally have had a more substantial impact on national voter preferences, as can be seen in Table 5.10, which ranks states both by the mean increase in percentage points for their primary winners and by the mean decrease in points for the losers. (The paucity of cases prohibits any two-way comparisons, for example, by state *and* party.)

Again, little more than the general direction of these mean percentage changes can be given much credence, considering the limitations of the data. It might be noted that candidates have tended to do better after losing—as compared to winning—in ten states (up from seven through the 1972 campaign), a fact pointing up the extraneous causal factors at work on party voter preferences. Despite these data limitations, however, there is a remarkable similarity of rankings in the current and earlier lists. It seems safe to conclude that state primaries have had relatively similar though opposite effects on national voter preferences for both winners and losers, and that those primaries most helpful to win (in terms of standing in the polls) have also been the most damaging to lose. There is also a remarkable similarity between the two lists and similar rankings of the same states through the 1972 campaign. If these findings are not surprising, they do provide a kind of external validation for the rankings of state primaries and suggest that the difference in the mean percentage changes might serve as a rough grouping of the primaries according to their impact on national opinion, as presented in Table 5.11. Again, there is a remarkable similarity between this ranking and a similar one for the same states through the 1972 campaign.

Readers familiar with primary election seasons over the past forty years may see in the Table 5.11 groupings still another hypothesis: earlier primaries (like New Hampshire and Wisconsin) appear to have a greater impact on national voter preferences than do later primaries. It seems safe to conclude as a generalization across all primaries and with varying degrees of exception that the earlier the primary the greater its effect on national voter preferences for those candidates that enter—greater gains for winners, greater losses for the losers. The data permit the testing of

TABLE 5.11

RANK OF STATE PRIMARIES BY DIFFERENCE IN MEAN PERCENTAGE CHANGES, FOR PRIMARY WINNERS AND LOSERS, IN NEXT GALLUP PREFERENCE POLL CONDUCTED AFTER THE PRIMARY, 1936-76

Rank	State Primary	Number of Candidates	Winner-Loser Difference in Mean Change in Next Poll
		Most Impact	
1	New Hampshire	35	+ 7.74
2	Wisconsin	50	+ 6.82
3	Illinois	42	+ 4.71
4	Pennsylvania	69	+ 4.17
5	Nebraska	47	+ 4.11
6	Oregon	56	+ 2.27
7	Maryland	15	+ 2.16
8	Florida	26	+ 1.54
9	Ohio	21	+ 0.81
10	New Jersey	34	+ 0.42
11	Massachusetts	44	− 0.03
12	California	25	− 0.18
13	Indiana	14	− 2.86
14	South Dakota	21	− 2.88
15	West Virginia	13	− 5.84
		Least Impact	
	All state primaries*	648	+ 2.46

Source: The Gallup Poll, Public Opinion 1935-1971, Volumes 1-3, New York, Random House, 1972; *The Gallup Opinion Index,* various numbers, Princeton, N. J., Gallup International, 1971-1976.

*Including those in the eighteen other states with too few primaries to be listed as individual states in this ranking.

still another widely held notion: primaries in states with larger populations have a greater impact on public opinion. Although the effect of state population is positive, it is small, particularly compared to the effect of the time of the primary. (Again the paucity of cases precludes a two-way analysis in terms of both temporal order and population size.)

The first question concerning interaction between polls and primaries has now been answered. The outcomes of individual state primaries often do cause immediate and substantial changes in national voter preferences and in the anticipated directions (up for winners, down for

TABLE 5.12
CANDIDATES' AGGREGATE PERCENTAGE CHANGE IN GALLUP PREFERENCE STANDING, OVER STATE PRIMARY SEASON, AS FUNCTION OF PERCENT OF PRIMARIES ENTERED WON, 1936-76

Percent of Primaries Entered Won	Percentage Change in Polls Over Primary Season				
	Down 6+	*Down 0-5*	*Up 1-5*	*Up 6+*	*Totals*
0	6 (22%)	13 (48%)	4 (15%)	4 (15%)	27 (100%)
1-49	5 (24%)	8 (38%)	4 (19%)	4 (19%)	21 (100%)
50-100	3 (13%)	5 (22%)	4 (17%)	11 (48%)	23 (100%)
Totals	14 (20%)	26 (37%)	12 (17%)	19 (27%)	71 (100%)

Source: The Gallup Poll, Public Opinion 1935-1971, Volumes 1-3, New York, Random House, 1972; *The Gallup Opinion Index,* various numbers, Princeton, N. J., Gallup International, 1971-1976.

Note: Some column totals may exceed 100 percent due to rounding of percentages.

losers), though this effect appears to be stronger for winners, for Democrats, and for states with early primaries (particularly New Hampshire and Wisconsin), but not much stronger for states with larger populations.

Is a candidate's overall primary performance related to an aggregate change in his standing in national opinion during the same period? This ought to be true, if the immediate effects of primaries on polls are indeed lasting and significant. The available data do suggest an answer in the affirmative, even though the relationship between overall primary performance and opinion change is only moderate.

The primary performances of seventy-one candidates (all those who entered two or more races) can be assessed as intervening between the last pre-primary poll and the first post-primary poll. Of these candidates, twenty-seven (38 percent) did not win any primaries, twenty-one (30 percent) won fewer than half the primaries they entered, and twenty-three (32 percent) won half or more of the primaries they entered; these percentages were virtually unchanged by the 1976 election. Table 5.12 summarizes the relationships between these primary performances and the trans-seasonal shifts in national voter preferences.

As Table 5.12 shows, there is a moderate positive relationship between the percent of primaries entered won and the change in percentage points over the primary season. This table does not address as closely as the previous analysis of immediate effects the question of causal direction between primaries and polls. It may be that the correlation between overall primary performance and aggregate opinion change is spurious, that both are affected by other factors (perhaps related to the nature of the campaigns waged by the candidates). Insofar as the finding here does not contradict the more controlled finding for individual primaries, however, it lends additional plausibility to the conclusion that state primary outcomes do cause changes in national opinion.

This conclusion appears to contradict the general model of presidential nomination campaigns constructed thus far. If the eventual nominee emerges, more often than not, in the first poll of the campaign, and if there is only a gradual increase in the probability that the poll favorite will receive the nomination, then the impact of the primaries would seem necessarily to be limited. Because it now appears certain that primary results do affect the preference polls, however, it becomes necessary to resolve the apparent contradiction by looking at the opposite causal relationship, the extent to which standing in the polls affects primary results.

Does national opinion, as measured and publicized by the preference polls, affect a candidate's fortunes in the state primary season? The data indicate not only that there is a relationship between the level of national party preference for a candidate and his primary chances, but that this relationship is indeed one of the strongest in the data.

The primary performances of eighty-seven candidates (all those who entered two or more races) can be compared to their standing in the last preference poll released prior to the primary season (the number of candidates is sixteen greater than in the preceding section because a post-primary poll is not required here). The results of this comparison are summarized in Table 5.13.

As Table 5.13 shows, there is a strong positive relationship between a candidate's standing in the last preference poll before the primary season and his performance in the primaries. Roughly half the variance in candidates' primary performances can be accounted for by the percentage of their party's voters favoring their election at the outset of the primary season (this relationship is virtually unchanged by the 1976 campaign).

Interestingly enough, the data do not reveal any immediate effects of changes in poll standings on subsequent performance in primaries. A total of 137 polls can be assessed as intervening between two or more primaries; the changes in opinion represented by these polls bear no relationship to subsequent changes in the candidates' primary perform-

TABLE 5.13
CANDIDATES' PERCENT OF PRIMARIES ENTERED WON, AS
FUNCTION OF THEIR PERCENTAGE IN LAST GALLUP
PREFERENCE POLL RELEASED BEFORE PRIMARY
SEASON, 1936-76

Percent Standing in Last Gallup Poll before First Primary	Percent of Primaries Entered Won			
	0	1-49	50+	Totals
0	5 (63%)	1 (13%)	2 (25%)	8 (100%)
1-9	19 (61%)	6 (19%)	6 (19%)	31 (100%)
10-19	9 (47%)	6 (32%)	4 (21%)	19 (100%)
20-29	2 (33%)	3 (50%)	1 (17%)	6 (100%)
30-39	2 (20%)	4 (40%)	4 (40%)	10 (100%)
40-49	0 (0%)	0 (0%)	2 (100%)	2 (100%)
50+	0 (0%)	1 (9%)	10 (91%)	11 (100%)
Total	37 (43%)	21 (24%)	29 (33%)	87 (100%)

ance (shifts in percentage of primaries entered won). Although primaries have immediate effects on national opinion, as measured by the polls, the reverse relationship does not appear to hold.

To summarize the dynamics of interaction between polls and primaries, then, primaries do influence polls, and not vice versa, in the short run, but the strongest relationships are the long-run effects in the opposite direction, the effects of national opinion on winning both the state primary elections and the presidential nomination. As often is true in the popular media, the week-to-week impact of primaries on polls obscures the fact that major changes in national public opinion are usually glacial. Thus, with only this minor qualification to accommodate the role of primaries, the previously described historical model of presidential nomination campaigns can stand.

Expanded Primary System Overshadowing Polls

Why, then, given this model derived from forty years of American political tradition, has the state primary election system decided the two out-of-power party nominees, McGovern and Carter, in the last two presidential nominating races? One reason is the steady increase in the number of primary states since 1968. For the previous forty years, from 1928 through 1968, the number of primaries had stabilized at around fifteen and included only about half of the dozen or so largest states. Following the Democrats' defeat in 1968, however, a number of party reforms, led by the McGovern-Fraser guidelines,[12] established new rules for delegate selection. The easiest way for state parties to comply with these rules without disrupting other party procedures was to put a presidential primary law through the legislature. By the 1972 campaign, seven states had added primaries, bringing the total to twenty-three (with the District of Columbia), including eleven of the twelve largest states and involving roughly two-thirds of all convention delegates. These changes allowed McGovern to enter seventeen primaries, more than any candidate since President Calvin Coolidge in 1924.

Had the historical model of presidential nomination campaigns been restored in 1976, the Democratic nomination would probably have fallen to Hubert Humphrey. Humphrey had been a Democratic leader for some twenty-five years, had served his party as vice president and presidential candidate, and had led Gallup polls of Democrats continually from October 1975, well into the primary season (even after a number of Carter's most stunning victories). As a strategy appropriate to this position, at least under the historical model, Humphrey decided not to enter the early primaries, expecting to win the nomination in a brokered convention.

Even while Humphrey formulated his 1976 plans, however, and as a largely unanticipated consequence, reforms in both parties had continued to work toward bolstering the importance of the state primary season. Another seven states added primaries after the 1972 election, bringing the total number of contests to thirty and involving thirteen of the fifteen largest states and nearly three-fourths of each party's convention delegates. When these developments were reported in the news media, most commentators warned that the larger number of primaries would further dilute the importance of any one, forcing candidates to pick and choose the states they would enter.

Jimmy Carter, perhaps alone among political strategists, perceived the new significance party reforms had given the much-expanded state primary schedule. Of all the presidential candidates, only Carter declared his intention to run in all thirty primaries (although he later chose to skip

West Virginia out of deference to favorite son Senator Robert Byrd). With a season record of seventeen victories, ten seconds, one third (New York), and one fourth (Massachusetts), Carter won more primaries than presidential candidates have traditionally had available to enter and more primary delegates than traditionally have been up for election. Not since President Woodrow Wilson won in nineteen states in 1916 had a nominee garnered more primary victories. The effect of Carter's primary performance on his standing among rank-and-file Democrats eclipsed even McGovern's unprecedented climb from obscurity four years earlier.

Evidence that the historical model of presidential nomination campaigns no longer prevailed also emerged from the Republican campaign in 1976. Under the historical model, President Ford would have had an easy time on his way to nomination for a full term in office. Instead, he was challenged by Ronald Reagan in a campaign no less unprecedented than those of McGovern and Carter. Not since Herbert Hoover in 1932 had an actively campaigning president lost more than a single state primary. Reagan topped Gerald Ford in twelve of twenty-nine Republican contests. No primary challenge of a sitting president has ever produced more victories than did Reagan's, nor more convention delegates—again because of the increased number of primary elections.

Thus, the historical model of presidential nomination campaigns derived from forty years of American political tradition has been shaken in the past two election years by the nomination campaigns of McGovern, Carter and Reagan. As shown here, however, there is still considerable evidence for basic elements of the historical model, including the dynamics of interaction among national opinion polls and state primary elections, including four major relationships:

(1) Standing in the preference polls has a strong direct effect on winning the presidential nomination; this relationship increases gradually as the convention approaches.

(2) Standing in the preference polls has little or no effect on changes in subsequent polls, that is, preference polls do not generate significant bandwagon movements.

(3) Standing in the preference polls has a direct positive effect on success in the state primary elections, still accounting for roughly half the variance in candidate performance in the primaries (although this relationship has been eroded by the McGovern and Carter campaigns).

(4) Outcomes of individual primary elections effect immediate changes in the polls, particularly for winners, Democrats, and early primaries; the overall primary season has a lesser aggregate effect on national opinion.

Despite these relationships, however, the nomination campaigns of 1972 and 1976 suggest that the historical model may be breaking down in favor of an increased role for state primary elections. The expanded number of state primary elections suggests that the more recent trend will continue, although it may remain true, as this author's earlier article concluded, that "there is no greater advantage than strength in the early polls for winning the presidential nomination."[13] At the same time, however, thanks to the proliferation of primaries and reforms in both parties, no longer will presidential nominations fall routinely to sitting presidents, long-established party leaders, and early front-runners in the opinion polls. In future campaigns we can expect other relatively obscure candidates—like McGovern and Carter—to attempt to use the state primary system to capture in a matter of weeks support that has traditionally taken several years and even several nomination campaigns to build. We can also expect serious challengers—like Ronald Reagan—to mount all-out nomination campaigns against sitting presidents. Barring major counter-reforms in the primary system, it is unlikely that any future candidate, including incumbent presidents, can be elected to the White House without a string of state primary victories.

Notes

1. The tables and analysis in the present chapter are updated versions of those first published in James R. Beniger, "Winning the Presidential Nomination: National Polls and State Primary Elections, 1936-1972," *Public Opinion Quarterly* 40 (Spring 1976): 22-38.

2. Ibid., p. 38.

3. William R. Keech and Donald R. Matthews, *The Party's Choice,* Studies in Presidential Selection (Washington, D. C.: Brookings Institution, 1976).

4. Beniger, "Winning the Presidential Nomination," p. 38.

5. Democratic and Republican nominations for each of the eleven presidential campaigns, 1936-76, excluding President Franklin Roosevelt's renomination in 1936, for which *The Gallup Poll, Public Opinion 1935-1971*, 3 vols. (New York: Random House, 1972) does not index a party preference poll. Hereafter, the phrase "twenty-one nominations" refers to those for which Gallup polls are available.

6. The phrase "eleventh-hour changes" as a category of presidential nomination campaign outcomes is introduced in Beniger, "Winning the Presidential Nomination," p. 29.

7. The phrase "genuine horseraces" as a category of presidential nomination campaign outcomes is introduced in ibid., pp. 39-40.

8. Ibid., p. 30.

9. The phrase "staved-off challenges" as a category of presidential nomination campaign outcomes is introduced in ibid., pp. 28-29.

10. *The Gallup Opinion Index,* no. 125 (November-December 1975): 1.

11. For Gallup polls, see *The Gallup Opinion Index,* various numbers (Princeton, N. J.: Gallup International, 1971-76). For primaries, see James W. Davis, *Presidential Primaries: Road to the White House* (New York: Crowell, 1967), pp. 290-305; *Facts on File Yearbook* (New York: Facts on File, 1968, 1972, 1976).

12. The McGovern-Fraser Commission, officially titled "The Commission on Party Structure and Delegate Selection," was a product of demands for reform that followed the ill-fated 1968 Democratic convention in Chicago. Chaired by George McGovern from 1969 to 1971 and by Minnesota Congressman Donald Fraser from 1971 to 1972, the commission published eighteen guidelines designed to reduce inequities in state delegate selection. See *Mandate for Reform,* Report to the Democratic National Committee (Washington, D. C.: Democratic National Committee, 1970). For background, see Austin Ranney, "Changing the Rules of the Nominating Game," in *Choosing the President,* ed. James David Barber (Englewood Cliffs, N. J.: Prentice-Hall, 1974), pp. 71-93.

13. Beniger, "Winning the Presidential Nomination," p. 38.

Voter Participation _____ 6
in Primaries

Voter turnout in key presidential primary states remains disappointingly low—less than 30 percent of the voting age population—despite the celebrity-level coverage by the television networks and the national press. In 1976, more states held presidential primaries than ever before, but the percentage of voters who registered a choice in the selection of presidential candidates in the primaries declined from previous years. Voting figures for the 1976 primary season, compiled by Austin Ranney, show that even though 5 million more voters expressed a preference for presidential nominees than in 1972, the actual percentage of participating voters in the primary states dropped by 4 percent.[1] This decline occurred despite the fact that both parties had intense nominating battles in 1976, whereas four years earlier only the Democratic party presidential nomination was seriously challenged. Voter turnout in presidential primaries since 1960 is listed in Table 6.1.

In this chapter we will first make a brief historic overview of voter turnout since the rise of presidential primaries in 1912. Next, we will compare voter participation in the 1972 and 1976 presidential primaries and then look more closely at participation in key primary states over the past two decades. Another task will be to compare voter turnout in primary and general elections. The impact of election laws and the level of competition on voter turnout in primaries will then be analyzed. Finally, we will explore some of the reasons why American citizens do not vote in presidential primaries and suggest possible ways of improving voter turnout in these springtime elections.

Historical Overview

Long-term voter turnout in the presidential primaries from 1912 through 1976 is charted in Figure 6.1. The steadily rising voter turnout in recent years can be attributed chiefly to the growing number of states adopting

TABLE 6.1
VOTER TURNOUT IN PRESIDENTIAL PRIMARIES, 1960-76

Year	Democrat	Republican	Total
1960	5,686,664	5,537,967	11,224,631
1964	6,247,435	5,935,339	12,182,774
1968	7,535,069	4,473,551	12,008,620
1972	15,993,965	6,188,281	22,182,246
1976	16,078,676	10,374,167	26,452,843*

Source: See Appendix.
*District delegate vote in Alabama, New York, and Texas unavailable.

the presidential primary, especially since 1968. In the 1968 primaries a total of slightly over 12 million votes was cast, which constituted approximately 8 percent of the national voting age population. In 1976 the total vote was approximately 29 million—slightly over 19 percent of the voting age population, estimated to be approximately 150 million. Thus, with the jump in the number of states holding presidential primaries from seventeen to twenty-nine between 1968 and 1976, almost two and one half times as many people participated in the 1976 presidential primaries as eight years earlier. Also, the broad increase in the total number of primary votes cast can of course be partially explained by the absolute growth of the U. S. population—which more than doubled between 1920 and 1975 (105 million to 213 million). But the upward trend of primary voting is disproportionate and reflective of factors other than population. As V. O. Key discovered many years ago, rank-and-file participation in a primary is greater in the majority party, especially in the later stages of its dominance.[2] Thus, the impact of the Progressive movement on the (majority) Republican party is reflected in the higher level of GOP voter participation between 1912 and 1928. Likewise, the higher turnout in the presidential primaries among (majority) Democrats is easily discerned during Franklin D. Roosevelt's New Deal era of the 1930s. More recently, the higher Democratic turnout in the 1960s and 1970s reflects the numerous currents—the anti-war and party reform groups and George Wallace— swirling about in the dominant Democratic party. Indeed, these voting data frequently echo Samuel Lubell's thesis that whatever the principal causes of political conflict may be, they are played out first in the conflict of groups, candidates and issues of the majority political party.[3] Further analysis of Republican party data also shows high turnout in the hotly contested Eisenhower-Taft 1952 nominating race and another peak turnout in the close Ford-Reagan struggle in 1976. These higher turnout figures reconfirm evidence marshalled later in the chapter indicating

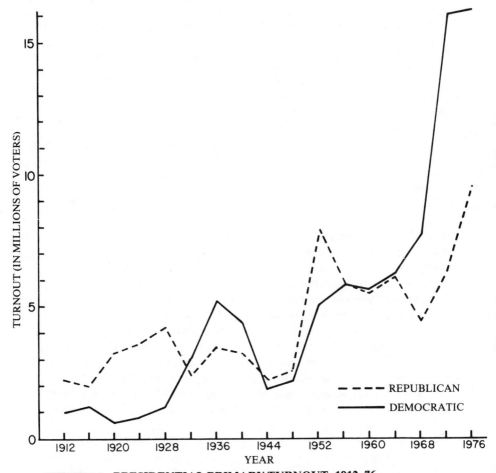

FIGURE 6.1   PRESIDENTIAL PRIMARY TURNOUT, 1912–76

that the level of competition in the primaries also affects the level of voter participation.

Throughout the chapter our chief interest will be focused on turnout in the recent primary elections, especially 1972 and 1976—the period in which the number of state primaries held nearly doubled (from fifteen to twenty-nine states) from the late 1960s. Because closely contested nominating races took place in both major parties, the 1976 presidential primaries are a good starting point for our analysis of voter turnout.

Presidential Primary Turnout in 1976

Although twenty-nine states and the District of Columbia held presidential primaries in 1976, only twenty-six states are used in Austin Ranney's analysis because data are unavailable or incomplete from three

TABLE 6.2
TURNOUT OF VOTERS IN PRESIDENTIAL PRIMARIES, 1976

State	Total Votes Cast	Estimated VAP	Percent of VAP Voting	Total Registered Voters	Percent of RV Voting
Alabama	665,855	2,501,000	26.6	1,792,582	37.1
Arkansas	534,341	1,503,000	35.5	961,399	55.6
California	5,709,853	15,294,000	37.3	7,701,888	74.1
Florida	1,910,149	6,326,000	30.2	3,381,750	56.5
Georgia	690,843	3,375,000	30.5	2,090,267	33.0
Idaho	164,960	567,000	29.1	457,965	36.0
Illinois	2,087,807	7,718,000	27.0	5,753,155	36.3
Indiana	1,245,715	3,640,000	34.2	2,910,086	42.8
Kentucky	439,534	2,374,000	18.5	1,545,915	28.4
Maryland	757,717	2,863,000	26.5	1,679,126	45.1
Massachusetts	941,950	4,173,000	22.6	1,766,812	53.3
Michigan	1,771,480	6,268,000	28.3	4,575,335	38.7
Montana	196,620	518,000	37.9	411,090	47.8
Nebraska	395,390	1,080,000	36.6	736,567	53.7
Nevada	122,991	424,000	29.0	198,073	62.1
New Hampshire	187,312	574,000	32.6	319,880	58.6
New Jersey	602,961	5,514,000	11.7	3,511,364	17.2
North Carolina	798,559	3,847,000	20.7	2,265,048	35.2
Oregon	730,167	1,653,000	44.2	1,177,909	62.0
Pennsylvania	2,183,122	8,441,000	25.9	5,023,278	43.5
Rhode Island	74,700	648,000	11.5	514,335	14.5
South Dakota	142,748	469,000	30.4	366,856	38.9
Tennessee	574,359	2,958,000	19.4	1,899,593	30.2
Texas	1,979,001	8,503,000	23.3	5,360,434	36.9
Vermont	72,270	327,000	22.1	266,649	27.1
West Virginia	528,269	1,281,000	41.2	1,042,502	50.7
Ohio	2,083,207	7,459,000	27.9	no statewide registration	
Wisconsin	1,333,373	3,211,000	41.5	no statewide registration	
Total	28,925,253	103,149,000		57,709,858	
Mean turnout			28.2		42.9

Source: Austin Ranney, *Participation in American Presidential Nominations, 1976* (Washington, D.C.: American Enterprise Institute, 1977), p. 20. The data on registration and votes cast in the 1976 primaries were compiled by the Congressional Research Service of the Library of Congress. The data on estimated voting age population are from U.S., Bureau of Census, *Current Population Reports, Series P-25,* no. 626, issued May 1976.

Note: "VAP" stands for Voting Age Population; "RV" stands for Registered Voters.

states, New York, Ohio and Wisconsin, and in the District of Columbia only the Democrats held a presidential primary.

Table 6.2 shows the total votes cast in each of the twenty-six presidential primaries, the estimated voting age population (VAP) as of November 1976, the turnout rate on the voting age population basis,

TABLE 6.3

**TURNOUT IN COMPETITIVE PRESIDENTIAL PRIMARIES AND
ENSUING GENERAL ELECTIONS, 1948-68**

State	Year	Percent Turnout in Primary*	Percent Turnout in General Election*	Difference
California	1952	42	68	26
Nebraska	1952	39	73	34
New Hampshire	1952	37	78	41
Ohio	1952	25	70	45
Oregon	1952	45	67	22
Pennsylvania	1952	19	66	47
South Dakota	1952	41	73	32
Nebraska	1968	43	63	20
New Hampshire	1968	38	71	33
Oregon	1968	55	66	11
Wisconsin	1968	49	69	20
Mean turnout		39	69	30

Source: Primary election returns, 1948-64, are taken from James W. Davis, *Presidential Primaries: Road to the White House* (New York: Thomas Y. Crowell, 1967), pp. 296-305. All general election returns and primary election returns for 1968 are taken from various volumes of Richard M. Scammon, ed., *America Votes* (Washington, D. C.: Governmental Affairs Institute and Congressional Quarterly). Estimates of populations of voting age for the states are taken from the *Statistical Abstract of the United States, 1969* (Washington, D. C.: Bureau of the Census, 1969), table 534, p. 369. See Austin Ranney, "Turnout and Representation in Presidential Primary Elections," *American Political Science Review* 66 (March 1972): 24.

*Turnout percentage is calculated, as in most studies, by dividing the total number of votes cast by the estimated population of voting age.

and the turnout on a registered voter (RV) basis. The twenty-six states in 1976 had a mean turnout rate of 27.6 percent on the VAP basis and 42.9 percent on the RV basis.[4] It will be noted further that there was considerable variation among the state turnout rates. Among registered voters the range was from California's high of 74.1 percent to Rhode Island's low of 14.5 percent.

In 1972, twelve of the states included in the 1976 analysis also held formally contested presidential primaries (that is, more than one candidate was on the ballot for each party in each of the twelve states). The mean registered voter turnout in 1972 was 46.7 percent, almost four percentage points higher than 1976.

Another comparison using the voting age population figures in contested primaries only for the 1948-68 period is also worth noting. A competitive primary has been defined by Austin Ranney as one in which two or more candidates or candidate-pledged slates appeared on each party's ballot, at least one major national contender appeared on each party's ballot and in neither party did the winning candidate or slate get more than 80 percent of the votes.[5] Austin Ranney found that for the eleven primaries that satisfied these criteria in the 1948-68 period (all of them in either 1952 or 1968), the mean voting turnout was 39 percent; the mean voting age population turnout in the ensuing general elections was 69 percent, an increase of thirty points from the primary to general elections (see Table 6.3). In 1972 no primaries qualified as competitive under the three criteria listed above. But using these criteria in 1976, twenty-two states (including Ohio and Wisconsin) qualified as competitive.[6] The mean turnout using the voting age population base was 28 percent in 1976, eleven percentage points below the figure for the 1948-68 period. Thus, although the nation had far more—and far more heavily contested—presidential primaries in 1976 than ever before, there was a sharp drop-off in voter turnout. This drop-off, moreover, was larger than the more widely discussed drop-off in voter turnout in presidential general elections during the past three decades. In 1948-68, the highest voting age population turnout in general elections was 62.8 percent in the closely contested Kennedy-Nixon 1960 elections; the turnout dropped to 54.4 percent in the 1976 general election. While this drop-off of 8.4 percentage points has led to widespread discussion about voter apathy, this figure is still smaller than the 11 percentage-point drop in competitive presidential primaries during the same period.

Participation in Several Key Primary States

In New Hampshire, the state that quadrennially basks in the limelight of the mass media for two months before its presidential primary, voter turnout has averaged only 35.3 percent of the voting age population for the past five presidential primaries, 1960-76.[7] (General election voter turnout during this period has averaged approximately 65 percent.) This relatively low primary turnout is made all the more disappointing by the fact that the citizenry of New Hampshire also held their annual town meetings—the last vestige of direct democracy in the United States—on the same day as the presidential primary, until 1976. If the local concerns of the New Hampshire populace—school levies, roads, fire and police protection and the salaries of town officials—have failed to bring out the voters on election day, it seems doubtful that future voter turnout in this presidential primary will ever increase much beyond one-third of the citizenry.

In only one state, Oregon, does the presidential primary voter turnout consistently approach half the voting age population. For the past five presidential primary elections (1960-76) 48.9 percent of the Oregon electorate have turned out to express their preference for presidential candidates and to participate in the selection of national convention delegates. Oregon also has the distinction of being the only state in the Union since the pre-World War I period to have over half of its potential voters turn out in a single presidential primary election. In 1968, approximately 55 percent of the Oregon electorate went to the polls to choose between Senators Eugene McCarthy and Robert Kennedy in the Democratic column and to register a preference between former Vice President Richard Nixon and California Governor Ronald Reagan in the GOP primary.

Close behind Oregon in primary voter turnout is Wisconsin, birthplace of the presidential primary movement. As front-line participants in such heavily fought contests as Kennedy-Humphrey in 1960, McGovern-Humphrey-Wallace-Muskie in 1972, and Carter-Udall and Ford-Reagan in 1976, Wisconsin voters have averaged almost 47 percent turnout in the past five presidential primary elections.

California, the nation's most populous state, has the third highest presidential primary voter rate in the country, 39.9 percent in the last five primary elections (1960-76). Why do these two West Coast states rank first and third in presidential primary voter turnout? Some observers would attribute it to the unique "political culture" of each of the two states—the early Progressive influence, widespread use of initiative and referendum measures, and strong concern about environmental issues. Voter turnout remains high, it should be noted, even though no gubernatorial primaries are held on presidential primary election day (both states elect governors in the off-year election). Senatorial primaries, however, are sometimes held on this date, depending upon which year in the cycle the six-year term of the incumbent ends. Illinois, on the other hand, holds its gubernatorial primaries on the same day as its presidential primary; yet voter turnout since 1960 has averaged only 16.4 percent of the voting age population.

Two Midwestern states with a long tradition of presidential primaries dating back to the famous Taft-Roosevelt contest in 1912—Nebraska and South Dakota—attract less than 30 percent of their citizenry to the polls on primary day. Nebraska, even though treated to such recent top-flight matches as those between Senators McCarthy and Kennedy in 1968, McGovern and Humphrey in 1972, Carter-Church and Ford versus Reagan in 1976, has averaged only 28.8 percent turnout since 1960. South Dakota, despite several big name contests in recent primaries, has averaged only 25.2 percent voter turnout since 1960. New Jersey, which joined the presidential preference primary club in 1972 (though it has had a delegate primary since 1912) possesses the unenviable record of

TABLE 6.4

PRESIDENTIAL PRIMARY TURNOUT, 1972 AND 1976

(PERCENT)

Primary	1972	1976	Net Change
New Hampshire	53.3	46.1	− 7.2
Massachusetts	28.7	32.2	+ 3.5
Florida	57.8	56.5	− 1.3
Illinois	22.6	36.2	+ 13.6
North Carolina	52.3	35.3	− 17.0
Pennsylvania	30.2	43.4	+ 13.2
District of Columbia	14.6	11.6	− 3.0
Indiana	43.1	42.8	− 0.3
Nebraska	56.5	52.1	− 4.4
West Virginia	50.3	47.8*	− 2.5
Maryland	44.0	44.8*	+ 0.8
Michigan	43.7	38.7	− 5.0
Oregon	62.3	58.9*	− 3.4
Tennessee	34.0	30.2	− 3.8
Rhode Island	9.2	14.5	+ 5.3
South Dakota	25.5	38.9	+ 13.4
California	63.5	70.1*	+ 6.6
New Jersey	9.4	10.1*	+ 0.7
Ohio	46.7	44.5*	− 2.2

Source: Congressional Quarterly Weekly Report XXXIV (July 10, 1976): 1808.

*Based on unofficial returns.

Note: Turnout is based on the number of eligible registered voters in each state. This table does not include the seven states that held primaries for the first time in 1976, or the results from the delegate selection primaries in New York, Texas and Alabama or from Wisconsin, where there is no statewide registration. For the states included in the table the national turnout rate was 42.6 percent in 1972, compared to 43.8 percent in the same states for 1976.

having the nation's lowest presidential primary voter turnout in recent years, 9.7 percent in the past two presidential primary elections (see Table 6.4).

How does voter turnout in presidential primaries compare with participation in the caucus-convention system, the other major method for selecting national convention delegates? In this era of presidential primaries it is sometimes forgotten that twenty-one states in 1976 with a combined voting age population of 33,000,000—approximately 22 percent of the national voting age population—selected their national convention delegates through a multi-tiered caucus-convention system.

Starting with precinct caucuses, delegates in these states are elected to congressional or legislative district conventions, which pick a majority of the delegates sent to the national convention. The remainder of the national (at-large) delegates are chosen at state party conventions.

The 1976 data, collected by the *Congressional Quarterly,* show that Democratic party member turnout (no data for Republicans were collected), in the caucus-convention states is much lower than in the primary states. According to Austin Ranney's figures, the mean proportion of the voting age population that participated in the Democratic precinct caucuses was 1.9 percent. By contrast, the mean proportion of the voting age population participating in the closed primary states (the best comparison since only registered party members can vote) was 18.6 percent, almost ten times higher than caucus participation.[8] The highest Democratic caucus turnout, according to the *Congressional Quarterly,* was in Connecticut, where 106,000 party members, approximately 19 percent of the state's registered Democrats, participated in the delegate-selection process.[9] Among the primary states, California had the highest turnout of registered Democrats in the presidential primary, 71.7 percent of the registered party voters. Selective reports on Republican turnout in caucus-convention states show no marked disparity from these figures in voter turnout. In any case, the level of party member participation in the caucus-convention system, despite efforts of the Democratic party reformers to open up the delegate selection process, was far below voter participation in the presidential primaries.

Comparison of Turnout in Primary and General Election

Nationwide, voter turnout in presidential primaries prior to 1976 averaged approximately 27 percent of the electorate during the period 1948-68.[10] For the states' ensuing general presidential elections, the mean turnout was 62 percent, a "surge" of thirty-five percentage points.

The data for the primaries, calculated by Austin Ranney, are based upon seventy-two presidential primaries held from 1948 through 1968 in which voters had an opportunity to vote directly for their preferences for party nominee (in presidential preference polls) or indirectly (in choosing slates of delegates pledged to particular aspirants, as in California). These figures, as Ranney pointed out, were somewhat misleading because in many of the seventy-two cases there was no contest, or no serious contest, in one or both parties' primaries, and in others the contestants did not include a major contender in at least one major party. To provide a more accurate reading of voter turnout under competitive conditions, Ranney chose eleven competitive presidential primaries held in 1952 or 1968. As can be seen in Table 6.3, compiled by Ranney, competitive primaries produced a primary-to-general-election "surge" of 30 percentage points, somewhat more than the surges for gubernatorial and senatorial election data described below.

Because voters are participating in a selection process for the highest office in the land, the reader might easily conclude that voter turnout in the presidential primaries would be much higher than in off-year gubernatorial and U.S. Senate primaries. But the election data for gubernatorial and senatorial primaries during the past fifty years do not support this conclusion. The late V. O. Key found that in fifteen non-Southern states from 1926 to 1952, the average voter turnout in gubernatorial primaries was 31 percent, while the turnout in the ensuing general elections averaged over 50 percent.[11] For the period 1952-60, Arthur C. Wolfe found a mean turnout rate in all primary elections for governor of 32 percent, as compared with a mean turnout rate in general gubernatorial elections of 53 percent. The corresponding turnouts for U.S. senator were 30 percent in the primaries and 54 percent in the general elections.[12] More recently, Austin Ranney has found similar patterns in twenty-eight states that he has classified as "two-party" competitive states for the period 1962-68. For gubernatorial races the mean voting turnout in the primaries was 28.1 percent in the primaries and 60.7 percent in the general election. For U.S. Senate races, the mean voting turnout in the primaries was 26.4 percent and 61.3 percent in the general election.[13]

That there is a wide variance in primary and general election turnout is not surprising, for data from the Survey Research Center, University of Michigan, on presidential elections and off-year congressional elections over the past two decades have shown a surge and decline in voter turnout not unlike that found in presidential primary and general elections. Angus Campbell, in a seminal article published almost two decades ago, noted that "one of the most dependable regularities of American politics is the vote decline in off-year congressional elections. The turnout in the off-year elections is invariably smaller than in presidential elections which they follow, usually by a margin of over 25 percent of the presidential vote."[14] Campbell also discovered that the off-year electorates are not merely smaller but representative versions of the presidential-year electorates. The two electorates differ significantly in several respects. Campbell compared "core voters" (those who voted in both elections) with "peripheral voters" (those who voted in presidential but not congressional elections). The core voters scored significantly higher on the socioeconomic dimensions of age, education, income and status of occupation. Even more important differences appeared on various dimensions of political interest and involvement.

Ranney, in a survey of the New Hampshire and Wisconsin 1968 presidential primaries, found that "presidential primary electorates, like those in gubernatorial primaries, are demographically quite unrepresentative of the nonparticipating party identifiers: they are older, of higher status in income and occupation, and more active in a variety of civic, religious, and political organizations."[15] The data analyzed by Ranney also showed that party-identifying primary participants in both states differed significantly from their nonparticipating fellow party members on a number of socioeconomic dimensions. But there were "substantially fewer significant differences between participating and non-participating independents."[16] In his study of New Hampshire and Wisconsin voters Ranney concluded, however, that "strong partisans of both parties are only slightly more likely than weaker partisans to vote in presidential primaries, and the relationship between intensity of party identification and voting in such primaries is much weaker than that between partisanship and voting in general elections."[17]

Election Law Impact on Turnout

In our analysis of voter participation in presidential primaries thus far we have not discussed the impact of electoral law upon levels of political participation. Do the various types of primaries—binding or advisory, closed or crossover, winner-take-all or the all-candidate blanket ballot primary first developed in Oregon—affect voter turnout? Data on voter turnout in primaries are still scarce. But a recent study by Morris and Davis has shed more light on the relationship between the type of presidential primary and the level of voter turnout.[18]

BINDING AND ADVISORY PRIMARIES

Despite the belief that voters are more likely to turn out in presidential primary contests if the delegates chosen are pledged to specific candidates, Morris and Davis discovered for the period 1964-72 that there is no statistically significant difference between binding and advisory presidential primaries on turnout in either party.[19] But Austin Ranney, in a study of 1976 presidential primaries, found that in the seven states using a non-binding presidential preference primary the mean turnout of registered voters—not the voting age population base used earlier in the chapter—was slightly lower (41 percent). In three states—Georgia, Maryland and Montana—the preference primary is binding on the delegates of one party but not the other; their mean turnout was 42.0 percent. In the remaining fourteen states using the binding preference primary in both parties, the mean turnout of registered voters was 44.9 percent. Ranney concluded, "the differences in mean turnouts among these groups of states were small; they did proceed in linear fashion: the more closely the presidential preference poll approached the ideal of binding the delegates, the higher—by a small margin—was the turnout."[20]

Why? Confirming data are inadequate, but a salient factor may be that the vast majority of primary voters are unaware of the distinction between pledged and unpledged delegates. Also, primary voters are more likely to be concerned with the presidential preferential primary—the "beauty contest"—rather than the selection of delegates. In 1976 some form of preferential primary was held in twenty-four states. In these states the voters in one or both parties cast votes for both their presidential choice and a list of delegates. Voters cannot be faulted because the preference primary results rather than delegate selection contests capture the headlines and the prime television network time. Besides, advisory primaries have sometimes had a powerful influence on the nominating process. John F. Kennedy's uphill victory in the 1960 West Virginia advisory primary is a classic example.

WINNER-TAKE-ALL PRIMARIES

One special form of binding primary—the winner-take-all contest—has produced higher voter turnout than all other types of binding competitive primaries. In the five competitive winner-take-all Democratic primaries held during 1964-72, the mean turnout was 64.02 percent (of registered voters), compared with a 53.62 percent mean turnout level for all other competitive binding contests.[21]

"LOOPHOLE" AND PROPORTIONATE REPRESENTATION PRIMARIES

As part of the post-1972 Democratic convention delegate-selection reforms, the national party's Commission on Delegate Selection and Party Structure, known as the Mikulski Commission, approved a system of proportionate representation for each state's delegation. According to Rule 11, each state's delegates were to be allocated in proportion to the popular votes cast for presidential contenders, "except that preferences securing less than 15 percent of the votes cast for the delegation need not be awarded any delegates."[22] But in a later ruling the Democratic National Committee authorized state parties, if they wished, to adopt a winner-take-all system for delegates selected at the congressional district level, a provision which soon came to be called the "loophole" primary, since it allowed a state to evade the national party's proportionality rule.

For the 1976 Democratic presidential primaries it is thus possible to compare turnout in states following the proportionality rule and those permitting a modified winner-take-all system. Of the twelve states requiring proportionality in both parties, Austin Ranney reports the mean registered voter turnout was 42.6 percent. In the ten states with loophole primaries for both parties, the mean turnout was 40.9 percent. For the four states requiring proportionality for the Democrats but not for

Republicans, the mean turnout was 47.9 percent. This figure, however, was heavily influenced by the inclusion of California, with its 74.1 percent turnout of registered voters, the highest in the land. If California is omitted from this group of states, the mean turnout of the other three states is 39.2 percent. Thus, it appears that only a small relationship exists between the extent of proportionate representation and primary turnout. Indeed, the party reformers' argument that voters would be more inclined to vote in a primary using proportionality, where presumably their votes would not be wasted, does not receive much support from Ranney's data.[23] Subsequently, the 1976 Democratic National Convention voted to ban all types of winner-take-all primaries, including the loophole primary, in the future nominating races. The Republicans, however, still permit winner-take-all primaries.

THE OREGON BLANKET BALLOT

Another ballot form, Oregon's blanket ballot, virtually assures a good competitive race in one or both parties. In 1959 Oregon solons, disappointed with their voter turnout in the presidential preference primary contests, approved an all-candidate primary ballot. Under this revised primary legislation the Oregon secretary of state has been empowered to list all "serious, nationally recognized candidates" on the ballot. Candidates are automatically listed without their consent. Experience has shown that the Oregon "laundry list" ballot usually guarantees the voters a wide choice of candidates and a lively nominating contest, at least in the out-of-power party. By 1968 Massachusetts, Nebraska and Wisconsin had also adopted modified forms of the Oregon plan. Fourteen states now use the Oregon type of preference primary. States that list all serious candidates, according to data compiled by Morris and Davis, have a greater voter turnout than those states listing fewer than the maximum number, "irrespective of campaign considerations."[24]

Among the fourteen blanket ballot states, Ranney's data for 1976 show the mean registered voter turnout was 44.5 percent. Among the ten states using the "volunteer ballot" preference system, in which aspirants have their names placed on the preference poll only if they or their supporters petition to do so, the mean turnout of registered voters in 1976 was 41.8 percent.[25] Two states—Alabama and Texas—do not use preference polls. Data were unavailable for New York, Ohio and Wisconsin.

CLOSED AND CROSSOVER (OPEN) PRIMARIES

Since the early days of the Progressive movement, it has frequently been argued that the "open," or what has come to be called the "crossover" primary, encourages greater voter participation because the voter can decide for himself which party primary contest interests him the most and does not restrict him to the party under which he or she is registered. Thus, if there is no important contest in his own party, the voter is free to vote in the opposition party presidential primary. The closed primary, which requires the voter to register his party preference several weeks before the election to be eligible to vote in his own party's primary, has been viewed as an obstacle to greater voter participation. Yet, Austin Ranney discovered in his analysis of the 1976 presidential primary races that voter participation in the closed primary states was considerably higher. The closed primary states had a mean turnout of 50 percent, whereas the crossover states had a mean turnout of only 34.9 percent.[26] What accounts for this unexpected turnout differential? No easy explanation is available. Ranney sought to find out if the higher turnout in closed primaries was an independent relationship or merely a reflection of other factors. By controlling for two factors that produce comparably large differences in turnout—educational level of the states' populations and levels of primary campaign spending—Ranney found that the differences in turnout in closed and crossover primaries remained essentially unchanged. In all four groups of states—higher education, lower education, higher campaign spending, lower campaign spending—the closed primary states had substantially higher mean levels of turnout than crossover states. Political scientists remain baffled as to why this should be the case. In an interview with columnist David Broder, Ranney speculated that in the closed primary states "parties have a more visible existence and the stress on party may make voting in the primaries more important."[27] But this is certainly not the case in California. More research is needed over a longer time span before any firm conclusions can be drawn on this phenomenon.

Level of Competition in Primary

Another factor affecting primary voter turnout is the level of competition in the primary. Morris and Davis found in the primaries before 1976 that as the index of candidate competition increases, voter turnout increases in presidential primaries, especially in the Democratic party.[28] Clearly, voters are attracted to a good horse race. Moreover, the national and state media coverage of a contested primary appears to help increase voter activity. The evidence indicates, however, that Republican and Democratic voters do not behave identically in primary elections. Republicans do not appear to react to competitiveness in primaries, regardless of whether the race appears close or one-sided.[29] The Republicans' consistently higher turnout rate is apparently related to socioeconomic status. Opinion poll data published by the Survey Research Center, University of Michigan, and other sources have for years indicated that upper socioeconomic status groups, which tend to be Republican, have a higher turnout rate than other socioeconomic groups.[30]

Democrats, on the other hand, are stimulated to go to the polls in greater numbers as the closeness of the primary races intensifies. The reason may be that the relative homogeneity of Republican voting coalition does not significantly affect GOP voter response. By contrast, the Democratic party consists of an uneasy coalition of union members, intellectuals, blacks, Southern conservatives and Catholics, and each element, either individually or jointly, may sponsor a candidate for the presidential nomination. In other words, party composition probably accounts for the higher level of competitiveness in the Democratic presidential primaries.[31] Regionally, the Republican turnout in Southern presidential primaries, however, has been considerably lower than the Democrats for two reasons. First, until 1968, Republicans rarely held presidential primaries in this predominantly Democratic sector of the country; instead, Republican state executive committees authorized the selection of national convention delegates by state party conventions. Second, until the close 1976 race between President Ford and Ronald Reagan, Southern Republican presidential primaries were considered rather insignificant by the candidates and the voters alike.

Morris and Davis have also found that as the index of the opposition party's campaign intensity increases, voter turnout increases.[32] In other words, as the competition heats up in one party, the primary competition stimulates increased voter turnout in the other major party. That this "spillover" effect occurs can probably be attributed, in part, to the nature of the mass media. Television and radio cannot restrict the impact of its advertising solely to the candidate's partisans. Members of the opposition party are exposed to the same commercial appeals to vote. Constant reminders from the media appear to influence partisans in the opposition party—even if their primary is uncontested—to go to the polls to endorse their candidate. Unopposed presidential candidates also frequently urge their supporters to go to the polls to demonstrate party strength for the impending general election race. The citizen's sense of civic duty may also impel him to go to the polls. However, in 1976, Austin Ranney reports, "there was no significant relationship in either party between the closeness of the presidential primary and the proportion of registered voters who voted in that primary."[33] Ranney calculated an index of competition for each of the parties and then averaged the two figures for an overall level of competition for the state; he also considered each of the parties separately. The formula for calculating the index of competition, developed by William Morris and Otto Davis, is percent of leading candidate divided by the difference between the percents of the two top candidates. The contradictory evidence on the impact of the level of competition upon voter turnout suggests that further study is in order before any conclusive judgment can be offered.

Effect of Campaign Spending on Turnout

Until passage of the Federal Election Campaign Act of 1971, no comprehensive presidential primary campaign spending data were available to measure the impact of campaign spending on voter turnout. The Federal Election Campaign Act put a ceiling on the amount of money candidates could spend on media advertising in presidential primaries, but this law did not take effect until April 7, 1972—half-way through the 1972 nominating campaigns. Prior to that date, presidential candidates were free to spend as much money as they could raise—or what they considered prudent to spend. John F. Kennedy, for example, kept his official spending in the 1960 campaign under $1 million to avoid charges that he and his wealthy father, Joseph P. Kennedy, were "buying" the Democratic nomination.

Under the new law the candidates' detailed reporting requirements to the Federal Election Commission make it possible to measure quantitatively the relationship between variations in the money spent in the 1976 presidential primary campaigns and variations in the size of the voting turnouts. To develop a standardized measure of campaign spending for purposes of comparing one state with another, Austin Ranney calculated the candidates' reported total actual expenditures in both parties as a percentage of their legal limit under the new 1974 federal law. For all twenty-six states in the analysis, the correlation between campaign spending and turnout of registered voters was .40—one of the strongest relationships among variables discussed in this section.[34] As a double check on the combined figures for the two parties (since only Jimmy Carter's spending figures were used in the Democratic party) Ranney took the data for Republicans Ford and Reagan in the thirteen closed primary states and correlated them with the turnout of registered Republican voters in those states. The correlation was .42, only two points higher than that for both parties combined. This information adds further confirming evidence to the hypothesis that campaign spending is one of the factors most strongly associated with primary turnout.

Registration Law Impact of Turnout

Political reformers have insisted for years that registration laws are major barriers to higher voter participation. Several recent studies have shown that variations in the states' registration laws affect voter turnout in presidential general elections.[35] An equally important concern is whether registration laws explain much of the variance of voter turnout in presidential primaries. In a study of twenty-eight presidential primary states, Austin Ranney used a scale of five Rosenstone-Wolfinger measures, which are considered the greatest inhibitions against voting in presidential elections.[36] In four states with only one restrictive law the mean turnout was 29.8 percent. The nine states with two restrictive measures had a mean turnout of 25.5 percent. But, surprisingly, seven states with three restrictive laws had a mean turnout of 33.5 percent—the highest turnout of all the presidential primary states! For the seven states with four restrictive laws the mean turnout was 29.8 percent, the same as the states with only one restrictive law. In the only state with five restrictive laws, Kentucky, the mean turnout was 18.5 percent.[37] Thus, while registration laws have been found to affect the level of voter turnout in presidential general elections, they do not seem to play a significant role in presidential primaries—at least based on the 1976 experience.

Why Don't Citizens Vote in Primaries?

As the evidence in this chapter shows, a large majority of eligible voters prefer to sit out the primaries. Why did so many citizens fail to make it to the polls? To find the answer, the Gallup organization recently queried a cross-section of prospective voters. Table 6.5 lists the major reasons given by citizens for not taking part in the 1976 primaries. Most reasons for not voting in the primaries are the same given for not participating in the general election: not registered, didn't like the candidates, illness, not interested in politics, and out of town or traveling.

Can voter participation be increased? The Gallup poll data suggest that a system of universal postcard registration would improve turnout in the primaries. Gallup's registration figures indicate, for example, that only half of young voters are presently registered to vote. State registration laws, according to Rosenstone and Wolfinger, reduced turnout in the 1972 presidential election by 9.1 percent. This figure would have translated into 12.2 million additional voters if the registration laws everywhere had been as lenient as in the most permissive state.[38] Survey data show that once a person is registered, the likelihood that he or she will vote increases substantially.[39] Some type of round robin television debates in the primaries might also enliven voter interest. The famous Kennedy-Nixon televised debates in the 1960 general election attracted a huge national audience— an estimated 75 million viewers in 30 million homes. In the 1972 California Democratic primary the three televised debates between Senators McGovern and Humphrey—each major TV network carried one debate—reached nationwide audiences in the mil-

TABLE 6.5
REASONS FOR NOT VOTING IN PRIMARIES, 1976
(PERCENT)

Not registered	31
Didn't like the candidates	17
Illness	9
Not interested in politics	7
Out of town/traveling	7
Working	5
New resident	5
No way to get to the polls	2
Registered as an Independent/Didn't want to declare a party affiliation	2
Don't believe in primary system	2
No particular reason	15
Miscellaneous/Don't know	0
Total	110*

Source: Gallup Opinion Index, no. 133 (August 1976): 28.
*Adds to more than 100 percent due to multiple responses.

lions. The three nationally televised 1976 Ford-Carter general election debates attracted an average of 75 million viewers. Proponents of a debate revival argue that televised candidate confrontations are needed to kindle political interest and activity among the electorate. Regular presidential primary debates are worth a try.

Notes

1. Austin Ranney, *Participation in American Presidential Nominations, 1976* (Washington, D. C.: American Enterprise Institute, 1977), p. 22.

2. V. O. Key, Jr., *American State Politics: An Introduction* (New York: Alfred A. Knopf, 1956).

3. Samuel Lubell, *The Future of American Politics,* 2nd ed. rev. (Garden City, N.Y.: Doubleday, 1955), p. 217; see also, Richard L. Rubin, "Presidential Primaries: Continuities, Dimensions of Change, and Political Implications" (Paper delivered at the 1977 annual meeting of the American Political Science Association, Washington, D. C., September 1-4, 1977), pp. 4-21.

4. Ranney, *Participation in American Presidential Nominations,* pp. 20-22. In New York no statewide data were collected for the number of persons who cast ballots for national convention delegates in the state's complicated and recently amended primary. For years neither Ohio nor Wisconsin has kept statewide figures on the number of registered voters. With only the Democratic party holding a primary in the District of Columbia, the turnout was misleadingly low compared with that of the other states, all of which held primaries in both parties.

5. Austin Ranney, "Turnout and Representation in Presidential Primary Elections," *American Political Science Review* 66 (March 1972): 21-37.

6. The following states were excluded from the 1976 competitive list: Georgia, where Carter received 82 percent of the votes in the Democratic primary; New Jersey and Pennsylvania, where only Ford was on the GOP ballot; and West Virginia, where favorite son Robert Byrd got 89 percent of the votes in the Democratic primary. Ranney, "Turnout and Representation," p. 22.

7. Data derived from presidential primary election returns in Appendix.

8. Ranney, *Participation in American Presidential Nominations,* p. 15.

9. *Congressional Quarterly Weekly Report XXXIV* (July 10, 1976): 1809. It has been estimated that in 1976 more than one million people nationwide (700,000 Democrats and 400,000 Republicans) participated in delegate selection in the nonprimary states. See Austin Ranney, "The Political Parties: Reform and Decline," in Anthony King, ed., *The New American Political System* (Washington, D. C.: American Enterprise Institute, 1978), pp. 218-19.

10. Ranney, "Turnout and Representation," pp. 23-24.

11. Key, *American State Politics,* pp. 134-38.

12. Arthur C. Wolfe, *The Direct Primary in American Politics* (Ph.D. diss., University of Michigan, 1966), table 4.6, p. 102.

13. Austin Ranney, "Parties in State Politics," in *Politics in American States: A Comparative Analysis*, ed. Herbert Jacob and Kenneth N. Vines, 2nd ed. (Boston: Little, Brown, 1971), table 3, p. 98.

14. Angus Campbell, "Surge and Decline: A Study of Electoral Change," *Public Opinion Quarterly* 24 (Fall 1960): 397-418. The article has been reprinted in Angus Campbell, et al., *Elections and the Political Order* (New York: John Wiley and Sons, 1966), pp. 40-62. The quotation cited is from this text, p. 51.

15. Ranney, "Turnout and Representation," p. 27.

16. Ibid., p. 26.

17. Ibid., pp. 28-29.

18. William D. Morris and Otto A. Davis, "The Sport of Kings: Turnout in Presidential Preference Primaries" (Paper delivered at 1975 annual meeting of the American Political Science Association, San Francisco, California, September 2-5, 1975), pp. 22-23.

19. Ibid., p. 22.

20. Ranney, *Participation in American Presidential Nominations*, p. 28.

21. Morris and Davis, "The Sport of Kings," p. 26. These data cover competitive primaries in which there were two or more candidates and the winner's margin was less than two to one.

22. "Democrats All," mimeographed (Washington, D. C.: Democratic National Committee, 1973), p. 18.

23. Ranney, *Participation in American Presidential Nominations*, pp. 28-29.

24. Morris and Davis, "The Sport of Kings," p. 32.

25. Ranney, *Participation in American Presidential Nominations,* p. 30.

26. Ibid.

27. Washington *Post*, April 20, 1977.

28. Morris and Davis, "The Sport of Kings," pp. 15-16.

29. Ibid.

30. Norman H. Nie, Sidney Verba, and John R. Petrochik, *The Changing American Voter* (Cambridge: Harvard University Press, 1976), p. 207.

31. Morris and Davis, "The Sport of Kings," p. 15.

32. Ibid., pp. 15-16.

33. Ranney, *Participation in American Presidential Nominations,* pp. 24-35.

34. Ibid., p. 33.

35. Steven J. Rosenstone and Raymond E. Wolfinger, "The Effect of Registration Laws on Voter Turnout," *American Political Science Review* 72 (March 1978): 22-43; Stanley Kelley, Jr., Richard E. Ayres, and William G. Bower, "Registration and Voting: Putting First Things First," *American Political Science Review* 61 (June 1967): 359-79; and Jae On Kim, John R. Petrochik, and Stephan N. Enokson, "Voter Turnout Among American States: Systematic and Industrial Components," *American Political Science Review* 69 (March 1975): 107-31.

36. The five restrictive measures are: (1) registration closed twenty-four days or more before the election; (2) voting rolls purged every three years or less; (3) registration offices not open in the evening or on Saturdays; (4) registration only at city level, not at the precinct level; and (5) no absentee registration allowing for registration of the sick, disabled and absent. See Steven J. Rosenstone and Raymond E. Wolfinger, "The Effect of Registration Laws on Voter Turnout" (Paper presented at the 1976 annual meeting of the American Political Science Association, Chicago, September 2-5, 1976), pp. 14-15, as quoted in Ranney, *Participation in American Presidential Nominations*, p. 26.

37. Ibid.

38. Rosenstone and Wolfinger, "The Effect of Registration Laws on Voter Turnout," *APSR*, p. 36.

39. Kelley, Ayres, and Bower, "Registration and Voting," p. 362.

Presidential Primaries _____ 7
and the Incumbent President

The same irresistible forces of the presidential primary system and the mass media that have pushed out-party candidates to announce their presidential intentions long before the first-in-the-nation New Hampshire primary now pressure incumbent presidents to announce their re-election plans much earlier than in the past. President Ford, anxious to head off a possible challenge in 1976 from former Governor Ronald Reagan of California, formally announced his candidacy from the Oval Office in July 1975, a year before the GOP convention. Ford's announcement was intended not only to have the effect of discouraging intraparty opposition to his nomination in 1976, but also to do away with the perception of Mr. Ford as a "lame duck" president in his dealings with Congress and his own party. His predecessor, Richard M. Nixon, had given the green light to establish an organization to promote his own renomination, the Committee to Re-Elect the President (CREEP) more than a year before the 1972 GOP convention. It will be recalled that members of this group and the White House "plumbers" organized the break-in of the Democratic National Committee in the Watergate complex in June 1972, and the resultant cover-up instigated by the White House eventually—two years later—cost Nixon the presidency.

Adoption of the Twenty-Second Amendment in 1951, which imposed a two-term limit on presidents, vitiates his influence during his second term in choosing his successor, with the consequent strengthened impact of presidential primaries upon the in-party nomination process. In this chapter we will focus our major attention on several points: the influence of White House incumbents upon in-party nominations; the role of second-term incumbents on the nomination process before passage of the Twenty-Second Amendment; the effect of the Twenty-Second Amendment upon an incumbent's role in picking a successor; and the potential threat the presidential primaries offer to in-party challengers anxious to unseat a sitting president.

Advantages of Incumbency

No challenger can ignore the historical truth that an incumbent president is hard to beat, especially for renomination of his party. Historically, no incumbent president in the twentieth century has been denied his party's nomination if he has sought another term. Nor have incumbents been reluctant to capitalize on the awesome authority and resources of the presidential office to retain their White House occupancy. As one veteran party watcher has noted, "The Presidency provides a forum from which occupants can attempt to proselytize voters without giving the appearance of campaigning."[1] In 1972, for example, President Nixon conducted his renomination campaign more as the President running the country than as a candidate. Throughout the pre-convention period he did little overt campaigning; indeed, it was not until the closing weeks of the general election that he deigned to leave the White House to do any political stumping.

In the case of President Ford four years later, he had the powers of office just as much as if he had been elected rather than appointed. Generally, presidential incumbents running in the primaries enjoy special built-in advantages that non-incumbents can only dream about. For an incumbent seeking renomination the presidency makes him the best known person in the country. Wherever the president goes and whatever he does make national news. Presidential speeches and news conferences usually are televised nationwide during prime time hours. White House occupants can orchestrate this advantage through the mass media seven days a week. President Nixon seeking renomination in 1972, for example, exploited this factor to the hilt. During the three weeks immediately preceding the New Hampshire and Florida primaries, where a half dozen Democratic candidates were scrambling to emerge from the pack, the three national television networks carried a total of 41 hours and 44 minutes of special programs and commentary of President Nixon's trip to the People's Republic of China.[2] Later, with an eye as much on the Democratic race as on the upcoming general election, President Nixon timed perfectly his trip to the Soviet Union. He arrived in Moscow one day before the late-round Oregon primary. His meetings with Soviet leader Brezhnev and company were heavily publicized in the midst of the crucial McGovern-Humphrey primary fight in California. President Nixon returned to the nation's capital on the day after the second McGovern-Humphrey debate. With a grand flourish Mr. Nixon arrived on the Capitol Hill grounds by helicopter at the prime time hour of 9 P.M., amidst floodlights and whirring television cameras, and walked into a joint session of Congress to report on his summit meeting. As Herbert E. Alexander commented, "It was grand theater and extraordinarily effective politics all staged as presidential business and at no cost to the campaign.''[2] Under these circumstances non-incumbents can only stand by helplessly as the sitting president monopolizes the American political stage.

Another major advantage in past years was the incumbent's ability to raise large sums of campaign money from wealthy contributors. But the new 1974 Federal Election Campaign Act, which sets a $1,000 limit on individual contributions, has eliminated this advantage. Still, the financial advantages of incumbency in a nominating race were never more visible than President Ford's dilatory tactics, which delayed lifting the federal matching subsidies freeze during nine crucial weeks—March 22 through May 21—of the 1976 primary season. While he and Congress wrangled over the revisions in the Federal Election Campaign Act of 1974 needed to overcome the Supreme Court's objections to the selection process of Federal Election Commission members, his GOP rival Ronald Reagan was denied more than $900,000 in federal subsidies for his financially starved campaign.[3] Reagan's campaign had been consistently running at a deficit. By late March Reagan's campaign debt was nearly $1 million, according to his report to the Federal Election Commission. President Ford, by contrast, ended the month $777,232 in the black.[4] To be sure, Reagan eventually collected large sums from private contributors, but most of this money reached his campaign coffers late in the spring, too late to help in the key middle primaries in New York, Wisconsin, Pennsylvania, Michigan and Maryland. Nine states held primaries during this critical nine-week subsidy freeze. Furthermore, twelve more primaries were scheduled between May 25 and June 8—hardly enough time for Reagan's managers to get vitally needed money into the campaign pipeline. Earlier, Reagan's campaign manager, John Sears, advised Reagan to make only a token effort to woo delegates in two big Eastern primaries, New York and Pennsylvania, and the late Ohio primary because the cost of mounting full-blown campaigns in these states (which provided President Ford's 117-delegate margin of victory at the GOP convention) was prohibitive. Commenting on President Ford's stalling tactics, the Washington *Post* editorialized:

It is impossible to tell how much the course of the primaries was affected by the staff engineered by Mr. Ford and his friends. What is perfectly obvious and inexcusable—and what cannot now be lightly dismissed simply because the President finally did the only thing he could after the game was up—is that one candidate used his high office and unique power in a way that not only unfairly handicapped his opponent in his own party but also gave him unwarranted and capricious influence over the outcome of the race for the Democratic nominations.[5]

As the incumbent, Mr. Ford enjoyed another built-in financial advantage that saved his campaign treasury several hundred thousand dollars.

On all campaign trips with *Air Force One,* his official plane, Ford was able to delay payment for campaign use of the aircraft for several weeks. Reagan, on the other hand, had to prepay for his chartered Boeing 727 each week before his plane would leave the ground. During the period of the subsidy freeze this figure alone reached an estimated $450,000. In the meantime, President Ford made political trips for three months early in 1976 without paying out campaign money for travel bills until long after the fact. Then, too, President Ford enjoyed another major incumbent fringe benefit: he used part of his huge White House staff on a virtually cost-free basis throughout the entire pre-convention campaign, while Reagan was forced to hire his full campaign staff. Travel arrangements were handled by a ten-person White House staff. Under a policy approved by the Federal Election Commission, Mr. Ford's campaign staff merely calculated the number of persons traveling with the president's entourage for political purposes on each trip and then repaid the government for their pro rata share. Mr. Ford was doing nothing different, of course, from what other incumbent presidents have always done, but Mr. Reagan and his aides complained loudly about the special advantage that President Ford took of his office.

Still another tremendous advantage of an incumbent president in a nominating or general election campaign is the huge amount of "free" help he can command every day of the week from his 500-person White House staff and government agencies. The incumbent president has at his fingertips a team of experts to advise him on every conceivable issue and problem—the Office of Management and Budget, the Council on Economic Advisers, the National Security Council, the secretary of state, the top brass of the military services and the intelligence community. Against these odds a challenger from within the president's own party normally needs the courage of a biblical David to take on a White House incumbent.

Legal ceilings on campaign fund raising and spending indirectly aid an incumbent president. Challengers must start early if they are to overcome the advantages a sitting president usually enjoys. The challenger must recruit a full-time staff, including campaign accountants, and much sooner than was the case before the 1974 Federal Election Campaign Act was passed. With the $1,000 limitation on individual contributions, it is no longer possible for a challenger to count on a few "fat cat" contributions for six-figure donations to launch a presidential drive. Instead, the challenger's fund raisers must develop long lists of potential contributors and contact them personally or via direct mail, a prodigious task. All the while, the incumbent president can detail some of his White House staff to set up fund-raising machinery and then turn over the money-raising assignment to an independent reelection committee to avoid open charges of using government employees for partisan purposes. Presidents Eisenhower, Johnson and Nixon all utilized the special perquisites of incumbency to build up their pre-convention campaign war chests well ahead of their potential intraparty challengers.

At the time the federal matching subsidy law was passed in 1974, it was freely predicted that the power of the incumbent would be diminished by passage of the new law. Some political observers felt that the matching dollars provided by Uncle Sam would, among other things, encourage more presidential aspirants from the in-party to challenge the incumbent. It is probably too early to pass judgment on this point because the only in-party challenger to jump into the ring in 1976, Ronald Reagan, would have had wide access to funds whether or not the federal subsidy law had been in effect. But the fact remains that the financial obstacles facing an in-party challenger are indeed formidable.

Pressured by the new campaign finance laws to start early, challengers also become fair game for sniping by the president's surrogates, for instance, the vice president, cabinet members, or leading senators, on major issues of the day. Generally, the president holds the trump cards on foreign policy by virtue of his private conversations with prime ministers and foreign secretaries and complete access to all State Department cable traffic. On the domestic front a president can rely on proposed legislation for tax cuts, reports on the latest employment figures and other economic data to make upbeat announcements to the American people during the nominating race. Whenever the president feels that his renomination drive may need an assist, he can call a press conference to discuss the latest foreign policy initiatives or a new environmental policy or to announce the veto of a high-cost spending bill passed by Congress. More often than not, the three television networks will preempt their regular programming to carry the president's news conference "live" as a public service. Also, the president can take time out from his regular campaigning to perform various "nonpolitical" duties—dedicate a new dam, tour an aircraft carrier, or deliver a special commencement address. Meanwhile, the presidential challenger and his campaign staff are forced to manufacture media events to attract the network cameras. Small wonder that most potential challengers think twice before trying to unseat an incumbent.

No challenger can match the excitement and the emotional lift that a presidential motorcade campaign visit has on local crowds. Washington reporter Jules Witcover has described one brief episode in the continuous uphill battle for voter support and media coverage that challenger Ronald Reagan had to wage against incumbent President Gerald Ford in the 1976 Florida primary:

What Ford was showing the Florida voters that day, in addition to his own fortitude, was the presidency itself—the impressive *Air Force One,* the big cars, and phalanxes of Secret Service agents, the stream of press buses and scurrying White House staff aides. Reagan, for all his movie-star celebrity, could not match the extravaganza of an American President in transit.[6]

Of all the advantages an incumbent president enjoys on the campaign trail, perhaps the greatest is the ability to capture the national media's attention and completely overshadow the opposition. Reagan, as indicated above, encountered this political fact of life repeatedly in the New Hampshire and Florida primaries. In Florida, for example, Reagan flew into the state on the heels of his narrow defeat in New Hampshire, hoping to regain the initiative from President Ford. The former California governor launched a new broadside on Ford's foreign policy in Tampa, only to discover that it coincided with President Ford's motorcade rallies on Florida's east coast. National media coverage of the Ford visit pushed the Reagan campaign story off the evening televised newscasts, and state newspapers relegated Reagan's kick-off speech to the inside pages.

During the campaign the powerful advantages of presidential incumbency are not limited to the trappings of office and virtually cost-free campaign staffing. The president can always resort to time-honored patronage favors—a judgeship for a woman in Florida, a sub-cabinet position for a man in New Hampshire.

Unlike a challenger, the president also can make numerous concrete promises on the campaign trail that generate heavy media coverage and eventually translate into more votes. During the 1976 primary campaign President Ford, for example, proved to be one of the champion promisers of recent political history. While touring Florida, Mr. Ford promised various windfalls to his local audiences: a Veterans Administration hospital for St. Petersburg, an interstate highway for Fort Myers, a contract for a large Florida aerospace plant and rapid transit assistance for Miami. The president's ability to pledge immediate federal action sets him apart from challengers who can only criticize and propose. Whether offering small favors or federal bonanzas, the president's promises of special projects in the primary states give him an important political and psychological advantage over his adversaries. During the 1976 primaries Ronald Reagan complained frequently about President Ford's extravagant campaign promises. Barnstorming through western North Carolina, Mr. Reagan returned to the subject again and again. "If he comes here with the same bag of goodies to hand out that he's been giving away elsewhere, the Californian said at one stop, the band won't know whether to play 'Hail to the Chief' or 'Santa Claus is Coming to Town.'"[7]

In some instances, the president also can play upon local sympathies by promising to block federal action that is locally unpopular—no dam on the New River in North Carolina, no shutdown of the Portsmouth (N.H.) Navy Yard, and so forth.

Equally important, an incumbent president generally benefits from the traditional reluctance of party members to turn out a sitting president. To cast an incumbent out of office in favor of an intraparty challenger is viewed by most party regulars as an admission of failure—failure to pick a well-qualified candidate four years earlier. While the position of incumbent president is far less secure now than before the Vietnam War era, majorities in both parties are still reluctant to ditch a one-term incumbent president. This traditional attitude, of course, did not save President Lyndon Johnson during the early weeks of his 1968 drive for renomination; he apparently decided against seeking reelection rather than face impending defeats in Wisconsin and other primary states. But the support-the-President syndrome helped President Ford weather the Ronald Reagan challenge in 1976. Political insiders in both parties are in virtually unanimous agreement that the advantages of incumbency spelled the difference between victory and defeat for President Ford in his cliffhanger triumph over challenger Reagan at the 1976 Republican National Convention. Columnist David Broder has summed up the realities of incumbency this way: "An incumbent president, no matter how much his leadership is suspect, operates with more political resources than any other player in the presidential election game."[8]

Incumbent President's Options before
Passage of Twenty-Second Amendment

Before the adoption of the Twenty-Second Amendment, an incumbent second-term president could maintain his freedom of action and, if he wished, undermine the operation of the presidential primary system by refusing to announce his intentions or by using stand-in favorite-son candidates in the presidential primaries to scare off potential contenders. Several incumbent presidents have had one or more reasons for not revealing their decision—a secret desire to be renominated, determination to dictate a successor or a wish to maintain control of the party.

Despite the tradition of the two-term limitation first established by President Washington, several twentieth-century incumbents never wrote off entirely the possibility of seeking another four years in the White House before passage of the Twenty-Second Amendment. There was frequently a marked reluctance to turn over the reins of leadership. The president sometimes felt that potential successors didn't measure up to the job of president, but he did not want to appear to be actively seeking another term. Consequently, he sometimes played a guessing game with the public and the press or remained silent and impassive to keep potential contenders within his party from becoming active candidates. But what if a retiring president, prior to the passage of the Twenty-Second Amendment, objected vehemently to the candidacy of a leading unannounced contender from his own party? Could the incumbent president block this man's nomination? Or could the candidate actively opposed by the president take his case directly to the people in the primaries? Because it was customary in the past for presidential aspirants from the in-party to maintain discreet silence until the president made a pronouncement about his own future plans, incumbent presidents on several occasions tried, sometimes successfully, sometimes not, to maintain control over the nominating process throughout the pre-convention period.

President Woodrow Wilson in 1920 unsuccessfully attempted to keep the door open for his own renomination for a third term, even though party leaders had already concluded that the state of his health after his stroke would not permit a third try. Wilson's manipulations fooled none of the big state party leaders who proceeded to select their own candidate—Governor James M. Cox of Ohio.[9]

President Calvin Coolidge's experience with the succession problem in 1928 is another interesting chapter. The retiring president, who was serving out his first full term of office following President Harding's death in 1923, expressed no public preference about his successor in the pre-convention period. William Allen White, Coolidge's biographer, tells us that "Silent Cal" did nothing to insure the nomination for his popular secretary of commerce Herbert Hoover. Although Coolidge at no time tipped his hand, the impression of several of his close associates was that he was hoping for a convention deadlock, out of which would come his own renomination.[10] In the spring of 1928, one Coolidge partisan, New York's Republican national committeeman, Charles D. Hilles, tried to prevent pre-convention endorsements in order to open the way for a "draft-Coolidge" movement, but he received no affirmative nod from the White House. Possibly President Coolidge felt that no further action had to be taken at the time, for as late as the middle of April there was still a marked feeling in some quarters that Coolidge could have the nomination if he gave the slightest hint that he would serve again, if drafted.[11] In the meantime, however, Hoover's political stock continued to rise as delegates from primary and convention states alike fell in line for him. By national convention time, Hoover was able to steamroller all opposition, including the remnants of the "draft Coolidge" movement.

Clearly, Hoover had used his performance in the primaries successfully to help capture the nomination without an endorsement from the White House.

President Franklin D. Roosevelt, anxious to preserve his maneuverability toward a possible third-term nomination in 1940, did nothing to discourage his would-be successors from entering the race and then left the Democratic hopefuls—Postmaster General James A. Farley, Secretary of State Cordell Hull, Montana Senator Burton K. Wheeler and Federal Security Administrator Paul V. McNutt—all dangling. By staying out of the primaries, yet working through pro-administration forces in the various primary states, Roosevelt kept all rival contenders off balance. Farley, for example, was put in the awkward position in the Massachusetts primary of having a slate of delegates pledged to him—but with the definite understanding that only if President Roosevelt didn't run for a third term would they support him.[12]

Pro-third term or uninstructed states favorable to the president were entered in almost all of the primary states. Roosevelt's use of the uninstructed delegations in 1940 was in marked contrast to 1932, when Roosevelt's managers were seeking free and open primaries against the "stop Roosevelt" forces, spearheaded by Jouett Shouse, the pro-Smith Democratic national chairman. A close friend of Alfred E. Smith, Shouse had attempted to subvert the presidential primary system by urging the selection of "uninstructed" delegations. In 1940, however, the leaders of the "draft Roosevelt" movement, according to one reporter, were "doing everything possible although wholly in absence of any definite word as to the President's own purposes to prevent the full operation even of such a primary system as the country has."[13] Roosevelt's strategy was effective, particularly in Ohio where one prospective contender, Senator Burton K. Wheeler (D, Mont.), backed away from a primary fight with a stand-in favorite son for fear, as he put it, that his entrance might be construed as opposing Roosevelt.[14] Only Vice President John N. Garner refused to fall into line. For his temerity, Garner was soundly trounced by the Roosevelt partisans in the California, Illinois, Oregon and Wisconsin primaries.

President Roosevelt continued to play political possum until the middle of the Democratic convention. When he was asked by a visitor in March 1940 whether he intended to be a candidate, he reportedly answered, "Keep the delegates in the bag. It is a long time until July 15 [the convention date], and no one can tell what will happen."[15] Thus, throughout the 1940 pre-convention period, Democratic contenders could not openly, or did not dare, use the primaries to build up their own candidacies unless they were prepared to break with the administration entirely—and none of them were, except Garner. As one news magazine phrased it, "while the anti-third-term Democrats fumed futilely, the name of Roosevelt dominated party ballots in eleven states."[16]

Twelve years later, President Truman, who was excluded from the two-term limitation of the Twenty-Second Amendment, tried to neutralize the influence of the presidential primary system in 1952—he called primaries just so much "eyewash"—by keeping his own candidacy intentions a secret until after the first two presidential primaries (New Hampshire and Minnesota) had been held and filing dates in several others had expired. President Truman's strategy, however, backfired in New Hampshire, where he was unexpectedly defeated by Senator Estes Kefauver. In the Minnesota primary, on the other hand, the president used Senator Hubert H. Humphrey to organize a pro-administration stand-in slate. Truman's Minnesota victory helped him keep his opponents in the dark a little longer.

President Truman also briefly lined up another stand-in candidate, Senator Brien McMahon of Connecticut. Entered in the Illinois primary at the eleventh hour, when it appeared that Kefauver would win by default, McMahon was reportedly a "stalking horse" for the Truman forces, anxious to hand Kefauver a stinging defeat and thus end once and for all his chances for the presidential or vice presidential nomination. The Connecticut senator was said to have been assured support by former Illinois Democratic Senator Scott Lucas, who blamed his defeat for reelection in 1950 on Senator Kefauver's timing of his Senate crime investigating committee hearing in Chicago. McMahon was also promised support by an influential segment of the state Democratic leadership. Less than a week later, however, McMahon suddenly withdrew from the Illinois race, too late for the administration forces to enter another candidate. McMahon's explanation was that he could not in good conscience campaign for himself, "when in my own mind I prefer someone else—Harry S. Truman."[17] There was considerable speculation that Senator McMahon may have inquired further and discovered that the support on which he based his entry in the Illinois primary would not be forthcoming without a hard fight. More likely, his withdrawal was for unrevealed reasons of health. He died of cancer on July 28, 1952, shortly after the Democratic National Convention. In any event, Kefauver's managers were relieved that they would not have a primary fight, because they had serious doubts about their candidate's ability to overcome the Illinois Democratic state organization. Actually, the Kefauverites should have welcomed the primary fight, for this was the only way that Kefauver could have won the nomination—by opposing a state organization-backed candidate and by demonstrating his wide popularity with the voters.

President Truman confounded all of his critics and supporters by withdrawing from the presidential race in late March 1952. But he had thoroughly upset the presidential primary machinery in several states by using stand-in slates. Yet, President Truman's hasty withdrawal from the nominating race after the New Hampshire primary was a left-handed acknowledgment of the growing influence of the primary system and portended future changes in the nominating process. Senator Kefauver had demonstrated that a two-term incumbent president alone could no longer dictate the choice of a successor without a serious challenge from within his party.

New Year's Day 1956 saw President Dwight D. Eisenhower still undecided on whether to seek a second term, following his heart attack in the fall of 1955. His not-always-loyal GOP Senate majority leader, William F. Knowland of California, who had presidential ambitions himself, announced that he could not wait beyond February 15 for President Eisenhower to make up his mind.[18] But February 15 passed without any statement from the president. Taking no chances on missing filing deadlines and thus being excluded from several important presidential primaries, Knowland had his name filed in four states—and also in the Territory of Alaska. In his home state of California, a stand-in slate was prepared. But on February 29, 1956, President Eisenhower announced that he considered himself physically fit and would seek reelection. In one blow this presidential announcement knocked Senator Knowland out of serious presidential contention. Several of the Knowland-pledged delegates remained listed on the ballot in a few states, but all were overwhelmed by President Eisenhower's supporters.

In the months following the tragic assassination of President John F. Kennedy in November 1963, the new chief executive, Lyndon B. Johnson, maintained a discreet silence on his political intentions for 1964. All press conference questions relating to his plans were parried or pushed aside, much as President Coolidge had done in the early months after President Harding's death. But there did not seem to be the slightest doubt in the minds of any national or state Democratic leaders, or the Washington press corps, that Mr. Johnson would seek a full term in the White House.

As the 1964 primary season approached, President Johnson's trusted associates in a number of presidential primary states quietly began lining up favorite son "stand-in" candidates and delegations. In Indiana, for example, Democratic Governor Matthew E. Welsh announced on March 20 his "favorite son" candidacy to make sure that Indiana's fifty-one votes at the national convention would go to President Johnson. Governor Welsh's move was also prompted by the expected candidacy of the arch-segregationist governor of Alabama, George C. Wallace, who otherwise might have run unopposed in Indiana. Members of the Indiana congressional delegation, who were all present for Governor Welsh's announcement, said that he had the consent of the White House.[19] Other stand-in favorite-son candidacies soon followed—Governor John Reynolds of Wisconsin, Senator Daniel B. Brewster of Maryland and Governor Edmund G. "Pat" Brown of California. To assure full control of the New Hampshire Democratic primary, President Johnson's friends in the Granite State filed a full slate of delegates "favorable" to his nomination, since as late as the end of February the President said he still had not decided about running.[20] (In New Hampshire, the consent of the candidate is not required for delegates to run as favorable to him. President Johnson's name did not appear on the presidential preference ballot because this would have required his consent.)

In Oregon's all-candidate primary, where the Oregon secretary of the state is authorized by law to list all candidates who are "generally advocated," supporters of President Johnson put his name on the ballot by petition moments before Oregon Secretary of State Howell Appling, Jr. held a press conference to announce the names of all candidates who would appear on the Democratic and GOP ballots.[21]

While national attention was focused on the California GOP presidential primary, Democratic Governor Edmund G. "Pat" Brown organized an "uninstructed" delegation but one that was known to favor President Johnson. To make certain no disloyal delegates might be chosen, Brown announced that he would serve as "chairman of the organizing committee."[22] This move, however, did not discourage Democratic Mayor of Los Angeles Samuel Yorty, a party maverick who had supported Nixon for president in 1960 against Kennedy, from forming a rival pro-Johnson delegation. Yorty's efforts to undercut Governor Brown failed, however, as the Brown slate carried the state by a two-to-one margin.

To prevent the Republicans from monopolizing the mass media during the presidential primary season, President Johnson played a cat-and-mouse game with the press over his own political intentions until late June. Then, with his own plans made known, he succeeded in making the prospective choice of his vice-presidential running mate the favorite topic of speculation at his press conferences. He kept the press and the aspiring hopefuls—Senator Hubert H. Humphrey, Attorney General Robert F. Kennedy, Secretary of Defense Robert McNamara, Senator Eugene McCarthy and Peace Corps Director R. Sargent Shriver—in suspense throughout July. The first indication as to who might be his choice as running mate was done in reverse fashion by the process of elimination. In mid-August President Johnson told a press conference that cabinet officials and other high officers in the administration should not be considered. This announcement nipped the Bobby Kennedy boomlet and seemed to open the door for Humphrey's vice-presidential nomination. But the president, wringing out every last ounce of publicity value regarding his preferred choice, refused to tip his hand until he appeared personally at the Democratic National Convention in Atlantic City, New Jersey, and told a packed Convention Hall that Senator Humphrey was the man he wanted as his running mate. In the case of Johnson, like Theodore Roosevelt's ascension to the presidency after McKinley's assassination, the vice-presidential takeover on the subsequent presidential nomination within the "in-party" differed little from that of an incumbent president seeking a second term.[23]

Effect of the Twenty-Second Amendment

Since only two presidents, Eisenhower and Nixon, have come under the two-term limitation of the Twenty-Second Amendment and because President Nixon was forced out of office midway in his second term, it may be premature to assess the effect of the two-term constitutional limitation on the nominating process because we don't have enough case studies. But we can speculate how a lame duck president will affect the operation of the presidential primary system.

President Eisenhower, after months of hesitation and qualified support, gave his full blessing to Vice President Richard M. Nixon in March 1960, shortly after the New Hampshire primary. One news columnist, however, considered Eisenhower's endorsement too late to affect decisively the nomination of Nixon, since the real struggle for the nomination had already been settled in favor of Nixon in December 1959.[24] At that time, New York Governor Nelson Rockefeller decided to withdraw from presidential contention after an unfruitful, nationwide scouting expedition to assess his prospects for winning the nomination. The almost unbroken series of cool receptions from Republican state party leaders, predominantly loyal to Nixon, convinced Rockefeller during his tour that his chances for the 1960 GOP nomination were bleak.[25]

What would be the effect of the Twenty-Second Amendment on White House aspirants if the incumbent president indicated no preference regarding his successor? At the minimum, of course, would be the general recognition that the second-term president is not running and that the presidential primaries are therefore open to potential successors. The incumbent might want to pick his successor, but the amendment makes it more difficult for him to do so. To control the succession, an incumbent president would probably have to find a successor who is able and willing to take on all challengers in the primaries, as Nixon was in 1960. This is probably one reason why President Eisenhower had to support him. Yet it is conceivable that the Twenty-Second Amendment, by making it clear that the incumbent is completely out of the running, might enable him to exert more influence on the choice of his successor plans.

But we can rely only the Eisenhower case since President Truman's incumbency in 1952 must be viewed in a different context.

President Truman was specifically exempted from coverage of the Twenty-Second Amendment, passed during his second administration. Thus, Truman could have sought another full term even though he had served seven and three-quarters years. But Senator Estes Kefauver, the crusading chairman of the Senate Committee to Investigate Organized Crime in Interstate Commerce, announced his entrance in the presidential race in January 1952, two months before Truman announced his retirement. Kefauver and his advisors had concluded earlier that Truman would not run again in 1952, and to get a flying start on other contenders Kefauver skipped the customary observance of waiting until the president spelled out his own future intentions.

From the time of Kefauver's crime investigation hearings in 1950, the Tennessee senator had not been a Truman favorite. The televised committee hearings had embarrassed Democratic party leaders in several Eastern states. Truman's displeasure with Kefauver was heightened by Kefauver's assertion in his candidacy announcement that the Truman administration was not doing enough to stamp out corruption in the country.[26] When Kefauver had the audacity to challenge—and then defeat—President Truman in the New Hampshire primary, the Tennessee senator became a prime target for Truman's wrath. Even before President Truman's formal announcement of his retirement, he and his lieutenants were working behind the scenes to snuff out Kefauver's drive for the nomination. Within a few days after Truman's retirement statement, a full slate of favorite-son candidates was in the field to help block Kefauver's path—Governor G. Mennen Williams of Michigan, Governor Paul Dever of Massachusetts, W. Averell Harriman of New York, and Senator Hubert H. Humphrey of Minnesota. At Truman's request, Senator Robert Kerr of Oklahoma had entered the Nebraska presidential primary earlier as a stand-in candidate for the president; also, Vice President Alben Barkley needed little urging from Truman to toss his hat into the ring, even though he was seventy-four years old at the time. The purpose of Truman's strategy, of course, was to tie up enough votes so that neither Kefauver nor anyone else could win the nomination on the first ballot. The big city Democratic leaders, working to preserve their bargaining power, were only too anxious to cooperate in this plan. Truman's kingmaker role was enhanced by the fact that among the plethora of candidates there was not one who could be called outstanding in terms of political "availability."

Undeterred, Kefauver won twelve primaries (mostly uncontested), losing only in Florida and the District of Columbia. Yet, Kefauver failed to win the nomination. His defeat was attributed in some quarters not so much to President Truman's opposition as to his own failings as a candidate: his habit of antagonizing middle-of-the-road delegations by charges of anti-Kefauver "plots" among the "big city bosses"; his anti-organizational tactics in a number of states; and his failure to win the endorsement of the Southern bloc with its 340 convention votes.[27] President Truman's hostility toward Kefauver and the president's support of Illinois Governor Adlai E. Stevenson for the nomination in 1952 was nevertheless a potent influence. News columnists Joseph and Stewart Alsop claimed that "an authoritative estimate" showed that President Truman could swing 400 Democratic delegates to any candidate the convention liked (615.5 votes were necessary to nominate) and give at least 200 votes to a candidate the convention did not like.[28]

President Lyndon B. Johnson indirectly helped Vice President Humphrey capture the in-party Democratic nomination in 1968 by his late withdrawal from contention (on March 31, 1968), which came after nearly all of the primary filing deadlines had passed. By delaying his candidacy announcement for another two weeks, Humphrey avoided having to take on his leading challengers, Senators Eugene McCarthy and Bobby Kennedy, in any of the remaining primaries. Several other factors also helped Humphrey. First, before passage of the McGovern-Fraser Commission party reform guidelines in 1972, the delegate-selection process in more than a dozen states favored the president's "crown prince" successor. Delegations in four states, for example, were handpicked by the state executive committee—and by the governor personally in two states. In another half dozen states the delegate selection process had commenced before the beginning of the presidential election year; all 110 national committee members from the fifty states—mostly pro-Humphrey—had been elected four years earlier.[29] Second, Senator Bobby Kennedy's assassination on the night of his big California presidential primary victory removed Humphrey's most serious competitor. Third, big-time labor and the Democratic big city party leaders and their delegates favored Humphrey, who had campaigned for almost two decades in their areas, helping Democratic congressmen and other prospective officeholders. But the 1968 experience involving a retiring president is inconclusive because Humphrey's leading challenger, Senator Bobby Kennedy, was gunned down by an assassin just as his drive for the presidency was gaining full momentum. It will, of course, never be known whether Kennedy could have overtaken Humphrey in a down-to-the-wire finish. During his whirlwind eighty-five-day campaign he had rolled up five victories in six primary contests, and the magic of the Kennedy name might well have carried him to the Democratic nomination. In any case, President Johnson's eroded influence within the Democratic party and his preoccupation with the Vietnam War probably could not have tipped the nomination away from a well-coordinated Kennedy pre-convention bandwagon push. In 1968 the decision of the anti-war activists to use the presidential primaries as a major instrument in the "dump Johnson" movement reinforces the belief that sitting presidents, mired down with an unpopular war or, hypothetically speaking, a severe economic recession at home are not immune from in-party presidential challengers. In the single historical case of an appointed president seeking a full-term nomination, President Ford in 1976, the record shows that an unelected president is even less immune to in-party rivals wishing to displace him.

The unusual set of circumstances surrounding the 1976 Republican nominating race deserves special mention.

An Unelected Chief Executive Faces In-Party Challenge

In 1976 President Ford, an unelected chief executive, faced the stiffest challenge to an incumbent since President William Howard Taft's bitter renomination battle against former President Theodore Roosevelt in 1912. Indeed, not since Herbert Hoover in 1932 had an actively campaigning incumbent president lost more than a single state primary. Ronald Reagan, former governor of California and chief spokesman for the Republican right wing, topped President Ford in ten out of twenty-six primaries but lost to Mr. Ford by approximately 800,000 popular votes nationwide. The former Hollywood star did not hoist the white flag until he lost the first ballot nomination to Ford 1,187 votes to 1,070 at the bruising GOP convention in Kansas City. While former President Theodore Roosevelt won a higher percentage of primaries (9 out of 10) against President Taft in 1912, no primary challenge to a sitting president has ever produced more victories than Reagan's performance in 1976.

In normal times an insurgent's challenge to his party's incumbent president has generally been regarded as politically suicidal or at best quixotic. Since the first season of state primaries in 1912, nominations within the party holding the White House have routinely gone to sitting presidents, even relatively unsuccessful ones. Reagan's strategists believed, however, that the unusual circumstances of Mr. Ford's elevation to the presidency would diminish the usual problems of opposing an incumbent. Reagan justified his bold challenge on the basis that Ford occupied the White House not by virtue of a popular mandate but as a result of President Nixon's forced resignation in face of impeachment charges growing out of the Watergate scandals.

Because the American voters had never passed judgment on Ford, Reagan made the case that the Republican nomination should be taken directly to the people. Reagan's handlers never passed up an opportunity to remind fellow Republicans that President Ford had never run for public office outside his old Grand Rapids, Michigan, congressional district; but for the unusual set of circumstances that lifted him into the presidency, he would have never been considered a serious candidate for the highest office in the land. Mr. Reagan, having twice been elected governor of the most populous state, could also make a reasonable claim to having won more popular support at the polls than Mr. Ford. An appointed president, Mr. Ford had neither the loyalties, party organization, nor personal prestige that normally accrue to an incumbent. Moreover, there were fewer who had a vested interest in keeping him in office than is usually the case with an incumbent. Despite potential charges of being a party wrecker, Reagan was in a position to avoid part of the normal incumbent party embarrassment in turning their own man out of office because Mr. Ford had never been the party's choice, or the country's, in an earlier election. In Ford's case, to repudiate him was one way to repudiate Richard Nixon all over again. Originally, the carefully conceived strategy of the Reagan camp was to portray President Ford as a pleasant fellow who lacked leadership ability and an officeholder trapped by the mind set of a quarter century on Capitol Hill. Later on in the campaign, President Ford's foreign policy detente with the Soviet Union and control of the Panama Canal became focal points of Reagan's attack.

Without a presidential primary system encompassing twenty-nine states, however, Reagan's candidacy might not have gotten off the ground because President Ford's supporters controlled the regular GOP organization in most states, especially those in the big-delegate Eastern states. The primary route, however, provides the opportunity for an incumbent challenger to appeal over the heads of party leaders directly to the voters. If the challenger unseats the incumbent, it will have been done fair and square. If he loses, he can partially defend his action of taking his case to the American people by pointing out that his primary challenge provided a good "tune-up" for the incumbent's general election campaign and prevented the out-of-power party from monopolizing the national media throughout the four-month nominating campaign.

Underlying changes in American politics appear to be reducing the renominating capacity of incumbent presidents. The Ronald Reagan challenge to President Ford within the Republican party in 1976 was not an aberration. In both 1968 and 1972, incumbent presidents faced challengers with varying strength. The Eugene McCarthy and Bobby Kennedy insurgencies in 1968 persuaded President Johnson to step down after the first-round New Hampshire primary. Four years later, on the other hand, the primary challenges of Representatives Paul N. "Pete" McCloskey and John Ashbrook against President Nixon constituted nothing more than a minor league exhibition game against the White House incumbent. Nevertheless, the challenges were made despite the hopelessness of the odds. With an expanded number of presidential primaries and the switch from closed to open caucuses in a number of states, along with the volatile impact of network television on insurgent candidacies, the prospect of more in-party challenges to sitting presidents seems likely in the years ahead. As British political scientist Anthony King has observed, "The proliferation of primaries also means that since incumbent Presidents can no longer control their party (there being hardly any party for them to control), they can no longer count on renomination."[30]

As the 1980 presidential primary season rapidly approached, the political grapevine in the nation's capital was full of rumors that first-term President Jimmy Carter would face a strong in-party challenge to his renomination from Senator Edward Kennedy or California Governor Edmund G. "Jerry" Brown (or both). As the weeks ticked by, both Kennedy and Brown sounded very much like presidential candidates, though neither potential challenger was prepared to tip his hand. Recent opinion polls offered little comfort to President Carter. The latest Gallup poll (June 1979) showed Senator Kennedy, who had previously turned down his supporters' requests to run in 1972 and 1976, leading Carter 52 percent to 17 percent, with Brown at 8 percent and others (which included Vice President Walter F. Mondale and Senator Henry M. Jackson of Washington), plus the undecideds and no preference, 23 percent.[31] In December 1978, the highly respected California poll, conducted by the Mervin D. Field organization, showed the largest state's voters favoring Kennedy 44 percent to Carter's 22 percent, with Governor Brown at 21 percent, and undecideds at 13 percent.[32] Subsequently, Senator Kennedy formally entered the 1980 Democratic presidential sweepstakes on November 7, 1979; Governor Brown officially tossed his hat in the ring one day later.

Clearly, presidential primaries are tailor-made for all kinds of grievance expressions against incumbent presidents. Faced with public clamor over long-term gasoline shortages, skyrocketing fuel oil heating costs, double-digit inflation, and frequent rising unemployment, every president from now on can anticipate being held personally accountable by the public for almost every national ill, except possibly the Caribbean-spawned hurricanes. This tension-charged atmosphere, which makes the president a prime target for his endless critics, provides of course a field day for ambitious in-party challengers. No wonder it is becoming increasingly apparent to party watchers that, with more than thirty states now holding primaries, incumbent presidents can expect as a matter of course an in-party popular referendum on their performance and record of their first term in office.

Notes

1. F. Christopher Atherton, "Campaign Organizations Confront the Media Environment," in *Race for the Nomination,* ed. James David Barber (Englewood Cliffs, N.J.: Prentice-Hall, 1978), p. 18.

2. Herbert E. Alexander, *Financing the 1972 Election* (Lexington, Mass.: D. C. Heath, 1976), p. 221.

3. After the revised campaign reform bill was passed on May 4, Mr. Ford took another week to decide whether to sign it, although he had known the exact provisions of the bill for a week, and then nearly another week to nominate the commissioners. Several more days elapsed before their final confirmation. Washington *Post,* May 22, 1977.

4. New York *Times,* April 13, 1976.

5. Washington *Post,* May 23, 1976.

6. Jules Witcover, *Marathon: The Pursuit of the Presidency, 1972-1976* (New York: Viking Press, 1977), p. 400.

7. New York *Times,* March 22, 1976.

8. Washington *Post,* July 4, 1979.

9. Wesley M. Bagby, *The Road to Normalcy: The Presidential Campaign and Election of 1920* (Baltimore: The Johns Hopkins University Press, 1962), pp. 55-66.

10. William Allen White's account is based on conversations with William Butler, Republican national chairman (1924-28), who had been selected for this job by Coolidge; Irwin H. Hoover, head usher of the White House during Coolidge's administration; and White's correspondence with William Jardine, secretary of agriculture under Coolidge. See, *A Puritan in Babylon* (New York: Macmillan, 1938), pp. 400-02.

11. Boston *Evening Transcript,* April 21, 1928.

12. New York *Times,* February 13, 1940.

13. Ibid., February 18, 1940.

14. Ibid., February 13, 1940.

15. Ibid., March 12, 1940.

16. "Primary Texts" *Newsweek* 15 (March 4, 1940): 14.

17. New York *Times,* January 26, 1952.

18. Ibid., February 11, 1956.

19. Ibid., March 21, 1964.

20. Ibid., March 2, 1964.

21. Ibid., February 29, 1964.

22. Ibid., February 13, 1964.

23. This assessment and upgrading of an elevated vice president's ability to control the next nomination on his own since Teddy Roosevelt's time agrees generally with the analysis made by Paul T. David, Ralph M. Goldman, and Richard C. Bain in *The Politics of National Party Conventions* (Washington, D. C.: Brookings Institution, 1960), pp. 111-13, 125-26. By contrast, the four nineteenth-century vice presidents elevated to the presidency— Tyler, Fillmore, Andrew Johnson and Arthur—were systematically dumped in favor of a new candidate. Ibid.

24. William S. White, Minneapolis *Morning Tribune*, March 21, 1960.

25. Theodore H. White, *The Making of the President, 1960* (New York: Atheneum, 1961), pp. 72-77.

26. Paul T. David, Malcolm Moos, and Ralph M. Goldman, eds., *Presidential Nominating Politics in 1952,* 5 vols. (Baltimore: The John Hopkins University Press, 1954), 1: 36.

27. Ibid., pp. 108-09.

28. Ibid., pp. 107-08.

29. *Mandate for Reform: Report of the Commission on Party Structure and Delegate Selection to the Democratic National Committee,* Senator George S. McGovern, Commission Chairman (Washington, D. C.: Democratic National Committee, 1970), p. 19.

30. Anthony King, "The American Polity in the Late 1970's: Building Coalitions in the Sand," *The New American Political System*, ed. Anthony King (Washington, D. C., American Enterprise Institute, 1978), p. 375.

31. For an incumbent president eligible for reelection to trail a potential rival is not unheard of, but it is unusual. In late March-early April 1952, using a list of candidates rather than one-on-one, the Gallup poll showed that 33 percent of Democrats chose Senator Estes Kefauver of Tennessee and 32 percent preferred President Harry Truman; others and undecided totaled 35 percent. In looking toward the 1968 Democratic nomination the Gallup organization sample in January 1968, using a list of candidates, showed Senator Bobby Kennedy ahead of President Lyndon Johnson 43 percent to 34 percent, with others and undecided at 23 percent. While two episodes do not forecast a trend, it is noteworthy that both times the incumbent president ran behind a party rival in the Gallup poll, the incumbent party lost the White House in the next presidential election. *Gallup Opinion Index,* no. 158 (September 1978): 6-7. The latest Gallup poll (December 9, 1979) on announced Democratic candidates showed Senator Kennedy ahead of President Carter 51 percent to 34 percent, with Governor Brown at 9 percent, and undecided/no opinion at 6 percent. The number of Democratic respondents in the poll was 728. Source: American Institute of Public Opinion, Princeton, N.J.

32. New York *Times,* January 11, 1979.

Outmoded and Long-Shot _____8
Presidential Candidacies

The presidential nominating field usually includes a wide variety of candidates who no longer figure prominently in the nomination: unannounced candidates, late blooming candidates, favorite sons, dark horses and draft candidates. For more than a century these candidates have enlivened presidential nominating races; but with the powerful interaction of presidential primaries, the national media and the opinion polls in recent years, the winner of the presidential primaries has overshadowed all these candidates and preempted the nomination, usually on the first ballot. Especially the efficient winnowing-out process of the presidential primaries has relegated all of these candidates to an "also ran" status. Nonetheless, because all of these types of presidential candidates are as much a part of American political folklore as campaign rallies and political platforms, each will be described and analyzed briefly.

The Unannounced Candidate

In U.S. politics, when a presidential aspirant announces his candidacy, he becomes a conspicuous target for all of his opponents. If he participates in the presidential primaries, he runs the risk of being knocked out of the race or being badly mauled. Meanwhile, the unannounced or shadow candidate can sit on the sidelines, avoid the bruising primary races, and hope that the front-runners become deadlocked or falter. In such an event, the unannounced candidate stands available to the national convention as a compromise nominee. But in playing the waiting game he may discover after the opening primaries that one of the front-running candidates is pulling so far ahead of the field that, unless the unannounced candidate makes known his intentions quickly, the nominating race may be over before he gets away from the starting gate. The basic strategy of the unannounced candidate, however, is to avoid the primaries in the belief that the "risks of running and losing far outweigh the possible benefits of running and winning." But it will be one of the basic arguments of this chapter that, as a result of the expanded presidential primary system, the day of the unannounced candidate has passed. The public no longer views them as viable candidates, and therefore national convention delegates will not give them serious consideration.

The unannounced candidate should not be confused with a draft candidate. The unannounced candidate merely refuses to pronounce officially his candidacy while he and his managers seek to round up enough delegates to nail down the nomination. The draft candidate, on the other hand, has been described as follows: "A true candidate for the draft must be able to persuade his friends that he is not running for the presidential nomination, and that he will wait until, through no fault of his own, his party thrusts its standard into his hands and anoints him the Man of the Hour."[1] More will be said about the draft candidate below.

Time and again, unannounced candidates have failed to realize that there is simply no longer enough time to set up an effective nationwide organization, including top-notch fund-raisers, and line up top-flight campaign managers in key states, or sufficient time to cultivate rank-and-file prospective delegates once the presidential primary campaign gets under way. Generally, a well-known candidate with several presidential primary victories under his belt looks too much like a winner to be ignored. These emerging front-runners can exert heavy pressure on the uncommitted delegates, who fear that to delay any longer in committing themselves to a candidate may mean missing the winning nominee's boat entirely. All the while, the unannounced candidate must agonize over his fate—and pray for a convention deadlock.

Despite the growing importance of presidential primaries over the past three decades, a number of candidates have quietly sought to capture the nomination—and all have failed—by maintaining the posture of the unannounced candidate until it was too late. In the section that follows we will retrace briefly the frustrating experiences of several of these unsuccessful candidates.

Unlike Adlai E. Stevenson, the 1952 Democratic nominee, and Senator Estes Kefauver of Tennessee, who was making his second try for the presidency in 1956, Governor W. Averell Harriman of New York attempted to maintain the fiction throughout the 1956 presidential primary campaign that he was not an active candidate. On the surface, Harriman's holding pattern strategy of waiting for Senator Kefauver to knock Stevenson out of his front-running position in the primaries appeared to have merit. Harriman and his managers reasoned that, with Stevenson out of the way, Kefauver still could not win the nomination because he was opposed by the Southern bloc and the Northern big city leaders. Therefore, the convention would most likely turn to Harriman. The Harriman board of strategists felt also that it would not be prudent to get involved in primary contests against such well-known campaigners as Stevenson and Kefauver. By staying out of the primaries, Harriman would emerge unscathed, and with the support of the big New York delegation and considerable strength in several other states, plus second-choice votes, his chances for the nomination would be excellent.

During the opening stages of the primary race Harriman's tactics seemed to be paying off. Stevenson's unexpected defeat in the Minnesota primary, according to one reporter, "set Governor Harriman's 'inactive' candidacy . . . clicking like a geiger counter at a uranium stockpile."[2] Harriman's political tutors—former President Truman, former Secretary of State Dean Acheson, former Secretary of Agriculture Charles Brannan, former Democratic National Committee Chairman Frank Kinney and Samuel I. Rosenman, veteran advisor of Presidents Roosevelt and Truman—persuaded themselves that the waiting game strategy was reaping dividends. But Stevenson refused to be counted out. By administering a series of primary defeats to Kefauver, he regained his front-running position to the point that he was clearly regarded as the convention choice by the time the primary season closed. It was Stevenson's impressive California primary victory, the final contest of the primary season, that visibly upset Harriman's wait-and-see strategy. Within four days, the New York governor announced "this hat is in the ring." Almost immediately, a Harriman for President organization blossomed out and established a national headquarters in Chicago.[3] But Harriman had waited too long. His transparent argument that he was not an "active" candidate had not impressed the elected delegates or the American public. Still, Harriman's managers tried to line up support from Senator Kefauver and his pledged delegates. But Kefauver announced his withdrawal from the race two weeks before the convention and promised his support to Stevenson who, Kefauver said, had been willing to campaign and fight it out with him in the primaries. Harriman's experience with the "inactive" candidacy suggests that convention delegates and the public are no longer impressed with the flimsy argument that a candidate is "not a candidate," even though he is running and breathing hard for the presidency. With the vast coverage that the American press and broadcasting media give to the nominating campaigns, especially the presidential primaries, it is becoming increasingly difficult for a candidate to feign inactivity.

Four years later, though, two Democratic presidential candidates, Senators Stuart Symington of Missouri and Lyndon B. Johnson of Texas, still failed to profit from Harriman's painful lesson of the unannounced candidacy. Symington, an unannounced candidate, learned that a nominating campaign based on avoidance of the presidential primaries can be a shortcut to political oblivion.

Fashioning himself as a compromise candidate who would emerge from the deadlocked 1960 Democratic National Convention with the nomination, Symington based his pre-convention strategy on several plausible arguments: that Senators Kennedy and Humphrey would fight an inconclusive battle in the primaries; that Johnson would be unable to shake off the Southern label and would, therefore, be politically unacceptable to Northern labor leaders; and that favorite sons Governor Edmund G. "Pat" Brown of California and Governor Robert B. Meyner of New Jersey could be dismissed because Brown, like leading contender Kennedy, was a Roman Catholic, and Meyner's handicap of being a "fallen away Catholic" who had left the Church was so serious he could not be regarded as a prime contender. Therefore, if the deadlock developed, who would be a more acceptable nominee than Symington? And if one wished to be the compromise candidate who was acceptable to all the various minority elements of the Democratic party—labor unions, black voters, the South, and big city political leaders—why, Symington reasoned, create opponents by antagonizing them in the presidential primaries?[4] It was with these assumptions that Symington commenced his quest for the nomination in the fall of 1959.

By early March 1960, however, Symington began to feel the intense heat of presidential primary politics, as the battle swayed between the Kennedy and Humphrey forces in Wisconsin with a nationwide audience looking on. Senator Kennedy, the front-runner, was getting such a big lead that Symington sensed that unless he jumped into the race soon he might find the field closed to him. Consequently, on March 24, 1960, he announced his candidacy—reportedly two months earlier than he had originally planned.[5] He said, however, that he wouldn't enter any presidential primaries, since he regarded them as an inadequate gauge of delegate sentiment. Actually, Symington's compromise candidate strategy had frozen him into an inflexible position. By the time he announced his candidacy, it was too late to think of entering the primaries. His only hope at this late date was to pray for a convention deadlock, but none developed. Senator Kennedy's powerful primary campaign stampeded the convention delegates into nominating him on the first ballot. Except for his formal nomination, Symington was almost entirely forgotten by the convention delegates.

Senate Majority Leader Lyndon B. Johnson was able to avoid announcing his candidacy throughout the spring of 1960 because he had almost 400 Southern and Rocky Mountain delegates pledged to him. He also had the manufactured excuse that his congressional leadership duties did not allow him sufficient time to campaign actively for the nomination. It is noteworthy that Senator Kennedy, in issuing challenges to all candidates to contest the primaries with him, sometimes excluded Johnson—on the same grounds that his duties as Democratic majority leader did not allow sufficient campaigning time.[6] Even though Johnson did not announce his candidacy formally until the eve of the Democratic convention, it became apparent by late May, after front-runner Kennedy's smashing victory in the West Virginia primary, that Senator Johnson was running for the presidency in everything but name. He booked each weekend full of speaking engagements at state party conventions, Democratic fund-raising dinners and dedications of reclamation projects—all with the view of displaying his political profile and advancing, however subtly, his candidacy. An unofficial national campaign organization, the "Citizens for Johnson National Committee," was established on June 2, 1960. Co-chairmen were Oscar Chapman, former secretary of the interior, and Mrs. India Edwards, vice chairwoman of the Democratic National Committee from 1950 to 1956. Few unannounced candidates have enjoyed such built-in insulation from presidential primary combat as Johnson was given. But, alas, his popularity and influence as Senate majority leader could not be transformed into grass-roots popularity or delegate votes.

As a result of his inactivity in the primaries, Senator Johnson was unable to overtake the long lead built up by Senator Kennedy during his victorious primary campaign drive. Powerless to halt Kennedy, Johnson—to the surprise of many observers—settled for the vice presidential nomination, little knowing that three and one-half years later an assassin's bullet would thrust upon him the office of the presidency that had eluded him in 1960.

As the 1964 GOP nominating race opened, two unannounced candidates—Governor William W. Scranton of Pennsylvania and former Vice President Richard M. Nixon—stood on the sidelines trying to decide whether or when to jump into the fray. Governor Scranton, reportedly the personal choice of former President Eisenhower, spent an agonizing five and one-half months carefully weighing the presidential entry question before making up his mind to plunge into the battle. A subject of frequent political speculation and mass media coverage as GOP politicians and newsmen traveled to and from the Pennsylvania capitol at Harrisburg, Scranton maintained an enigmatic silence about his intentions. The word from the state capital was that the governor was not a candidate but that he was keeping "an open mind" to a possible draft.[7] This continued to be Scranton's posture throughout the heated primary fights between Senator Goldwater and Governor Rockefeller.

In the early stages of the primary race, Scranton's unannounced candidacy seemed to be paying off. Goldwater and Rockefeller both were rejected by the New Hampshire voters in favor of Ambassador Henry Cabot Lodge, also an unannounced candidate. Scranton's "brain trust" concluded that even if Rockefeller won a big California primary victory, he would still have only 300 to 400 delegates, not anywhere near the 655 needed to nominate. Moreover, Rockefeller's divorce and remarriage were considered big campaign liabilities. Senator Goldwater, while viewed a formidable challenger, was not regarded as unbeatable. His dismal New Hampshire primary performance had shown that. Moreover, he had demonstrated a remarkable ability for making rash statements on a variety of subjects: putting Social Security on a voluntary basis, selling the Tennessee Valley Authority, defoliating the South Vietnamese jungles with nuclear weapons to get at the Viet Cong guerrillas and giving NATO field commanders authority to use nuclear missiles without prior clearance from Washington. These off-the-cuff statements were thought to have left Goldwater vulnerable and unacceptable to many GOP delegates—or at least so it seemed. Because the political stock of former Vice President Nixon had fallen precipitously after his defeat in the 1962 California gubernatorial race, Scranton calculated that Nixon would not be a serious threat. Another potential contender, Governor George Romney of Michigan, had received a sharp rebuff from a GOP-dominated legislature that rejected his package of tax reforms. Scranton's advisors reasoned, quite accurately, that if Romney could not control his own legislature, how could he be viewed as the dynamic leader the Republican party was searching for. Also, the national public opinion polls showed Goldwater lagging behind both Nixon and Lodge. After Rockefeller's victory in the mid-May Oregon primary, it appeared to the Scranton people as if Goldwater's steady accumulation of delegates in the party convention states would not help him surmount the odds that had been building up against him in the primaries. But all of these pleasant dreams were shattered by Goldwater's surprise, come-from-behind victory in California. Suddenly, the Goldwater bandwagon surged forward. Instead of a long-odds challenger facing them, the Scranton staff discovered through the maze of the California election returns that Goldwater had broken away from the pack of challengers and moved into a commanding lead for the nomination.

Leaders of the moderate wing of the party, who had previously counted Goldwater out of the running as a man who could not win, now began a series of desperate, eleventh-hour maneuvers to get Scranton to run. The scene was at the annual Governors' Conference, starting June 5 in Cleveland. Not only were all the GOP governors on hand, but many of the party dignitaries, including former Vice President Nixon, had stopped by to do some politicking. Nixon urged Scranton—and also Governor Romney—to run. At the conference it was revealed that General Eisenhower had set up a private meeting the previous weekend and urged

Scranton to enter the race. But shortly before Scranton was to appear on a nationwide telecast, he reportedly received another phone call from Ike that apparently dampened his enthusiasm. It was later reported that Eisenhower's former Secretary of the Treasury George M. Humphrey, a staunch Goldwater backer, had pressured Ike to back away from endorsing Scranton.[8] Following four more days of indecision, Scranton—some critics called him "the Hamlet of Harrisburg"—finally announced before the Maryland State Republican convention that he would enter the race, though he conceded the hour was late. Indeed, the hour was too late.

Scranton's supporters had calculated that with his bloc of friendly Eastern Republican delegates, plus Oregon, and the wavering and undecided delegates, he had a mathematical chance to win. But there was no stampede to join his crusade against Goldwater. In state after state Scranton received a cordial reception but few pledges of support. The plain fact of the matter was that Scranton, the unannounced candidate, had entered the race in the fourth quarter, too late to win the nomination in the age of presidential primaries. He had not availed himself of the opportunities the primaries offered: to become better known (some people still confused him with the city of Scranton, Pennsylvania); to prove his vote-pulling power; and to demonstrate his ability to face the issues and manage a far-flung nomination campaign. Scranton's late entry also meant that many of the state party convention-elected delegates who might have backed Scranton earlier had now committed themselves to Goldwater; several favorite sons had made deals with Goldwater, and many of the financial nabobs in the GOP had placed their money on the Arizonan. At the Republican National Convention, Scranton managed to collect a scattering of delegate votes from twenty-two states, the District of Columbia, Puerto Rico and the Virgin Islands. In only eight states did Scranton collect ten or more votes. The final tally showed Goldwater 883 votes and Scranton 214, with 206 votes scattered.

Another unannounced candidate who sought "to have his cake and eat it" was former Vice President Nixon. Perhaps Nixon had no other choice in 1964 than to wait until all of the leading combatants had killed off one another and then emerge as the knight in shining armor. His stunning defeat in the 1962 California gubernatorial race, in which he attempted to recoup his loss of the 1960 presidential election, was thought to have ruined his political careeer. Tired and disheveled, he had declared before the TV cameras the day after his California defeat that he was "through with politics." Months later, he gave up his California residence and moved to New York to join a prestigious law firm. In effect, he gave up his base of political power to begin what proved to be a lucrative law practice. Under the circumstances, he apparently felt that he could not openly seek the presidential nomination again, even though he had lost the 1960 race by only 118,000 popular votes. So, as the 1964 presidential sweepstakes opened, Nixon disavowed any interest in seeking the nomination, but he did not close the door to a possible draft. Appearing on a national television show in late January 1964, Nixon said that he would accept a draft for the Republican nomination. The former vice president asserted that he did not anticipate a draft but "if the opportunity should come I would accept it."[9] Nixon maintained the posture of elder statesman and ambassador of goodwill among all groups of Republicans. While testifying in Washington before a Senate subcommittee on the subject of presidential disability and succession, he was besieged by reporters. He reiterated that he was "available" for a second nomination, but that he was not actively seeking it. He told reporters that he would not ask that his name be removed from the Oregon primary ballot, because to do so required him to sign an affidavit that he would not accept the nomination. Nixon said, however, that he had asked the Florida secretary of state to withdraw a slate of Nixon delegates in that state, since he understood that it was his prerogative to have the names stricken.[10]

At a New York press conference in mid-March, Nixon applauded Ambassador Henry Cabot Lodge's surprise write-in victory in New Hampshire and reminded the reporters not to count out Goldwater and Rockefeller. But Nixon also declared, "I feel that there is no man in this country who can make a case against Mr. Johnson more effectively than I can."[11] Throughout April and May, Nixon maintained a wait-and-see attitude. The underlying thought in the Nixon camp apparently was that Goldwater could not win the nomination on a record of ultraconservatism. For that reason, Nixon did not want to alienate Goldwater supporters who might come his way after a first or second round of inconclusive balloting at the national convention. In top Republican circles it was reported that Nixon had an informal understanding with Goldwater that, if the Arizona senator failed to collect enough delegates to get the nomination, Goldwater would throw his support to Nixon. Nixon denied this story. Nevertheless, the impression prevailed that Nixon's friends were backing Goldwater, particularly in the late stages of the California race when the polls began to indicate that Rockefeller would win.[12] But Goldwater upset these delicate calculations by winning the California primary. Immediately, Nixon tried to shift gears and begin a rescue operation. His early solution had been "let Rocky do it." But, since he now saw Goldwater as the chief contender and probable convention nominee, it was necessary to find someone other than Rockefeller to stop the Arizonan. The cornerstone of the Nixon strategy was to find a "third man" to block Goldwater; then, Nixon could emerge as the compromise choice of the San Francisco convention. Nixon's desperate search for a "stop Goldwater" candidate continued at the national Governors' Conference in Cleveland. Before arriving at the conference from a London trip, he learned that Scranton was still unenthusiastic about running. Soon after landing, he buttonholed Michigan Governor Romney and urged him to run. Romney, after several hours of meditation, declined and suggested that Mr. Nixon take on the assignment himself.[13] Nixon later denied that he had promised to support Mr. Romney as a "third force" candidate but did not specify to the press just what he had told Romney. In any event, Nixon added that he had no intention of taking on the job himself. Both Nixon and Romney, however, had some uncomplimentary things to say about Goldwater.

Scranton's belated entry in the race restored, at least for the time being, the "third force" candidate that Nixon had been looking for earlier. But Nixon, sensing the hopelessness of his case by the time Scranton made up his mind, declined to support Scranton. Upon his return from a brief European business trip, Nixon acidly observed, "If a man receives a phone call and changes his mind, he isn't a very strong man. He's got to make his own decisions and not appear to be a puppet maneuvered by someone else."[14] (This reference was to the phone call from Eisenhower to Scranton mentioned earlier in this chapter.) For the next two weeks Nixon remained in the background while making a political tour through the Midwest and the South. On July 1, Senate Minority Leader Everett M. Dirksen of Illinois described Scranton's chances as futile and observed that the Goldwater drive could not be stopped, even by General Dwight D. Eisenhower. Nixon apparently agreed, for the news was leaked to the press that Nixon had given up all hope of winning the nomination. In conversation with political associates, Nixon conceded that Goldwater had won, and he relegated himself to the role of a party unifier behind Goldwater.[15] Thus, the unannounced candidacy of Richard M. Nixon ended for 1964. But four years later, Mr. Nixon emerged phoenix-like as a full-bloom active candidate who soon outdistanced his chief rivals in the primaries. Reviewing the 1964 GOP pre-convention maneuvers, it is evident that Scranton came to recognize in the closing days before the San Francisco convention that his try for the nomination was "too little and too late." Neither Scranton nor Nixon had profited from the experience of other unannounced candidates in recent years.

Until the closing days before the 1968 GOP convention, California Governor Ronald Reagan maintained the posture of an unannounced "favorite son," in hopes that he would be nominated at the convention without his being an open candidate for the presidency. When asked about primary campaigning, Reagan told his questioners that this would only create "divisiveness," the one thing he most wanted to avoid.[16]

Nevertheless, he permitted his name to be entered in several primaries. But his "non-candidate" candidacy must be assessed as a failure. Reagan's primary vote track record was equally unimpressive: New Hampshire, 1 percent; Wisconsin, 11 percent; Nebraska, 22 percent; and Oregon, 23 percent. The only victory in the campaign was his home state of California, which he won unopposed, collecting eighty-six delegates. Reagan persisted in playing the unannounced candidate game until the eve of the 1968 GOP convention, when he finally announced his "candidacy." As one cynical GOP governor remarked on this announcement, "It's like a woman who's eight and a half months pregnant announcing she's going to have a baby."[17] Reagan might have started a stampede among Southerners before Nixon arrived on the scene. The first and only convention ballot totals gave Nixon 692 (25 more than the needed 667 votes); Rockefeller, 277; Reagan, 182; favorite sons and others, 182. If Reagan had decided to meet Nixon head on in the primaries, he may well have thwarted Nixon's first ballot victory. In the process he might have persuaded many of the earlier uncommitted Southerners who, with no ultraconservative in the race, ultimately joined up with Nixon, but who in their hearts would have preferred Reagan, had he been an announced candidate. But, unfortunately, Reagan failed to learn from other unannounced candidates in recent years—Harriman, Symington and Scranton—that to capture the nomination the candidate must be willing to take on all challengers in the primaries. Reagan's failure to pursue an active candidacy may have cost him the grand prize. The California governor learned too late that it is virtually impossible for an unannounced candidate to mount a full-fledged national campaign once the presidential primary season opens. It is noteworthy that Reagan did not repeat this error in his second try for the presidency eight years later. The retired California governor formally announced that he would challenge incumbent President Ford for the GOP nomination in mid-November 1975, nine months before the 1976 Republican convention. Reagan, in his third try for the White House, announced his candidacy for the 1980 GOP nomination in mid-November 1979.

The continued spread of presidential primaries from sixteen states in 1968 to twenty-nine states and the District of Columbia in 1976 has virtually terminated the unannounced candidate strategy. In 1972, for example, only one Democratic contender out of the thirteen-candidate field, Congressman Wilbur Mills of Arkansas, maintained the posture of an unannounced candidate. Though $730,000 was spent on his behalf, mostly in the New Hampshire ($200,000) and Massachusetts ($150,000) primaries, Mills's candidacy never got off the ground.[18] The Draft Mills Committee ceased operations before the 1971 Federal Elections Campaign Act, with its stringent disclosure provisions, went into effect on April 7, 1972. But Mills's supporters, well-financed by funds from national-level business and professional groups affected by tax legislation originating in the House Ways and Means Committee, chaired by Mills, continued to woo delegates right up to and at the Democratic National Convention. Few unannounced candidates have persisted with their silent candidacies as long as Mills against such hopeless odds. Without continued heavy funding from pressure groups affected by Mills's committee, his unannounced candidacy probably would not have continued beyond New Hampshire.

Documents in the Watergate Committee's files revealed that Mills received several illegal corporate contributions. Several corporate officials and an oil company lobbyist were convicted, fined and, in two instances, sentenced to jail for making illegal contributions to Mills's presidential drive.[19] Mills emerged unscathed from the Watergate investigation, but his entire political career soon went into eclipse after news of his affair with a Washington nightclub stripper, Fannie Foxe, hit the headlines, following Miss Foxe's leap into the Washington Tidal Basin.

No better illustration of the plight of the unannounced candidate will ever be found than Senator Hubert H. Humphrey's pathetic, last-gasp attempt in 1976 to keep alive his flickering presidential hopes in the final weeks of the primaries. Even though he had announced in late April that he would not contest the last-round New Jersey primary, held on the same day as the Ohio and California primaries, Humphrey indicated that he would probably become an active candidate if Jimmy Carter stumbled in these primaries. But Carter's 126-delegate victory in Ohio, which gave him a grand total of more than 1,100 delegates (1,505 were needed to win), clinched the nomination for the Georgian. Within the next forty-eight hours Governor George Wallace and Senators Henry "Scoop" Jackson and Frank Church released their delegates and asked them to support Carter.

With these concessions, Humphrey's twenty-year quest for the White House came to a tearful end. In January 1976, Humphrey had indicated that he would be available if the Democrat convention was deadlocked but that he would not contest the nomination in the primaries. He said he wanted to leave a clear field for the candidates in the primaries to win or lose. With this wait-and-see, unannounced candidate strategy Humphrey and his allies were banking on favorite-son candidates and uncommitted slates to prevent any of the twelve candidates in the primaries from emerging as a clear-cut front-runner to claim the nomination. Humphrey's hopes, in short, rested on a "brokered" convention in which the delegates would turn to him, the unannounced candidate, after failing to agree on a nominee from the field of relatively even-matched contenders. Humphrey may have been lulled into overconfidence early in the primary season when the New York *Times*/CBS polls conducted on election day in several Northern primary states showed that had Humphrey been on the ballot he would have outpolled Carter.[20] Also, a comparable Washington *Post* primary survey in Pennsylvania, based upon 2,794 voters, showed similar results (see Table 8.1).

TABLE 8.1
PRE-PRIMARY POLL IN PENNSYLVANIA, 1976
(PERCENT)

	Without Humphrey in Race	With Humphrey in Race
Humphrey gets	0	46
Carter gets	35	22
Jackson gets	23	8
Udall gets	24	13
Wallace gets	7	5
Others get	11	4

Source: Washington *Post,* April 29, 1976.
Note: Based on responses from 2,239 Pennsylvania Democratic primary voters. The sample slightly underrepresents Jackson's and Wallace's actual vote and slightly over-represents Udall's vote.

After Carter's stunning victory in Pennsylvania in late April 1976, Humphrey wavered for nearly forty-eight hours on his unannounced candidacy strategy. Under heavy pressure from many of his old supporters and friends, and facing a 4 P.M., April 29th deadline to file in New Jersey—the last filing deadline in the nation—Humphrey painfully announced in the old Senate Caucus Room, the traditional stage for the proclamation of presidential candidacies, that he would neither enter the New Jersey primary nor authorize a committee to solicit support among delegates on his behalf. Humphrey said, however, that he would still be willing, in the event that a deadlocked convention so wished, to accept the nomination. According to the "Happy Warrior," who unsuccessfully sought the presidency in 1960, 1968, and 1972, his decision was based on the belief that he had insufficient time, money, and organizational strength for "the kind of hard-hitting campaign that I'm accustomed to."[21] (Possibly his decision may have been influenced, in part, by the threatened recurrence of a bladder malignancy, which subsequently claimed his life in January 1978). Humphrey, clinging to a vain hope, may have felt that there was still time between the late April New Jersey filing deadline and the end of primaries on June 8th to mount a last-minute drive for the nomination. In the four weeks after his decision not to enter the New Jersey primary Humphrey nevertheless spent more time there (parts of five days) than any of the announced presidential candidates, ostensibly campaigning for congressional candidates and "fulfilling long-standing commitments." His prime objective, of course, was to generate support for the uncommitted slate of delegate candidates unofficially supporting him and, in some districts, Governor Edmund G. "Jerry" Brown of California. But all of this effort went down the drain as Carter inched closer to the nomination each week of the remaining primaries. The uncommitted New Jersey slate bested Carter, but the former Georgia governor won the New Jersey preference primary with 56 percent of the popular vote. Far more important, Carter's overwhelming victory in Ohio—he picked up 126 delegates—opened the floodgates for his nomination. Once again, the history of eleventh-hour candidates who finally shed their unannounced status shows that, since the end of World War II, they are destined to fail. Humphrey was no exception.

Looking ahead, it seems fair to predict the operation of 33 presidential primaries will probably "smoke out" most unannounced candidates before the primary season opens. The dilemma of the unannounced candidate is also compounded by the expanded use of the Oregon-type blanket ballot primary, which lists all serious candidates. Now used in 18 states, the Oregon system requires the secretary of state (or a special commission) to list all candidates "generally advocated or recognized by national news media." The only way an unannounced candidate can keep his name off the ballot is to sign an affidavit that he or she is not a candidate. Most aspirants, even unannounced candidates, do not wish to make such flat-out, categorical withdrawals from the race. Also, the new federal matching subsidy law for underwriting individual presidential campaigns is a tantalizing plum which most presidential aspirants do not wish to pass up. By formally announcing their candidacies and by raising $5,000 in each of twenty states in amounts of $250 or less, the candidate can qualify for up to $5 million in matching subsidies. Few are the unannounced candidates who are willing to pass up these juicy federal subsidies. In 1976, fifteen candidates, including President Gerald Ford and Ronald Reagan, an arch-opponent of big government, signed up for Uncle Sam's matching funds in the primaries. Under these new nominating conditions, unannounced candidates would seem to be facing extinction.

The Late-Blooming Candidate

The year 1976 saw the emergence of a special kind of unannounced, late-blooming contender within the Democratic party—the late-entry candidate. Instead of announcing many months before the New Hampshire primary, as most of the dozen Democratic aspirants had done,

Senator Frank Church of Idaho and Governor Edmund G. "Jerry" Brown of California waited until all but three contenders had been mortally wounded on the primary field of battle before entering the nominating fray. While the late-entry candidate may not face extinction in the immediate years ahead, the long-term prospects of survival for this candidate species are probably no better than those of the favorite son. Let's examine why by looking chiefly at the 1976 presidential nominating experience.

Senator Church's explanation for his delayed entry was that his chairmanship of the Senate Select Committee on Intelligence consumed so much of his time that he could not campaign effectively until this assignment was completed. Reminded by the press and some of his advisors that "the late, late strategy" was at best a long-shot gamble, Church declared: "It's never too late—nor are the odds too great—to try."[22] From the start, Church faced three nearly insurmountable obstacles: lack of money, lack of a broad political base beyond his native state of Idaho, and too close identification with the liberal wing of the party in a year when half a dozen liberal candidates had fallen by the wayside. His response to these mountainous obstacles: "Meet the Don Quixote of this campaign."[23]

Senator Church's last-minute campaign catapulted off the launching pad with a surprise first-round victory in Nebraska. He followed this unexpected triumph with an upset victory over Jimmy Carter in the Oregon primary, a key primary state. Two weeks before the final round of primaries, Church won his home state of Idaho's primary and that of neighboring Montana, but then his campaign ran out of gas—and money. He finished third in Nevada, Rhode Island, Ohio and California and fourth in New Jersey. Despite his four victories, the New York *Times* delegate count gave him only seventy-one (other counts gave him as many as seventy-nine) votes. Although he had outdueled front-runner Jimmy Carter west of the Mississippi, he was no match for Carter in the late-round, big delegate states of Ohio and New Jersey, or Governor Brown on his home turf in California, or in Rhode Island or New Jersey.

Church was immobilized during part of the final week of the California campaign with a severe throat infection. Then, shortly after he returned to the hustings in Ohio, the news of the Teton Dam disaster in northeastern Idaho forced him to return to his home state to survey the devastating flood damage. But Church refused to use any of these excuses in his withdrawal statement, in which he described Carter as "truly a candidate whose time has come."[24] Church's Gallup poll ratings, it might be noted, never exceeded 4 percent during the primary season.

Governor Brown, in his characteristic unorthodox way, called four newsmen into his office in mid-March for an amiable chat and offhandedly announced that he would run a "full and serious" favorite-son candidacy because no "clear-cut front-runner" had emerged from the early primaries—and because his "new ideas and fresh thoughts deserve a hearing."[25] By late April, Brown decided to expand his favorite-son candidacy into a broader campaign covering five of the last dozen primaries—Maryland, Nevada, Oregon, Rhode Island and New Jersey. But Brown's "late, late strategy" limited him to such a narrow field of action that he did not have enough time to build a big delegate base or to knock anyone else out of the race. Late-starting candidates, if they check the primary schedule, will discover, as did Governor Brown, that time runs out early. (By the end of March 1980, for example, a late entrant would be able to get on the ballot in just seven primary states, none of major importance except New Jersey.) Brown's procrastination in entering the presidential nominating race contained the seeds for the eventual failure of his late-starting campaign. His reluctance to enter the presidential sweepstakes until mid-March, for example, prevented him from forming slates of committed delegates in Maryland until it was too late to file. Consequently, Brown's spectacular triumph in Maryland's "beauty contest" preferential primary was largely neutralized by Jimmy Carter's one-sided victory in the Maryland delegate contest; Carter won thirty-three delegates to twenty for the Brown-leaning uncommitted slate. Although Carter absorbed his worst licking since his fourth-place finish in the New York primary, he continued, nevertheless, to inch his way closer and closer to the nomination. His thirty-three Maryland delegates pushed his delegate total to nearly 700, more than 2.5 times as many as his closest rival, Senator Jackson, who by then had become an inactive candidate.

Because Governor Brown had failed to announce his candidacy before the Oregon primary filing deadline (March 16, 1976), he was forced to mount a time-consuming and difficult write-in campaign for this late-round West Coast primary. Brown's whirlwind campaign and his well-organized write-in drive netted over 100,000 write-in votes, enough to win a third-place finish behind Senator Church and Jimmy Carter, who had led the Portland *Oregonian* poll throughout the campaign until Church displaced him on the final week before the primary. After all the write-ins had been tallied, Governor Brown's supporters claimed a new record (24 percent) for the most successful write-in campaign in the long history of the Oregon primary, far surpassing Governor Nelson Rockefeller's 11 percent write-in vote in 1968. But Brown's third-place showing in Oregon could hardly be claimed a victory. On the same six-primary Tuesday, Carter won three primaries—Arkansas, Kentucky and Tennessee; Church picked up a second victory in his home state of Idaho; and Brown's solo triumph was in the Nevada primary. By this late May date, only six primaries were left. Brown successfully campaigned for an uncommitted slate in Rhode Island the following Tuesday, upsetting the favored Carter slate 32 to 30 percent. On the final primary day Brown overwhelmed Carter in the California primary and gained added satisfaction at Carter's expense by leading (actually, sharing the leadership with undeclared candidate Humphrey) the New Jersey uncommitted delegate slate to a convincing victory over Carter's ticket (42.1 to 27.9 percent). But, like a professional basketball team rallying for a come-from-behind victory that falls short, Brown ran out of time and primaries to win.

Although the California governor and the uncommitted delegates he backed captured five of the six primaries in which Brown competed, Carter was able to outlast Brown and the other two remaining active candidates—Church and Udall—and lay claim to the nomination within forty-eight hours after the California primary polls closed. The 218 Carter delegates elected on "Super Bowl Tuesday" gave him a grand total of more than 1,100 delegates, enough to convince Mayor Richard J. Daley of Chicago, Governor George Wallace and Senator Jackson to shift their support (roughly 400 delegates) to Carter and thereby assure the nomination for the smiling Georgian. But Governor Brown, declaring the nomination was "still open," flew off to Louisiana to campaign for delegates in this caucus-convention state. Though he won the support of Governor Edward Edwards and the bulk of Louisiana's forty-one-member delegation, Brown appeared in the eyes of most Democratic professionals to be the captain of a lost cause. Quixotically, he continued his hopeless challenge: "Jimmy Carter, wherever you are, I'm looking for you. I want to debate you."[26] Brown's managers scheduled a cross-country visit for the California governor to Connecticut to woo uncommitted delegates, but the trip was eventually cancelled. Finally, more than two weeks after Carter had locked up the nomination, Governor Brown purchased one-half hour of network television time to talk to the American voters about the need for a "new generation of leadership." In the course of the telecast he acknowledged that Jimmy Carter had collected enough delegates to win a first-ballot nomination. But Brown, determined to maintain his national reputation as the most promising Democrat of the under-forty generation, refused to issue a concession statement. This did not come until the eve of Carter's nomination in New York City. From the start of his longshot bid for the Democratic presidential nomination, Governor Brown knew that he could win the nomination for president only one way: through an early-ballot deadlock followed by an auction among the candidates and other power brokers controlling large blocs of votes. Brown gambled and lost. But the nation has probably not heard the last from the young governor of the nation's most populous state.

The Favorite Son

Almost as old as the two-party system itself, favorite sons are a familiar part of the American political landscape. Unlike yesteryear, however, when favorite-son candidates frequently were chosen as presidential nominees—and sometimes successfully elected—it is probably safe to say that the favorite sons will not be nominated in future presidential election years.

In political parlance a favorite son is a home-state presidential aspirant who may or may not be (usually the latter) a serious contender for the presidential nomination. Over the years, state parties have sometimes advanced a governor or U.S. senator as a favorite-son candidate for president, with the intent of using his candidacy and state delegation to win a seat at the bargaining table if the nomination is to be "brokered." Some favorite sons have hoped against hope that political lightning might strike and make them the party nominee. But, realistically speaking, this has been an empty hope for almost a half century. The last favorite-son candidate to win the nomination—and the presidency—was Warren G. Harding, Ohio's Republican favorite son in 1920. Harding was chosen on the tenth ballot after three leading contenders—Frank O. Lowden, Leonard Wood and Hiram Johnson—became hopelessly deadlocked. For the Democrats, the last favorite son nominated was John W. Davis of West Virginia, selected on the 103rd ballot of the marathon 1924 Democratic National Convention. Davis was overwhelmed by the Coolidge landslide in November.

In the past, favorite-son candidates sometimes have possessed enough delegate "clout" to block some early front-running candidates. At the crucial stage of a multiple-ballot convention, they have delivered their delegates to another candidate in return for some political consideration, perhaps even the vice presidential nomination. John Nance Garner of Texas did that in 1932 to become Franklin Delano Roosevelt's running-mate. But the changing forces in the nominating process—especially the powerful influence of presidential primaries—have, for all practical purposes, ruled out the possibility of a favorite son ever winning the party nomination again.

The types of favorite sons and the roles they perform in both the primary and caucus-convention states can be classified generally into six categories:[27]

1. "Outstanding" favorite sons usually come from large pivotal states and may become serious contenders when the field is wide open. Their political influence and contacts extend considerably beyond their state's borders.
2. "Rising" favorite sons are usually governors or leading members of Congress who have gained prominence in their states. They are interested in spreading their names beyond their state borders and usually are most concerned with future presidential elections since they cannot be expected to compete on even terms with nationally known candidates or outstanding favorite sons.

3. "Token" favorite sons, usually the state party leaders, assume this role to demonstrate their control over the state party organization or to forestall encroachments upon their control of the party. Later they may choose to swing delegate support behind a particular candidate.
4. "Stand-in" favorite sons, usually handpicked by the state organizations, are selected to reflect the wishes of the party and are on the ticket because the presidential primary laws of such states—for example, Ohio—require that a candidate be listed.
5. "Nuisance" favorite sons are marginal candidates, sometimes without solid organizational support even in their own state. They have no chance of winning the nomination but crave the publicity that attends their entry in the presidential race. Occasionally these candidates cast themselves in the role of "spoilers," that is, they try to prevent front-running candidates from obtaining a clear victory in a primary contest.
6. "Quasi" favorite sons are the more-or-less active presidential candidates whose campaigns seem to have real prospects of success only in their home states. Spawned partly by the new matching federal subsidy campaign finance law of 1974, quasi favorite sons hope to have a seat at the bargaining table if a convention deadlock develops and the nomination has to be brokered.

Examining these categories in more detail, the outstanding favorite son usually enters one or more presidential primaries outside his state as part of his quest for the nomination. While not a front-runner, he is well up in the pack, within striking distance of the nomination should a convention deadlock develop between two leading candidates. In 1948, for example, Senator Arthur Vandenberg, Michigan's outstanding favorite son who declined to campaign actively for the nomination, was considered by a number of observers as the logical compromise if Governor Thomas E. Dewey and Senator Robert A. Taft became stalemated.

Since the outstanding favorite son almost invariably comes from a large pivotal state, he has a bloc of delegates to serve as the nucleus for a stretch drive. The outstanding favorite son usually is acquainted with other important state leaders who may be willing under certain circumstances to assist his candidacy rather than see the convention deadlocked. The chief handicap of most outstanding favorite sons, however, has been their lack of nationwide recognition or organization to compete on even terms with a nationally known candidate.

Rising favorite sons usually are privy to the inner councils of the party but, lacking full stature, comprise the second team of presidential candidates. Front-running candidates treat them with respect and, in turn, expect the rising favorite son to step aside when the smaller islands of delegates begin breaking up and gravitating toward the nationally known candidates. This works no great hardship on the rising favorite son. He has had the opportunity to bask in the limelight of the convention, to be wooed by the national candidates' political managers, or to be promised certain political favors in the event the party nominee wins in November. The rising favorite son may even be considered a long-shot vice-presidential candidate. Or, more likely, the rising favorite son will be consigned to the second team or destined for political oblivion. In 1956 the Democratic governor of New Jersey, Robert B. Meyner, came to be classified in the latter category.

Token favorite sons are usually veteran party leaders who want to exert powerful influence in the choice of the party nominee. The token favorite son maintains tight control over his delegations so he will be in a position to swing behind the candidate he considers best qualified as the party's standard-bearer in November. If he wishes, he may serve as a stalking horse for a leading presidential contender who needs his support at a vital point in the balloting. The token candidate is almost never in the thick of presidential contention. For a variety of reasons, he is not politically "available"—he may come from a "safe" Republican or Democratic state, be too old, be heavily tarnished with a machine politics label, be too closely identified with a large pressure group, or be unacceptable to important minority groups. Democratic Senator Robert F. Byrd of West Virginia in 1976 would undoubtedly be rated a token favorite son.

Stand-in favorite sons are largely products of certain presidential primary laws and are never serious contenders for the nomination. Stand-in candidates are entered to comply with filing laws that require the consent of the presidential candidate to enter. Delegates in these states are usually formally pledged. In some instances, stand-in favorite sons also are used by incumbent presidents who, for either reasons of health or political expedience, do not want to announce their intentions. In the case of President Harry S Truman in 1952, a stand-in favorite son was used in the Minnesota primary (Senator Hubert H. Humphrey) until the president finally made up his mind not to seek reelection. When President Truman asked that his name be withdrawn from the California presidential primary, Attorney General Edmund G. "Pat" Brown was pressured by the state organization to serve as the Democratic stand-in candidate to keep Senator Estes Kefauver from winning the primary by default. Subsequently, Brown graduated from the stand-in to the outstanding favorite son category by winning the California governorship in 1958 and by turning back Richard Nixon's effort to unseat him in 1962. Brown's defeat by Ronald Reagan in 1966, however, removed him from further presidential contention.

Nuisance favorite son candidates, the fifth category, are usually unknown to most American voters. Who, for example, could identify Riley

Bender, favorite-son candidate for president in the 1944 Illinois Republican primary and preference winner in the 1948 Republican primary? Driven more by the desire for publicity than a willingness or ability to organize a full-fledged campaign, the nuisance candidates rarely cause sleepless nights for front-running candidates. Although the nuisance candidates are often the first to admit that they have no possibility of winning the nomination, they sometimes delight in assuming the "spoiler" role. For example, Democratic Senator Wayne B. Morse of Oregon waged a "stop Kennedy" crusade throughout the 1960 primary campaign. He singled out the Massachusetts senator for his "reactionary" voting record, especially his vote for the Landrum-Griffin labor reform law. Yet Morse was the first to concede that his own chances for the nomination were utterly hopeless. Undoubtedly, as long as there are presidential primary laws there will be nuisance favorite son candidates, but they never will be considered as having any greater chance of becoming president than does the average state senator.

Quasi favorite sons have an ambivalent position in the pre-convention race. In the two-year period before the primary season opens they may nurture hopes of making a national race, but the realities of their poor Gallup poll ratings and low-level acceptance by party professionals usually force the quasi favorite son to scale down his aspirations. In 1976, for example, Senator Lloyd M. Bentsen, Jr. of Texas, an early announced candidate, began laying plans for a national race months before the 1974 Democratic party's mini-convention in Kansas City. But the tepid response to his nationwide drive for support convinced him to retrench to a regional effort in the South. When he fared badly in the early Mississippi and Oklahoma caucuses, he then announced that he would concentrate on the Texas presidential primary, termed the "Lloyd M. Bentsen primary" by his critics, who insisted this new primary law was passed by his friends in the Texas legislature solely to boost his presidential candidacy. Bentsen's faltering White House hopes were dashed in the Lone Star State by Jimmy Carter, who walked off with ninety-three out of ninety-eight delegates at stake in the primary. Carter won despite the fact that Bentsen had virtually all the well-known local Democrats on his slates as well as active support from virtually all top state officials, including Governor Dolph Briscoe. Also, Governor Milton J. Shapp of Pennsylvania launched his 1976 drive for the White House as a quasi favorite son candidate. But Shapp, a popular vote-getter in Pennsylvania, failed to generate any enthusiasm for his candidacy elsewhere. Following his failure of trial runs in the Massachusetts and Florida primaries, where he finished seventh and fourth respectively, Shapp removed himself from further presidential contention.

No one, except possibly the candidate himself, takes a favorite son candidacy seriously any longer. They played no role, for example, in determining the outcome of the 1968, 1972 or 1976 conventions in either party. The most recent failure that comes to mind is Senator Robert Byrd, the Democratic favorite son from West Virginia, in 1976. Jimmy Carter, who entered twenty-nine out of thirty primaries, did not even bother to enter the Mountaineer State primary and campaign against Senator Byrd because he figured, correctly, that he would have Byrd's West Virginia votes in the end anyway. Commenting on the Byrd candidacy, newsman Martin Schram observed,

It is the sham of the American political process that when Byrd announced his candidacy early in the campaign year, he swore that he was more than just a one-state candidate, that he would be running a truly national campaign. It is proof of the strength of the American political process that no one believed him.[28]

Favorite sons are simply no match for the active, nationally recognized candidates who monopolize exposure in the national press and the television network news programs. In 1976, for example, two Democratic governors and favorite sons, Daniel Walker of Illinois and Hugh Carey of New York, fielded partial slates of uncommitted delegates in hopes that in the event of a convention deadlock the delegates might eventually turn to one of them, or at least that their performances would entitle them to a seat at the bargaining table. But these candidacies—especially Carey's attempt to field "an empire slate for the Empire State"—failed as badly as those of their predecessors.

In recent years both major parties have sought to discourage favorite-son nominations at their national conventions. In 1972 the Democratic National Committee approved a new rule requiring all prospective nominees to file a petition with fifty delegate signatures, including at least twenty delegates from one state, one day before nominations are to be made.[29] Republican rule makers at the 1972 Miami Beach GOP convention, in a special effort to maintain the themes of harmony and unity, drafted an instant change in the convention rules which guaranteed that only President Nixon's name would be put in nomination. This was done by adopting a rule that no candidate could be nominated unless he had support from the majority of three or more state delegations, and this excluded all candidates but President Nixon.[30] Within the next decade favorite-son candidates may well become an endangered species.

The Dark Horse

Despite its long-time usage in American political parlance, the term "dark horse" has never been generally agreed upon by scholars or politicians. The term seems to imply an unanticipated or minor candidate, perhaps a favorite son, whose victory surprises the general public.[31] The basic strategy of a dark horse candidate must rest on a convention deadlock. Lacking initial strong support, the dark horse candidate and his handlers seek in a quiet, unassuming way to line up supporters or present their strategy to political professionals around the country—and cross their fingers for a convention stalemate. James K. Polk, in 1844, was the first genuine dark horse candidate to be nominated. Until the eighth ballot, he had received no votes whatsoever, yet he was nominated on the ninth! Eight years later, Franklin Pierce was totally ignored until the thirty-fifth ballot, when Virginia gave him fifteen votes; on the forty-eighth he had only fifty-five votes. But then a stampede occurred that put him over the top on the next ballot at the 1852 Democratic convention. Although dark horse candidates were more prevalent and successful in the nineteenth century—Polk, Pierce and Hayes all reached the White House—the only twentieth-century dark horse, favorite-son candidate to win the nomination and presidency since the emergence of presidential primaries has been Senator Warren G. Harding, the GOP victor in 1920. Two other dark horses in this century have won their party's nomination but have lost the presidential election—John W. Davis, the 1924 Democratic nominee, and Wendell Willkie, the 1940 GOP standard-bearer. Neither participated in the presidential primaries in the year of their nomination.

Most of the conditions that over the years fostered dark horse candidates have disappeared. Within the Democratic party, for example, the repeal of the two-thirds rule in 1936 sharply reduced the possibility of national convention deadlock (see Table 8.2). Under this century-old rule, one-third of the delegates plus one could exercise a veto over prospective nominees. Southern Democrats were the staunchest defenders of the two-thirds rule, since it enabled the South to veto candidates displeasing to the region. Of the twenty-six Democratic conventions held under the two-thirds rule, fourteen took more than one ballot to select a nominee. Three in the twentieth century took more than forty ballots: 1912 (46), 1920 (43) and 1924 (103). Once this rule was eliminated, the chances of a convention deadlock declined abruptly; thus the possibility of the convention turning to a dark horse, compromise candidate diminished accordingly. The Republicans throughout history have required only a simple majority to nominate. As a result, the GOP has had few protracted conventions. Their last multi-ballot convention was in 1948, when Dewey was nominated on the third ballot. Since the party's birth in 1854, only two Republican conventions have run ten or more ballots. In the pre-radio, pre-television era, the tactic of awaiting or even promoting a convention stalemate was made easier by the absence of reliable, detailed information on the candidates and their relative standing in the delegate count. With this paucity of information, dark horse candidates often felt they had as good a chance as the next in a wide open nominating race.

TABLE 8.2

NUMBER OF BALLOTS AT LAST SIX OPEN DEMOCRATIC CONVENTIONS PRIOR TO AND SINCE REPEAL OF TWO-THIRDS RULE IN 1936

Year	Number of Ballots Before Repeal	Nominee
1908	1	William Jennings Bryan
1912	46	Woodrow Wilson
1920	44	James M. Cox
1924	103	John W. Davis
1928	1	Alfred E. Smith
1932	4	Franklin D. Roosevelt
Year	Number of Ballots After Repeal	Nominee
1952	3	Adlai E. Stevenson
1956	1	Adlai E. Stevenson
1960	1	John F. Kennedy
1968	1	Hubert H. Humphrey
1972	1	George S. McGovern
1976	1	Jimmy Carter

Source: Richard C. Bain and Judith H. Parris, *Convention Decisions and Voting Records,* 2nd ed. (Washington, D. C.: Brookings Institutions, 1973), pp. 171-343.

Before the advent of national television, it probably didn't matter much what the press said about the first few primaries, since prior to 1948 the influence of the primaries and mass media on the nominating process was much less. But it matters now. This is the basic reason why the dark horse candidate no longer plays a significant role in the candidate selection process. The national media's emphasis on these early victories—and defeats—have made journalistic assessments of candidates' performance a key factor in the nominating race. Under these circumstances the dark horse candidate who stands prancing on the sidelines soon finds the leading presidential contenders and the national media passing him by. Without any proven record in the primaries, the dark horse candidate simply is not regarded a serious contender. If a dark horse has any doubt about his candidate standing, he need only consult the periodic pre-convention delegate count, conducted by the Associated Press, the New York *Times* or the Washington *Post.* As for his ratings in the Gallup and Harris opinion polls published throughout the primary season, the dark horse candidate can consider himself lucky if he finds himself listed among the serious contenders, since he usually lacks the name recognition needed to build up his ratings in the polls.

Equally important, a change in Democratic national party rules has encouraged more primary states to require delegates running in the primaries to be pledged to a specific candidate. This mandatory pledge has reduced the formerly large pool of unpledged delegates to a relatively small minority at the national convention. Thus, the task of the dark horse, which is to wean away delegates pledged to other candidates, is compounded.

Theoretically, the wide open field of candidates that prevails under the presidential primary system would seem to favor dark horse candidates, since the odds of one candidate outpacing the field would seem rather low. But the primary system has not functioned in this manner. The spread of presidential primaries to thirty-three states has been an anathema to dark horse candidates. Before the rapid proliferation of presidential primaries and the growth of network television, the dark horse candidate could remain hidden in the pack as the candidates moved into the home stretch without endangering his chances for the nomination. But the dark horse candidate, now operating under the glare of network television cameras, can no longer avoid the scrutiny of the national media. The advent of nationwide television (the transcontinental coaxial cable was completed in 1952) and the expansion of the national press corps have led to a quantum jump in the coverage of the presidential nominating races, especially in the early round presidential primary states. As one team of authors noted almost two decades ago, "Under modern conditions, so much information is systematically collected and published concerning the attitudes of voters, party officials, and convention delegates that the range of opportunity for the tactics of deadlock has been reduced."[32] In the era of presidential primaries, mass media and nationwide opinion polls the convention's choice of nominees has been narrowed to the winner of the primaries. In other words, much of the convention's business—especially the convention's choice—has been settled before the convention has met. This transformation of the nominating process has threatened to make dark horse candidates an endangered species, too.

The Draft Candidate

The same strategic considerations that militate against unannounced candidates, favorite sons and dark horses winning the presidential nomination also discourage the draft candidate. Indeed, so remote is the possibility that a presidential candidate will be "drafted" in the age of television that one commentator has declared, "Presidential drafts are like blue moons. They are only said to occur, or, when they do, they are unbelievable."[33] The scarcity of draft candidates can also be attributed to the basic fact that the overwhelming majority of those figures in public life who are likely to be regarded by their party and the electorate as presidential timber are not modest about making their candidacies or their willingness to serve known. Consequently, presidential nomination vacancies at convention time are virtually nonexistent. The long period of vigorous and open pre-convention campaigning gives all willing candidates ample opportunity to demonstrate their vote-getting ability and national leadership qualities. The best chance that a potential draft candidate can hope for is either a convention deadlock or a plethora of candidates with none possessing outstanding qualifications.

James A. Garfield of Ohio was the only draft candidate ever to be elected president. In 1880 Garfield was drafted on the thirty-sixth ballot after fellow Ohioan, Senator John Sherman, convinced his own chances were hopeless after twenty-eight ballots and a convention deadlock, shifted his support to Garfield. Since the inception of the presidential primary system only two candidates have been drafted: Charles Evans Hughes, a Republican, in 1916, and Adlai E. Stevenson, a Democrat, in 1952.

Hughes, an associate justice on the U.S. Supreme Court, was drafted by the 1916 GOP Convention on the third ballot. As a member of the High Court, Hughes could not, of course, have been an active candidate without first tendering his resignation, but he gave no indication that he wished to step down from the bench. His name did appear on the Oregon primary, despite his request to have it removed.[34] In several other primary states Hughes kept his name off the ballot. Overall, the pre-convention results showed that the primaries and caucus-convention states had produced a host of favorite sons, none very strong and none willing to bargain or align themselves with another candidate. Thus, the first prerequisite for a draft candidate had been met.

More important, the Republican party was still suffering from the deep wounds of the Taft-Roosevelt schism and the Progressive insurgency in 1912. Regular or old-guard Republicans were unwilling to support Theodore H. Roosevelt or Hiram Johnson, his Bull Moose running-mate, or others who had bolted the party four years earlier. The Progressives refused to support any regular Republicans, such as Elihu Root, the 1912 convention chairman, Henry Cabot Lodge, or any others involved in the Taft "steamroller" in 1912. With this split still haunting the party, the GOP convention faced the unenviable task of nominating a candidate acceptable to both major factions. Since almost all active Republicans had been involved one way or the other in the 1912 party bloodletting, the only hope was to find a public figure who had been out of the country (as Buchanan had been for the Democrats in the stormy years before 1856) or who held an office that legitimately entitled him to stay above the battle. The one office that fulfilled this requirement was, of course, the Supreme Court.

Many organizational Republican leaders would have preferred a candidate other than Hughes, who as a reform governor of New York earlier had displayed a record of independence from the regular organization. But they lacked another first-rate candidate. Roosevelt, who did not like Hughes personally, suggested Henry Cabot Lodge as the prospective nominee. Knowing that Lodge was unacceptable to the GOP progressives, Roosevelt was probably using this ploy to keep the door open for his own renomination. But Teddy subsequently did not repudiate his floor leader when he announced for Hughes. None of the favorite-son candidates had been able to form a winning coalition so they, too, accepted Hughes by default. On the third roll call Hughes received 949.5 of the 987 convention votes, and his nomination was then made unanimous.[35] Not until after the balloting had been completed, however, did Hughes formally assent to serve as the GOP's standard-bearer and resign from the Supreme Court. (Later, in 1930, President Hoover appointed Hughes to be chief justice.)

The third presidential draft grew out of vastly different circumstances. In 1952 the Democratic party, which had occupied the White House for twenty consecutive years, faced a near political vacuum after President Harry S Truman unexpectedly announced his retirement in late March, following his surprising defeat by Senator Estes Kefauver in the New Hampshire primary. Though he won a dozen primaries mostly unopposed, Kefauver was unacceptable to most Southern Democrats and big city party leaders. None of the Truman stand-ins, or outstanding favorite sons or Senator Richard B. Russell of Georgia, the South's leading contender, generated much enthusiasm within the party. Yet the major state party leaders were painfully aware that Senator Kefauver was the front-running candidate and that in order to head off the Tennessee senator they needed an alternate candidate with broad appeal to major factions within the party and among political independents. Throughout the primary season Governor Adlai E. Stevenson of Illinois, the eventual nominee, time and again disclaimed interest in the presidency; only the persistence of a small, volunteer, home state Stevenson for President Committee kept his draft campaign alive.

Three weeks before the convention Stevenson read a statement at the National Governors' conference in Houston, saying, "I have not nor will I participate, overtly or covertly, in any movement to draft me."[36] Three days before the Chicago convention he reiterated, "I'll do everything possible to discourage any delegate from putting me in nomination."[37] Nevertheless, Stevenson's name bobbed up repeatedly on presidential handicappers' lists. As governor of the host state to the 1952 Democratic convention in Chicago, Stevenson greeted the delegates at the opening session with a graceful, literate welcoming address. Still reluctant to run, Stevenson nevertheless gave a weak go-ahead signal two days later, after Governor Henry F. Schricker of Indiana nominated him. Thirteen other Democratic hopefuls, including Kefauver, Vice President Alben W. Barkley and Hubert Humphrey, were also nominated. Kefauver led on the first two ballots, but Stevenson, aided by strong backstage support from President Truman, carried the nomination on the third ballot with 617.5 votes of the total 1,230. Stevenson had been drafted with only one and one-half votes to spare!

The draft of Adlai Stevenson may well have been the last presidential draft in this century. As one observer put it some years ago, "The mass news media . . . have made it difficult for a draft candidate to play possum, and they have left him no place to hide."[38] Because national television makes everything immediate and visible, the coy candidate who trifles with the public and feigns disinterest in the presidency will probably be taken at his word and dismissed from mind as a presidential contender. Outright dissembling with the public while waiting, hope against hope, for draft-like conditions to develop will probably create a stronger negative public reaction.

In 1976, Senator Hubert H. Humphrey, while not ruling out a presidential bid even after his "final" withdrawal statement in late April, appeared to be banking his last flickering hopes for reaching the White House on a last-minute "Draft Humphrey" surge. But, alas, Jimmy Carter's decisive victory in the Pennsylvania primary knocked out Senator Henry "Scoop" Jackson, the last potential road-blocking opponent who might have created the needed convention deadlock to open the way for Humphrey's nomination.

In light of widespread talk of drafting Senator Edward M. "Ted" Kennedy to replace President Jimmy Carter as the 1980 Democratic nominee, however, it may be premature to write the final obituary for the draft candidate. To qualify the point, however, most of the "Draft Kennedy" scenarios have focused on an early Kennedy entry into the 1980 presidential primaries, not a traditional convention draft. Before Kennedy officially entered the race in November 1979, Kennedy supporters predicated their strategy on President Carter's continued faltering performance in the opinion polls and a Kennedy write-in victory in the New Hampshire primary. According to their now discarded script, Kennedy was to have been drafted to enter the second round of presidential primaries to head off California Governor Edmund G. "Jerry" Brown and push Carter into involuntary retirement. Thus, if all had gone according to the original plan, the youthful Massachusetts senator would have arrived at the 1980 Democratic convention as the party's uncrowned nominee. Under these circumstances the two prerequisites listed earlier in the chapter for the traditional draft candidate—a convention deadlock or a plethora of candidates with none possessing outstanding qualifications—would still remain valid.

In any case, it seems unlikely in the years ahead that a last-minute draft candidate, no matter how carefully he charts his course, will be able to overcome the tremendous momentum that the victor of the presidential primaries generates in the mass media and persuade a large number of pledged national convention delegates to suddenly switch their political allegiance. Mandated to select a nominee who has all the earmarks of a "winner," most convention delegates are not going to discard casually a presidential aspirant who has successfully tested his vote-getting strength in the primaries and caucus-convention states for an untested, long-shot draft candidate. Similarly, as discussed earlier in the chapter, the presidential prospects of unannounced candidates, late entries, favorite sons, and dark horse candidates have also nearly vanished in the era of presidential primary-media politics.

Notes

1. Henry F. Graff, "Playing Political Possum Isn't Easy," New York *Times Magazine,* June 16, 1960, p. 13.

2. New York *Times,* March 22, 1956.

3. Charles A. H. Thomson and Frances M. Shattuck, *The 1956 Presidential Campaign* (Washington, D.C.: Brookings Institution, 1960), pp. 65-66.

4. Theodore H. White, *The Making of the President, 1960* (New York: Atheneum, 1961), pp. 38-39.

5. New York *Times,* March 27, 1960.

6. But often Kennedy referred to all of his inactive opponents. "If the voters don't love them in March, April, or May," he told a New Hampshire audience, "they won't love them in November." Theodore C. Sorenson, *Kennedy* (New York: Harper & Row, 1965), p. 128.

7. New York *Times,* December 10, 1963.

8. "I Am a Candidate," *Time* 83 (June 19, 1964): 13-14.

9. St. Paul *Pioneer Press,* January 24, 1964.

10. New York *Times,* March 6, 1964.

11. Ibid., March 12, 1964.

12. Minneapolis *Morning Tribune,* May 11, 1964.

13. New York *Times,* July 3, 1964.

14. "I Am a Candidate," p. 15.

15. New York *Times,* July 3, 1964.

16. Lewis Chester, Godfrey Hodgson, and Bruce Page, *An American Melodrama* (New York: Viking Press, 1969), p. 199.

17. Ibid., p. 437.

18. Herbert E. Alexander, *Financing the 1972 Election* (Lexington, Mass.: D. C. Heath, 1976), pp. 194-97.

19. Ibid., p. 195.

20. New York *Times,* March 4, April 29, 1976. Gary R. Oren, who served as a consultant for the New York *Times*/CBS polls during the 1976 presidential primaries, reports that when the interviewers asked primary voters whether they would have voted for Humphrey if he had been on the ballot, the pollsters discovered that "Humphrey would theoretically have won every primary save New Hampshire's occurring before the end of his 'active-noncandidacy' on April 30." Afterwards, according to Oren, "Carter's support, which had been 'soft' in face of Humphrey's potential candidacy, dramatically crystallized." Gary R. Oren, "Candidate Style and Voter Alignment," in *Emerging Coalitions in American Politics,* ed. Seymour Martin Lipset (San Francisco: Institute for Contemporary Studies, 1978), p. 149.

21. New York *Times,* April 30, 1976.

22. Ibid., March 19, 1976.

23. Ibid.

24. Ibid., June 15, 1976.

25. Ibid., March 14, 1976.

26. "Stampede to Carter," *Time* 107 (June 21, 1976): 9.

27. Material in this section is based, in considerable part, upon the discussion of favorite sons found in Paul T. David, Malcolm Moos, and Ralph M. Goldman, eds., *Presidential Nominating Politics in 1952,* 5 vols. (Baltimore: The Johns Hopkins University Press, 1954), 1: 186-88. Additional information on favorite-son candidates may be obtained in Clarence A. Berdahl, "Presidential Selection and Democratic Government," *Journal of Politics* 11 (February 1949): 35-40.

28. Martin Schram, *Running for President* (New York: Pocket Books, 1976), p. 166.

29. See *Call to Order*, Commission on Rules of the Democratic National Committee, James G. O'Hara, Chairman (Washington, D. C.: Democratic National Committee, 1972), pp. 56-57.

30. Detroit *Free Press,* August 17, 1972.

31. Paul T. David, Ralph M. Goldman, and Richard C. Bain, *The Politics of National Nominating Conventions* (Washington, D. C.: Brookings Institution, 1960), p. 119.

32. Ibid., p. 432.

33. Graff, "Playing Political Possum," p. 9.

34. Louise Overacker, *The Presidential Primary* (New York: Macmillan, 1926), pp. 37-38.

35. Richard C. Bain and Judith H. Parris, *Convention Decisions and Voting Records,* 2nd ed. (Washington, D. C.: Brookings Institution, 1973), p. 197.

36. David, Moos, and Goldman, *Presidential Nominating Politics,* p. 109.

37. Ibid., p. 110.

38. Graff, "Playing Political Possum," p. 41.

Presidential Nominating _____ 9
Finance

The bicentennial year 1976, commemorating the Republic's two hundredth anniversary, also marked the dividing line between new and old styles of financing presidential nominating campaigns. On the surface, the sharply contested primaries in both parties and the marathon coast-to-coast campaigning looked and sounded very much like past national campaigns, but these pre-convention races were conducted under a fundamentally different set of ground rules which almost certainly affected the final outcome. Candidates seeking presidential nominations from the two major parties in 1976 spent $66.9 million—an all-time record—even though new federal spending limits were imposed in the primaries.[1] But more important than this huge outlay of money, the passage of the 1974 Federal Election Campaign Act, with its matching dollar-for-dollar federal subsidy feature and its $1,000 ceiling on individual campaign contributions to a presidential candidate, produced a radical change in nominating finance.[2] Before the 1976 primary season opened Congress decided, in the aftermath of the Watergate scandals, that candidates without personal wealth or rich associates deserved some federal financial support during the primaries. In supporting matching federal subsidies for primary campaigns, the congressional majority left no doubt that absolute limits should be imposed on candidates with unlimited resources so that promising outsider candidates would not be wiped out automatically, as often in the past, by better financed, better known competitors.

New Financial Ground Rules for Primary Campaigns

For the first time in history, presidential candidates in 1976 were able to collect matching federal funds, up to $5 million, if they first raised $100,000 on their own initiative—$5,000 in each of twenty states in denominations of $250 or less. Federal subsidies had widespread ramifications on candidate strategy and fund-raising tactics. Indeed, the establishment of federal matching funds helped Jimmy Carter, an obscure former governor of Georgia, to win the Democratic nomination despite his narrow initial base of geographical and financial support.

As expected, the get-rich-quick appeal of Uncle Sam's matching dollars for the presidential nominating race attracted a record number of presidential contenders, thirteen aspirants in the out-of-power Democratic party. The same public subsidization of primary competition also helped Ronald Reagan, the former GOP governor of California, mount an intense nomination challenge against President Gerald Ford which very narrowly missed toppling the incumbent president.

Federal matching dollars also encouraged candidates, including those with marginal financial resources, to throw their hats in the ring far in advance of the spring nominating season. By February 1975, seventeen months before the 1976 nominating convention, five Democratic presidential hopefuls (Udall, Carter, Harris, Jackson and Bentsen) had already entered the fray, even though under the new law no U. S. Treasury matching dollars could be released until January 1976.

Equally important, the new law's $1,000 limitation on individual contributions forced a major revision in pre-convention—as well as general election—fund-raising tactics. The 1974 law made it impossible for a few wealthy contributors to bankroll or "buy a piece of the candidate" in the primaries. Formerly, the lesser known, outsider candidate could turn to a handful of financial "angels" to underwrite his campaign; for instance, in 1968 Senator Eugene McCarthy obtained more than $300,000 from Stewart Mott, son of a General Motors magnate. Four years later, Mott gave Senator George McGovern over $400,000 for his pre-convention drive.[3] But with the big contributions banned, a McCarthy or McGovern-type candidate could no longer rely on his millionaire friends to supply the six-figure sums that served so effectively as "seed money" and day-to-day operating funds in the 1968 and 1972 pre-convention races. However, the new limit on individual contributions, as indicated earlier, did not result in the drying up of pre-convention campaign funds.

The thirteen Democratic presidential hopefuls who qualified for federal matching funds in 1976 spent $40.7 million, $8 million more than their Democratic counterparts in 1972 (see Table 9.1). The two Republican contenders, President Ford and Ronald Reagan, spent over $26 million— compared with the $5 million spent by President Nixon's campaign staff in 1972, when he had only token opposition. Various independent and minor party candidates accounted for the remaining $5 million pre-convention expenditures in 1976. Further evidence that the new campaign

TABLE 9.1

**MAJOR PRESIDENTIAL CANDIDATES' PRE-NOMINATION
FINANCES, JANUARY 1, 1975 THROUGH AUGUST 30, 1976
(IN MILLIONS OF DOLLARS)**

Candidate	Receipts	Expenditures	Matching Funds Received
Ronald Reagan	$14.2	$12.6	$ 5.1
Gerald R. Ford	14.0	13.6	4.6
Jimmy Carter	11.6	11.4	3.4
George C. Wallace	7.8	7.9	3.3
Henry M. Jackson	5.4	6.2	2.0
Morris K. Udall	4.6	4.5	1.9
Lloyd Bentsen	1.6	2.4	0.5
Edmund G. Brown, Jr.	1.7	1.8	0.6
Frank Church	1.5	1.5	0.6
Fred Harris	1.4	1.4	0.6
Birch Bayh	1.2	1.1	0.5
Milton J. Shapp	0.9	0.8	0.3
Terry Sanford	0.6	0.6	0.2
R. Sargent Shriver	0.8	0.6	0.3
Ellen McCormack	0.5	0.2	0.2
Total	$67.8	$66.9	$24.1

Source: FEC Disclosure Series, No. 7: *1976 Presidential Campaign Receipts and Expenditures*, Washington, D. C.: Federal Election Commission, May 1977, pp. 11, 15-17.

reform act was not an insurmountable barrier to fund raising during the 1976 pre-convention period can be found in the fact that nine Democratic hopefuls raised at least $1 million each—another record. Carter led all Democratic contenders, spending $11.4 million, followed by Governor George Wallace with expenditures of $7.9 million and Senator Jackson with $6.2 million. Overall, federal matching funds accounted for $24.1 million, approximately one-third of all pre-convention funds raised.

Campaign finance experts and political aides inside and outside Jimmy Carter's campaign agree that the new federal election law in 1976 reduced the built-in advantage that otherwise might have gone to presidential candidates with established power bases, for example, the chairman of a powerful congressional committee, such as Senator Henry Jackson. Under the old system, special interest groups normally funneled campaign funds to influential legislators, since these favors were useful even if the chairman did not reach the White House. The new law, which limits both total spending and the size of individual contributions, also protected

Mr. Carter's campaign from a money blitz by Democratic contenders who formerly had access to big money contributors. As explained by Carter's campaign treasurer, Robert Lipshutz, "Several of our opponents had the potential for attracting big money, more than we did and the limits helped equalize the competition."[4]

The new law's leveling influence gave Mr. Carter an even chance against such established Democratic aspirants as Senators Jackson, Bayh, and Bentsen, and R. Sargent Shriver, the 1972 Democratic vice presidential nominee. Furthermore, Mr. Carter conducted an effective, frugal campaign that enabled him to stretch his dollars further than most of his intraparty opponents. Carter, for example, paid his chief campaign staffers only one-third the salaries Senator Jackson's top aides received.[5] As a result, the Carter campaign faced no severe cash crunch during the nine-week freeze on federal subsidies from mid-March to late May when federal matching funds were cut off following the Supreme Court's partial invalidation of the 1974 Federal Election Campaign Act. By contrast, Representative Morris Udall, starved for campaign funds during the nine-week matching fund moratorium, found it necessary to forage off the land as best he could, relying almost exclusively on limited direct-mail solicitations from his liberal Democratic supporters. In the future, presidential contenders will probably not have to face the shut-off of federal matching funds experienced by the 1976 aspirants. But federal primary campaign subsidies still cannot be regarded as a panacea for presidential contenders. While the subsidies provided several million dollars to candidates who had raised funds early, such as Senator Jackson and Governor Wallace, the federal matching funds could not compensate ultimately for the candidates' failure to attract votes in the primaries. Even Governor Wallace's $7.9 million expenditure and Senator Jackson's campaign outlay of $6.2 million failed to save their candidacies.

While several candidates found themselves woefully short of campaign funds in the primaries as a result of a U.S. Supreme Court decision in January 1976, the real cash flow problem for several Democratic aspirants could be more directly attributed to their poor showings in the early primaries. Senator Birch Bayh of Indiana, heavily in debt after only two primaries—he finished third in New Hampshire and fourth in Massachusetts—abandoned his campaign before the New York primary, where he was expected to do well. Pennsylvania Governor Milton Shapp, R. Sargent Shriver, and former North Carolina Governor Terry Sanford, all facing serious financial problems, also dropped out of the race in the first quarter. Former Oklahoma Senator Fred Harris, flat out of money, put his candidacy on "inactive status" after the early Massachusetts primary in hopes of replenishing his treasury. But he was never able to attract the money needed to resume active campaigning.

Federal subsidies created a financial illusion in the minds of most contenders. In 1975, the year before the presidential election, the eleven active Democratic and Republican candidates raised a total of $13,337,000. But these same eleven hopefuls spent $12,992,000 of the $13,337,000 in 1975. By the time the 1976 primary season opened most of these Democratic candidates were in financial straits. The candidates had been lulled into a false sense of financial security by the impending federal subsidies. After defeats in the early primaries these candidates, unable to attract additional money and faced with big campaign debts, had no choice but to withdraw. By contrast, Carter's successful campaign fund-raising activities during the first four months of 1976 helped him widen his front-runner lead over his competitors. Carter's contributions increased from $125,000 in January to $400,000 in February, $612,000 in March, and $732,000 in April 1976.[6] If one lesson stands out above all others in pre-convention campaign management during 1976, it would be the need for a candidate to have a secure financial base. Jimmy Carter, the successful Democratic nominee, frequently turned to his home state of Georgia to sustain his drive for the presidency. As one veteran reporter put it, "At several junctures in the campaign—particularly during the early months, as Mr. Carter struggled to become a viable, known candidate—contributions from Georgians were crucial."[7] Georgia money was especially vital throughout 1975, when his home state contributors gave almost half of the $900,000 Mr. Carter collected between January and November. Carter's home state contributions were also indispensable in April 1976, when court action temporarily cut off matching federal money just as the crucial Pennsylvania primary campaign was getting under way. Fellow Georgians contributed about half the $465,000 Mr. Carter spent to win in Pennsylvania. Other Democratic contenders in that contest, notably Senator Jackson, were hamstrung by a lack of campaign funds.

According to Robert Lipshutz, Carter's campaign treasurer, almost one of every five dollars collected by Mr. Carter during the pre-nomination period came from Georgia. Put another way, Georgians gave $1.5 million of the $7.9 million of private funds collected before the Democratic convention in New York City. "If one had to choose the single most important element to Jimmy Carter's successful drive for the Democratic presidential nomination," Lipshutz said in an analysis of the campaign's financing, "it would have to be the unwavering support and tremendous generosity of Jimmy Carter's fellow Georgians."[8]

Five Democratic candidates—Carter, Wallace, Jackson, Udall and Bentsen—raised or spent at least $2 million each in their quest for the nomination. But the other four were unable to maintain Carter's pace once the heavy spending in the early primaries had drained their war chests. The truth of the matter is that without a smooth fund-raising operation there is no way in the midst of the furious primaries for candidates to replenish their treasuries fast enough, since the costly primaries run almost consecutively for fifteen Tuesdays from late February until early June. The new 1974 Federal Election Campaign Act with its $1,000 limit on individual contributions makes the fast raising of large sums of money extremely difficult, as most candidates discovered in the 1976 nominating race. To be sure, federal matching funds have become an integral part of the candidate's financial arsenal. But the records of the Federal Election Commission reveal these funds constitute only slightly more than one-third of the funds spent by the six leading Democratic contenders, except for Governor George Wallace, who, with his well-geared direct mail operation, received almost half of his campaign money from Uncle Sam.

Before the 1976 presidential primary season opened, campaign finance experts freely predicted that the federal matching subsidies would encourage more candidates to enter early and stay in the race longer because Uncle Sam would be picking up half of the tab. Even if the candidate captured only small batches of delegates in the primaries under the party's new proportional representation rules, many veteran party watchers reasoned that these also-ran candidates would hang on longer, hoping against hope that they might be able to win some late-round primaries. Experience in the 1976 Democratic pre-convention race, however, showed a faster candidate attrition rate than four years earlier. In 1972 the first drop-out, Democratic New York Mayor John Lindsay, did not pull out of the race until after the Wisconsin primary in early April. To be sure, the primary season started earlier in 1976 because New Hampshire moved its primary ahead one week and Massachusetts shifted from a late April to early March primary, but by mid-March six Democratic hopefuls— Bentsen, Bayh, Shapp, Sanford, Harris and Shriver—had withdrawn from the race or shifted to an inactive status. Early shrinkage of the candidate field could probably be attributed as much, if not more, to repeated defeats in the primaries as to the shortage of campaign funds. Indeed, these two factors are directly related. Inadequate campaign funds lead to defeats in the primaries. Weak showings in the primaries, in turn, seriously reduce the flow of campaign money. Based upon the experience of a single primary season, it seems evident that matching federal funds under the new law are not in and of themselves sufficient financial nourishment to keep weak candidates in the race until convention time.

Did the federal program open up the nominating process? Did it give more candidates a fair chance to capture the grand prize? On paper, at least, the answer would appear to be in the affirmative. But it seems doubtful that the Democratic contenders who fell by the wayside early in the race—Bayh, Shriver, Shapp, Bentsen, Harris and Sanford—think the new campaign reform law improved their chances. The truth of the matter is that under either the old laissez faire system or the new subsidy system the ability to raise large sums of pre-convention funds privately is a basic prerequisite for winning the nomination. Even with the passage of the federal matching funds law, candidates must still develop efficient fund-raising operations if they are to have enough staying power to become serious contenders. Unless drastic revisions are made in the 1974 Federal Election Campaign Act, the lesson learned once again in 1976 will probably prove equally valid for some time to come.

Ability to raise big money—$6-10 million—during the pre-convention period is still a major factor in affecting the outcome of the presidential nominating race. Indeed, a big campaign war chest collected by the individual candidate and his staff are as likely to shape our political choices during the primary season as they did in the days when there were no federal matching subsidies or public disclosure laws.

With the spread of primaries to more than thirty states, candidates will now have to stretch their budgets to the limit. After Senator Edmund S. Muskie, the early 1972 front-runner, faltered so badly trying to campaign in over twenty primaries, party experts were convinced that in future pre-convention races candidates would have to pick and choose their primaries more carefully or risk financial bankruptcy. Muskie, after a narrow victory in New Hampshire and three fourth-place finishes in Florida, Wisconsin and Pennsylvania, discovered that his $7 million campaign war chest was empty. He withdrew from active campaigning following his defeat in the Pennsylvania primary. One of the major reasons given for Muskie's failure in 1972 was that he had tried to campaign in too many primaries, that he spread his money too thinly in those primaries. Four years later, however, former Georgia Governor Jimmy Carter defied the political experts and campaigned in all of the primary states except West Virginia, chalking up seventeen victories in his successful nomination drive.

The other leading 1976 contenders, frightened by Muskie's ill-fated experience in 1972, were fairly selective in picking primaries to enter. Privately, they discounted Carter's run-everywhere strategy just as they underestimated Carter as a serious contender before the opening of the primary season. But, when the former Georgia governor triumphed in the mid-January Iowa precinct caucuses and captured the early-round New Hampshire, Vermont and Florida primaries, the political experts and his rival contenders realized that Carter had clearly outmaneuvered them.

When Carter knocked Senator Jackson out of the Pennsylvania primary in late April and then continued to pick up primary victories in the Southern states, even though his new rivals, Senator Frank Church and California

Governor Jerry Brown, defeated him in Nebraska, Maryland, Idaho, Montana, Nevada, Oregon and California, the political pundits finally acknowledged that it was indeed possible to run everywhere—and still win the nomination. But to do so requires not only a combination of skillful handling of the issues, masterful use of the national media, frugal management of campaign and staff expenditures, and an effective grassroots organization in the primary states, but also, as indicated earlier, an efficient fund-raising committee.

Carter's heaviest primary campaign expenditures were, in order: California, $654,000; Florida, $568,000; Ohio, $534,000; Pennsylvania, $465,000; New York $464,000; New Jersey, $431,000; Maryland, $212,000; and New Hampshire, $209,000.⁹ It will be noted that Carter lost three of the six states in which he had invested the largest sums—California, New York and New Jersey. But, under the Democratic party's new proportional representation rules, Carter nevertheless collected almost 200 delegates from these three states. Thus, the expenditure of $1,547,000 in these three states was far from a business loss to Carter. Even though the costs of campaigning all across the land are high and the danger of political mine fields along the campaign trail are ever present, the possibility of winning the richest prize of all, the presidential nomination, will probably induce many future candidates to throw caution to the winds and adopt the Carter run-everywhere strategy.

Though it had been predicted that the limits on spending imposed by the Federal Election Campaign Act would lead to reduced pre-convention expenditures, President Ford and Ronald Reagan, the two GOP contenders, spent $26.2 million dueling for the Republican nomination. Reagan led all the fund raisers. Although Reagan's bid to unseat Ford fell short by 117 delegates at the GOP convention, the former California governor raised $14.2 million, including $5.1 million collected in federal matching subsidies. An avowed opponent of big government, Reagan nevertheless accepted the $5.1 million subsidy; indeed, with the new $1,000 limit on individual contributions, it seems unlikely that he could have mounted as hard-hitting a national campaign as he did without Uncle Sam's money.

Regulation of Nominating Finance

It was the early twentieth-century Progressive movement, spawned largely out of protests over the close relationship between big business and the government, that first aroused serious public interest in the role of money in politics. Huge under-the-table corporate campaign contributions to pervert the voter's will in state legislatures were, the Progressives declared, undermining the democratic process. Progressive leaders, such as Senator Robert M. LaFollette, Sr., of Wisconsin, and Governor Hiram Johnson of California, proposed the adoption of the direct primary, including the presidential primary, to help neutralize corporate political power and return political responsibility to the people. But the Progressives soon learned that presidential primary nominating campaigns cost as much, if not more, than the special interest-dominated caucus-convention system. The Progressive movement died out long before any effective public action was taken to deal with the crucial role of big money in presidential nominations. Indeed, more than half a century passed before public attention was again focused on this critical issue. Not until the Watergate scandals erupted following President Richard Nixon's landslide reelection in 1972 did Congress see fit to grapple seriously with nomination and election finance.

Until passage of the Federal Election Campaign Act of 1971, federal corrupt practices acts did not cover presidential primaries. Early in the twentieth century an amendment to the Corrupt Practices Act of 1907, passed in 1911, extended coverage to primaries and conventions for the nomination. But in 1921, the Supreme Court's decision in *Newberry* v. *United States,* involving excessive expenditures in a Michigan senatorial primary election, cast doubt on the right of Congress to regulate federal nominations.[10] Congress cleared up this misunderstanding in the Corrupt Practices Act of 1925, by specifically exempting congressional nominations from the coverage of the law. Until 1955, when Congress passed a law to permit a presidential primary in the District of Columbia, federal lawmakers had not seen fit to intrude into this field of legislation. The traditional attitude of Congress had been that only by constitutional amendment could the federal government regulate presidential primaries. After passage of the Federal Election Campaign Act of 1971, which set limits on the amount of money a presidential candidate could spend on mass media advertising in presidential primary campaigning, the constitutional issue of federal regulation virtually disappeared—until the court challenges against the new 1974 law.

In late 1971, Congress also took its first step toward helping candidates raise funds by authorizing tax credits to encourage more citizens to contribute to candidates of their choice. Under the Revenue Act of 1971, an individual taxpayer was allowed to take a tax credit of $12.50 ($25 for a joint return) or a deduction of $50 ($100 for a joint return) for political contributions in primaries or general elections.[11] Signed into law in February 1972, the new legislation came too late to provide much financial help in the 1972 nominating race, especially for the out-of-power Democrats.

Though the direct connection between the Senate Watergate investigation and presidential primary finance was not clearly perceived during the televised hearings, the first real breakthrough in the public funding of presidential nominating races came as a result of the Watergate scandals. Testimony collected by the Senate Watergate Investigation Committee in 1973 revealed that huge, illegal contributions had been made by corporate donors during the 1972 primary and general elections. These startling revelations provoked widespread demands, both inside and outside Congress, for campaign reform. Even long-time opponents to public financing, such as conservative columnist James J. Kilpatrick, conceded, "It is an idea whose time has just about come."[12]

Congress passed its first public subsidy campaign finance bill in late 1974. Reluctantly signed by President Ford, the measure (1) provides a public subsidy of $20 million (later adjusted upward slightly to reflect inflationary costs) for the general election to Republican and Democratic presidential candidates, with lesser amounts to minor party candidates, and limits presidential candidate spending to $20 million each in the general election and $10 million (later adjusted upward to $10,910,000) each in the nomination race; (2) provides for federal matching subsidies, dollar for dollar, up to a $5 million limit, for every candidate who can first raise $5,000 in individual contributions of $250 or less in each of twenty states for a total of $100,000; (3) permits presidential candidates to spend another $2 million (also adjusted upward to reflect increased costs) to underwrite fund-raising costs during the pre-convention period; (4) authorizes the expenditure of $2 million in federal funds to underwrite costs of each major party's national nominating convention; (5) limits individual contributions to $1,000 to a candidate for federal office in any primary, run-off or general election campaign; (6) curbs the advantage wealthy candidates have enjoyed in presidential nominating races by limiting to $50,000 the amount a presidential candidate can contribute to his own campaign; thus, the huge family fortunes of a John F. Kennedy or a Nelson A. Rockefeller can no longer be used to the same degree to advance the presidential ambitions of their "favorite son"; and (7) establishes an independent agency—the Federal Election Commission—to administer the new system.[13]

Passage of the Federal Campaign Finance Reform Act of 1974, with its provision for public financing of presidential primaries, subsequently upheld by the Supreme Court, removed any lingering doubt about the constitutionality of Congress moving into the area of pre-convention campaigning. In signing the 1974 act, however, President Ford expressed reservations that the $10 million spending ceiling for presidential primary campaigning and the $1,000 limit on individual contributions might impinge on First Amendment guarantees of free speech.[14] Critics of the new campaign law, led by former Democratic presidential candidate Eugene McCarthy, challenged its constitutionality the day after it went into effect on the grounds that it violated First Amendment rights. However, in a landmark decision, handed down January 30, 1976, the Supreme Court upheld public financing of presidential primary and general elections, the limits on how much may be contributed by individuals to any election race, and strict requirements for reporting both contributions and expenditures.[15] At the same time, however, the high court struck down as unconstitutional all limits on spending in a campaign for president—with one major exception: The court ruled that presidential candidates who accept federal financing—matching funds in the primaries and full payment of the campaign bill in the general election—must abide by congressionally established limits on spending. It is noteworthy that all Democratic and Republican candidates for president in 1976 accepted federal subsidies and thereby came under the spending limits prescribed in the new law. The Supreme Court also ruled that the Federal Election Commission, created to implement the reform legislation, had to be restructured within thirty days or cease exercising all but a few of its powers. Subsequent disagreement between President Ford and Congress over this invalidated section of the law caused a nine-week freeze on federal matching subsidies. But Supreme Court approval of the Federal Election Campaign Act of 1974 marked the beginning of a new era in presidential primary and general election campaign finance. In some respects, however, the old system of private financing of presidential nominating races was not that much different from the new era of federal subsidies, at least in the overall cost of pre-convention nominating races. Both methods were expensive, as will soon be explained.

Soaring Costs of Primary Campaigning

In his losing try for the 1976 Democratic nomination, Senator Henry Jackson spent $1.34 million in February and $1.1 million in March 1976, an outlay of $2.4 million in two months. The high cost of primary campaigning, however, is not a new phenomenon. As early as 1920, Republican aspirant General Leonard Wood, the General Douglas MacArthur of his era, spent a total of about $1,773,000 (in an era with a much lower cost of living) in the thirteen primary states where he campaigned. Primary expenses have continued to mount as jet air transportation, chartered buses, increased mail and phone costs, higher office rents and hotel bills, large full-time campaign staffs and the skyrocketing cost of television broadcasts consume huge bundles of money. The passage of the new federal matching fund law has helped alleviate—but not remove—the high cost of seeking the presidential nomination.

For a candidate of modest means the rising costs of presidential primary campaigning have become a critical problem in several ways. Above all else, a presidential candidate must base his strategy on realistic estimates of available money. High costs have often determined how many primaries he could enter and, more importantly, reduced his chances of winning the nomination. In 1960, for example, in announcing his first try for the presidency, Senator Hubert H. Humphrey stated that the number of primaries he would enter was contingent on available campaign funds. After declaring he would enter the primaries in Wisconsin, the District of Columbia, Oregon and South Dakota, Humphrey added,

I would like to enter other primaries. But each of these is an election contest in itself and is expensive. Quite frankly, the financial resources available to me are limited. If financial support permits, I will enter other primaries and will make known my decision on these when the time comes.[16]

Not only did money affect the number of primaries a candidate could realistically enter, it also influenced campaign strategy. A candidate with limited means could not afford a full-scale television and radio advertising campaign unless he had the money in hand. Regulations of the Federal Communications Commission require that all broadcasting time be paid in full before the candidate goes on the air. Moreover, this advertising time must be booked weeks in advance to assure "prime-time" listener coverage for spot ads and also to prevent rival candidates from buying up all available time. Airlines also now require pre-payment of leased campaign aircraft (approximately $50,000 a week for a Boeing 727), and phone companies insist on huge deposits before phone banks are installed in a campaign headquarters.

One observer has suggested that a wealthy candidate in the past has also enjoyed an important psychological advantage over his opponents. In 1960, Hubert Humphrey dared not risk incurring a large debt because he still needed to seek reelection to the U.S. Senate if his quest for the presidency failed; but the wealthy Kennedy could confidently undertake expensive primary contests because he knew he could always draw on his own private fortune or that of his family.[17] In other words, Senator Kennedy could threaten to invade favorite-son states, such as California and Ohio, and run the risk of the heavy expense, if necessary, in challenging the state organizations. As it turned out, the Ohio Democratic leader, Governor Michael DiSalle, capitulated without a primary fight and agreed to head a slate pledged to Kennedy. In California Senator Kennedy, after threatening to enter this West Coast primary, came to an "understanding" with Governor Edmund G. "Pat" Brown, assuring partial delegation support without an expensive primary fight. It has been estimated that avoidance of these two primary battles alone saved Kennedy at least $1 million—probably more.[18]

Campaign finance expert Alexander Heard was certainly correct in 1960 when he observed that "no person can actively seek a presidential nomination without a good deal more money at his disposal than most politicians can command."[19] Even if a candidate had the resources of a Kennedy or a Nelson Rockefeller, he had to depend on a corps of wealthy backers and personal admirers who were willing to contribute generously of their money and time, and sometimes their time could be more valuable than a cash contribution during this crucial launching period. The presidential candidate who contested the primaries without these wealthy backers entered with an almost insurmountable handicap. But with the passage of the 1974 Federal Election Campaign Act prohibiting all contributions exceeding $1,000 the ground rules for seeking the presidency changed. In return for the ban on big contributions Congress agreed to provide candidates with matching federal funds, up to $5 million, to help underwrite their presidential primary campaigning expenses. That the new law did not dry up campaign contributions is evidenced by the record-breaking receipts of $67.8 million collected in 1976. But the problem of zooming primary costs still remains.

Let's take a brief look at the record of campaign costs over the past fifty years. From 1928 through 1948, the approximate cost of participating in a single contested presidential primary rose from $50,000 to $100,000. Part of this increase could be attributed to inflation. But, since World War II and the era of mass communication, public relations men, advertising agencies and the massive increase in the number of people reaching voting age, presidential primary candidates have been forced to spend larger and larger sums in primary campaigns and general elections to compete for audience attention. By 1960, the cost of a single primary against a top-flight opponent had risen to $200,000. Four years later, the average cost of a single contested primary jumped to over $400,000 and, barring legal ceilings, showed no sign of declining in future campaigns. Until passage of the Federal Election Campaign Act of 1971, which imposed a ceiling on mass media expenditures, most campaign managers felt $1 million was the rock bottom cost (some experts said this figure was too low) for mounting a California-sized primary.

To illustrate where the money goes, the 1964 California Goldwater committees' $1 million expenditures were divided as follows: television and radio, $400,000; staff salaries and expenses, $200,000; headquarters and publicity, $400,000. An additional $1 million raised by the local Goldwater committees in California went for printing, television, billboards, office space, telephone and postage.[20] In 1972, Senator McGovern spent an all-time high amount for a single state in the California primary, $4,175,000. This sum constituted 35 percent of the total cost of McGovern's

TABLE 9.2
1972 PRE-CONVENTION EXPENDITURES BY
DEMOCRATIC PRESIDENTIAL CANDIDATES
(THOUSANDS OF DOLLARS)

Candidate	Expenditures
George McGovern	12,000
Edmund Muskie	7,000
George Wallace	2,400
Henry Jackson	1,500
John Lindsay	1,000
Terry Sanford	850
Wilbur Mills	730
Birch Bayh	710
Eugene McCarthy	475
Fred Harris	330
Shirley Chisholm	300
Vance Harke	260
Sam Yorty	250
Harold Hughes	200
Patsy Mink	15
Wayne Hays	3
Edward Coll	2
Total	32,725

Source: Reprinted by permission of the publisher, from Herbert E. Alexander, *Financing the 1972 Election* (Lexington, Mass.: Lexington Books, D. C. Heath and Company, Copyright 1976, D. C. Heath and Company), p. 98.

drive for the nomination. In Table 9.2, both pre- and post-April 7, 1972 (the date new 1971 campaign law on media expenditures went into effect), expenditures are listed. The cost of maintaining Senator Muskie's national headquarters during his abortive quest for the presidency in 1971-72 was $2.5 million.[21]

The trend toward longer campaigns in most of the primary states has pushed pre-convention expenses to new highs. Unlike candidates Herbert Hoover and Alfred E. Smith in 1928, and Franklin D. Roosevelt in 1932, presidential candidates no longer can rely on "front porch" campaigns. Candidates begin to hit the campaign trail two years or more before the national convention. By January of the presidential election year they campaign virtually full time until the end of the primary season in June—unless they are knocked out of the race. The standard campaign practice of repeated, short visits to hotly contested primary states has boosted costs even higher. Frequent three-day visits, for example, marked the 1960 Wisconsin presidential primary campaigns of both Senators Kennedy and Humphrey. Between January 1 and April 5, 1960, Kennedy made seven stop-offs for a total of twenty days campaigning in Wisconsin. During the same period Senator Humphrey barnstormed the Badger State seven times for a total of twenty-eight days.

Four years later, Governor Nelson Rockefeller spent a total of twenty-four days (nine trips) between January 1 and mid-March in an unsuccessful attempt to capture the New Hampshire primary. His arch-rival, Senator Barry Goldwater, devoted eighteen days (five trips) in an equally futile effort to pull out a victory in this New England primary. In the 1964 GOP California primary, where these two political gladiators fought a no-holds-barred struggle to the finish, Goldwater followed his original battle plan and stumped the Golden State for a total of thirty days (twelve trips); the New York governor campaigned there twenty-five days (nine trips) between New Year's Day and early June 1964.

By 1972, the out-party Democratic presidential hopefuls—McGovern, Humphrey, Muskie and the lesser names—were campaigning at such a hectic pace that some citizens in primary states may have thought the candidates had taken up permanent residence in those states. Senator McGovern spent virtually every weekend in New Hampshire during the first eight weeks of the 1972 primary campaign, to say nothing of the frequent earlier visits in 1971. The McGovern and Humphrey presidential primary campaign caravans moved from one primary state to another, much as carnival shows shift from one county fair to the next. For the late-round California primary, with its grand prize of all 271 delegates, McGovern and Humphrey both tossed aside virtually all their duties in the U. S. Senate and spent the final two weeks of campaigning without interruption on the West Coast. Four years later, Jimmy Carter visited New Hampshire on more than a dozen separate occasions to campaign in the first-in-the-nation primary. Congressman Morris Udall equalled or exceeded Carter for the amount of time spent in this New England state. Several other key states—Massachusetts, Florida, Wisconsin, New York and Pennsylvania—received almost as much attention from the field of Democratic contenders. The two Republican antagonists, challenger Ronald Reagan and, to a lesser extent, President Ford, also devoted huge blocs of campaign time to New Hampshire, Florida and other crucial states.

Rising primary costs can be attributed, in large part, to inflation and the need for greater saturation advertising among the voters. Because so many mass-circulation newspapers, radio and television stations, billboards and direct-mail campaign literature now compete for the reader's or listener's attention, it is often necessary to advertise simultaneously in several newspapers and radio and television stations to increase the probability that the campaign message will reach the potential voter at least once.

Television and radio advertising are estimated to account for at least one-quarter (and sometimes more) of the cost of modern primary campaigning. In Jimmy Carter's 1976 pre-convention campaign, media advertising accounted for about one-third of the money spent in the primary states.[22] Prior to passage of the 1971 Federal Election Campaign Act limiting mass media expenditures in primaries and the general election, one veteran Washington newspaperman commented, "Television campaign expenses will continue to rise and their only limit, because of holes in the federal expenditures law, will be the availability of money."[23]

Private polling is another formidable campaign cost for presidential candidates. It has been estimated by one finance expert, Herbert E. Alexander, that in the 1960 primaries and general election between $1 million and $1.5 million was spent on political polls. Alexander calculated that private poll-taking costs in the 1964 primaries and general election at all levels totaled more than $5 million.[24] Polling costs continued at about this level through 1976.

Massive direct-mail solicitation—the path followed in 1972 by Senator McGovern and Governor George Wallace—appeared to be a trend-setting pattern. Both of these candidates had built up extensive mailing lists from their 1968 campaigns. By February 1972, the McGovern organization reported that appeals for help to more than 2 million potential contributors had netted $1.2 million.[25] These contributions furnished McGovern with a solid base of proven donors for future appeals, especially as McGovern approached the expensive, late-round primaries. Another purpose for announcing the list of donors was evidently to dramatize the broad base of McGovern's campaign. His contributor list of 42,000, according to his campaign manager, gave McGovern "about 40,000 more than anybody else."[26] Wallace, who spent $2.4 million on his 1972 pre-convention campaign, used direct-mail solicitation to pay almost 80 percent of this bill. Until recently, most presidential contenders have not been farsighted enough to develop computerized mailing lists; it was always easier to turn to the big contributors.

Late in 1975, Jimmy Carter enlisted the fund-raising services of Maurice Dees, the young, Southern direct-mail wizard who had raised millions by mail for Senator McGovern four years earlier. Unlike the direct-mail blitz of 1972, Mr. Dees focused Mr. Carter's money-raising effort on direct, personal solicitation by regional finance committees set up in various cities. According to Dees, direct mail was less valuable to a "centrist" candidate such as Mr. Carter or in a campaign that lacked a single compelling issue, such as the war in Vietnam.[27] Some of the most successful fund-raising events were the old political standbys—the $100-a-person cocktail party and the telethons. A local telethon in Georgia, called "Spend Valentine's Day with Jimmy Carter," yielded the campaign $328,000.

Mr. Carter's pre-convention fund raising was divided into three stages. In late 1974, while Mr. Carter was still governor, he and his aides raised some $47,000 to be used as a "nest egg" to pay for office space and a small staff. During 1975 Carter's supporters raised almost $1 million, mainly in Georgia, to underwrite the nationwide campaigning Mr. Carter was undertaking at the time. The heavy Carter financial push did not begin until Mr.Dees joined the Carter team. Dees's arrival coincided with the opening of the primary season. In the next eight months the Carter staff under his direction collected approximately $8 million, plus $3.4 million in federal matching funds.

As in previous campaigns, Governor Wallace relied heavily on direct-mail solicitations from his long-time supporters. Under the direction of Richard Viguerie, the Washington, D.C.-based direct-mail specialist for conservative causes, the Wallacites collected $4.3 million from January 1, 1975, through August 30, 1976. Most of this money was raised before Wallace's disastrous losses to Jimmy Carter in the Florida and North Carolina primaries. Senator Henry Jackson, who rivaled Wallace as a superb fund raiser in 1975, was unable to maintain the pace in early 1976. Although Jackson's fund raisers collected a grand total of approximately $6.2 million, including $2 million in federal subsidies, his treasury was virtually bare before the final two weeks of his showdown Pennsylvania primary battle against Carter. Jackson's loss in the Keystone State left his presidential quest in shambles; four days later he indicated that he was no longer an active candidate.

Sources of Funds

For more than a half a century surprisingly little was known about one of the most important ingredients for winning the presidential nomination: money. Until the publication in 1960 of Professor Alexander Heard's pioneering study, *The Costs of Democracy*,[28] nominating finance was a neglected phase of American politics. As Professor Heard observed, "The opaque mists that enshroud nomination finances in general also envelope presidential nominations."[29] More recently, Herbert E. Alexander's exhaustive research on campaign money has shed more light on presidential finances.[30] Over the years, however, candidates and their fund raisers have been extremely tight-lipped about the sources of their funds and the amount of their expenditures. There were sound political reasons for not revealing nominating costs. Many candidates were apprehensive that they would appear to be in a position of buying votes with huge campaign expenditures. This was particularly true of wealthy candidates who wished to avoid the charge that only money kept them afloat in the nominating race. In 1960, Senator John F. Kennedy was a target for such charges, even from within his own party. In the Wisconsin presidential primary, Senator Hubert H. Humphrey said that he was running not only against Jack Kennedy but against "Jack's jack."[31] Humphrey continued his attack against Kennedy in the West Virginia primary, declaring that he was running against "a suitcase full of money and an open-end checkbook" as well as against Kennedy's millionaire father, Joseph P. Kennedy. In the Oregon primary campaign, Senator Wayne B. Morse, the favorite-son candidate, accused Kennedy of "wallpapering" the state with money. In the general election campaign, Republicans had a field day using this ammunition originally produced by Kennedy's intraparty rivals. Although no evidence was unearthed to prove excessive Kennedy expenditures during the pre-convention race, the young Massachusetts senator was extremely sensitive to these charges.

Several candidates—Herbert Hoover, Franklin D. Roosevelt, Robert A. Taft, Adlai E. Stevenson, and Kennedy—have been wealthy men who could afford, if necessary, to invest their own funds in their nomination campaigns. On the other hand, candidates such as Senators Robert M. LaFollette, Hiram Johnson, Estes Kefauver, Hubert Humphrey, George McGovern and Morris Udall have been men of limited means who would not have been able to run for president without heavy private financial backing. Jimmy Carter, the peanut farmer-businessman-politician, would be classified as moderately wealthy; his assets, estimating conservatively, totaled $800,000. Without heavy support from fellow Georgians, however, he would not have made it past the early primaries.

Looking back into the earlier history of the presidential primary movement, Governor Franklin D. Roosevelt in 1932 depended almost exclusively on rich friends for financial support during his nomination drive. Leading contributors included Frank C. Walker, New York attorney and later postmaster general, $5,000, and William H. Woodin, industrialist and later secretary of the treasury, $5,000. Among Roosevelt's other financial "angels" were Joseph P. Kennedy, Boston financier and the father of the assassinated president; Edward J. Flynn, Democratic leader from the Bronx; Jesse I. Strauss, New York merchant; Robert W. Bingham, a Louisville publisher; and Herbert Lehman, who succeeded Roosevelt as governor of New York.[32]

The post-World War II period, marked by the growing importance of presidential primaries, has seen a much more wide open type of pre-convention campaigning. But there was not much more data available on sources of campaign funds until after passage of the Federal Election Campaign Act of 1971, which required listing the full name, address and occupation of all contributors after April 6, 1972, in campaign financial reports.

In 1952, General Eisenhower received his heaviest financial backing from Eastern industrialists, Midwestern automobile magnates and wealthy magazine publishers—the same group that had supported Dewey in 1948 and 1944, and Willkie in 1940. It was no secret that Senator Taft derived his major financial support from conservative Midwestern businessmen in all three of his presidential tries, 1940, 1948, and 1952. But his finance directors never gave out any figures.

It has been commonly assumed that Senator Estes Kefauver, a maverick Democrat, conducted his 1952 presidential primary race on a shoestring. This is not entirely true. As early as December 1951, Tennessee friends of Kefauver, led by Democratic Governor Gordon Browning, organized a testimonial dinner attended by 250 well-heeled Tennessee businessmen. Pledged to $1,000 apiece, they contributed $250,000, the sinews of Kefauver's hard-hitting primary campaign.[33]

Stevenson's 1956 presidential primary campaign consumed sizable amounts of money. The combined disbursement of the national Stevenson for President Committee and the Stevenson Campaign Committee came to $783,000. But no list of individual sources was released, although in December 1955 it was reported that Stevenson raised $100,000 during a three-day fund-raising tour of New York City.[34]

Before and after the 1960 Democratic convention, unconfirmed rumors circulated that the major cost of Senator Kennedy's extensive primary campaigning was picked up by his multimillionare father. However, the Kennedy family has denied this, and the data reported by the St. Louis *Post-Dispatch* after the 1960 convention tend to refute the charge. According to the newspaper, five Kennedy for President committees contributed $543,949 to the campaign.[35] Part of this amount came from Massachusetts Democrats, who allocated a quarter of the proceeds from their $100-a-plate Jefferson-Jackson Day dinner in January 1960 to the Kennedy war chest, a total of $50,000. Members of the Kennedy family contributed $90,000 and the senator himself chipped in $60,000 to bring the total to $693,939. The national Citizens for Kennedy-Johnson Committee assumed the pre-convention deficit of $217,000. In addition, members of the Kennedy family also formed a Ken-Air Corporation to buy a $385,000 Convair airplane, which was leased to the senator at the rate of $1.75 a mile.[36] Another valuable contribution which cannot be measured in dollars was the massive volunteer campaign help from members of the Kennedy "clan" and Boston friends, who all worked without salary and paid their own travel expenses.

In 1964, the Goldwater for President Finance Committee, headed by Daniel C. Gainey, a Minnesota printing executive and a former Harold Stassen backer, concentrated its fund-raising drive in four states: California, New York, Texas and Illinois. Three of the top fifteen-member committee were oilmen. The best-known names of the committee, however, were two former Eisenhower cabinet members: Postmaster General Arthur Summerfield and Treasury Secretary George Humphrey. With Goldwater's poor showing in the New Hampshire primary, however, promised funds from some big contributors failed to materialize. But, as his bag of delegates collected in the caucus-convention states began to swell, a far-flung 2.5 million-piece direct-mail solicitation campaign began to pay off with a steady flow of contributions. Not all of the Goldwater support, however, could be measured in dollars alone. Tremendous grass-roots support and statewide volunteer organizations furnished incalculable aid to his winning drive. For example, in Los Angeles County, a 15,000-member army of volunteers swarmed over this populous county— the key to a state victory—ringing doorbells and distributing campaign literature as if Armageddon were just around the corner. One national commentator called the volunteer effort of the national Goldwater movement his greatest asset.[37]

Governor Nelson Rockefeller's unsuccessful $5 million bid for the presidency in 1964 was paid for mostly out of his own pocket. All but approximately $100,000 of the funds spent in Rockefeller's pre-convention campaign came from Rockefeller's checking account and members of his family.[38] The remainder came from a few close friends and general contributors. The heavy emphasis upon volunteer fund-raising which characterized the Goldwater campaign was obviously ignored. In California, for example, Rockefeller held private luncheons with members of the San Francisco "establishment," but money raising was not the main topic of conversation. Rockefeller, however, did have Leonard Firestone of the automobile tire family, former Standard Oil of California President T. S. Peterson, and Justin Dart of Rexall Drug soliciting funds on his behalf.[39]

With the rising costs of primary campaigning, presidential contenders had reached a point in the mid-1960s that would soon force them to reassess the ways to meet these rocketing costs. Their choices were to depend heavily upon influence-peddlers to underwrite nominating campaigns, devise a revolutionary means of fund raising, or go deeply into debt.

Former Vice President Richard M. Nixon, the 1968 out-party challenger, chose to base his pre-convention campaign almost exclusively on "fat cat" contributors from the oil, chemicals, auto and related industries— "national" money. During the seven-month pre-convention period Maurice Stans, a New York-based investment banker who had served in Eisenhower's cabinet and a fund-raiser par excellence, collected and spent approximately $10 million (see Table 9.3). As Theodore H. White described the Stans fund-raising operation, "there was the root-Republican money, the hate Johnson money, the smart money, the little money, and then there was the big, big money from the classic contributors, nursed out of them personally be regional chiefs who spread over a geographical

TABLE 9.3
1968 PRE-CONVENTION EXPENDITURES BY
REPUBLICAN PRESIDENTIAL CANDIDATES
(THOUSANDS OF DOLLARS)

Candidate	Expenditures
Richard Nixon	10,000
Nelson Rockefeller	8,000
George Romney	1,500
Ronald Reagan	750
Harold Stassen	90
Total	20,340

Source: Reprinted by permission of the publisher, from Herbert E. Alexander, *Financing the 1968 Election* (Lexington, Mass.: Lexington Books, D. C. Heath and Company, Copyright 1971, D. C. Heath and Company), pp. 10-29.

and ideological spectrum."[40] So well programmed was the Stans fund-raising system that state Nixon chairmen did not have to give more than a passing thought to fund raising during the primary season.

Senator George McGovern's 1972 primary finances depended upon a combination of personal solicitation of big contributors, special loans from these big donors, extensive computerized direct-mail operations targeted on small contributors, and a series of concerts organized by movie star Warren Beatty. All told, the McGovern fund raisers collected $12 million in private funds, a new record for Democratic presidential contenders (see Table 9.2).

Failure of Ronald Reagan's daring challenge to grab the 1976 GOP nomination away from President Ford could not be attributed to the shortage of campaign dollars, but largely to their too-late arrival. As Herbert E. Alexander has pointed out, "In dollars raised the Reagan fund drive was extremely successful, but the bulk of the contributions arrived too late to ease the most severe financial problems."[41] Loans played a crucial role in easing the Reagan cash crunch during the nine-week freeze of Federal Election Commission funds. The Citizens for Reagan Committee, for example, borrowed $1 million from the National Bank of Washington during February 1976. During the matching-fund cutoff, Reagan loans aggregated to $3,346,226.[42] All loans, it might be noted, were repaid by the summer of 1976. But Reagan's solvency came too late to affect the nomination outcome. Direct mail solicitations furnished a major share of the $14.2 million Reagan's money-raisers collected during the nomination campaign. Of the $3,569,727 received in private contributions by the Citizens for Reagan Committee during the first three months of 1976, for example, over $2 million came through direct mail. Between August 1975 and April 1976 the Reagan organization sent out more than seven million pieces of mail. But direct mail is expensive. Consequently, the net gain from this type of solicitation is much lower than from $1,000-a-plate dinners and receptions. Since most of these contributions were in denominations of $100 or less, however, virtually all of this money could be used to qualify for federal matching funds (only the first $250 of any private contribution can be used to qualify for federal dollars). As the favorite candidate of right-wing Republicans, Reagan and his staff returned time and again to his conservative supporters for financial help. One nationwide TV speech and appeal for funds, following his first primary victory over President Ford in North Carolina, netted almost $1.2 million. Even though Reagan suffered a severe cash flow problem during the nine-week cut-off of federal matching funds after the U.S. Supreme Court ruled that the appointment process for Federal Election Commission members had to be changed, the Ronald Reagan duel against President Ford in 1976 was the best financed nominating challenge in party history.

The President Ford Finance Committee experienced some initial funding problems in 1975 because its first chairman, whose recognized talent had been in raising $25,000 individual contributions under the old system, could not adjust to the new federal campaign law based on the smaller contributor. But soon after his successor took over, the Ford Committee's fund-raising machinery moved into high gear, collecting $500,000 in December 1975, $800,000 in January 1976, and $324,000 in the first week of February via direct mail solicitation, large fund-raising events, and the president's state campaign organizations. Each state was given a quota, and the quotas, for the most part, were met. Ford's surprise victories in the New Hampshire and Florida primaries also helped open regular party coffers (see Figure 9.1). Exploiting the advantages of incumbency, President Ford encountered no further funding difficulties, collecting a grand total of $14 million during his nomination drive.

Reporting requirements of the 1974 Federal Election Campaign Act have removed the foggy mist that formerly enshrouded presidential nominating finances. Indeed, so stringent are the Federal Election Commission's public disclosure requirements that the size of a typical presidential candidate's accounting staff now almost equals his regular campaign staff—and may be more important for his political survival than his campaign strategists.

Spending in the Primaries

Until the 1960s, pre-convention expenditures varied from campaign to campaign, depending more on the intensity of competition than on the cost-of-living index. More than sixty years ago, the combined pre-conven-

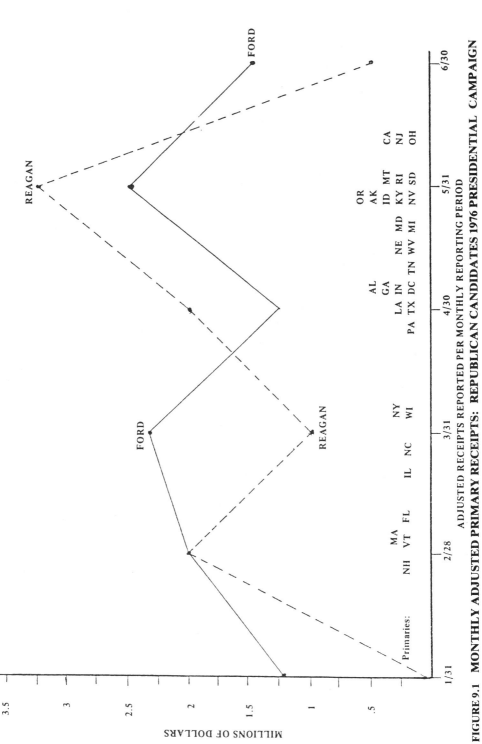

FIGURE 9.1 MONTHLY ADJUSTED PRIMARY RECEIPTS: REPUBLICAN CANDIDATES 1976 PRESIDENTIAL CAMPAIGN (2 CANDIDATES)

Source: Federal Election Commission

TABLE 9.4
REPUBLICAN AND DEMOCRATIC CANDIDATE EXPENDITURES
IN NOMINATING RACES, 1952-76
(MILLIONS OF DOLLARS)

Year	Republicans	Democrats
1952	5.8	0.8
1956	0.5	2.5
1960	0.5	2.1
1964	10.0	1.0
1968	20.0	25.0
1972	5.7	32.7
1976	26.2	40.7

Source: 1952 and 1956 figures are from Alexander Heard, *The Costs of Democracy* (Chapel Hill: University of North Carolina Press, 1960), pp. 334-38; the data for 1960-72 are from Herbert E. Alexander's studies: *Financing the 1960 Election* (Princeton, N. J.: Citizens Research Foundation, 1962), *Financing the 1964 Election* (Princeton, N. J.: Citizens Research Council, 1966), and reprinted by permission of the publisher, from Herbert E. Alexander, *Financing the 1968 Election* and *Financing the 1972 Election* (Lexington, Mass.: Lexington Books, D. C. Heath and Company, Copyright 1971 and 1976, D. C. Heath and Company); figures for 1976 are from FEC Disclosure Series No. 7: 1976 *Presidential Campaign Receipts and Expenditures* (Washington, D. C.: Federal Election Commission), p. 9.

tion expenditures of President Taft and former President Roosevelt in 1912, reflecting the heated competition between these bitter rivals, totaled more than $1.1 million. General Wood's pre-convention spending record of $1,773,000 in 1920 against Illinois Governor Lowden and California Senator Hiram Johnson was not surpassed until the hot fight between Eisenhower and Taft in 1952. Since 1960, however, pre-nomination expenditures have skyrocketed, as Table 9.4 shows. The rapidly expanded use of television advertising, especially the saturation type, indicated that the cost of future presidential primary campaigns would rise sharply, much faster than mere cost-of-living increases or population growth.

From the beginning of the primary era, data have showed that presidential candidates who fought for the nomination in the primaries spent more money than candidates who avoided these "trial heat" elections. But the difference in amounts was not as big as might be expected—at least until 1968. As late as 1964, it was still possible for a presidential contender to spend more funds in the caucus convention states than in the primaries. Senator Goldwater in 1964, for example, spent an estimated $3 million in the caucus-convention states versus $2.5 million in the primaries. Since then, however, spending in the primary states has far exceeded campaign outlays in the caucus-convention states.[43] Three reasons explain the rapid increase in primary spending. First, the number of states adopting presidential primaries has doubled—from fifteen to thirty-three states—since 1968. Second, the large field of candidates, especially in the Democratic party, has intensified the competition. Third, the inflationary spiral of higher travel costs, especially jet aircraft charters and full-time campaign staffs, has pushed expenditures in the primaries to new highs (see Table 9.4).

The 1952 Republican presidential nominating race was the most expensive on record to that date. On the basis of incomplete but substantial information, it has been estimated that the Eisenhower 1952 pre-convention campaign, which included primaries and state party conventions alike, totaled $2.5 million. The principal Eisenhower campaign group, Citizens for Eisenhower, reportedly spent between $500,000 and $600,000 in states where presidential primaries were held. Although no official information is available on Senator Taft's campaign, Alexander Heard concluded that Taft's expenses equaled and probably exceeded those spent on behalf of Eisenhower, chiefly because Taft's campaign matched Eisenhower's in scope and intensity and because Taft's campaign was launched earlier.[44] Oddly enough, it was not one of the Taft-Eisenhower primary contests that set a new spending record. Instead, it was the bitter fight in California between Governor Earl Warren and Thomas Werdel, a political unknown representing the conservative faction of the Republican party. The anti-Warren forces were reported to have spent between $500,000 and $600,000 in an attempt to upset the popular California governor, but some estimates placed the Werdel committee expenditures as high as $1 million.[45] To counter the vitriolic Werdel campaign, the Warren managers were compelled to dip heavily into their treasury.

The cost of Stevenson's 1956 pre-convention campaign has been calculated at $1.5 million. Senator Kefauver's pre-convention expenditures probably equaled the $356,000 figure spent in the 1952 campaign, although he personally listed his 1956 presidential primary expense total as $250,000.[46]

In 1960, the combined expenses of the five major contenders for the Democratic nomination were approximately $2.1 million, according to Herbert Alexander. But this figure does not include amounts spent on behalf of some candidates by state and local committees.[47] Approximately half this amount was spent by the Kennedy forces. In response to a question at a televised Kennedy press conference before the Democratic convention (called to answer former President Truman's charges of a Kennedy-rigged convention), the young Massachusetts senator called attention to the estimated $2.5 million spent on behalf of General Eisenhower's 1952 pre-convention campaign. Kennedy calculated his own costs at one-third that figure, or approximately $830,000.[48]

Kennedy's pre-convention costs were held down, it has been pointed out, by the following factors: the unusually heavy press coverage and free publicity he received because of his famous family, his wealth, his war record and his youth; the fact that Senator Humphrey, who lacked big money, was his only major opposition in the primaries; and tactical success in avoiding full-fledged campaigns against favorite sons in the expensive primary states of Ohio and California.

In the 1960 Republican nominating race, Vice President Richard M. Nixon, the only announced GOP candidate, had no serious opposition. He did not campaign openly, preferring to maintain the posture of a dedicated, hard-working vice president. But his name or Nixon-pledged slates were entered in ten primaries to help maintain interest among Republican voters, to satisfy the legal requirements for electing delegates, and to demonstrate vote-drawing power comparable to that of Senator Kennedy and other Democratic aspirants. Financial data on Nixon's low-key 1960 campaign are limited. Herbert Alexander, who served as chief staff member of the President's Commission on Campaign Costs (1961-62), has estimated that Nixon spent an average of $35,000 a primary, or about $350,000.[49] This figure seems about right. Alexander concluded that, overall, $500,000 would appear to be a rock-bottom estimate for Nixon's total outlay to win the 1960 GOP nomination.

The cost of the 1964 presidential nominating campaigns in the out-party GOP was the highest on record, approximately $10 million. There were two reasons for this heavy expenditure. First, Governor Nelson Rockefeller, with a private fortune estimated as high as $150 million, was prepared to spend unlimited personal and family funds in his quest for the Republican nomination. Second, Senator Barry Goldwater, a millionaire himself, was able to match the Rockefeller expenditures dollar for dollar in each primary because he had attracted enough wealthy and middle-income supporters while serving as chairman of the Republican Senate Campaign Committee for several years and because his staff's direct-mail fund raising tapped new, undeveloped sources of wealth.

Though it was the habit of the Goldwater strategists to talk "poor mouth" whenever they compared their campaign spending with Rockefeller's, the overall cost of the Arizonan's pre-convention race actually exceeded that of the New York governor—$5.5 million to Rockefeller's $5 million. From December 1962 until January 1964, the National Draft-Goldwater Committee collected $751,000. This sum, plus another $50,000 reportedly raised in early 1962, represented the largest fund ever collected publicly prior to a candidate's formal announcement for the presidency. The Goldwater for President Finance Committee, made up of a nucleus of former Republican national finance committee members and the "draft" committee, reportedly raised $2.7 million to finance

Goldwater's national headquarters activity in the six months preceding the 1964 San Francisco convention.[50]

Rockefeller's 1964 out-of-pocket nominating campaign expenditures totaled $2,927,135. These figures do not include costs of travel for Rockefeller and his personal staff, including much of the large field staff spread throughout the country, and the use of the family airplane. If all these unlisted expenses were tabulated and added to the bill, the overall Rockefeller campaign bill would be in the $5 million range.[51] Rockefeller actively campaigned in only four primaries, New Hampshire, West Virginia, Oregon and California; but he had formal organizations working on his behalf in thirty-five of the fifty states and informal groups in eleven other states.

It is impossible to estimate closely how much Rockefeller spent in the caucus-convention states, but it was less than in the primaries. Mr. Rockefeller provided most of the money from his own exchequer for his local campaign organizations throughout the country. As one member of the Rockefeller staff commented, "This is one of our best talking points. We can go to the pros all over the country and tell them we'll put in the dollars to help their local candidates as well as ourselves."[52]

The costs of seeking the presidential nomination in 1968 took a quantum jump. Combined expenditures by presidential aspirants of both major parties totaled $41 million, or four times the pre-convention costs in 1964. "By comparison," Herbert E. Alexander notes, "the much publicized clash between Hubert Humphrey and John F. Kennedy in 1960 seems, in retrospect, as if it took place in another era."[53] There were several reasons for the high cost in 1968: intense nominating struggles in both parties; multiple candidacies in both parties; two wealthy candidates, Robert F. Kennedy and Nelson Rockefeller; and a highly volatile issue (Vietnam) which brought new partisans and new money into the political process.

The six Democratic aspirants in 1968 spent approximately $25 million (see Table 9.5), but deficits and debt settlements on unpaid bills reduced the total outlay to about $21 million.[54] Senator Eugene McCarthy, an outsider candidate with limited financial means at the outset of his campaign, surprisingly led all Democratic contenders with expenditures of $11 million. McCarthy's opposition to the Vietnam War attracted a number of millionaire liberal Democrats and a new clientele of issue-oriented donors.

Senator Robert Kennedy's whirlwind eighty-five-day campaign, which ended in tragedy, cost $9 million. The combined campaigns of President Johnson (before his withdrawal in late March), Vice President Humphrey and their Indiana and California stand-in candidates (Branigan and Lynch) totaled approximately $5 million. Senator George McGovern's

TABLE 9.5
1968 PRE-CONVENTION EXPENDITURES BY
DEMOCRATIC PRESIDENTIAL CANDIDATES
(THOUSANDS OF DOLLARS)

Candidate	Expenditures
Eugene McCarthy	11,000
Robert Kennedy	9,000
President Lyndon B. Johnson, Vice President Hubert Humphrey and stand-in candidates	5,000
George McGovern	74
Lester Maddox	50
Total	25,124*

Source: Reprinted by permission of the publisher, from Herbert E. Alexander, *Financing the 1968 Election* (Lexington, Mass.: Lexington Books, D. C. Heath and Company, Copyright 1971, D. C. Heath and Company), pp. 30-68.

*Debt settlements on unpaid campaign bills reduced this figure to approximately $21 million.

entry (after Kennedy's assassination) cost $74,000, and segregationist Governor Lester Maddox of Georgia spent $50,000 in his abbreviated quest for the nomination.

GOP presidential aspirants spent more than $20 million in the 1968 pre-convention race (see Table 9.3). Former Vice President Richard M. Nixon, the nominee, accounted for more than one-half of this outlay. Governor Rockefeller, even though he did not enter the primaries, spent $8 million. Michigan Governor George Romney's abortive campaign, which collapsed before the New Hampshire primary, cost $1.5 million.[55] California Governor Ronald Reagan, although he did not formally announce his candidacy for the presidency until the opening day of the GOP national convention, waged a close-to-the-vest nominating campaign for almost two years that cost $750,000. Perennial candidate Harold Stassen, a five-time "also-ran," spent about $90,000. While most of this Republican money was expended during the spring of 1968, considerable campaign planning money was committed earlier, in 1966-67. By contrast, virtually all Democratic nominating costs in 1968 were incurred in the eight months preceding the Chicago convention.

Pre-convention spending for Democratic presidential contenders in 1972 rose to $32.7 million, approximately $7 million more than the previous record-shattering $25 million in 1968. Senator George McGovern, the nominee, led the fifteen-candidate field with an outlay of about $12 million; Senator Edmund Muskie, the early front-runner who faltered in the primaries, was the second highest pre-convention spender with campaign bills of $7 million. Senator Hubert H. Humphrey, making his third try for the presidency, spent approximately $4.7 million.[56] Table 9.2 listed the estimated costs for all Democratic candidates—the front-runners, the "morning glory" candidates who folded early, the dark horses, and the favorite sons.

Senator McGovern's pay-as-you-go pre-convention campaign was financed, in part, by a loyal army of 150,000 small contributors. At least $3.2 million came from these rank-and-file donors during the primaries. Without this steady stream of money flowing into his national headquarters it seems doubtful that McGovern, in the early stages of his pre-convention campaign, would have been able to mount his successful dual-pronged strategy of capturing key primaries while also collecting approximately 300 delegates from the caucus-convention states. Also, the McGovern computerized direct-mail solicitation brought in large sums of money from previously untapped or seldom-tapped sources. During the primary season the McGovern strategists fostered the belief that the South Dakotan's campaign depended almost exclusively on the small-fry contributor. The postseason record shows, however, that almost one-half ($5.7 million) of the $12 million collected by McGovern's fund raisers came from the "fat cats."[57] Even outsider candidates, if they were to capture the nomination, had to turn to the financial heavy hitters.

Senator Humphrey, in his third presidential bid, relied chiefly on large contributors, as did Senator Muskie. As campaign finance specialist Herbert E. Alexander told the *Christian Science Monitor,* "Without large contributors, Senator Muskie and Humphrey would probably have been out of the race well before convention time—if, indeed, they would have made the race at all."[58] Governor George Wallace, knocked out of the race by an assassin's near-fatal attempt on his life the day before the Maryland primary, financed his hard-hitting campaign mostly by postal solicitation from small donors. Plumbers, farmers, factory workers and housewives helped underwrite his late-starting campaign which netted six primary victories before gunshot wounds and the resulting paralysis forced his withdrawal from active campaigning.

In 1972, the highest outlay by a candidate in a single primary was $4,175,000 (by Senator McGovern) in California. As Alexander explains, "California was the linchpin of McGovern's strategy from the beginning, and his investment in the state represented a full third of his pre-nomination costs."[59] No attempt has been made to put a price tag on the value of McGovern's estimated 50,000 volunteer workers in the California primary. But if they were calculated at $100 per person, this figure would have come to $5,000,000! To most members of the national press corps this huge army of volunteers was the difference between victory and defeat for McGovern. Senator Humphrey, desperately short on funds, spent about $500,000 in the same West Coast primary in a last-ditch stand to halt McGovern's drive for the nomination. Alexander has noted that Humphrey's financial resources were not enough to mount a strong challenge to McGovern. Public opinion polls showed Humphrey running twenty percentage points behind before the final campaign push, but he finished less than six percentage points behind McGovern in the Golden State primary. Alexander has observed that "had Humphrey adequately financed his campaign in California, the outcome could have been different."[60] Originally, the Humphrey plan for California called for spending $460,000 on media advertising, the ceiling allowed by the Democratic candidates' joint agreement. Most of this sum was raised by the late Eugene Wyman, Humphrey's veteran fund raiser, but more than $250,000 of it was sent to the national headquarters in Washington to meet urgent obligations. As a result, Humphrey was able to spend only $234,800 for radio and television, about one-half as much as had been planned.

By the time the 1972 GOP convention assembled in Miami Beach, the Committee for the Re-Election of the President (CREEP) had spent almost $5 million in the primary and caucus-convention states and in laying plans for his general election campaign, which cost an estimated $61 million.[61] A precise calculation of GOP pre-convention expenditures was impeded by the fact that the reporting requirements of the Federal Election Campaign Act of 1971 did not take effect until April 7, 1972, three months after the primary season got underway. CREEP fund raisers worked frantically before this deadline to collect and commit as much money as possible for the general election—Nixon had no major opposition in the primaries—to avoid the new reporting requirements.

President Nixon did, however, face two weak GOP challengers, one from the left, Representative Paul N. McCloskey, Jr., the other from the right wing of the party, Representative John Ashbrook, Ohio. McCloskey, the liberal Republican, challenged Mr. Nixon in the New Hampshire primary, mainly over the issue of continued U. S. involvement in Vietnam. But he dropped out of contention when he received only 20 percent of the New Hampshire vote. McCloskey concluded that further campaigning was futile, especially after some of his big contributors indicated that he could not count on them for further help. Though no longer a candidate, McCloskey's name nevertheless remained on the ballot in ten states. He won one delegate vote in New Mexico, thus preventing President Nixon from winning a unanimous nomination. All told, McCloskey spent approximately $550,000 in his hopeless challenge, a symbolic protest against the Vietnam War.[62]

Representative Ashbrook's conservative challenge against Mr. Nixon's foreign and domestic policies, especially opposition to Mr. Nixon's reconciliation policy toward China and the arms limitation agreement with the Soviet Union, was no more successful than McCloskey's. Although Ashbrook was soundly trounced in the New Hampshire, Florida and California primaries (he did not win a single delegate), he refused to bow out of the nominating race until his last-gasp bid for votes among right-wing Republicans in the California primary. But he won only 219,000 votes out of 2.2 million cast, less than 10 percent. Estimated total cost of his futile campaign was $740,000.[63]

In the record-breaking 1976 nominating races, the thirteen Democratic contenders outspent the two Republican candidates, President Ford and Governor Ronald Reagan, $40.7 to $26.2 million (see Table 9.1) during the period January 1-August 30, 1976. But on an individual basis, President Ford led all candidates in preconvention expenditures with $13.6 million. Challenger Reagan was not far behind in second place with a total preconvention campaign bill of $12.6 million.[64] Not since former President Theodore Roosevelt challenged President Taft in 1912 had the Republicans seen a sitting president so seriously threatened for renomination. Democratic nominee Jimmy Carter was in third place with a 1976 pre-convention campaign bill of $11.4 million. Nine Democratic hopefuls raised more than $1 million apiece, but three of them—Bentson, Harris and Bayh—dropped out of the race before the primary season had reached the end of the first quarter. As recently as 1960, the figure of $1 million was considered large enough to make a hard run for the presidency. By 1976, though, this figure was only large enough to see a candidate through the first three weeks of primary competition. The spending ceilings on individual state primaries established by the Federal Election Commission for the 1976 campaign reflect the high cost of modern-day electioneering (see Table 9.6).

Out-of-State Financing

Long ago the huge costs of presidential primary campaigning forced candidates to rely upon out-of-state financing to underwrite their campaigns. To expect the frugal citizens of New Hampshire to support out-of-state candidates to the tune of $1.5 million—the amount spent in their 1976 primary—is absurd. Inevitably, all candidates who invite themselves to New Hampshire must turn to their national headquarters to provide the cash for this primary campaign and the thirty-two primaries that follow.

The continued dependence on out-of-state financing arises from the very nature of the nominating process itself. As Alexander Heard has explained, "The leadership of a presidential nominating campaign must be focused at the top (at the national headquarters) because most wealthy contributors are concentrated in a few Eastern states."[65] In the past

TABLE 9.6
FEDERAL ELECTION COMMISSION SPENDING CEILINGS FOR
PRIMARY STATES IN 1976
(IN THOUSANDS OF DOLLARS)

State	VAP (in thousands)	Spending Ceiling*
Alabama	2,439	$ 426
Arkansas	1,449	253
California	14,840	2,590
District of Columbia	515	153
Florida	6,020	1,051
Georgia	3,294	575
Idaho	542	218
Illinois	7,654	1,336
Indiana	3,601	629
Kentucky	2,316	404
Maryland	2,812	491
Massachusetts	4,097	715
Michigan	6,145	1,073
Montana	503	218
Nebraska	1,065	218
Nevada	402	218
New Hampshire	559	218
New Jersey	5,102	891
New York	12,781	2,231
North Carolina	3,736	652
Ohio	7,357	1,284
Oregon	1,606	280
Pennsylvania	8,363	1,460
Rhode Island	653	218
South Dakota	463	218
Tennessee	2,895	505
Texas	8,225	1,436
Vermont	320	218
West Virginia	1,255	219
Wisconsin	3,134	547

Source: Federal Election Commission.

*The per-state spending limit for presidential candidates is determined by (1) multiplying 8¢ times the Voting Age Population (VAP) of each state, (2) adding to that figure the 9.1 percent cost-of-living increase applicable for the 1976 limits, and (3) doubling that adjusted figure. In states where 8¢ times the Voting Age Population is less than $100,000, the minimum $100,000 figure is used instead. Limitations apply only to those presidential candidates receiving federal matching funds.

two decades, it might be added, the Sun Belt states of the Southwest have also become important sources of campaign funds. While out-of-state financing of nominating campaigns antedates the presidential primary system, expensive primary contests have accentuated the need to bring in large sums of money from outside to pay the huge campaign bills. States such as New Hampshire, Wisconsin and Oregon do not have the heavily industrialized base that produces large numbers of affluent citizens, the potential contributors. Nor can candidates turn to their party as a source of campaign revenue. In an intraparty contest among several presidential contenders the state and national parties generally remain above the battle until the nominee has been safely chosen at the national convention. Faced with these barriers, candidates must develop their own contributor lists and rely on their old supporters to see them through the primaries. But this is not an insurmountable problem because contributors almost universally prefer to give to candidates, not parties.

In 1960, the Kennedy national headquarters transferred approximately $470,000, or more than half the admitted Kennedy pre-convention expenditures, to state primary campaigns. The Oregon presidential primary was a typical example of out-of-state financing. According to the Oregon secretary of state's report, the campaign managers for both Kennedy and Nixon relied almost exclusively on outside funds. The Oregon Kennedy for President Committee's contributions totaled $55,835, of which the Massachusetts Kennedy for President Committee furnished $51,010, and the national Kennedy for President Committee, $1,400. The Oregon for Nixon Committee received $47,000 of its total contributions of $48,702 from the Dick Nixon Club in Washington, D.C.[66]

Governor Rockefeller's 1964 pre-convention campaign, as indicated earlier, was financed largely by himself and a few close friends. The winner of the 1964 Oregon GOP primary, Governor Rockefeller was far and away the biggest spender in this West Coast primary. Almost all of his funds came from out of state. The Rockefeller for President National Committee furnished $447,884 out of the New Yorker's total reported expenditures of $459,943. Of Senator Barry Goldwater's reported Oregon expenditures of $99,687, the Goldwater for President National Committee supplied $60,900.[67]

In the 1964 California primary, Senator Goldwater showed for the first time that a presidential primary campaign could, with sufficient organizational work, be financed exclusively with home state funds. To defray the costs of the $2 million primary campaign, the eighteen state and local Goldwater committees raised $1 million, more than half of this at two $100-a-plate dinners. The other $1 million came from county and local fund-raising efforts, mostly in the conservative counties of southern California. So successful were the California Goldwater money raisers, led by Henry Salvatori, a Los Angeles oilman, that they contributed at least $150,000 to the national Goldwater campaign between January 3 and March 10, 1964.[68]

Four years later, former Vice President Richard Nixon did not have to make further huge outlays in the primaries after his decisive victory in New Hampshire for three main reasons: Michigan Governor George Romney dropped out of the race early; Nelson Rockefeller, after first taking himself out of the nominating race, did not enter any primaries after he threw his hat into the ring again; and California Governor Ronald Reagan's waiting-game strategy of avoiding an open confrontation with Nixon in the primaries also kept Nixon's primary costs down. But in the first-round New Hampshire primary the Nixon team spent money as if there were no tomorrow. Dozens of television ads, billboards ("Nixon's the One"), receptions, advance and scheduling teams and major campaign headquarters in the two leading cities pushed the bill to almost $500,000, with virtually all the tab being picked up by the national Nixon committee in Washington.[69] Likewise, Governor Romney's abortive New Hampshire primary campaign was financed almost exclusively by national campaign money. The only in-state money was an unsolicited $200 contribution. Of the $83,000 the Romney organization reported in receipts in Wisconsin, only one in-state $500 contributor was listed; the balance came as transfers from eleven committees located in Detroit.[70]

Senator Robert Kennedy's whirlwind primary campaign in 1968 also depended almost exclusively upon out-of-state financing. The State of Oregon official campaign finance report, for example, showed that of the $310,620 listed in contributions, $309,842 came from the national campaign. Most of the $2.4 million California primary campaign was supplied from the national campaign headquarters, though exact details have never surfaced.[71]

In 1972, McGovern's national headquarters in Washington, D. C., provided about half the financing for his ten primary victories. Washington headquarters raised approximately $4.7 million for the period after April 7, 1972, and the thirty-five states with reporting committees raised just over $5.7 million for the same period.[72] Though McGovern was able to attract more young political activists than Senator McCarthy for his primary campaigns, his state campaign organizations relied almost exclusively on money from the national headquarters to pay for the salaries of state party workers and the media campaigns.

Senator Muskie's 1972 fiasco in the primaries cost his backers $7 million. As an early front-runner, Muskie attracted sizable chunks of cash from establishment Democrats, especially in the East—the so-called limousine liberals—and, secretly, from wealthy disaffected Republicans who disliked Nixon. Of the approximately $7 million spent by the Muskie campaign, an estimated $5-$5.5 million was doled out by the national headquarters in Washington, D. C. The remaining $1.5-$2 million was spent by the various state and local committees.[73] But Muskie's poor showing in the early primaries discouraged his backers and soon brought him to the end of the financial line.

Former Vice President Hubert H. Humphrey relied heavily on big contributors, many of the same big givers who had bankrolled his two previous tries for the presidency. But as his political fortunes in the primaries sagged, Humphrey was forced more and more to borrow heavily from his wealthy benefactors. When Humphrey finally dropped out of the race on the second day of the Democratic convention, he owed approximately $1 million in primary campaign debts.[74] Until forced out of the race by a would-be assassin's bullet, George Wallace depended heavily in 1972 upon his massive national headquarters direct-mail operation first developed during this third-party candidacy drive in 1968.[75]

President Richard Nixon's renomination drive against token opposition was paid for almost entirely by funds raised by CREEP from its national headquarters in the nation's capital.[76] State and local campaign organizations in the presidential primary states, it seems clear, have usually been long on enthusiasm and short on cash. They have had to rely heavily on the candidate's national headquarters for money to operate their presidential primary campaigns.

Four years later, Jimmy Carter relied on a tripartite combination of home state and out-of-state contributions—and borrowing—for his successful nominating campaign. By late May 1976, Federal Election Commission records showed that the Democratic front-runner, Jimmy Carter, had accumulated $2.1 million in debts. To meet the cash flow pinch from the Pennsylvania and later primaries, Carter borrowed nearly $1 million from two Atlanta banks, the Fulton National and the Citizens and Southern National.[77] An additional $646,000 was owed to his media consultant, Jerry Rafshoon, a fellow Georgian. Once Carter had in effect locked up the nomination after the Pennsylvania primary, out-of-state campaign contributions began flowing steadily from all over the country into the Carter treasury (see Figure 9.2). With the resumption of matching payments and a deluge of contributions in May, June and July, the Carter committee actually had a surplus of almost $450,000 by late July. Such are the advantages of winning the nomination!

Out-of-state financing of primary campaigns, until the passage of the 1974 Federal Election Campaign Act, was encouraged by the fact that state laws requiring presidential candidates to reveal sources and amounts of their expenditures were grossly inadequate. Funds could be collected and disbursed from outside the state by the candidate's national headquarters, without the public knowing about the transactions. Under the

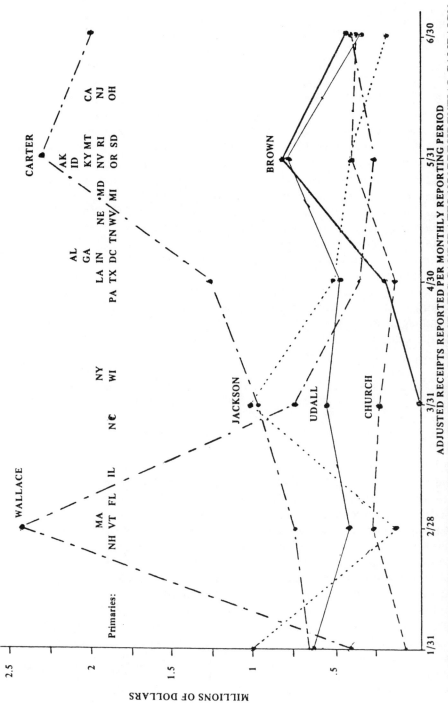

FIGURE 9.2   MONTHLY ADJUSTED PRIMARY RECEIPTS: DEMOCRATIC CANDIDATES 1976 PRESIDENTIAL CAMPAIGN
(6 CANDIDATES)
Source: Federal Election Commission

1971 and 1974 campaign reform finance laws, out-of-state money will continue to be used to underwrite many state presidential primary campaigns, but it will no longer be done under the table.

Looking ahead, what changes can be anticipated in light of the experience gained from the first federally subsidized presidential nominating campaigns in U. S. history?

Federal Subsidies and Future Primary Campaigns

The U. S. Treasury has become the new "fat cat" of American politics; indeed, the new matching federal subsidy law proved so popular in 1976 that it will be continued—but with minor revisions. The Federal Election Commission (FEC) issued two regulations in the late stages of the 1976 pre-convention race that will undoubtedly affect the pre-convention strategies of future presidential contenders.

First, to prevent presidential candidates knocked out of the primaries from continuing to collect federal subsidies after becoming "inactive" candidates, the Federal Election Commission ruled in June 1976 that presidential candidates will get no more federal matching money except to pay campaign debts incurred before they bowed out of the nominating races. Under this new ruling, Representative Morris Udall became inactive on June 14, 1976, on the basis of his public statement that he was no longer seeking the nomination and that delegates pledged to him could now vote for Carter. Senator Jackson's release of delegates on June 16 made him inactive as of that date.[78]

Second, the amended legislation reviving the Federal Election Commission and signed by President Ford on May 11, 1976, also cuts off any matching funds to a candidate thirty days after he receives less than 10 percent of the vote in a second consecutive primary in which he (or she) actively competed.[79]

The FEC regulation pertaining to inactive status may dissuade some candidates who have been hopelessly outclassed in the early primaries from withdrawing entirely before convention time, since they will be unable to collect additional matching funds while they are phasing out their candidacies. Senator Birch Bayh's campaign manager has commented that "closing the operation down—it's like liquidating a national business."[80] On the other hand, the second FEC regulation setting a minimal 10 percent of the vote in two consecutive primaries to qualify for additional matching funds will aid the natural selection process of thinning out the candidate field. Weak candidates in the past were inclined to linger on in the race, hoping that their prospects would improve. But faced with the cut-off of federal matching funds, they will probably drop out of the race sooner.

Rapid escalation of the cost-of-living index will require that spending ceilings for presidential contenders be raised in the years ahead, especially since candidates now face competition in more than thirty primaries.[81] Beyond this recommendation and the two speculative observations made above, it seems wise, in the words of Governor Edmund G. "Jerry" Brown, Jr., of California, "to let the process evolve" before passing further judgment.

Notes

1. This figure is for adjusted expenditures. As originally reported, gross expenditures in the two major parties were $78.3 million, but elimination of loan repayments, duplicative reporting, refunded contributions, and transfers to and from affiliated committees brought the net figure down to $66.8 million. This sum includes fund-raising, legal and accounting fees which are exempt from spending limitations. See FEC Disclosure Series, No. 7, *Presidential Campaign Receipts and Expenditures* (Washington, D. C.: Federal Election Commission, May 1977), pp. 16-17.

2. Public Law 93-443, 93rd Congress, S.3044, October 15, 1974, cited as Federal Election Campaign Act Amendments of 1974.

3. Herbert E. Alexander, *Financing the 1972 Election* (Lexington, Mass.: D. C. Heath, 1976), pp. 294-95.

4. New York *Times,* July 20, 1976.

5. Carter's manager Hamilton Jordan received an annual salary of $16,000; Robert Keefe, Jackson's manager, was paid $45,000 per year. Ibid.

6. Ibid., June 17, 1976.

7. B. Drummond Ayres, Jr., Ibid., November 18, 1976.

8. Ibid.

9. Herbert E. Alexander, *Financing the 1976 Election* (Washington, D. C.: Congressional Quarterly Press, 1979), pp. 241-44.

10. 256 U. S. 232.

11. Herbert E. Alexander, *Money in Politics* (Washington, D. C.: Public Affairs Press, 1972), p. 313.

12. Detroit *Free Press,* August 3, 1973.

13. Public Law 93-443 (1974). Subsequently, the Federal Election Commission authorized a cost-of-living adjustment and a 20 percent exemption for fund-raising purposes in the primaries to raise the total spending limit to $13,092,000 per presidential candidate.

14. New York *Times,* January 31, 1976.

15. *Buckley et al.* v. *Valeo, Secretary of the United States Senate, et al.,* 424 U. S. 1; see also New York *Times,* January 31, 1976.

16. New York *Times,* December 31, 1959.

17. Herbert E. Alexander, *Financing the 1960 Election* (Princeton, N. J.: Citizens Research Foundation, 1962), p. 27.

18. Ibid.

19. Alexander Heard, *The Costs of Democracy* (Chapel Hill: University of North Carolina Press, 1960), p. 341.

20. Herbert E. Alexander, *Financing the 1964 Election* (Princeton, N. J.: Citizens Research Foundation, 1966), p. 21.

21. Alexander, *Financing the 1972 Election,* pp. 131-32.

22. New York *Times,* November 18, 1976.

23. Charles Bartlett, Minneapolis *Morning Tribune,* August 6, 1963.

24. "It was a 200 Million Dollar Political Campaign," *U. S. News and World Report* 57 (November 9, 1964): 41-42.

25. New York *Times,* February 29, 1972.

26. Ibid.

27. Ibid., May 28, 1976.

28. Heard, *The Costs of Democracy,* p. 493.

29. Ibid., p. 333.

30. Since the 1960 presidential election, Dr. Alexander has been publishing his widely acclaimed studies every four years. His most recent volume is *Financing the 1976 Election* (Washington, D. C.: Congressional Quarterly Press, 1979).

31. Alexander, *Financing the 1960 Election,* p. 15.

32. James A. Farley, *Behind the Ballots* (New York: Harcourt, Brace and World, 1938), p. 72.

33. Columnists Joseph and Stewart Alsop, Pittsburgh *Post-Gazette,* May 3, 1952.

34. St. Louis *Post Dispatch,* December 9, 1955.

35. Ibid., August 7, 1960.

36. Alexander, *Financing the 1960 Election,* pp. 16-17.

37. Robert D. Novak, *The Agony of the GOP 1964* (New York: Macmillan, 1965), pp. 342-47.

38. Alexander, *Financing the 1964 Election,* p. 24.

39. Ibid., p. 25.

40. Theodore H. White, *The Making of the President 1968* (New York: Atheneum, 1969), p. 329.

41. Alexander, *Financing the 1976 Election*, p. 321.

42. *Christian Science Monitor*, July 17, 1972.

43. In 1972 the McGovern campaign won 376 committed delegates in the nonprimary states with a per-delegate cost figure of about $1,200. This was still only about one-seventh the direct cost (excluding national headquarters spending) of more than $8,350 per delegate won in the presidential primary states ($8,085,000 for 967 delegates). Alexander, *Financing the 1972 Election,* pp. 120-21. The 1976 cost-per-delegate figures for Jimmy Carter, President Gerald Ford and Ronald Reagan are available in Thomas R. Marshall, "Caucuses versus Primaries: How Much Do Delegate Selection Institutions Really Matter?" (Paper delivered at the 1977 annual meeting of the American Political Science Association, Washington, D. C., September 1-4, 1977), pp. 9-10, Table 2.1.

44. Heard, *The Costs of Democracy,* p. 334.

45. Paul T. David, Malcolm Moos, and Ralph M. Goldman, eds., *Presidential Nominating Politics in 1952,* 5 vols. (Baltimore: The Johns Hopkins University Press, 1954), 5: 227-28.

46. Letter to author from Senator Kefauver, dated March 9, 1959.

47. Alexander, *Financing the 1960 Election,* p. 21.

48. New York *Times,* July 5, 1960.

49. Alexander, *Financing the 1960 Election*, p. 22.

50. Alexander, *Financing the 1964 Election,* p. 17.

51. New York *Times,* June 17, 1964.

52. Ibid., March 27, 1964.

53. Alexander, *Financing the 1968 Election*, p. 7.

54. Ibid.

55. Though it is impossible to pinpoint all of Romney's expenditures, approximately $280,000 was spent in New Hampshire; $100,000 for pre-primary activity in Wisconsin and $30,000 in Oregon. Ibid., p. 12.

56. Alexander, *Financing the 1972 Election,* p. 151.

57. Ibid., p. 121.

58. *Christian Science Monitor,* July 17, 1976.

59. Alexander, *Financing the 1972 Election,* p. 243.

60. Ibid., p. 244.

61. Ibid., p. 227.

62. Ibid., p. 223.

63. Ibid., pp. 223-24.

64. Herbert E. Alexander lists the total 1976 Democratic primary spending at $46.3 million and Republican 1976 primary spending at $26.7 million. Alexander, *Financing the 1976 Election*, pp. 170-73.

65. Heard, *The Costs of Democracy,* p. 19.

66. Howell Appling, Jr., comp., *Summary Report of Campaign Receipts and Contributions 1960 Primary Election* (Salem, Ore.: Secretary of State, 1960), pp. 10-11.

67. Howell Appling, Jr., comp., *Summary Report of Campaign Contributions and Expenditures* (Salem, Ore.: Secretary of State, 1964), pp. 12-17.

68. Alexander, *Financing the 1964 Election,* pp. 20-21.

69. Alexander, *Financing the 1968 Election,* p. 18.

70. Ibid., p. 16.

71. Ibid., p. 58.

72. Alexander, *Financing the 1972 Election,* p. 113.

73. Ibid., p. 131.

74. Ibid., p. 158.

75. Ibid., pp. 169-73.

76. Ibid., pp. 217-23.

77. Richard Reeves and Barry M. Hager, "The Good Old Boy Network," *The New Republic* 177 (September 6, 1977): 6-9; see also "Those Carter Loans," *Newsweek* 93 (February 12, 1979): 33-34. Herbert E. Alexander reports that Carter's preconvention deficit reached its height of $1,684,800 in late May. Alexander, *Financing the 1976 Election*, p. 240.

78. Governor George Wallace was declared inactive as of June 9, when he endorsed Governor Carter. Senator Birch Bayh of Indiana, Fred Harris of Oklahoma, Governor Milton Shapp of Pennsylvania, and Sargent Shriver of Maryland were ruled inactive as of May 11, the day the new law concerning inactive status took effect. Washington *Post,* June 24, 1976.

79. New York *Times,* May 12, 1976.

80. Ibid., March 12, 1976.

81. The Federal Election Commission (FEC) spending limits are so low for the 1980 presidential primaries that one major GOP presidential candidate—John Connally—is considering rejecting federal matching funds for the New Hampshire primary. Instead, his campaign staff would plan to spend unlimited private funds in hopes of having maximum impact in the nation's first primary. (By rejecting Uncle Sam's matching dollars a candidate could avoid the FEC-imposed spending ceilings in state primaries.) Their reasoning, according to one source, is that a dismal showing in New Hampshire, where the chips are so high, could in effect force Connally out of the race and make adherence to state spending limitations moot thereafter. Until the Connally episode, the FEC had not specifically ruled on the loophole of whether a candidate could decline money early in the race—freeing him from the federal limits in the early, critical primaries—and then come in later to quality for U.S. Treasury funds. As a result, the FEC started processing a regulation in late August 1979 to deny federal money in later primaries to any presidential candidate who violates the limit in the early primaries. To be valid, however, the proposed FEC regulation must first be approved by Congress. See Fred Barbash, "FEC Moves to Close Campaign Spending Limit Loophole," *Washington Post*, September 1, 1979.

An Overview of the —————————10
Presidential Primary System

Although all four victorious presidential nominees in the out-of-power party since World War II—Eisenhower, Kennedy, Nixon and Carter—have clinched their party's nomination by virtue of their winning performances in the presidential primaries, the intricate nominating process by which they became the party standard-bearer has only recently begun to come under close scrutiny in Congress and many state capitals. The existing "mixed" system, a combination of presidential primaries and caucus-convention elections, is so complicated to the average citizen that an increasing number of reform-minded legislators and party activists have demanded that it be simplified and, in some cases, made more responsive to popular will.

Renewed Interest in Primary Reform

Proposals for some kind of federalized presidential primaries have been discussed more widely on Capitol Hill in the past decade than anytime since the Progressive era. What explains the revived interest in presidential primaries? Especially within the Democratic party the new concern can be explained as an unanticipated consequence of the sweeping changes made in the party rules regulating the presidential nominating process over the past ten years. Reform in the presidential nominating process came first as an outgrowth of the Eugene McCarthy protest movement against inadequate representation at the strife-torn 1968 Democratic National Convention. The subsequent McGovern takeover of the Democratic presidential nominating machinery in 1972 also helped push along primary reform in the states. Fourteen states adopted presidential primaries between 1969 and 1976. As a result, the number of states using the presidential primary in 1976 reached twenty-nine, exceeding the previous highwater mark established in 1916, when twenty states used this unique Progressive invention to select delegates to national conventions. Since then, four more states—Connecticut, Kansas, Louisiana and New Mexico—have been added to the list, making a grand total of thirty-three states for the 1980 primaries. While most members of the McGovern-Fraser Commission of Party Structure and Delegate Selection favored a reformed convention rather than establishment of regional or national primaries, the new party rules triggered unexpectedly heavy activity on the state level. Legislative leaders in several states concluded that a state presidential primary law would give rank-and-file citizens a more direct voice in the selection of state delegates to represent them at the national conclaves. Other state legislators decided that the most effective way to prevent the new national delegate selection rules from upsetting traditional ways of handling state and local party business, especially in the South, would be to split off presidential nominating procedures entirely from all other party activity. Still, legislators in other states felt that the new national party rules left caucuses and conventions much more vulnerable than a presidential primary to a takeover by a small, highly organized cadre of ideologues.

In the halls of Congress, the national primary movement has been pushed along by a twin drive for a constitutional amendment to abolish the Electoral College and substitute direct election of the president without regard to state lines. As explained by Austin Ranney, "Most of the arguments against the Electoral College and in favor of direct national elections can also be made against the national party convention and in favor of a direct national primary."[1] Both the Electoral College and the national convention, the critics insist, are artificial devices thrust between the sovereign voters and their choosing of a president. Both of these time-honored institutions make possible the selection of a president by a minority of voters, whereas direct election of the president and a national presidential primary will always reflect the popular will, the equally weighted votes of individual citizens.

Both reforms—direct election of the president and a national primary to select the party nominees—enjoy broad public support as measured by the Gallup poll. In February 1976, a Gallup survey showed 68 percent favoring a national primary and only 21 percent preferring national conventions.[2] Polls have consistently shown that well over two-thirds of the general population favor direct national election of presidents. With increased popular attention and interest focused on the presidential nomination and election process, the need to examine carefully the existing system and proposed alternatives takes on growing importance.

Discussion of proposed reform of the presidential nominating process has always been handicapped by a lack of general understanding of the highly complicated nature of the existing "mixed" presidential-primary-caucus-convention system. By contrast, the deceptively simple appeal of a single national direct primary to choose presidential candidates seems, on the surface at least, a sensible alternative. But is it the easy solution? Our tasks in this chapter will be twofold: first, to determine whether or not the existing primary system best serves the needs of the country for choosing nominees; second, to analyze the existing primary system and proposed alternatives for nominating presidential candidates and weigh the advisability of further reform.

Despite our generally favorable assessment of the presidential primary system in this study, some fundamental questions may still remain as to how the present nominating system measures up to the needs of the American voters:

1. Does the nominating system represent a consensus of party leaders and rank-and-file voters?
2. Does it maintain party responsibility?
3. Does it produce candidates with marked leadership potential, men and women who can command allegiance and active support of divergent elements with the party?
4. Does it avoid rampant factionalism and prolonged deadlocks?
5. Does it permit opportunities for negotiation and compromise among various sectional factions, special economic groups and minorities?
6. Does it preserve the two-party system?

The existing presidential primary system, operating within the framework of the national nominating convention, better meets all of these tests—when considered as a single package—than would other nominating systems based exclusively on a national presidential primary law or the caucus-party convention principle. The reasons merit further discussion.

The Existing Primary System: Pro and Con

Over the years the major arguments in favor of the primary system have been made by such persons as former Senate Democratic Majority Leader Mike Mansfield, Montana, and Senator William Proxmire, Wisconsin, the late Democratic Senator Paul Douglas, Illinois, former Republican Senators Margaret Chase Smith, Maine, George Aiken, Vermont, and the late Democratic Senator Estes Kefauver of Tennessee. All have favored a national presidential primary law, instead of the continuance of the existing "mixed" or patchwork system.[3] In this section, however, we will confine our analyses to the basic arguments for and against the existing mixed primary system. Later we will discuss the regional primary proposals and the case for and against the national primary.

ADVANTAGES

There are six major arguments in favor of the existing mixed primary system. The existing system permits rank-and-file voters in thirty-three states to participate directly in the selection of presidential candidates by electing convention delegates or expressing candidate preferences (or both), without destroying the nominating function of the national convention. Indeed, the existing primary-convention system avoids the revolutionary changes that a national primary would have upon the nomination system. By permitting the state delegations to retain a direct voice in the nominating process for the highest office in the land, the mixed system reinforces the confederate nature of the U. S. party system. States are still free to adopt, revise or discard their primary laws in favor of the caucus-convention arrangement, if they prefer, with minimal national party regulation.

As it exists today, the mixed primary system serves as a national forum and testing ground for the presidential candidates. There is no better "school for presidents" than the presidential primaries. They give the national convention delegates and the voting public the opportunity to assess first hand, over a period of several months, a presidential candidate's behavior, reaction under pressure and statesman qualities—a comprehensive "on-the-job" training program. The thirty-plus state primaries put a premium on a candidate's organizing ability—his deployment of campaign funds, management of campaign staff and his own time, and his decisiveness. Also, the primaries test the candidate's capacity to recover from campaign gaffes, his reaction to the unexpected, and, above all, his physical stamina. The present system furnishes an invaluable measuring stick for comparing candidates' qualifications. The primaries subject the candidates to a variety of election conditions, shifting sets of competitors and close scrutiny by the national media. A single national primary would tell us much less about candidates than the long, arduous, state-by-state grind. Under the present system the candidates are tested in a sequential series of primaries over a four-month period to an intensive degree never contemplated by our Founding Fathers—and all the time under the relentless lenses of the television camera. The present system also provides an excellent round robin elimination contest, a broad cross-sampling of voter opinion in various geographical sections—a form of regional primary—without the necessity of holding presidential primary elections in each of the fifty states. In fifteen weeks the primaries weed out with relentless efficiency the weak vote-getters.

One of the chief virtues of the existing string of primaries spaced over a period of several months is that the sequential nature of the mixed system permits the outsider or insurgent candidate to build success upon good showings in one state at a time. The "start-up" costs of a presidential primary campaign are relatively modest. A presidential candidate with a modest budget and a corps of volunteer workers (such as Jimmy Carter, George McGovern or Eugene McCarthy) can concentrate all of his resources and firepower on a single primary in the early stages of the campaign. If he is successful, say, in New Hampshire, he can move all of his troops and wagon trains to Florida or Wisconsin and repeat the process, thus building up presidential support gradually among the delegates and in the polls. If the outsider candidate had to focus on a single national primary, without the benefit of the slow buildup, he or she would be hopelessly outclassed. Also, the serialized testing of candidates enables them to assess their chances after one or two forays in the primaries. In the case of Michigan Governor George Romney in 1968, and Senator Birch Bayh in 1976, some candidates may find that they do not have the necessary vote-drawing power or finances after one or a few primaries—and so can conveniently pull out of the race. Better this arrangement than wasting the huge sums it would cost to compete in a national primary to find out the same thing.

When the primary returns are all in and the results have been fully assessed, the majority of the convention delegates are still free to make their choice of the candidate they feel best merits the nomination. The convention can still operate, if there is no popular choice, as a broker to reconcile differences and factions of the party with a compromise candidate and draft a platform acceptable to the various constituencies within the party. The national convention still remains far and away the best forum for putting together a winning ticket combination and platform that are most likely to appeal across party lines and to the millions of independent voters (now more than one-third of the electorate). A factional winner of a national direct primary, on the other hand, would be hard-pressed to produce such a combination.

Finally, the existing mixed system of primaries retains the national convention to legitimize the winner of primaries. As pointed out throughout this study, the national nominating convention has become chiefly a ratifying body and provides a coronation for the primary winner. Clearly, this has become the case since the recently adopted rule changes, especially in the Democratic party, have embedded the primary results even more firmly into the structure of the convention roll call. But the primaries alone still are not enough to anoint the nominee. Partisans and observers alike may have forgotten that in the 1976 primaries Jimmy Carter was the choice of only 39 percent of the approximately 16 million participating Democratic voters. In the hotly contested GOP nominating race, President Ford outpointed challenger Ronald Reagan by less than a total of 800,000 votes in the twenty-six preference or delegate encounters (Ford won sixteen and Reagan ten). By utilizing the national convention for the legitimization of the presidential choice, parties are able to foster consensus building after the tension-filled rivalry of the primary campaign. Candidates can secure the nomination by plurality victories in the primaries, as both Carter and Ford did in 1976, without necessarily being accepted by the majority of adherents of their own party. But, as David Broder has commented, "It is the acquiescence of others in their party demonstrated in convention hall that tells the voters that the nominees are legitimately the party standard-bearer."[4] Thus, the presidential primaries and national convention serve as reciprocal parts of the highly complex but remarkably responsive leadership selection machinery of this fifty-state federal Republic.

DISADVANTAGES

Senator Adlai E. Stevenson III (D, Ill.), like his father, the twice-defeated Democratic presidential nominee (1952 and 1956), has been one of the most articulate critics of the existing nominating process. In declining overtures to run for the 1976 Democratic nomination, Stevenson commented, "A candidacy today triggers a thousand skirmishes, a welter of endless, draining detail. . . . It plunges the candidate into a morass of unintelligible regulations and dervish-like activity, all largely beyond his control and comprehension."[5] With such an oversized field, Stevenson continued, ". . . [T]he press is beleaguered and spread too thin. Commentators gauge the viability of candidates by the most superficial devices: the size of campaign bankrolls or the volume of applause at joint appearances. . . . And television, the dominating medium," he said, "offers episodes and spectacles, and the citizen is hard put to fathom their significance." More specifically, the main arguments against the existing presidential primary system have been made on the basis of both mechanical and substantive defects.[6] But, as our discussion of each of the alleged defects will show, the shortcomings are not as serious as the opponents of the presidential primary system may make them. Indeed, some so-called defects can more accurately be listed as distinct advantages.

In the first place, primaries are held in only certain states, not all of them. This, however, is not a glaring defect but an advantage, for it reduces the expense and campaign burden of presidential candidates. It is not essential to hold a primary election in every state of the Union to learn who is the popular favorite and strongest vote-getter. Nor is it necessary for the front-running candidate to enter and win all thirty-three presidential primaries—though it is important that he or she capture a majority of the primaries against serious contenders. Also, presidential candidates are not required to enter all primaries; consequently, candidates can pick and choose only the primaries that offer the best prospects of victory. Actually, the voluntary participation of candidates in the primaries is no longer the serious deficiency critics have painted it to be. With over 75 percent of the delegates now selected in the presidential primary states, all major contenders know they must compete for this huge batch of delegates in the primaries if they are ever to reach the White House. The Oregon-type blanket ballot primary, which requires the inclusion of all candidates "generally advocated," has reduced candidates' options in at least eighteen states. Under the Oregon plan all candidates' names are listed on the primary ballot, whether they like it or not, unless they sign an affidavit that they are not a candidate—a step which disqualifies them for any federal matching campaign subsidies. While it is true that presidential candidates may pick or choose races in about half the primary states, few serious contenders dare avoid key primary fights because they would risk losing all the delegates in those states. Furthermore, this action would be interpreted by the national media and convention delegates in other states as an obvious sign of weakness.

The dates of the various primaries are so widely scattered—from late February until June—that the presidential candidates must campaign like traveling salesmen. With the wide diversity of election dates, victories in the early primaries, according to the critics, may unduly influence the results in later primary states, which is true. Actually, the absence of a uniform date for all presidential primaries is equivalent to a "shake-down" cruise and is invaluable training to a candidate for a successful general election campaign. Indeed, it tests a presidential contender for his ability to deal with the same types of crises and deadlines that he will, if nominated and elected, have to face in the White House. As Arthur Schlesinger, Jr., has observed, "Primary contests not only give a candidate exposure to the country but the country exposure to the candidate. Both sides learn from the experience. It is especially beneficial when candidates must campaign in parts of the country with which they are not familiar and which are not familiar with them."[7]

Is there a "domino effect" in the primaries? That is, do early-round primary victories help a candidate win in subsequent primaries? Sometimes they do; sometimes they don't. The outcome of the lead-off New Hampshire primary certainly helped Jimmy Carter in his drive for the nomination in 1976. But a New Hampshire victory did not transform Senator Edmund Muskie into the Democratic nominee in 1972 or Ambassador Henry Cabot Lodge into the 1964 GOP standard-bearer. More important, the four-month primary season permits cumulative demonstrations of strength by the leading candidates. Recent nominating races in the out-of-power party have been characterized at the outset by multiplicity of candidates and occasional voter confusion, but with a thirty-three-state obstacle course clear lines of choice usually become apparent before the end of the primary season as the defeated candidates drop one by one from the race.

Too much psychological importance is attached to early-round primary victories. It has been pointed out, for example, that a victory in New Hampshire, a predominantly Republican state (at least until the late 1960s) in which fewer than 1.4 percent of the American voters live, is not an accurate reflection of American public opinion of various presidential candidates. Obviously, the New Hampshire primary is not a barometer of how the American public will vote in November; but the national media use it as an early-season measurement of candidate popularity, and party leaders and prospective national convention delegates, their sensitive political antennae rotating in all directions, are anxiously looking for early signals about voter attitudes toward the candidates. Critics of the primary system have sometimes overlooked that the total population of the states holding presidential primaries now exceeds 167 million people (approximately 80 percent of the total population of the United States in 1970). Moreover, the total electoral vote of this group of states under the reapportionment following the 1970 census is 424 electors, almost 79 percent of the Electoral College.

It is said that presidential primaries create a divisive influence within the party, making it difficult to heal the painful wounds inflicted during the primary in time to form a united front against the rival party in the fall campaign. This was certainly true of the McGovern-Humphrey battle in the 1972 Democratic primaries. But four years later Jimmy Carter, winner of the primaries, captured the Democratic nomination with a minimum of bitterness among his defeated rivals and then went on to win the presidency. The narrow margin of Carter's general election victory, the polls showed, has generally been attributed to his own campaigning errors and the amazing general election campaign comeback by President Ford, not the residue of earlier candidate rivalries in the Democratic primaries.

Critics have always contended that primary contests spawn conflicts within the state organization. This is sometimes true. But a review of nominating battles since 1912 doesn't indicate a greater degree of intraparty conflict in the primary states than in the caucus-convention states. No presidential primary has produced the white heat of intraparty strife that developed in 1952 in Texas between the Taft and Eisenhower wings of the Republican party at the district and state conventions and the subsequent "rump" state convention. In fact, the presidential primary may reduce party bitterness by convincing the defeated candidate that he has been beaten in a fair, open contest, thus simplifying the reconciliation of party factions. George Wallace's 1976 presidential bid is a case in point. Wallace had a full, fair and well-financed shot at the Democratic nomination. As a result of a series of primary defeats in Massachusetts, Florida, North Carolina and elsewhere—Wallace won only his Alabama home state primary in 1976—he had to concede that his failure was the result of the people's judgment and not the machinations of political insiders. Speaking of Wallace's political demise, David Broder observed, "It is infinitely healthier for the political process that he was beaten cleanly and openly in the same game he had previously exploited, rather than being victimized by a back-room convention cabal."[8]

Another virtue of the primary sometimes overlooked is that it helps eliminate the seating contests between rival delegations from the same state at the national convention, such as the Taft and Eisenhower factions in 1952 wrangling furiously over the seating of contested delegations from the caucus-convention states of Georgia, Louisiana and Texas. More recently, however, credentials challenges among primary state delegates at the 1972 Democratic convention over the newly established "quotas" for minority groups and the interpretation of the California winner-take-all primary law versus the national party guidelines suggest that credentials fights can sometimes be acrimonious, no matter what the method of delegate selection used. The Democrats in 1976, however, unlike their other recent conventions, did not have a single contested delegation challenge. But the Republicans, torn apart by the heated nominating battle between the Ford and Reagan forces, had a series of bitter confrontations over the rules governing the interpretation of delegates' mandate under the various state primary laws. The problem arose because some states choose the actual convention delegates in a separate process from the presidential primary. In North Carolina and Florida, for example, many Reagan backers were pledged to vote for Ford by the proportional representation primary results, while in Indiana and Illinois the opposite was true. Fearful that "closet" Reagan supporters might flaunt their official pledge to support Ford and switch to Reagan on the first ballot, the Ford-controlled Convention Rules Committee and then the full GOP convention approved a party rule that barred any bolts by delegates bound by the state primary laws.[9]

Defeat in a single primary may cut down a leading contender in the out-of-power party and eliminate him from the race, even though he may be the most able candidate in his party. Ever since Wendell Willkie was defeated in the 1944 Wisconsin presidential primary and then withdrew from the Republican nominating race, the charge has been made repeatedly that primaries do not select nominees but merely destroy them. This may have been true on a few occasions in the past, but it is no longer the case. In 1956, Adlai Stevenson recovered after an early upset in the Minnesota primary by Senator Kefauver and then went on to capture renomination. In 1964, Senator Goldwater lost two important primary contests in New Hampshire and Oregon before he rebounded to win the crucial California primary in June, the last popular contest before the GOP national convention. Eight years later, Senator George McGovern lost the first three state primaries in which his name was entered—New Hampshire, Florida and Illinois. Yet, he was able to recover from these early setbacks and win the 1972 Democratic nomination by capturing ten of the final thirteen primaries held, including seven victories in a row. With the spread of presidential primaries to thirty-three states, candidates are no longer expected to win every primary in the early rounds to stay in the race. President Carter, it should not be forgotten, lost eleven contests during his long march through the primaries on his way to the White House in 1976. But a series of primary defeats without any large state victories in between will sound the death knell for most presidential contenders in the out-of-power party. Even so, Senator Eugene McCarthy in 1968 carried his nomination battle right down to the wire, despite his loss of four of the last five primaries to the late Senator Bobby Kennedy. Representative Morris Udall, a perennial second-place finisher behind Carter in the 1976 primaries (he was runner-up in eight primaries and placed third in seven contests), stayed in the race all the way to the Democratic convention balloting.

A common argument against the existing system is that presidential primary elections have been turned into massive popularity contests: candidates are chosen not on the basis of professional competence but on their handshaking ability. There is undoubtedly some truth in this charge. During the 1956 general election campaign Adlai Stevenson complained, "The idea that you can merchandise candidates for high office like breakfast cereal . . . is the ultimate indignity to the democratic process."[10] But this shift to a personalist type of primary campaigning is part of the changing electioneering style. Front-porch campaigns disappeared from the political scene long ago. In a vast, rapidly growing country of 220 million people, politicians and their managers, taking a tip from the motivational researchers, have concluded that it may be more important that their presidential candidate create a favorable "image" with the voters than concentrate on the issues. Perhaps the advent of more television debates will focus sharper attention on the issues in the primary and general elections alike. But in this age of the mass media and the physical impossibility of a candidate personally meeting more than a small percentage of the voters, it seems doubtful that popularity and a candidate's political "image" will cease to be major criteria for selecting presidential candidates and presidents.

Today's primaries are criticized as voracious consumers of candidates' time, money and physical energy. Presidential primary campaigning begins, at least informally, more than two years in advance of the national conventions and does not stop until the last primary and state conventions in June, usually a month or six weeks before the national conclave. The late Vice President Hubert H. Humphrey, who had been through the primary wars more than once, observed, "Physically, the presidential primaries are no harder than a campaign for the Senate—except that they just go on and on. As soon as you are through one, there is another."[11] There is considerable merit to this nonstop campaigning charge. Still, the question remains: Is traveling in two dozen or more primary states, talking and shaking hands with thousands of voters, attending dozens of political barbecues, becoming immersed in local problems, and being short on sleep throughout the long weeks of the primary season too great a price to pay for permitting the public to participate in the presidential nominating process? Public life, as all participants know, is a severe taskmaster. Greater use of television may help reduce the frightening burden of attempting to reach thousands of voters during each state primary, but probably no candidate would wish to rely exclusively on the television cameras to win elections, even if he could.

The most serious objection to the presidential primary system is that it weakens party responsibility by taking the power to make the nomination away from the party professionals and turning it over to rank-and-file voters. Defenders of party rule insist that the party function of selecting presidential candidates to provide national leadership and carry out the party program is wrecked if the primary voters are permitted to substitute their choice for that of the responsible party officials.[12] Members of the party-responsibility school maintain that a party can't carry out its nominating function if the power of selection is taken out of its hands and given to the voters. These critics argue that the rank and file may nominate a candidate who is incapable of unifying the party after a hard-fought national convention and who, if elected, may be unable to obtain the cooperation of party members in Congress to implement the party program. The party-responsibility advocates contend that democracy in a heavily populated modern state should mean popular control over government through periodic general elections, not popular participation in party matters, such as nominations. Popular control, according to this group, means voter choice between competing political parties, not control of intraparty business. While the primaries have undoubtedly weakened intraparty democracy and the hold of the party on the nominating machinery, the primaries have nevertheless had a salutary effect upon the nominating process by making potential nominees more responsive to the popular will. This change has occurred without forcing party leadership to relinquish ultimate control over the final selection of the party nominee at the national convention.

In the long run, there is probably no satisfactory alternative selection process to the existing system, short of parliamentary government, except the return to the straight party caucus-convention system or the adoption of a national direct primary law. The return to the straight party caucus-convention system (or the oligarchic Congressional Caucus) is almost unthinkable in this era of greater participatory democracy. The potential mischief a national primary poses for the American party system makes it less acceptable than a return to the nineteenth-century caucus-convention system.

The Case Against the Straight Party Convention System

Three main arguments against a return to the straight party convention system have been made repeatedly over the years.[13]

First, the nineteenth-century national convention was not representative, since the rank-and-file voter was given no voice or opportunity at any point in the process to participate in the selection of convention delegates within the states. Decisions at the national convention, according to critics, were actually made by "kingmakers," a handful of professional politicians, while the delegates picked at boss-controlled precinct caucuses and congressional district conventions sat by passively.

Second, the national convention was easily susceptible to capture by the vested interests working behind the scenes in the individual states with the local political rings to control the delegate selection process. Since the old-fashioned caucus-party convention system was not subject to state regulation (in most states today the caucus-convention system is regulated in much the same way as the primary), local party machines working with corporate wealth could tightly control the national convention delegate selection process at all levels in many states—and virtually dictate the convention choice.

Third, the national convention machinery with its hundreds of delegates is too cumbersome and unwieldy, and the carnival-like atmosphere of the convention is not a suitable place for the selection of candidates for the highest office of the land.

Because so many objections have been raised against the caucus-convention system, against the existing crazyquilt presidential primary structure, and against the proposed national direct primary, Senator Robert Packwood (R, Ore.) in March 1972 came up with a compromise proposal: regional primaries.[14]

Regional Primaries

PACKWOOD PLAN

Under the Packwood plan the national nominating convention would be left intact, but a system of five regional primaries would be held, one a month from March to July. The states would be grouped in clusters generally corresponding to the following geographical areas: The Northeast (ten states); the Midwest (six states); the South (nine states, plus the District of Columbia and three territories); the Great Plains (twelve states stretching from the Canadian border to the Gulf); and the Far West (thirteen states and one territory). The order of the primaries would be determined by lot by a five-member federal elections commission. The time sequence of the primaries for each of the five regions would be released only seventy days before the primary date, with the view of cutting down heavy campaigning in the "early bird" primaries.

No state would be allowed to conduct its own primary. Each regional primary ballot would include the names of all candidates judged to be serious contenders by the federal commission. Candidates not chosen by the commission could win a place on the ballot by petition. To have his or her name removed from the ballot, a candidate would sign a statement that he or she was not and did not intend to become a candidate. One would have to withdraw separately from each regional primary. Under the Packwood proposal a presidential candidate would be authorized to select delegates in proportion to the vote he received in that state. In other words, the Packwood plan would be based on proportionality and eliminate winner-take-all primaries. No candidate receiving less than 5 percent of the vote in a state would be entitled to any delegates. Each delegate would be committed to support the candidate who appointed him for two ballots, or until the candidate's total fell below 20 percent of the convention total—or until he released them.[15]

The chief advantage of the Packwood plan is that it reduces the number of primary races to five while retaining the staggered time sequence of the present system. By spreading the regional primaries over five months the Packwood plan would give the less well-known, inadequately financed candidate an opportunity to gain national recognition through strong showings in an early-round regional primary, such as was done in individual primaries by Senator McGovern in 1972 and Jimmy Carter in 1976. Regional primaries would also cut down travel time, the wear-and-tear on candidates, and allow more personal campaigning in each region. The regional plan also allows weaker candidates some prospects for winning the nomination. If a candidate failed to attract favorable voter support in the early primaries, he could withdraw gracefully. The Packwood plan would permit each state to decide for itself whether or not to hold a primary, but the state would have no choice of dates; it would have to use the same date stipulated for all states of the region.

The Oregon senator's plan, however, is not a panacea. Although Packwood's regional primary system would preserve the national nominating convention, the proportional allocation of delegates on the basis of each state's primary vote might well lead to a return of the bitter, multi-ballot conventions of yesteryear. Unlike the present convention system, which usually contains several hundred unpledged or uncommitted delegates willing to shift their preferences, a national convention under the Packwood plan would consist almost entirely of pledged delegates ideologically loyal to the candidate who appointed them—and probably much less willing to compromise and shift their choices of candidates, even in the face of a convention deadlock. In short, the Packwood plan lacks an easy mechanism to allow state party leaders to negotiate and switch their choice toward a compromise candidate. Under the present convention system uncommitted delegates perform this role. Undoubtedly, Packwood's provision for the release of delegates after two ballots or after a candidate's support falls below 20 percent of the convention total would help reduce the possibility of convention stalemate, but the threat of deadlock would frequently hover over the convention.

The Packwood plan would not cut down the length of the primary season. It would still be long and expensive, though the regional concept might cut down travel costs. Candidates from minor parties could qualify for entry.

The major departure from the existing system would be the introduction of a congressionally approved, presidentially appointed national primary election commission to act as a certification body and administrative manager of the nominating campaign—a radical departure in U. S. nominating politics. More will be said about the threat of greater federal control of presidential nominations later in the chapter.

UDALL PLAN

Several other presidential nominating proposals—variations on the Packwood plan—were also put forward in 1972. Congressman Morris Udall (D, Ariz.), a candidate for president four years later, offered a plan that would not require states to hold primaries but would compel those states holding them to do so on one of three dates in April, May or June. No regional grouping of primaries would be required, and each state could select any date it wanted.[16] As in the Packwood plan, the names of presidential candidates would be put on the ballot by a candidate designation committee; Udall would have national party leaders serve on this committee. Under the Udall plan delegates would be awarded to candidates in proportion to the votes they received—but with two important differences from Packwood's proposal. First, a presidential candidate winning a majority of the vote in a state would be entitled to all its delegates. Second, a contender receiving less than 10 percent of the vote would *not* be entitled to any delegates.

Udall's 50 percent winner-take-all provision (which violates the 1976 Democratic delegate selection ground rules) would permit a candidate to gain momentum with a series of convincing victories and thus reduce the chances of a deadlocked convention. But it would also preserve proportional representation in states where the vote was evenly divided. Thus, in the 1972 California Democratic presidential primary, for example, the Udall plan would have wiped out Senator McGovern's clean sweep of 271 delegates and given him only 45 percent, with 40 percent of the delegates going to Humphrey.

Similar to Packwood's plan, the Udall proposal would virtually force each contender to compete seriously for a portion of the delegation in every state. The Udall plan would probably encourage a proliferation of minor candidates who, although they could not win many delegates themselves, would hope to prevent any rivals from gaining a majority of delegates. Udall, a perennial second-place finisher in the 1976 presidential primaries, believes that his system is better than others because it does less violence to the existing nominating system.[17]

Several other objections to the optional regional primary plan immediately come to mind. To establish an equitable sequence of regions holding primaries would not be easy. An impressive candidate performance in the first regional primary might have a powerful impact on subsequent primaries. The outcome of a regional plan could vary greatly depending upon which states were included within a region. The arbitrary division of the country into regions, some critics argue, could heighten regional tensions or sectional rivalries. For states without presidential primaries the regional plan, even if it did not mandate that states must have primaries, would probably have the effect of pressuring states, even against their best judgment, to move to primaries.[18] In a close nominating race decided at a "brokered" convention, outsider states might feel left out of key decision making if they were not a member of the regional primary coalition.

MANDATORY REGIONAL PRIMARIES

In 1976 Representative Richard Ottinger (D, N.Y.) introduced a mandatory regional primary bill.[19] Although the Ottinger bill resembles the Packwood regional primary plan, it has one major difference: the Ottinger bill *requires* every state to hold a presidential primary; the Packwood plan leaves that decision to each state. The Ottinger compulsory regional primary assigns each state to one or another of five regions (the same regions designated in the Packwood bill). Primaries are to be held simultaneously in all states of a region on the first Tuesday of April and on Tuesdays of the third, sixth, ninth, and twelfth succeeding weeks, ending in June. As in the Packwood plan, the Federal Election Commission (FEC) would determine by lot which region votes first. Then, the FEC would hold a drawing twenty days prior to the next scheduled date to determine by lot which region would hold the next regional primary.

Ballots in each state must include the names of all candidates whom the FEC has declared eligible for federal matching funds. Other presidential aspirants may also get their names on the ballot in particular states by submitting petitions to the secretaries of state or equivalent officers.

The Ottinger bill requires that in all states each party's primary must be closed to all but registered members of the party and directs the FEC to prescribe a system of party registration for any state that does not already have it.

The Ottinger plan's provision for proportional allocation of delegates, binding the delegates' votes at the convention, selection of vice presidential candidates and reimbursement of the states for the costs of holding primaries are identical to those in the Packwood plan.

The major difference, then, between the Ottinger and Packwood plans is that the former requires all states to hold primaries under conditions stipulated by federal law, while the Oregon senator's plan imposes these conditions only on those states which decide to hold a presidential primary.

Most of the objections to the voluntary regional primary apply as well to the compulsory regional primary: lack of an adequate "brokering" mechanism for shifting delegate support at conventions, determining the order of the sequential regional primaries, and potential heightening of tension between regions supporting different candidates.

Though the Packwood plan and, to a lesser extent, the Ottinger mandatory regional primary have attracted the attention of party reformers, none of the bills has been reported out of committee. State legislatures in three sections of the country, however, gave serious consideration to the regional primary in 1975.

STATE ACTION ON REGIONAL PRIMARIES

In New England, where five of the six states (Massachusetts, New Hampshire, Vermont, Rhode Island and Connecticut) now hold primaries, the regional primary idea has become a frequent topic of discussion. Especially in Massachusetts, the Democratic party leadership has been anxious to cut in on the favorable publicity and nationwide attention that the New Hampshire primary has enjoyed since 1952. Under the guidance of Lt. Governor Thomas P. O'Neill III, son of House Speaker Thomas P. "Tip" O'Neill, Democrats have been eager to push through the Massachusetts legislature a bill changing the Bay State primary date to coincide with New Hampshire's late February election. New Hampshire Governor Meldrim Thomson, Jr. and state legislators, however, jealous to maintain their state's position as the first-in-the-nation primary, were cool to this proposal. To counter the anticipated opposition from New Hampshire, Massachusetts legislators introduced a bill to empower the secretary of state to adjust the primary date, depending on whatever New Hampshire did.[20] Eventually, however, the Bay State solons gave up this idea.

Neighboring Vermont joined the presidential primary club in January 1976. After failing to pass the primary bill a year earlier, the Vermont legislature made it the first order of business of the session—just in time to join the 1976 round robin competition. But the Vermont preference primary was held one week later than New Hampshire and on the same day as the Massachusetts primary.

Next door in Rhode Island, the Democratic party chieftains were, according to one source, less enthusiastic about a regional primary. Reportedly, they sought to push their present late May primary into early June to let the field of candidates narrow down, thus enhancing their chances of backing the leading contender and getting to the national convention as pledged delegates for him.[21] But the Democratic-controlled legislature decided to take no further action on the date shift. Rhode Island voters in the 1976 primary, it might be noted, opted for an uncommitted delegation backing California Governor Edmund G. "Jerry" Brown, Jr., not the party nominee, Jimmy Carter.

Election officials representing the six New England states failed again in March 1979 to agree on a single date for a regional presidential primary in 1980. Bitter resistance from New Hampshire politicians intent on keeping their first-in-the-nation primary spot on the calendar and indifference among Rhode Island officials to a joint enterprise blocked agreement on a uniform date.[22] The Rhode Island primary is scheduled for early June, and state officials have expressed little interest in shifting this date. But Connecticut, Massachusetts, Vermont and Maine representatives reached an agreement to work for a mutual date early next March, even though Maine legislators finally decided not to pass a presidential primary law. This modified regional primary, held early in a presidential election year, would have given New England a political prominence outweighing its relatively small population. The joint date would also enable candidates to make maximum use of the regional nature of television broadcasting in New England. (Boston TV stations attract thousands of viewers in New Hampshire, Rhode Island and Maine; indeed, presidential candidates in the New Hampshire primary have for years relied almost exclusively on these Boston stations to carry their political advertising.)

New Hampshire, which has held the nation's first primary since 1948, has vehemently defended this distinction ever since. In 1978, for example, the New Hampshire legislature passed a law requiring that its primary precede that of any other state, no matter how early. William Gardner, the New Hampshire secretary of state, refused to change that position at the New England summit meeting. "It's a tradition, since we have always had it first," he said. "We'll do whatever we have to to maintain that."[23]

When the 1978 Puerto Rico Commonwealth Legislature approved a February 17 primary date for 1980 (the Democratic primary is scheduled for Sunday, March 16), the New Hampshire lawmakers promptly responded by tentatively scheduling its famed presidential primary on February 11, two weeks earlier than previously scheduled. Maine legislators originally proposed to have their primary on whatever date the New Hampshire primary is held. But New Hampshire officials retaliated by threatening to keep the exact date of their primary secret until the last minute. (The 1980 primary will be held on February 26).

New Hampshire's presidential primary has become the state's favorite natural resource—the chief means for developing national visibility and a big moneymaker for the tourist industry. Granite State public officials appear to be prepared to pay almost any price to maintain its premier quadriennial status. Recently, the Republican Party Board in Florida voted to hold a presidential preference convention and straw vote in November 1979, but New Hampshire legislators chose to ignore this challenge.[24]

Massachusetts and Vermont currently have plans to hold primaries on March 4, 1980, a date that conflicts with the new rules promulgated by the Democratic National Committee calling for a shortened primary season limited to the thirteen-week period from the second Tuesday in March to the second Tuesday in June. The GOP National Committee has no rules stipulating dates on which primaries may be held.

In 1975 in the Midwest, liberal Democratic legislators in Minnesota attempted to lay the groundwork for a regional primary consisting of Wisconsin, Minnesota and South Dakota, but they were stymied in the state senate after a presidential primary bill had passed in the Minnesota House of Representatives.

For a time the best prospects for a regional primary appeared to be in the Pacific Northwest. In 1975, Idaho passed a presidential primary law, to be held on the same date as the widely publicized Oregon primary. Montana, which for the third time in its state history passed a presidential primary law in 1975, set it for the first Tuesday in June, one week later than the Oregon and Idaho primaries. The state of Washington was also expected to fall in line, with legislative supporters of Senator Henry "Scoop" Jackson pushing for a home state primary to enhance his presidential nomination prospects. A bill providing for a winner-take-all primary at the congressional district level passed both houses, but it was vetoed by Republican Governor Daniel J. Evans. Since the Democrats lacked the two-thirds majority to override the veto, Washington remained in 1976 one of the twenty-one states using the caucus-convention system to select delegates.

Recent signs point to a special "Dixie" regional primary in 1980. Encouraged by President Carter's campaign operatives, three Southern states—Alabama, Florida, and Georgia—have been reportedly piecing together what amounts to a regional presidential primary. By mid-summer 1979 Florida and Alabama had set their presidential primaries for March 11, 1980. Carter's home state of Georgia, which in 1976 held its first presidential primary in forty-four years, was expected to follow suit. This action had been quietly promoted by Carter's southeastern campaign manager, who conceded in an Associated Press interview that the White House wanted a simultaneous early primary in these three states.[25] According to political insiders, the Carter strategists were anxious to move up the election dates of several Southern primaries, where President Carter is expected to do well, to help neutralize threatened first-round Carter primary defeats in New Hampshire, Massachusetts, Vermont and Connecticut. In 1976 Carter's victories in a half dozen Southern primaries helped maintain his pre-convention momentum and offset a series of primary losses, especially in five Western states at the hands of Senator Frank Church and California's Governor Edmund G. "Jerry" Brown, Jr. Carter's campaign staff appeared to be aiming for a successful repeat performance in primaries below the Mason Dixon line in 1980. In face of President Carter's record low poll ratings and widespread complaints about his ineffective leadership, especially from Democratic leaders in Congress and the state capitols, the timing of the new Dixie primary has taken on special importance to the beleaguered president. Recently, Senator Henry Jackson, one of Carter's 1976 Democratic protagonists, predicted that unless the president suddenly recaptured public support, he would not be a viable candidate and should consider withdrawing from the race if he lost several early 1980 primaries. Obviously, a strong Carter showing in three early Southern primaries would not only help blunt public criticism of his presidential leadership but also minimize the importance of the New England primaries—Senator Kennedy's home base.

The regional primary concept, designed as a middle ground between the present thirty-three state primaries and a single national primary, can be expected to remain one of the major alternatives to the existing system.

National Direct Primary

Proponents of regional primaries, however, must now share equal time with advocates of a national direct primary. Under most national direct primary proposals the national nominating convention would be abolished and replaced by a one-day national direct primary held in all fifty states.

Federal legislation to establish a national presidential primary, as indicated earlier, dates back to the Progressive era. The first bill to federalize the legal machinery for nominating presidential candidates was introduced in 1911 by Representative Richard P. Hobson (D, Ala.).

Under his plan presidential candidates were to be nominated by direct national primaries regulated by law instead of by the traditional national convention governed by party rules. Former President Theodore Roosevelt, running as the Bull Moose third-party presidential candidate in 1912, urged adoption of a national primary. From 1911 to 1977, according to one source, over 250 presidential primary proposals have been introduced in Congress, including thirteen in 1977.[26]

The national direct primary, the oldest reform proposal, has also been the most frequently introduced type of bill on Capitol Hill; approximately one-half of the 250-plus presidential primary bills have called for some version of a national direct primary election.[27]

Probably the best-known model is the Mansfield-Aiken bill, introduced in March 1972.[28] The jointly sponsored proposal would establish by constitutional amendment a single national primary in early August for any party whose candidate received at least 10 percent of the national vote in the previous presidential election. Candidates would become eligible for the primary by submitting petitions signed by voters numbering at least 1 percent of that party's total vote in the previous national election. Another provision would establish a minimum level of support in at least seventeen of the fifty states, presumably to prevent a candidate with only regional popularity from gaining a spot on the primary ballot. Each party's nomination would go to the candidate with the most primary votes, a plurality rather than a majority. If no candidate received 40 percent of the vote, a run-off between the top two would be held four weeks later. Under the Mansfield-Aiken bill, national conventions still would be held to select vice presidential candidates and presumably to adopt a platform.

More recently, proposals to establish a direct national primary were introduced in 1977 by Representatives Joseph Gaydos (D, O.), and Albert Quie (R, Minn.), and Senator Lowell Weicker (R, Conn.).[29] Typical of the most recent bills put in the legislative hopper is the Quie plan, which provides that "the official candidates of political parties for President and Vice President shall be nominated at a primary election by direct popular vote." Under the Quie plan all intermediaries between the voters and the nomination—in other words, state party leaders and national convention delegates—would be eliminated in the selection process. Held in all fifty states on the same day, the Quie plan sets the national primary date as the first Tuesday after the first Monday in August of presidential election years.

Like most of the direct national primary bills, the Quie proposal calls for a closed primary, though no provision is made for federally supervised party registration. Senator Weicker's bill, however, permits persons registered as independents to vote in either party's primary.

Candidates acquire positions on the ballot by filing with the president of the Senate petitions bearing a number of signatures equal to at least 1 percent of the total number of popular votes cast in the nation for all candidates in the most recent presidential election. Candidates for vice president would be required to petition separately and appear on the ballot in a separate group. No person would be allowed to run for both the presidential and vice-presidential nominations.

To win nomination a presidential candidate would have to receive a majority of popular votes. (The Gaydos bill allows a candidate to win the first primary with 45 percent or more of the votes.) If no candidate received an absolute majority on the first ballot, the two top vote-getters would face each other in a run-off primary four weeks later. The winner of the run-off would be the party nominee. The same conditions would prevail for the vice presidential primaries.

ADVANTAGES

The main advantages of a national primary are its directness and simplicity. Former Senate Majority Leader Mike Mansfield (D, Mont.), a major sponsor, insists that even with a run-off election, the national primary would come closest to the Democratic ideal of citizens choosing their nominees on a one-person, one-vote basis. Proponents of a national primary avow that it would be more representative in the sense that the nominee would be the choice preferred by most rank-and-file identifiers. Nominations would be done in the voting booths of America and not in the circus-like, mass rally atmosphere of the national convention.

Advocates of the national primary assert that this election could be understood much more easily by the rank-and-file voter. If the selection rules are simplified and made the same in all fifty states, proponents argue, more rank-and-file members of the electorate will understand the nominating process and therefore participate in the primary instead of waiting until November to vote. Further, the national primary would eliminate the chance for a presidential hopeful to manipulate the existing primary system by picking and choosing certain primaries and skillfully avoiding strong opponents on their own turf.

Robert Bendiner has argued that the national primary would cut down the "bandwagon" effect, the process whereby a candidate can move from a victory in one primary to make a strong showing in another carefully selected state.[30] The national direct primary would, of course, eliminate the excessive influence of the first-round state primaries, which give the early front-runner heavy media attention and national recognition, and help attract organizational and financial support.

Another argument made by proponents of a national primary is that it would shorten the pre-nomination season, thus helping lessen the physical strain on the candidates. Over and above these advantages, candidates in a national primary would probably be unable to campaign personally in all fifty states; instead, they could take their campaign to the voters via television. Thus, instead of the present hit-and-miss system of primaries, the national primary would give the voters in every state a chance to judge the qualifications of every candidate. Candidates could focus their campaigns on issues instead of jetting from one primary to another in frantic search of votes.

DISADVANTAGES

Deceptively appealing, the national primary would have revolutionary implications on the presidential nominating process and would probably shatter our already weakened party system. Indeed, adoption of a national direct primary would constitute as great an alteration in the American party system and in our way of choosing a president as did the changes in the early 1800s, when the rise of political parties transformed the electoral college into an instrument for popular election of the president.[31] On paper, the national primary concept appears eminently sensible. All fifty states would hold a national primary on a single day and choose their favorite as the party nominee for president. If no candidate received a majority of the votes—or 40 percent of the votes under some plans—a second or run-off primary between the top two candidates would be held to pick a winner to run in the November general election. What could be more simple? But a closer examination of the national primary reveals that it is filled with political boobytraps. Several of the worst features of the national primary warrant a detailed review.

The single national direct primary would abolish the sequential nature of presidential nominating contests. Unlike the present four-month, extended "candidate review" process in thirty-three primary and seventeen caucus-convention states, the party nominee would be selected during a one-day twelve-hour election. Delegates, the parties, the national media, and the public would be denied the present opportunity to defer final judgment on prospective nominees while they assess the candidates' appeal in a variety of electoral settings and over several months of intense scrutiny. Although the initial delegate selection process begins with the mid-January caucuses in frosty Iowa, the final list of delegates is not picked until June. As a matter of fact, almost 50 percent of the delegates nationwide were selected or apportioned during the last six weeks (May 4-June 8) of the 1976 primary season and the final-round district and state party conventions. Under the present system all interested constituencies have ample opportunity to assess the early front-runners, the political unknowns, the favorite sons, the late entries, and the strong finishers before the opening gavel is sounded at the national convention. This deferred decision making—the strongest feature of the existing nominating system—would all be lost if a national primary were adopted.

National primaries would most likely favor candidates with the best known names—Kennedy, Rockefeller, Reagan. A single national primary would make it next to impossible for relatively unknown candidates, such as Eugene McCarthy in 1968, George McGovern in 1972, or Jimmy Carter in 1976, to capitalize on early victories in state primaries to attract a growing number of supporters in the latter stages of the nominating campaign. With all the chips riding on a single national primary, the best known names would enjoy a tremendous advantage over the political unknowns, since voters generally prefer to vote for someone they know something about over someone unknown. Political visibility or name recognition, party professionals readily concede, is an important factor in any successful local, state or national campaign. The first task of any aspiring presidential contender is to become better known. Table 10.1 shows how well known various Democratic hopefuls for the 1976 nomination were nine months before the New York City convention. It stretches the imagination to conclude that eleventh-ranked Jimmy Carter, without the benefit of his victories in the Iowa caucuses, the New Hampshire, Vermont, Florida, North Carolina, Wisconsin and twelve other primaries, would have been able to build his name recognition high enough to compete on even terms with a Kennedy or a Humphrey in a single national primary contest. Carter needed more than four months of intensive media coverage to become an established national political figure. Fortunately for him also was the fact that four of the five best-known candidates— Kennedy, Humphrey, McGovern and Muskie—chose not to enter the 1976 Democratic sweepstakes.

TABLE 10.1
NAME RECOGNITION OF DEMOCRATIC PRESIDENTIAL
HOPEFULS IN OCTOBER 1975
(PERCENT)

Candidate	Recognition	Candidate	Recognition
Kennedy	96	Bayh	50
Wallace	93	Udall	47
Humphrey	91	Shapp	31
McGovern	89	Carter	29
Muskie	84	Bentsen	24
Shriver	76	Harris	22
Jackson	64	Sanford	21

Source: Gallup Opinion Index, no. 125 (November-December 1975): 98.

The national direct primary would appear to favor candidates with strong ideological ties to the extreme left or right wings of the party, at the expense of middle-of-the-road candidates. Because a national primary would attract a large field of entrants in each party—the Democrats in 1976 had a dozen serious aspirants—the prospect of a run-off primary would be extremely high. With a large field of candidates drawn mostly from the moderate wings of the two parties, it is more than likely that one or two candidates from the extreme wings of the party would be in the run-offs because the centrist candidates would cancel each other out in the primary. Also, as the Republicans learned in 1964 and the Democrats in 1972, a Goldwater or McGovern-type candidate attracts a strong, committed activist following which can be mobilized for the primary campaign, while the moderate, low-key candidate encounters serious problems in arousing support among the apathetic rank-and-file electorate. These voters invariably prefer to wait until November before going to the polls. Thus, the ideologically oriented candidate can turn out his factional supporters in large numbers on primary day to defeat middle-of-the-road candidates. But, paradoxically, this extremist candidate, who can carry the primaries with his enthusiasts, lacks the broadbased support among rank-and-file party members and independent voters needed to win the general election.

If there were a large field of candidates, such as in 1972 and 1976—and presidential primaries encourage more entrants—the winner of the national primary could conceivably be a divisive personality unacceptable to a majority of his party. Theoretically, a presidential candidate could win the nomination with 40 percent of the primary vote, even if he were the last choice of the remaining 60 percent. Nevertheless, his party would be forced to accept him as the nominee. As a vehicle to democratize nominations, the national primary would probably have the opposite effect.

The national primary also lacks the "safety-valve" feature of the present mixed convention system which permits a last-minute "draft" should the rapid turn of events—strategic considerations, a personal scandal, or health reasons—require a switch in candidates.

The cost of financing a national primary in fifty states would be almost prohibitive, even with the new federal matching-fund feature of the 1974 Federal Election Campaign Act. Assuming that no candidate received 40 percent of the votes—despite his one-sided victory in the 1976 Democratic nominating race, Jimmy Carter won only 39 percent of the total primary vote—a run-off national primary would have to be held between the two top contenders. Thus, two or more national elections would escalate the original cost to the candidates—and the fifty states conducting the elections. With three national elections the cost of television time, radio commercials, airline tickets, billboards, computerized direct mailings, organization and headquarters costs would reach an all-time high. For the candidates the task of soliciting primary campaign contributions would be a mammoth job requiring a large staff of fund raisers and accountants to assure compliance with the new 1974 Federal Election Campaign Act. Because it is doubtful that many men of modest means would be able to raise a large war chest, even with the new matching fund formula, a national primary would favor wealthy candidates.

To reduce the general election campaign period, sponsors of national primary legislation have scheduled (in those bills listing a specific date) the election for the last half of August or at the end of the first week of September, just after the Labor Day holiday weekend. Thus, the national primary would be held at the end of the summer political dog days, when voter interest is generally considered at its lowest ebb by most professional politicians. Voter turnout would probably be extremely light—the 1976 primary turnout averaged 29 percent. With the anticipated large field of contenders—a dozen or more in the out-of-power party would not be surprising—voters would be less likely to be familiar with the candidates' relative merits, policy positions and shortcomings.

Though holding the national primary in late August-early September would obviously shorten the general election campaign, the late primary date would most likely result in a longer national primary campaign, probably longer than the present ten-month primary-general election campaign. In the past two nominating campaigns the trend for presidential aspirants has been to make their official announcements earlier than ever. By February 1975, sixteen months before the 1976 Democratic convention, five Democratic hopefuls, including Jimmy Carter, had tossed their hats in the ring. The first candidate to announce his entry in the 1980 primaries (Representative Philip Crane, R, Ill.) tossed his hat in the ring in August 1978, nearly two years before the next GOP national convention and almost twenty-seven months before the 1980 presidential election. Under a national primary the intense desire of relatively unknown candidates to become nationally recognized would likely lead to even earlier announcements and consequently a longer primary campaign.

Although the informal nominating campaign would probably start at least two years before the primary election day, the successful candidate for the presidency and his opponent would have to face three national elections (assuming a run-off primary) within approximately seventy days. The thought of three elections within a ten-week period makes most political scientists and campaign managers shudder. For the average citizen three trips to the polls within three months might begin to overtax his or her patience with the democratic process. Voter reaction might well take the form of lower voter participation, which now averages less than 55 percent in presidential elections, the lowest among the Western democracies.[32] While high voter participation is not necessarily a sign of robust political health for a nation, the likelihood of 70-80 million or more potential voters sitting on the sidelines in an election to pick the highest officeholder in the land does not bode well for the nation's future.

A national primary would further weaken the party structure and, as indicated earlier, lead to intensive factionalism within each major party. This disruptive influence would become serious every time two major candidates became involved in a run-off primary. The result would be a bitter collision between candidates of opposing philosophies, with party wounds deepened and moderates forced to move to one extreme wing of the party or the other. This factionalism, usually slow to dissipate, would undermine the party throughout the general election campaign. It might lead to a multi-faction, or multi-party system, instead of the present, viable two-party system. The existing nominating system, haphazard as it may sometimes be, nevertheless allows minority factions to have more bargaining power for seeking concessions to their point of view from the nominee, for example, in the choice of vice presidential nominee, platform changes, political appointees or support for legislation favorable to the minority group. These give-and-take negotiations usually enable the nominee to approach the general campaign with a more united party behind him. A presidential candidate selected in a national primary could ignore the party apparatus, preempt the party label for his personal campaign organization and capture the nomination with minimal communication with the party leadership. Any national primary would enhance the importance of candidate organizations at the expense of the parties.

More fundamentally, a one-day national direct primary would effectively shut out national and state party organizations from any active role in the sifting and winnowing nominating process that narrows down the theoretical list of millions of potential presidential candidates who meet the constitutional qualifications to a manageable "short list" of, say, ten or fifteen serious possibilities. The growing trend toward personalist politics and individual candidates' organizations, fostered by the emergence of television as a universal form of communication between the candidates and voters, would come to dominate presidential nominating machinery as the parties lose their ability to influence and control the selection process. With the "dismantling" of the party organizations, the national news media would continue to expand their already pervading influence and perhaps tilt the outcome of presidential nominating contests. By shaping most voters' perceptions of how the various contenders stand in the race, the national television and radio networks, major newspapers, and wire services not only could tip the outcome of the nominating races but heighten tensions between candidates and rival campaign organizations. Instead of the moderating influence of a political party that strives to facilitate bargaining, consensus and reconciliation in the presidential selection process, the national news media focus their coverage on the conflicts and rivalries between candidates to attract viewer and reader interest.[33] To the national news media executives, presidential nominating races are treated chiefly as political Olympics or pennant races: who's the favorite, who's ahead, who's behind? While these headlines-producing stories make good entertainment, they are a poor substitute for the role parties have generally performed in the nominating process.

Adoption of a national direct primary, one can predict with confidence, would turn political parties into little more than empty shells with only the covering labels of Democrat and Republican visible to the electorate. Presidential nominating races would consist almost exclusively of competition among rival entrepreneurial candidate organizations as reported by the national news media. These conditions would not be unlike the one-party—indeed, no-party—politics of the Old South, typified by intense factionalism and demagogic politicians. National primaries would most likely resemble traditional Southern Democratic gubernatorial primaries, depicted by the late V. O. Key, Jr., as gigantic popularity contests based on personalities rather than issues and characterized by the office seeker's lack of accountability to organized party electorates.[34] As Jeane Kirkpatrick has observed, ". . . any national primary would accelerate the trend toward personalist politics, exacerbate intraparty divisions, increase the likelihood of selecting unrepresentative candidates and an unrepresentative President, render the parties still more irrelevant to the presidential contest, and enhance the importance of candidate organizations."[35]

Passage of a national direct primary or mandatory regional primary would also signal the end of experimentation with various types of primary or caucus-convention systems within the states. Since the Progressive era, states have served as "laboratories" for testing various kinds of primaries and caucus systems.[36] In some cases, states have adopted the primary for a time and then switched to the caucus system, only to return to the presidential primary system again later on. Under the present mixed system, it is possible to observe and monitor the various delegate selection and candidate preference rules—closed primary versus crossover voting, binding versus advisory preference polls and proportional representation versus winner-take-all—and their impact on voter turnout and types of candidates favored. If a uniform system of primary rules were adopted for all fifty states, it would, of course, be impossible to analyze the impact and consequences of these various nominating practices. A national primary would mean that one and only one set of rules would govern the selection process across the nation. Uniformity seems too high a price to pay for the replacement of a confederate political system that has operated with only limited failings in selecting presidential candidates over the past 150 years.

In summary, establishment of regional or national primaries could have many unintended consequences that would be harmful to the national political process. Expansion of the primary to include all, or virtually all, of the fifty states would further weaken the already shaky national and state party structures. Nationwide or mandatory regional primaries would lessen the capacity of parties to articulate, aggregate and represent voter concerns. Instead, the mass communications media, especially the television networks, would become the chief agencies for sorting out the candidates, designating the front-runner candidate and discarding the "also-rans" from further serious consideration. As a result of this rank-ordering of candidates, the national media would, in effect, be defining the voters' choices.[37]

Most of the regional and national primary proposals contain provisions for a federal committee to certify candidates to compete in elections and to establish common procedural standards. Most proposals would also establish rigid delegate commitment rules. This would inhibit political "brokering" at the conventions and effectively block the type of state delegate shifts (even from pledged delegates) that in recent years have helped put Dwight D. Eisenhower, John F. Kennedy and Jimmy Carter over the top on the first ballot. Some of the measures also reimburse the states for their expenditures in primary elections, a carrot-type inducement to encourage states to adopt this method of delegate selection. Overall, the thrust of these bills would eventually leave little discretion to the states or the national parties. As William J. Crotty has observed, "Regardless of intention, they would insinuate the federal government into a process that despite its serious faults is best left to the states."[38] By and large, these proposals, which attempt to deal with problems in presidential nominations, tend to introduce more severe difficulties into the selection process than currently exist. In Crotty's words, "The present system is preferable to what is likely to evolve from a national specification of rules for nominating operations no matter how benevolent the goal of its creators."[39]

Suggested Modifications in the Present Nominating System

The asserted superiority of the mixed system over a national direct primary, a regional primary system, or a straight caucus-convention system does not mean, necessarily, that the present mixed nominating system of approximately two-thirds primary states and one-third caucus-convention states should not be altered. There are a number of modifications—not drastic changes—that could be introduced to improve the existing system.

The presidential primary season should be shortened. It is already longer than the general election campaign. Officially, the primary season commences the day after New Year's Day, with the candidates trudging off to snow-covered New Hampshire. Unofficially, candidates from the out-of-power party, recognizing the importance of an early start, have begun nonstop stumping for the presidential nomination almost two years before the next national convention. President Jimmy Carter announced his candidacy in December 1974, almost twenty months before the 1976 Democratic conclave in New York City. Throughout 1974 Carter was also informally campaigning, making personal contacts with party leaders and congressional candidates, in his capacity as chairman of the Democratic National Campaign Committee. Four years earlier, Senator George McGovern won the Democratic nomination after a nineteen-month state-by-state campaign. The final curtain for the springtime primary campaign season does not ring down until the first ten days of June. This unofficial eighteen-month and official four-month primary campaign could be shortened. Except for the fierce pride of the New Hampshire citizenry, there is no reason why that primary could not be moved back to late April or early May, with a comparable rescheduling of the primaries in Wisconsin, West Virginia, Oregon, California and other states. Recognizing the excessive length of the pre-convention campaign, the Democratic National Committee has voted to shorten the 1980 nominating season by confining all caucuses and primaries to a thirteen-week period—the so-called window concept—from the second Tuesday in March to the second Tuesday in June. However, another party rule will allow New Hampshire to keep its late February primary and Iowa its late January caucuses—where Jimmy Carter scored his first two victories in 1976—at least through 1980.[40] With a shorter delegate selection period, primaries and caucuses will, of course, be clustered closer together, reducing somewhat the possibilities that any one state's results, except New Hampshire's, would receive overwhelming attention.

One of the original reasons the primaries were held so early was that the national conventions at the turn of the twentieth century were held earlier than now. The Republicans gathered at their national conclaves during the second week in June. The Democrats generally followed two weeks later. In the pre-television era of the railroad and telegraph, the campaign moved along at a more leisurely pace. The presidential nominee was not officially "notified" until a delegation from the national convention visited him personally at his home several days afterwards to "inform" him of his nomination. Though more than four months elapsed between convention time and election, the colorful whistlestop campaign did not seem too long or onerous. Nowadays, each contested presidential primary is a national election in microcosm. The physical demands alone upon the candidates require the stamina of a bull ox. Consequently, any proposal to shorten the campaign is almost acceptable on face value.

More geographical balance is needed in the presidential primary schedule. Of the first eighteen primaries held in 1976, eight were held in the East, five in the Midwest, and five in the South. None were held further west than Texas and Nebraska, even though one-fourth of the states and almost one-fifth of the electoral votes (102) are found in the western United States. With the total disfranchisement of the West in the first half of the primary season, candidates from west of the Mississippi River operate under a serious disadvantage. It was therefore not surprising in 1976 that the three Western candidates—Reagan, Church and Brown— did not gain momentum until the second half of the primary season. By the time the Western primary season started, public opinion had largely crystallized, especially for Jimmy Carter. Of fourteen primaries held by both parties in the West after May 1, and contested by the three candidates, only one was lost by a Western candidate—Reagan to Ford in Oregon.

Primaries should be "closed." Voters should be restricted to vote only in the primary of the party in which they are registered. This requirement, which has been adopted by the Democratic party, cuts down crossover voting or "raiding" of the opposition party by rival party supporters who may wish to nominate a weak candidate in order to defeat him or her more easily in November.[41]

The presidential preference primary (the so-called beauty contest) and the selection of national convention delegates should be combined on the ballot to avoid confusion in a few states over a possible dual mandate, with one candidate winning the preference primary and another candidate a majority of the delegates.

Presidential contenders who receive at least 15 percent of the primary vote should receive their proportionate share of the state's national convention delegation.[42] If a contender wins a majority of the state vote, however, he or she would receive all the state's convention vote. (Suggested by Congressman Morris Udall, this majoritarian principle, which corresponds to the criterion of success for most elections, would be in conflict with the present Democratic party ban on all winner-take-all primaries.)

Delegates should be obligated to support the candidate who wins their votes in the primary for at least two ballots, unless released by the candidate, or until the candidate drops below a certain percentage of the convention vote.

Delegates should not be allowed to offer themselves on behalf of a presidential candidate without his or her written consent. Prospective delegates or slates of delegates should have their candidate affiliation or their uncommitted status printed on the ballot.

The federal government should continue to underwrite on a matching basis the primary electioneering costs of presidential candidates who have demonstrated the ability to raise a specified minimal amount of money in twenty states (as now provided by federal law).

These suggested reforms amount to little more than tinkering with the existing machinery. With these mechanical adjustments, however, the major flaws in the present nominating procedures would be corrected, if the maximum number of primaries can be kept at approximately two-thirds of the states. Retention of the caucus-convention system in at least one-third of the states should help halt further deterioration of our already badly weakened party system. Also, these additional reforms would help meet the six tests listed early in the chapter for assessing the viability of the American presidential nominating system. More importantly, by averting further federal intervention, the management of the present mixed primary and caucus-convention system would be left jointly in the hands of the state and national parties, thus avoiding any revolutionary changes in the existing decentralized but responsive presidential nominating system.

Notes

1. Austin Ranney, *The Federalization of Presidential Primaries* (Washington, D. C.: American Enterprise Institute, 1978), p. 4.

2. *Gallup Opinion Index*, no. 129 (April 1976): 30.

3. See Paul O. Douglas, "Let the People In," *New Republic* 126 (March 31, 1952): 14-15; Estes Kefauver, "Why Not Let the People Elect Our President?" *Colliers* 131 (January 31, 1953): 34-39; and William E. Proxmire, "Appeal for the Vanishing Primary," New York *Times Magazine* (March 26, 1960): 22, 82-83.

4. David Broder, Washington *Post,* September 1, 1976.

5. Jules Witcover, *Marathon: The Pursuit of the Presidency, 1972-1976* (New York: Viking Press, 1977), p. 190.

6. A concise summary of the anti-primary arguments may be found in David S. Broder, "One Vote Against the Primaries," New York *Times Magazine* (January 31, 1960): 6, 62. See also Wilson Carey McWilliams, "Down with the Primaries," *Commonweal* 103 (July 2, 1976): 427-29; Malcolm E. Jewell, "A Caveat on the Expanding Use of Presidential Primaries," *Policy Studies Journal* (Summer 1974): 279-84.

7. Arthur Schlesinger, Jr., New York *Times,* April 5, 1975.

8. Washington *Post,* April 7, 1976.

9. New York *Times,* August 18, 1976.

10. Adlai E. Stevenson, "Choice by Hullaballoo," *This Week Magazine* (February 28, 1960): 9-15.

11. Minneapolis *Morning Tribune,* May 22, 1960.

12. For a brief summary of this argument by a leading spokesman of the party-responsibility school, see E. E. Schattschneider, *The Struggle for Party Government* (College Park, Md.: Program in American Civilization, 1948). A more detailed exposition will be found in Pendleton Herring, *The Politics of Democracy* (New York: W. W. Norton, 1940); Herbert Agar, *The Price of Union* (Boston: Houghton Mifflin, 1950); and E. E. Schattschneider, *Party Government* (New York: Rinehart, 1942). See also, Herbert McClosky, "Are Political Conventions Undemocratic?" New York *Times Magazine* (August 4, 1968): 10-11, 62-68.

13. See, for example, James Reston, "Convention System: A Five-Count Indictment," New York *Times Magazine* (July 11, 1948): 7, 36-37; Hugh A. Bone, *American Politics and the Party System,* 4th ed. (New York: McGraw-Hill, 1971), pp. 313-15.

14. For a discussion of the Packwood plan, see U.S., Congress, Senate, *Congressional Record,* 92d Cong., 2d sess., 1972, 118, pt. 12: 15231-42.

15. "Presidential Primaries: Proposals for a New System," *Congressional Quarterly Weekly Report* 30 (July 10, 1972): 1653-54.

16. Ibid.

17. Ibid.

18. See Democratic National Committee, *Openness, Participation and Party Building Reforms for a Stronger Democratic Primary,* Report of the Commission on Presidential Nomination and Party Structure (Washington, D. C.: Democratic National Committee, 1978), pp. 33-35.

19. U.S., Congress, House, *Regional Presidential Primaries Act of 1979,* 94th Cong., 2d sess., H.Rept. 12161, pp. 4653-54.

20. New York *Times,* April 11, 1975.

21. Jules Witcover, Washington *Post,* May 23, 1975.

22. New York *Times,* March 3, 1979.

23. Ibid.

24. To attract nationwide attention both parties scheduled preference conventions in Florida in 1979. Jimmy Carter won a similar Florida preference convention in the fall of 1975 and also a straw vote in Iowa that helped launch his successful primary campaign the following year. Four years later, the bumper crop of straw polls in the fall of 1979 showed President Carter winning the Iowa and Florida Democratic party straw polls against Senator Kennedy. Within the Republican party. George Bush, former Director of Central Intelligence, captured the Iowa and Maine straw votes and Ronald Reagan outpointed John Connally and Bush in Florida's informal poll. See Adam Clymer New York *Times,* November 12, 1979.

25. *Bellingham* (Washington) *Herald,* August 5, 1979.

26. Joseph B. Gorman, *Federal Presidential Primary Proposals* (Washington, D. C.: Library of Congress, 1976), as quoted by Ranney, *The Federalization of Presidential Primaries,* p. 1.

27. Ibid., p. 7.

28. U.S., Congress, Senate, *Senate Journal,* 92d Cong., 2d sess., 1972, 118, pt. 7: 8014-16.

29. Ranney, *The Federalization of Presidential Primaries,* pp. 7-8.

30. Robert Bendiner, "The Presidential Primaries are Haphazard, Unfair, and Wildly Illogical," New York *Times,* February 27, 1972.

31. Ranney, *The Federalization of Presidential Primaries,* pp. 39-40.

32. Voter turnout in the 1976 presidential election was 54.6 percent, the lowest since President Truman's victory over Dewey in 1948.

33. Ranney, *The Federalization of Presidential Primaries,* pp. 36-37.

34. V. O. Key, Jr., *Southern Politics* (New York: Alfred A. Knopf, 1949), esp. chaps. 18-22.

35. Jeane J. Kirkpatrick, *Dismantling the Parties: Reflections on Party Reform and Party Decomposition* (Washington, D. C.: American Enterprise Institute, 1978), p. 27.

36. Ranney, *The Federalization of Presidential Primaries,* p. 38.

37. Ibid., p. 37.

38. William J. Crotty, *Political Reform and the American Experiment* (New York: Thomas Y. Crowell, 1977), p. 232.

39. Ibid.

40. Washington *Post,* August 8, 1979.

41. Wisconsin, Michigan and Montana, which still use the "open" primary, will either have to pass legislation restricting the Democratic primary to Democrats before the 1980 primaries or choose their Democratic delegates by a caucus system—unless the Democratic National Committee grants another waiver. The Republican delegate-selection process in these states will, of course, continue to be governed by the state primary law—or by party rules in Montana.

42. Under its 1980 rules, the Democratic National Committee has set the maximum cut-off point for sharing in the district delegates at 25 percent for primary states and 20 percent for caucus-convention states, with even lower cut-offs possible at the preliminary stages of caucus-convention states. State parties are required to set the percentage at least ninety days before their caucus. In 1976, 15 percent was the required minimum in all primaries and caucuses within the Democratic party—60 percent of the delegates were chosen in the period in which the 25 percent minimum is now required. Late starters, such as California Governor Edmund G. "Jerry" Brown or Senator Frank Church in 1976, or any narrowly based "protest" candidates, will be heavily disadvantaged under these new rules. New York *Times,* June 10, 1978.

Appendix A: Presidential Primary Election Vote, 1912-76

TABLE A.1
1912 PRIMARIES

	Republican Votes	%	Democratic Votes	%
March 19 North Dakota				
Robert M. LaFollette (Wis.)	34,123	57.2		
Theodore Roosevelt (N.Y.)	23,669	39.7		
William H. Taft (Ohio)	1,876	3.1		
John Burke (N.D.)[1]			9,357	100.0
March 26 New York[2]				
April 2 Wisconsin				
LaFollette	133,354	73.2		
Taft	47,514	26.1		
Roosevelt	628	.3		
Others	643	.4		
Woodrow Wilson (N.J.)			45,945	55.7
Champ Clark (Mo.)			36,464	44.2
Others			148	.2
April 9 Illinois				
Roosevelt	266,917	61.1		
Taft	127,481	29.2		
LaFollette	42,692	9.8		
Clark			218,483	74.3
Wilson			75,527	25.7
April 13 Pennsylvania				
Roosevelt	282,853[3]	59.7		
Taft	191,179[3]	40.3		
Wilson			98,000[3]	100.0
April 19 Nebraska				
Roosevelt	45,795	58.7		
LaFollette	16,785	21.5		
Taft	13,341	17.1		
Others	2,036	2.6		
Clark			21,027	41.0
Wilson			14,289	27.9
Judson Harmon (Ohio)			12,454	24.3
Others			3,499	6.8

TABLE A.1 (continued)

	Republican			Democratic	
	Votes	%		Votes	%
April 19 Oregon					
Roosevelt	28,905	40.2	Wilson	9,588	53.0
LaFollette	22,491	31.3	Clark	7,857	43.4
Taft	20,517	28.5	Harmon	606	3.3
Others	14	—	Others	49	.3
April 30 Massachusetts					
Taft	86,722	50.4	Clark	34,575	68.9
Roosevelt	83,099	48.3	Wilson	15,002	29.9
LaFollette	2,058	1.2	Others	627	1.2
Others	99	.1			
May 6 Maryland					
Roosevelt	29,124	52.8	Clark	34,021	54.4
Taft	25,995	47.2	Wilson	21,490	34.3
			Harmon	7,070	11.3
May 14 California					
Roosevelt	138,563	54.6	Clark	43,163	71.5
Taft	69,345	27.3	Wilson	17,214	28.5
LaFollette	45,876	18.1			

280

May 21 Ohio

Roosevelt	165,909	55.3	Harmon	96,164	51.7
Taft	118,362	39.5	Wilson	85,084	45.7
LaFollette	15,570	5.2	Clark	2,428	1.3
			Others	2,440	1.3

May 28 New Jersey

Roosevelt	61,297	56.3	Wilson	48,336	98.9
Taft	44,034	40.5	Clark[4]	522	1.1
LaFollette	3,464	3.2			

June 4 South Dakota

Roosevelt	38,106	55.2	Wilson[5]	4,694	35.2
Taft	19,960	28.9	Clark[5]	4,275	32.0
LaFollette	10,944	15.9	Clark[5]	2,722	20.4
			Others	1,655	12.4

TOTALS

Roosevelt	1,164,765	51.5	Wilson	435,169	44.6
Taft	766,326	33.9	Clark	405,537	41.6
LaFollette	327,357	14.5	Harmon	116,294	11.9
Others	2,792	.1	Burke	9,357	1.0
			Others	8,418	.9
	2,261,240			974,775	

1. Burke was the "favorite son" candidate, according to the North Dakota secretary of state.
2. Primary law optional in 1912. Republicans elected pledged delegates but figures not available.
3. Unofficial figures.
4. Write-in.

5. No presidential preference. Three sets of delegates ran: one labelled "Wilson Bryan" which came out openly for Wilson: one "Wilson-Clark-Bryan" which became identified with Clark; one Champ Clark which was accused by the Clark people of being a scheme to split the Clark vote The "Wilson-Clark-Bryan" list polled 4,275 and the Champ Clark list 2,722. The delegates were given to Wilson by the convention.

	Republican			Democratic	
	Votes	%		Votes	%
March 7 Indiana					
Charles W. Fairbanks (Ind.)[1]	176,078	100.0	Woodrow Wilson (N.J.)	160,423	100.0
March 14 Minnesota					
Albert B. Cummins (Iowa)	54,214	76.8	Wilson	45,136	100.0
Others	16,403	23.2			
March 14 New Hampshire					
Unpledged delegates	9,687	100.0	Wilson	5,684	100.0
March 21 North Dakota					
Robert M. LaFollette (Wis.)	23,374[2]	70.4	Wilson	12,341	100.0
Others	9,851[2]	29.6			
April 3 Michigan					
Henry Ford (Mich.)	83,057	47.4	Wilson	84,972	100.0
William A. Smith (Mich.)	77,872	44.4			
William O. Simpson (Mich.)	14,365	8.2			
April 4 New York					
Unpledged delegates	147,038	100.0	Wilson	112,538	100.0

April 4 Wisconsin

LaFollette[1]	110,052	98.8	Wilson	109,462	99.8
Others	1,347	1.2	Others	231	.2

April 11 Illinois

Lawrence Y. Sherman (Ill.)[1]	155,945	90.2	Wilson	136,839	99.8
Theodore Roosevelt (N.Y.)[3]	15,348	8.9	Others	219	.2
Others	1,689	1.0			

April 18 Nebraska

Cummins	29,850	33.7	Wilson	69,506	87.7
Ford	26,884	30.3	Others	9,744	12.3
Charles E. Hughes (N.Y.)[3]	15,837	17.9			
Roosevelt[3]	2,256	2.5			
Others	13,780	15.6			

April 21 Montana

Cummins	10,415	89.9	Wilson	17,960	100.0
Others	1,173	10.1			

April 25 Iowa

Cummins	40,257	100.0	Wilson	31,447	100.0

April 25 Massachusetts

Unpledged delegates at large[4]	60,462	57.3	Wilson	19,580	100.0
Roosevelt[4]	45,117	42.7			

April 25 New Jersey

Roosevelt[3]	1,076	73.7	Wilson	25,407	100.0
Hughes[3]	383	26.3			

	Republican			Democratic	
	Votes	%		Votes	%
April 25 Ohio					
Theodore E. Burton (Ohio)[1]	122,165	86.8	Wilson	82,688	97.2
Roosevelt[3]	1,932	1.4	Others	2,415	2.8
Ford[3]	1,683	1.2			
Hughes[3]	469	.3			
Others	14,428	10.3			
May 2 California					
Unpledged delegates	236,277	100.0	Wilson	75,085	100.0
May 16 Pennsylvania					
Martin G. Brumbaugh (Pa.)[1]	233,095	86.3	Wilson	142,202	98.7
Ford[3]	20,265	7.5	Others	1,839	1.3
Roosevelt[3]	12,359	4.6			
Hughes[3]	1,804	.7			
Others	2,682	1.0			
May 16 Vermont					
Hughes[3]	5,480	70.0	Wilson	3,711	99.4
Roosevelt[3]	1,931	24.6	Others	23	.6
Others	423	5.4			
May 19 Oregon					
Hughes	56,764	59.8	Wilson	27,898	100.0
Cummins	27,558	29.0			
Others	10,593	11.2			

May 23 South Dakota

Cummins	29,656	100.0	Wilson	10,341	100.0

June 6 West Virginia

5		5

	Wilson	1,173,220	98.8
	Others	14,471	1.2
		1,187,691

TOTALS

Unpledged delegates	453,464	23.6
Brumbaugh	233,095	12.1
Cummins	191,950	10.0
Fairbanks	176,078	9.2
Sherman	155,945	8.1
LaFollette	133,426	6.9
Ford	131,889	6.9
Burton	122,165	6.4
Hughes	80,737	4.2
Roosevelt	80,019	4.2
Smith	77,872	4.0
Simpson	14,365	.7
Others⁶	72,369	3.8
	1,923,374	

1. Source for names of "favorite son" candidates: The New York Times.
2. Source for vote breakdown: North Dakota secretary of state.
3. Write-in.
4. No presidential preference vote but one set of delegates at large was for Roosevelt and the other set unpledged.

5. Figures not available. Republican winner was Sen. Theodore E. Burton (R Ohio) and Democratic winner was Woodrow Wilson, according to The New York Times.
6. In addition to scattered votes, "others" includes Robert G. Ross who received 5,-506 votes in the Nebraska primary; Henry D. Estabrook who received 9,851 in the North Dakota primary and 8,132 in the Nebraska primary.

285

TABLE A.3
1920 PRIMARIES

Republican			Democratic		
	Votes	%		Votes	%
March 9 New Hampshire					
Leonard Wood (N.H.)[1]	8,591	53.0	Unpledged delegates[1]	7,103	100.0
Unpledged delegates	5,604	34.6			
Hiram Johnson (Calif.)[1]	2,000	12.3			
March 16 North Dakota					
Johnson	30,573	96.1	William G. McAdoo (N.Y.)[2]	49	12.6
Leonard Wood[2]	987	3.1	Others[2]	340	87.4
Frank O. Lowden (Ill.)[2]	265	.8			
March 23 South Dakota					
Leonard Wood	31,265	36.5	**Others**	6,612	100.0
Lowden	26,981	31.5			
Johnson	26,301	30.7			
Others	1,144	1.3			
April 5 Michigan					
Johnson	156,939	38.4	McAdoo	18,665	21.1
Leonard Wood	112,568[3]	27.5	Edward I. Edwards (N.J.)	16,642	18.8
Lowden	62,418	15.3	A. Mitchell Palmer (Pa.)	11,187	12.6
Herbert C. Hoover (Calif.)	52,503	12.8	Others	42,000	47.5
Others	24,729	6.0			
April 6 New York					
Unpledged delegates	199,149	100.0	Unpledged delegates	113,300	100.0

April 6 Wisconsin[4]

Leonard Wood[2]	4,505	15.0	James M. Cox (Ohio)[2]	76	2.2
Hoover[2]	3,910	13.0	Others	3,391	97.8
Johnson[2]	2,413	8.0			
Lowden[2]	921	3.1			
Others	18,350	60.9			

April 13 Illinois

Lowden	236,802	51.1	Edwards[2]	6,933	32.3
Leonard Wood	156,719	33.8	McAdoo[2]	3,838	17.9
Johnson	64,201	13.8	Cox[2]	266	1.2
Hoover[2]	3,401	.7	Others	10,418	48.6
Others	2,674	.6			

April 20 Nebraska

Johnson	63,161	46.2	Gilbert M. Hitchcock (Neb.)	37,452	67.3
Leonard Wood	42,385	31.0	Others	18,230	32.7
John J. Pershing (Mo.)	27,669	20.3			
Others	3,432	2.5			

April 23 Montana

Johnson	21,034	52.4	Others[2]	2,994	100.0
Leonard Wood	6,804	17.0			
Lowden	6,503	16.2			
Hoover	5,076	12.6			
Warren G. Harding (Ohio)	723	1.8			

April 27 Massachusetts

Unpledged delegates	93,356	100.0	Unpledged delegates	21,226	100.0

287

TABLE A.3 (continued)

	Republican		Democratic		
	Votes	%		Votes	%
April 27 New Jersey					
Leonard Wood	52,909	50.2	Edwards	4,163	91.4
Johnson	51,685	49.0	McAdoo[2]	180	4.0
Hoover	900	.9	Others	213	4.7
April 27 Ohio					
Harding	123,257	47.6	Cox	85,838	97.8
Leonard Wood	108,565	41.9	McAdoo[2]	292	.3
Johnson[2]	16,783	6.5	Others	1,647	1.9
Hoover[2]	10,467	4.0			
May 3 Maryland					
Leonard Wood	15,900	66.4	[5]		
Johnson	8,059	33.6			
May 4 California					
Johnson	369,853	63.9	Unpledged delegates	23,831	100.0
Hoover	209,009	36.1			
May 4 Indiana					
Leonard Wood	85,708	37.9	[5]		
Johnson	79,840	35.3			

Lowden	39,627	17.5
Harding	20,782	9.2

May 18 Pennsylvania

Edward R. Wood (Pa.)	257,841	92.3	Palmer[6]	80,356	73.7
Johnson[2]	10,869	3.8	McAdoo	26,875	24.6
Leonard Wood[2]	3,878	1.4	Edwards[2]	674	.6
Hoover[2]	2,825	1.0	Others	1,132	1.0
Others[2]	4,059	1.5			

May 18 Vermont

Leonard Wood	3,451	66.1	McAdoo[2]	137	31.4
Hoover[2]	564	10.8	Edwards[2]	58	13.3
Johnson[2]	402	7.7	Cox[2]	14	3.2
Lowden[2]	29	.5	Others	227	52.1
Others	777	14.9			

May 21 Oregon

Johnson	46,163	38.4	McAdoo	24,951	98.6
Leonard Wood	43,770	36.5	Others	361	1.4
Lowden	15,581	13.0			
Hoover	14,557	12.1			

May 25 West Virginia

Leonard Wood	27,255	44.6	
Others	33,849[7]	55.4	[5]

TABLE A.3 (continued)

Republican	Votes	%	Democratic	Votes	%
June 5 North Carolina					
Johnson	15,375	73.3	[5]		
Leonard Wood	5,603	26.7			
TOTALS					
Johnson	965,651	30.3	Unpledged delegates	165,460	28.9
Leonard Wood	710,863	22.3	Palmer	91,543	16.0
Lowden	389,127	12.2	Cox	86,194	15.0
Hoover	303,212	9.5	McAdoo	74,987	13.1
Unpledged delegates	298,109	9.4	Hitchcock	37,452	6.6
Edward R Wood	257,841	8.1	Edwards	28,470	5.0
Harding	144,762	4.5	Others[9]	87,565	15.3
Pershing	27,669	.9			
Others[8]	89,014	2.8			
	3,186,248			571,671	

1. Source: Louise Overacker. The Presidential Primaries (1926), p. 238-39. There was no preference vote. In the Republican primary, figures given were for delegates at large favoring Wood and Johnson. In the Democratic primary, although delegates were un-pledged, the organization (Robert Charles Murchie) group was understood to be for Hoover. The highest Democratic Hoover delegate received 3,714 votes.
2. Write-in.
3. Source: Overacker. op. cit., p. 238
4. No names entered for presidential preference in the Republican primary. The real contest lay between two lists of delegates, one headed by Robert M. La Follette and the other by Emanuel L. Philipp.

5. No names entered and no preference vote recorded
6. Source for name of "favorite son" candidate: The New York Times.
7. Most of these votes were received by Sen. Howard Sutherland (R W.Va.). The figure is unofficial.
8. In addition to scattered votes, "others" includes Robert G. Ross who received 1,698 votes in the Nebraska primary.
9. In addition to scattered votes, "others" includes Robert G. Ross who received 13,179 in the Nebraska primary.

TABLE A.4
1924 PRIMARIES

Republican	Votes	%	Democratic	Votes	%
March 11 New Hampshire					
Calvin Coolidge (Mass.)	17,170	100.0	Unpledged delegates	6,687	100.0
March 18 North Dakota					
Coolidge	52,815	42.1	William G. McAdoo (Calif.)	11,273	100.0
Robert M. LaFollette (Wis.)	40,252	32.1			
Hiram Johnson (Calif.)	32,363	25.8			
March 25 South Dakota					
Johnson	40,935	50.7	McAdoo[1]	6,983	77.4
Coolidge	39,791	49.3	Unpledged delegates[1]	2,040	22.6
April 1 Wisconsin[2]					
LaFollette[3]	40,738	62.5	McAdoo	54,922	68.2
Coolidge[3]	23,324	35.8	Alfred E. Smith (N.Y.)[3]	5,774	7.2
Johnson[3]	411	.6	Others	19,827	24.6
Others	688	1.1			
April 7 Michigan					
Coolidge	236,191	67.2	Henry Ford (Mich.)[4]	48,567	53.4
Johnson	103,739	29.5	Woodbridge N. Ferris (Mich.)[4]	42,028	46.2
Others	11,312	3.2	Others	435	.5

291

TABLE A.4 (continued)

	Republican			Democratic	
	Votes	%		Votes	%
April 8 Illinois					
Coolidge	533,193	58.0	McAdoo	180,544	93.9
Johnson	385,590	42.0	Smith[3]	235	.1
LaFollette[3]	278	—	Others	1,724	.9
Others	21	—			
April 8 Nebraska					
Coolidge	79,676	63.6	McAdoo[3]	9,342	57.3
Johnson	45,032	35.9	Smith[3]	700	4.3
Others	627	.5	Others[3]	6,268	38.4
April 22 New Jersey					
Coolidge	111,739	89.1	George S. Silzer (N.J.)[5]	35,601	97.7
Johnson	13,626	10.9	Smith[3]	721	2.0
			McAdoo[3]	69	.2
			Others	38	.1
April 22 Pennsylvania					
Coolidge[3]	117,262	87.9	McAdoo[3]	10,376	43.7
Johnson[3]	4,345	3.3	Smith[3]	9,029	38.0
LaFollette[3]	1,224	.9	Others[3]	4,341	18.3
Others	10,523	7.9			
April 29 Massachusetts					
Coolidge	84,840	100.0	Unpledged delegates at large[6]	30,341	100.0

April 29 Ohio					
Coolidge	173,613	*86.3*	James M. Cox (Ohio)[5]	74,183	*71.7*
Johnson	27,578	*13.7*	McAdoo	29,267	*28.3*
May 5 **Maryland**					
Coolidge	19,657	*93.7*			
Unpledged delegates	1,326	*6.3*			
Johnson[3]	3	—			
May 6 **California**					
Coolidge	310,618	*54.3*	McAdoo	110,235	*85.6*
Johnson	261,566	*45.7*	Unpledged delegates	18,586	*14.4*
May 6 **Indiana**					
Coolidge	330,045	**84.1**	[7]		
Johnson	62,603	**15.9**			
May 16 **Oregon**					
Coolidge	99,187	*76.8*	McAdoo	33,664	*100.0*
Johnson	30,042	*23.2*			
May 27 **West Virginia**					
Coolidge	162,042	*100.0*	[7]		

TABLE A.4 (continued)

	Republican		Democratic	
	Votes	%	Votes	%
May 28 Montana				
Coolidge / McAdoo	19,200	100.0	10,058	100.0

TOTALS

	Republican			Democratic	
Coolidge	2,410,363	68.4	McAdoo	456,733	59.8
Johnson	1,007,833	28.6	Cox	74,183	9.7
LaFollette	82,492	2.3	Unpledged delegates	57,654	7.5
Unpledged delegates	1,326	—	Ford	48,567	6.4
Others	23,171	.7	Ferris	42,028	5.5
			Silzer	35,601	4.7
	3,525,185		Smith	16,459	2.2
			Others	32,633	4.3
				763,858	

1. No presidential preference vote, as McAdoo's was the only name entered, but a contest developed between "McAdoo" and "anti-McAdoo" lists of delegates. Figures are average votes cast for these lists.

2. In Wisconsin the real contest in the Republican primary was between two lists of delegates, one led by La Follette and one by Emanuel L. Philipp. In the Democratic primary, the real contest was between two lists of delegates, one favoring Smith and one favoring McAdoo.

3. Write-in

4. Source for names of "favorite son" candidates: Michigan Manual, 1925.

5. Source for names of "favorite son" candidates: The New York Times.

6. No presidential preference vote provided for. There were nine candidates for the eight places as delegates at large, one of whom announced his preference for Smith during the campaign and received the second highest number of votes.

7. No names entered and no presidential preference vote taken.

TABLE A.5
1928 PRIMARIES

	Republican		Democratic	
	Votes	%	Votes	%
March 13 New Hampshire				
Unpledged delegates at large[1]	25,503	100.0	Unpledged delegates at large[1]	9,716	100.0
March 20 North Dakota				
Frank O. Lowden (Ill.)	95,857	100.0	Alfred E. Smith (N.Y.)	10,822	100.0
April 2 Michigan				
Herbert C. Hoover (Calif.)	282,809	97.6	Smith	77,276	98.3
Lowden	5,349	1.8	Thomas Walsh (Mont.)	1,034	1.3
Calvin Coolidge (Mass.)	1,666	.6	James A. Reed (Mo.)	324	.4
April 3 Wisconsin				
George W. Norris (Neb.)	162,822	87.1	Reed	61,097	75.0
Hoover	17,659	9.4	Smith	19,781	24.3
Lowden	3,302	1.8	Walsh	541	.7
Coolidge	680	.4			
Charles G. Dawes (Ill.)	505	.3			
Others	1,894	1.0			
April 10 Illinois				
Lowden	1,172,278	99.3	Smith	44,212	91.7
Hoover	4,368	.4	Reed	3,786	7.9
Coolidge	2,420	.2	William G. McAdoo (Calif.)	213	.4
Dawes	756	.1			
Others	946	.1			

Republican	Votes	%	Democratic	Votes	%
April 10 Nebraska					
Norris	96,726	91.8	Gilbert M. Hitchcock (Neb.)	51,019	91.5
Hoover	6,815	6.5	Smith	4,755	8.5
Lowden	711	.7			
Dawes	679	.7			
Coolidge	452	.4			
April 24 Ohio					
Hoover	217,430	68.1	Smith	42,365	65.9
Frank B. Willis (Ohio)	84,461	26.5	Atlee Pomerene (Ohio)	13,957	21.7
Dawes	4,311	1.4	Victor Donahey (Ohio)	7,935	12.3
Lowden	3,676	1.2			
Others	9,190	2.9			
April 24 Pennsylvania					
2			2		
April 28 Massachusetts					
Hoover[3]	100,279	85.2	Smith	38,081	98.1
Coolidge[3]	7,767	6.6	Walsh	254	.7
Alvin Fuller (Mass.)	1,686	1.4	Others	478	1.2
Lowden[3]	1,040	.9			
Others	6,950	5.9			
May 1 California					
Hoover	567,219	100.0	Smith	134,471	54.1
			Reed	60,004	24.1
			Walsh	46,770	18.8
			Others	7,263	2.9

	Republican			Democratic		
May 7 Indiana						
	James E. Watson (Ind.)	228,795	53.0	Evans Woollen (Ind.)	146,934	100.0
	Hoover	203,279	47.0			
May 7 Maryland[4]						
	Hoover	27,128	83.3	[5]		
	Unpledged delegates	5,426	16.7			
May 8 Alabama						
[5]				Unpledged delegates at large[6]	138,957	100.0
May 15 New Jersey						
	Hoover	382,907	100.0	Smith[3]	28,506	100.0
May 18 Oregon						
	Hoover	101,129	98.7	Smith	17,444	48.5
	Lowden	1,322	1.3	Walsh	11,272	31.3
				Reed	6,360	17.7
				Others	881	2.5
May 22 South Dakota						
	Unpledged delegates at large[7]	34,264	100.0	Unpledged delegates at large[7]	6,221	100.0
May 29 West Virginia						
	Guy D. Goff (W.Va.)	128,429	54.0	Smith	81,739	50.0
	Hoover	109,303	46.0	Reed	75,796	46.4
				Others	5,789	3.5

TABLE A.5 (continued)

Republican

June 5 Florida	Votes	%
5		

Democratic

	Votes	%
Unpledged delegates at large[8]	108,167	100.00

	Votes	%		Votes	%
TOTALS					
Hoover	2,020,325	49.2	Smith	499,452	39.5
Lowden	1,283,535	31.2	Unpledged delegates	263,061	20.8
Norris	259,548	6.3	Reed	207,367	16.4
Watson	228,795	5.6	Woollen	146,934	11.6
Goff	128,429	3.1	Walsh	59,871	4.7
Willis	84,461	2.1	Hitchcock	51,019	4.0
Unpledged delegates	65,293	1.6	Pomerene	13,957	1.1
Coolidge	12,985	.3	Donahey	7,935	.6
Dawes	6,251	.2	McAdoo	213	—
Fuller	1,686	—	Others[10]	14,411	1.1
Others[9]	18,980	.5			
	4,110,288			1,264,220	

1. Winning Republican delegates were unofficially pledged to Hoover and winning Democratic delegates were unofficially pledged to Smith, according to Walter Kravitz. "Presidential Preferential Primaries: Results 1928-1956" (1960), p. 4.
2. No figures available.
3. Write-in.
4. Source: Kravitz, op. cit., p. 5.
5. No primary
6. The Montgomery Advertiser of May 3, 1928, described the delegates as independent and anti-Smith.

7. Winning Republican delegates favored Lowden and winning Democratic delegates favored Smith, according to Kravitz, op. cit., p. 5.
8. The Miami Herald of June 6, 1928, described the delegates as unpledged and anti-Smith.
9. In addition to scattered votes, "others" includes Robert G. Ross who received 8,280 votes in the Ohio primary
10. In addition to scattered votes, "others" includes Poling who received 7,263 votes in the California primary; and Workman who received 881 in the Oregon primary and 5,789 in the West Virginia primary.

TABLE A.6
1932 PRIMARIES

	Republican			Democratic		
		Votes	%		Votes	%
March 8 New Hampshire						
	Unpledged delegates at large[1]	22,903	100.0	Unpledged delegates at large[1]	15,401	100.0
March 15 North Dakota						
	Joseph I. France (Md.)	36,000[2]	59.0	Franklin D. Roosevelt (N.Y.)	52,000[2]	61.9
	Jacob S. Coxey (Ohio)	25,000[2]	41.0	William H. Murray (Okla.)	32,000[2]	38.1
March 23 Georgia						
[3]				Roosevelt	51,498	90.3
				Others	5,541	9.7
April 5 Wisconsin						
	George W. Norris (Neb.)	139,514	95.5	Roosevelt	241,742	98.6
	Herbert C. Hoover (Calif.)	6,588	4.5	Alfred E. Smith (N.Y.)[4]	3,502	1.4
April 12 Nebraska						
	France	40,481	74.4	Roosevelt	91,393	63.5
	Hoover	13,934	25.6	John N. Garner (Texas)	27,359	19.0
				Murray	25,214	17.5
April 13 Illinois						
	France	345,498	98.7	James H. Lewis (Ill.)	590,130	99.8
	Hoover	4,368	1.2	Roosevelt	1,084	.2
	Charles G. Dawes (Ill.)	129	—	Smith	266	—
				Others[4]	72	—

| | Republican | | Democratic | |
	Votes	%		Votes	%

April 26 Massachusetts

Republican	Votes	%	Democratic	Votes	%
Unpledged delegates at large[5]	57,534	100.0	Smith[5]	153,465	73.1
			Roosevelt[5]	56,454	26.9

April 26 Pennsylvania

Republican	Votes	%	Democratic	Votes	%
France	352,092	92.9	Roosevelt	133,002	56.6
Hoover	20,662	5.5	Smith	101,227	43.1
Others	6,126	1.6	Others	563	.2

May 2 Maryland

Republican	Votes	%	Democratic	Votes	%
Hoover	27,324	60.0	[6]		
France	17,008	37.3			
Unpledged delegates	1,236	2.7			

May 3 Alabama

Republican	Votes	%	Democratic	Votes	%
[3]			Unpledged delegates[7]	134,781	100.0

May 3 California

Republican	Votes	%	Democratic	Votes	%
Hoover	657,420	100.0	Garner	222,385	41.3
			Roosevelt	175,008	32.5
			Smith	141,517	26.3

May 3 South Dakota

Republican	Votes	%	Democratic	Votes	%
Johnson[8]	64,464	64.7	Roosevelt	35,370	100.0
Others	35,133	35.3			

May 10	**Ohio**					
	Coxey	75,844	58.9	Murray	112,512	96.4
	France	44,853	34.8	Roosevelt⁴	1,999	1.7
	Hoover	8,154	6.3	Smith⁴	951	.8
				George White (Ohio)	834	.7
				Newton D. Baker (Ohio)	289	.2
				Garner⁴	72	—
May 10	**West Virginia**					
	France	88,005	100.0	Roosevelt	219,671	90.3
				Murray	19,826	8.2
				Others	3,727	1.5
May 17	**New Jersey**					
	France	141,330	93.3	Smith	5,234	61.9
	Hoover	10,116	6.7	Roosevelt	3,219	38.1
May 20	**Oregon**					
	France	72,681	69.0	Roosevelt	48,554	78.6
	Hoover	32,599	31.0	Murray	11,993	19.4
				Others	1,214	2.0
June 7	**Florida**					
	³			Roosevelt	203,372	87.7
				Murray	24,847	10.7
				Others	3,645	1.6

TABLE A.6 (continued)

Republican

	Votes	%
TOTALS		
France	1,137,948	48.5
Hoover	781,165	33.3
Norris	139,514	5.9
Coxey	100,844	4.3
Unpledged delegates	81,673	3.5
Johnson	64,464	2.7
Dawes	129	—
Others[9]	41,259	1.8
	2,346,996	

Democratic

	Votes	%
Roosevelt	1,314,366	44.5
Lewis	590,130	20.0
Smith	406,162	13.8
Garner	249,816	8.5
Murray	226,392	7.7
Unpledged delegates	150,182	5.1
White	834	—
Baker	289	—
Others[10]	14,762	.5
	2,952,933	

1 Hoover delegates won the Republican primary and Roosevelt delegates won the Democratic primary, according to Kravitz, op. cit., p. 6.

2 Unofficial figures.

3 No primary.

4 Write-in.

5 Delegate-at-large vote in Republican and Democratic primaries. Hoover delegates won the Republican primary, according to Kravitz, op. cit., p. 6. The New York Times of April 26, 1932, also reported that the Republican delegates were pledged to Hoover.

6 No names entered, according to the Maryland Record of Election Returns.

7 These were unpledged delegates who favored Roosevelt, according to Kravitz, op. cit., p. 6.

8 The winning Republican delegation supported Hoover, according to Kravitz, op. cit., p. 7.

9 In addition to scattered votes, "others" includes Bogue who received 35,133 in the South Dakota primary.

10 In addition to scattered votes, "others" includes Leo J. Chassee who received 3,645 in the Florida primary and 3,727 in the West Virginia primary; and Howard who received 5,541 votes in the Georgia primary.

Republican

Democratic

	Votes	%		Votes	%
March 10 New Hampshire					
Unpledged delegates at large[1]	32,992	100.0	Unpledged delegates at large[1]	15,752	100.0
April 7 Wisconsin					
William E. Borah (Idaho)	187,334	98.2	Franklin D. Roosevelt (N.Y.)	401,773	100.0
Alfred M. Landon (Kan.)	3,360	1.8	John N. Garner (Texas)	108	—
			Alfred E. Smith (N.Y.)	46	—
April 14 Illinois					
Frank Knox (Ill.)	491,575	53.7	Roosevelt	1,416,411	100.0
Borah	419,220	45.8	Others[2]	411	—
Landon	3,775	.4			
Others[2]	205	—			
April 14 Nebraska					
Borah	70,240	74.5	Roosevelt	139,743	100.0
Landon	23,117	24.5			
Others	973	1.0			
April 28 Massachusetts					
Landon[2]	76,862	80.6	Roosevelt[2]	51,924	85.9
Herbert C. Hoover (Calif.)[2]	7,276	7.6	Smith[2]	2,928	4.8
Borah[2]	4,259	4.5	Charles E. Coughlin (Mich.)[2]	2,854	4.7
Knox[2]	1,987	2.1	Others[2]	2,774	4.6
Others[2]	5,032	5.3			

TABLE A.7 (continued)

Republican | Democratic

Republican	Votes	%	Democratic	Votes	%
April 28 Pennsylvania					
Borah	459,982	100.0	Roosevelt	720,309	95.3
			Henry Breckinridge (N.Y.)	35,351	4.7
May 4 Maryland					
[3]			Roosevelt	100,269	83.4
			Breckinridge	18,150	15.1
			Unpledged delegates	1,739	1.4
May 5 California					
Earl Warren (Calif.)	350,917	57.4	Roosevelt	790,235	82.5
Landon	260,170	42.6	Upton Sinclair (Calif.)	106,068	11.1
			John S. McGroarty (Calif.)	61,391	6.4
May 5 South Dakota					
Warren E. Green[4]	44,518	50.1	Roosevelt	48,262	100.0
Borah	44,261	49.9			
May 12 Ohio					
Stephen A. Day (Ohio)	155,732	93.4	Roosevelt	514,366	94.0
Landon	11,015	6.6	Breckinridge	32,950	6.0
May 12 West Virginia					
Borah	105,855	84.8	Roosevelt	288,799	97.3
Others	18,986	15.2	Others	8,162	2.7

May 15 Oregon

Borah	91,949	90.2		Roosevelt	88,305	99.8
Landon	4,467	4.4		Others	208	.2
Others	5,557	5.4				

May 19 New Jersey

Landon	347,142	79.2		Breckinridge	49,956	81.1
Borah	91,052	20.8		Roosevelt[2]	11,676	18.9

June 6 Florida

[3]				Roosevelt	242,906	89.7
				Others	27,982	10.3

TOTALS

Borah	1,474,152	44.4		Roosevelt	4,814,978	92.9
Landon	729,908	22.0		Breckinridge	136,407	2.6
Knox	493,562	14.9		Sinclair	106,068	2.0
Warren	350,917	10.6		McGroarty	61,391	1.2
Day	155,732	4.7		Unpledged delegates	17,491	.3
Green	44,518	1.3		Smith	2,974	.1
Unpledged delegates	32,992	1.0		Coughlin	2,854	.1
Hoover	7,276	.2		Garner	108	—
Others[5]	30,753	.9		Others[6]	39,537	.8
	3,319,810				5,181,808	

1. Delegates favorable to Knox won the Republican primary and Roosevelt delegates won the Democratic primary, according to Kravitz, op. cit., p. 8.

2. Write-in.

3. No preferential primary held.

4. These delegates were unpledged but favored Landon, according to Kravitz, op. cit., p. 9.

5. In addition to scattered votes, "others" includes Leo J. Chassee who received 18,986 votes in the West Virginia primary.

6. In addition to scattered votes, "others" includes Joseph A. Coutremarsh who received 27,982 votes in the Florida primary and 8,162 votes in the West Virginia primary.

	Republican			Democratic	
	Votes	%		Votes	%
March 12 New Hampshire					
Unpledged delegates at large	34,616	100.0	Unpledged delegates at large[1]	10,501	100.0
April 2 Wisconsin					
Thomas E. Dewey (N.Y.)	70,168	72.6	Franklin D. Roosevelt (N.Y.)	322,991	75.4
Arthur Vandenberg (Mich.)	26,182	27.1	John N. Garner (Texas)	105,662	24.6
Robert A. Taft (Ohio)	341	.4			
April 9 Illinois					
Dewey	977,225	99.9	Roosevelt	1,176,531	86.0
Others[2]	552	.1	Garner	190,801	14.0
			Others[2]	35	—
April 9 Nebraska					
Dewey	102,915	58.9	Roosevelt	111,902	100.0
Vandenberg	71,798	41.1			
April 23 Pennsylvania					
Dewey	52,661	66.7	Roosevelt	724,657	100.0
Franklin D. Roosevelt (N.Y.)	8,294	10.5			
Arthur H. James (Pa.)	8,172	10.3			
Taft	5,213	6.6			
Vandenberg	2,384	3.0			
Herbert C. Hoover (Calif.)	1,082	1.4			
Wendell Willkie (N.Y.)	707	.9			
Others	463	.6			

April 30 **Massachusetts**					
Unpledged delegates at large[3]	98,975	100.0	Unpledged delegates at large[3]	76,919	100.0
May 5 **South Dakota**					
Unpledged delegates	52,566	100.0	Unpledged delegates	27,636	100.0
May 6 **Maryland**					
Dewey	54,802	100.0	[4]		
May 7 **Alabama**					
[4]			Unpledged delegates at large[5]	196,508	100.0
May 7 **California**					
Jerrold L. Seawell[6]	538,112	100.0	Roosevelt	723,782	74.0
			Garner	114,594	11.7
			Unpledged delegates[6]	139,055	14.2
May 14 **Ohio**					
Taft	510,025	99.5	Unpledged delegates at large[7]	283,952	100.0
Dewey[2]	2,059	.4			
John W. Bricker (Ohio)	188	—			
Vandenberg[2]	83	—			
Willkie	53	—			
Others	69	—			

TABLE A.8 (continued)

| | Republican | | Democratic | |
	Votes	%	Votes	%
May 14 West Virginia				
R. N. Davis (W.Va.) / H. C. Allen (W.Va.)	106,123	*100.0*	102,729	*100.0*
May 17 Oregon				
Charles L. McNary (Ore.) / Roosevelt	133,488	95.9	109,913	87.2
Dewey / Garner	5,190	3.7	15,584	12.4
Taft / Others	254	.2	601	.5
Willkie	237	.2		
Vandenberg	36	—		
May 21 New Jersey				
Dewey / Roosevelt[2]	340,734	*93.9*	34,278	*100.0*
Willkie[2]	20,143	*5.6*		
Roosevelt[2]	1,202	.3		
Taft[2]	595	.2		
Vandenberg[2]	168	—		

TOTALS

Dewey	1,605,754	49.7
Seawell	538,112	16.7
Taft	516,428	16.0
Unpledged delegates	186,157	5.8
McNary	133,488	4.1
Davis	106,123	3.3
Vandenberg	100,651	3.1
Willkie	21,140	.7
Roosevelt	9,496	.3
James	8,172	.3
Hoover	1,082	—
Bricker	188	—
Others	1,084	—
	3,227,875	

Roosevelt	3,240,054	71.7
Unpledged delegates	734,571	16.4
Garner	426,641	9.5
Allen	102,729	2.3
Others	636	—
	4,468,631	

1. Roosevelt delegates won, according to Kravitz, op. cit., p. 10.
2. Write-in.
3. An unpledged Republican slate defeated a slate of delegates pledged to Dewey, according to Kravitz, op. cit., p. 10. Sixty-nine James A. Farley delegates and three unpledged delegates won in the Democratic primary, according to Kravitz, ibid. The New York Times of May 1, 1940, also reported that most Democratic delegates favored Farley.
4. No primary.
5. Winning delegates were pledged to "favorite son" candidate William B. Bankhead, then Speaker of the U.S. House of Representatives, according to Kravitz, op. cit., p. 10, and the Montgomery Advertiser of May 8, 1940.
6. The Los Angeles Times of May 8, 1940, reported that the Republican delegation was unpledged. In the Democratic primary, according to Davis, p. 293, unpledged slates were headed by Willis Allen, head of the California "Ham and Eggs" pension ticket which received 90,718 votes; and by Lt. Gov. Ellis E. Patterson, whose slate, backed by Labor's Non-Partisan League, received 48,337 votes.
7. Democratic delegates were pledged to Charles Sawyer (Ohio), according to Ohio Election Statistics, 1940, and Kravitz, op. cit., p. 10.

Republican

	Votes	%
March 14 New Hampshire		
Unpledged delegates at large[1]	16,723	100.0
April 5 Wisconsin		
Douglas MacArthur (Wis.)	102,421	72.6
Thomas E. Dewey (N.Y.)	21,036	14.9
Harold E. Stassen (Minn.)	7,928	5.6
Wendell Willkie (N.Y.)	6,439	4.6
Others	3,307	2.3
April 11 Illinois		
MacArthur	550,354	92.0
Dewey	9,192	1.5
Everett M. Dirksen (Ill.)	581	.1
John W. Bricker (Ohio)	148	—
Stassen	111	—
Willkie	107	—
Others	37,575	6.3
April 11 Nebraska		
Stassen	51,800	65.7
Dewey	18,418	23.3
Willkie	8,249	10.5
Others	432	.5

Democratic

	Votes	%
Unpledged delegates at large[1]	6,772	100.0
Franklin D. Roosevelt (N.Y.)	49,632	94.3
Others	3,014	5.7
Roosevelt	47,561	99.3
Others	343	.7
Roosevelt	37,405	99.2
Others	319	.8

April 25 Massachusetts

Unpledged delegates at large	53,511	100.0

April 25 Pennsylvania

Dewey[2]	146,706	83.8
MacArthur[2]	9,032	5.2
Franklin D. Roosevelt (N.Y.)	8,815	5.0
Willkie[2]	3,650	2.1
Bricker[2]	2,936	1.7
Edward Martin (Pa.)	2,406	1.4
Stassen[2]	1,502	.9

May 1 Maryland

Unpledged delegates	17,600	78.9
Willkie	4,701	21.1

May 2 Alabama

3

May 2 Florida

3

May 2 South Dakota

Charles A. Christopherson[6]	33,497	60.2
Others[6]	22,135	39.8

Unpledged delegates at large	57,299	100.0

Roosevelt	322,469	99.7
Others	961	.3

3

Unpledged delegates at large[4]	116,922	100.0

Unpledged delegates at large[5]	118,518	100.0

Fred Hildebrandt (S.D.)[6]	7,414	52.4
Others[6]	6,727	47.6

TABLE A.9 (continued)

Republican / Democratic

	Republican Votes	Republican %		Democratic Votes	Democratic %
May 9 Ohio					
Unpledged delegates at large[7]	360,139	100.0	Unpledged delegates at large[7]	164,915	100.0
May 9 West Virginia					
Unpledged delegates at large	91,602	100.0	Claude R. Linger (W.Va.)	59,282	100.0
May 16 California					
Earl Warren (Calif.)	594,439	100.0	Roosevelt	770,222	100.0
May 16 New Jersey					
Dewey	17,393	86.2	Roosevelt	16,884	99.6
Roosevelt[2]	1,720	8.5	Thomas E. Dewey (N.Y.)	60	.4
Willkie	618	3.1			
Bricker	203	1.0			
MacArthur	129	.6			
Stassen	106	.5			
May 19 Oregon					
Dewey[2]	50,001	78.2	Roosevelt	79,833	98.7
Stassen[2]	6,061	9.5	Others	1,057	1.3
Willkie[2]	3,333	5.2			
Bricker[2]	3,018	4.7			
MacArthur[2]	191	.3			
Others	1,340	2.1			

TOTALS

MacArthur	662,127	29.1
Warren	594,439	26.2
Unpledged delegates	539,575	23.8
Dewey	262,746	11.6
Stassen	67,508	3.0
Christopherson	33,497	1.5
Willkie	27,097	1.2
Roosevelt	10,535	.5
Bricker	6,305	.3
Martin	2,406	.1
Dirksen	581	—
Others[8]	64,789	2.9
	2,271,605	

Roosevelt	1,324,006	70.9
Unpledged delegates	464,426	24.9
Linger	59,282	3.2
Hildebrandt	7,414	.4
Dewey	60	—
Others[9]	12,421	.7
	1,867,609	

1. Nine unpledged and two Dewey delegates won the Republican primary, and Roosevelt delegates won the Democratic primary, according to Kravitz, op. cit., p. 12.

2. Write-in.

3. No primary.

4. The Montgomery Advertiser of May 3, 1944, reported that these delegates were pro-Roosevelt but uninstructed.

5. The New York Times of May 3, 1944, reported that a contest for delegates took place between supporters of Roosevelt and supporters of Sen. Harry F. Byrd (D Va.). A vote breakdown showing Roosevelt and Byrd strength is unavailable.

6. The winning Republican slate was pledged to Stassen, the losing Republican slate to Dewey and the two Democratic slates to Roosevelt, according to the office of the South Dakota secretary of state and Kravitz, op. cit. p. 12.

7. Bricker delegates won the Republican primary and Joseph T. Ferguson delegates won the Democratic primary, according to Kravitz, op. cit., p. 13.

8. In addition to scattered votes, "others" includes Riley A. Bender who received 37,575 votes in the Illinois primary and Joe H. Bottum who received 22,135 in the South Dakota primary.

9. In addition to scattered votes, "others" includes Powell who received 6,727 votes in the South Dakota primary.

Republican

	Votes	%
March 9 New Hampshire		
Unpledged delegates at large[1]	28,854	100.0
April 6 Wisconsin		
Harold E. Stassen (Minn.)	64,076	39.4
Douglas MacArthur (Wis.)	55,302	34.0
Thomas E. Dewey (N.Y.)	40,943	25.2
Others	2,429	1.5
April 13 Illinois		
Riley A. Bender (Ill.)	324,029	96.9
MacArthur	6,672	2.0
Stassen	1,572	.5
Dewey	953	.3
Robert A. Taft (Ohio)	705	.2
Others[2]	475	.1
April 13 Nebraska		
Stassen	80,979	43.5
Dewey	64,242	34.5
Taft	21,608	11.6
Arthur Vandenberg (Mich.)	9,590	5.2
MacArthur	6,893	3.7
Earl Warren (Calif.)	1,761	.9
Joseph W. Martin (Mass.)	910	.5
Others	24	—

Democratic

	Votes	%
Unpledged delegates at large[1]	4,409	100.0
Harry S Truman (Mo.)	25,415	83.8
Others	4,906	16.2
Truman	16,299	81.7
Dwight D. Eisenhower (N.Y.)	1,709	8.6
Scott Lucas (Ill.)	427	2.1
Others[2]	1,513	7.6
Truman	67,672	98.7
Others	894	1.3

April 20 New Jersey[3]

Dewey	3,714	41.4
Stassen	3,123	34.8
MacArthur	718	8.0
Vandenberg	516	5.8
Taft	495	5.5
Dwight D. Eisenhower (N.Y.)	288	3.2
Joseph W. Martin	64	.7
Alfred E. Driscoll (N.J.)	44	—
Warren	14	.2

Truman	1,100	92.5
Henry A. Wallace (Iowa)	87	7.3
Others	2	.2

April 27 Massachusetts

Unpledged delegates at large[4]	72,191	100.0

Unpledged delegates at large[4]	51,207	100.0

April 27 Pennsylvania

Stassen[2]	81,242	31.5
Dewey[2]	76,988	29.8
Edward Martin (Pa.)	45,072	17.5
MacArthur[2]	18,254	7.1
Taft[2]	15,166	5.9
Vandenberg	8,818	3.4
Harry S Truman (Mo.)	4,907	1.9
Eisenhower	4,726	1.8
Henry A. Wallace (Iowa)	1,452	.6
Others	1,537	.6

Truman	328,891	96.0
Eisenhower	4,502	1.3
Wallace	4,329	1.3
Harold E. Stassen (Minn.)	1,301	.4
Douglas MacArthur (Wis.)	1,220	.4
Others	2,409	.7

May 4 Alabama

5

Unpledged delegates at large[6]	161,629	100.0

May 4 Florida

5

Others[7]	92,169	100.0

TABLE A.10 (continued)

	Republican			Democratic		
		Votes	%		Votes	%
May 4 Ohio						
	Unpledged delegates at large[8]	426,767	100.0	Unpledged delegates at large[8]	271,146	100.0
May 11 West Virginia						
	Stassen	110,775	83.2	Unpledged delegates at large	157,102	100.0
	Others	22,410	16.8			
May 21 Oregon						
	Dewey	117,554	51.8	Truman	112,962	93.8
	Stassen	107,946	47.6	Others	7,436	6.2
	Others	1,474	.6			
June 1 California						
	Warren	769,520	100.0	Truman	811,920	100.0
June 1 South Dakota						
	Hitchcock[9]	45,463	100.0	Truman[9]	11,193	58.3
				Unpledged Delegates[9]	8,016	41.7

TOTALS

Warren	771,295	29.1
Unpledged delegates	527,812	19.9
Stassen	449,713	16.9
Bender	324,029	12.2
Dewey	304,394	11.5
MacArthur	87,839	3.3
Hitchcock	45,463	1.7
Edward Martin	45,072	1.7
Taft	37,974	1.4
Vandenberg	18,924	.7
Eisenhower	5,014	.2
Truman	4,907	.2
Wallace	1,452	.1
Joseph W. Martin	974	—
Driscoll	44	—
Others[10]	28,349	1.1
	2,653,255	

Truman	1,375,452	63.9
Unpledged delegates	653,509	30.4
Eisenhower	6,211	.3
Wallace	4,416	.2
Stassen	1,301	.1
MacArthur	1,220	.1
Lucas	427	—
Others	109,329	5.1
	2,151,865	

1. Six unpledged and two Dewey delegates won in the Republican primary, and Truman delegates won in the Democratic primary, according to Kravitz, op. cit., p. 14.
2. Write-in.
3. Source: Kravitz, op. cit., p. 14.
4. The Boston Globe of April 28, 1948, reported that the Republican delegation was "generally unpledged" but was expected to support the "favorite son" candidacy of Sen. Leverett Saltonstall (R Mass.) on the first convention ballot. The Globe reported that Democratic delegates were presumed to favor Truman's nomination.
5. No primary.

6. Unpledged, anti-Truman slate, according to Kravitz, op. cit., p. 15.
7. Unpledged slate, according to Kravitz, ibid.
8. Taft won 44 delegates and Stassen nine in the Republican primary, and W.A. Julian won 55 delegates and Bixler one in the Democratic primary, according to Kravitz, ibid.
9. Republican delegates were unpledged, according to Kravitz, op. cit., p. 15. In the Democratic primary, according to Davis, p. 297, the slate led by South Dakota Democratic Party Chairman Lynn Fellows endorsed Truman and the slate headed by former Rep. Fred Hildebrandt (D.S.D.) ran unstructed.
10. In addition to scattered votes, "others" includes Byer who received 15,675 votes and Vander Pyl who received 6,735 votes in the West Virginia primary.

Republican

Democratic

	Votes	%		Votes	%
March 11 New Hampshire					
Dwight D. Eisenhower (N.Y.)	46,661	50.4	Estes Kefauver (Tenn.)	19,800	55.0
Robert A. Taft (Ohio)	35,838	38.7	Harry S Truman (Mo.)	15,927	44.2
Harold E. Stassen (Minn.)	6,574	7.1	Douglas MacArthur (Wis.)	151	.4
Douglas MacArthur (Wis.)[1]	3,227	3.5	James A. Farley (N.Y.)	77	.2
Others	230	.3	Adlai E. Stevenson (Ill.)	40	.1
March 18 Minnesota					
Stassen	129,706	44.4	Hubert H. Humphrey (Minn.)	102,527	80.0
Eisenhower[1]	108,692	37.2	Kefauver[1]	20,182	15.8
Taft[1]	24,093	8.2	Truman[1]	3,634	2.8
Earl Warren (Calif.)[1]	5,365	1.8	Dwight D. Eisenhower (N.Y.)	1,753	1.4
MacArthur[1]	1,369	.5			
Estes Kefauver (Tenn.)	386	.1			
Others	22,712	7.8			
April 1 Nebraska					
Taft[1]	79,357	36.2	Kefauver	64,531	60.3
Eisenhower[1]	66,078	30.1	Robert S. Kerr (Okla.)	42,467	39.7
Stassen	53,238	24.3			
MacArthur[1]	7,478	3.4			
Warren[1]	1,872	.9			
Others	11,178	5.1			
April 1 Wisconsin					
Taft	315,541	40.6	Kefauver	207,520	85.9
Warren	262,271	33.8	Others	34,005	14.1
Stassen	169,679	21.8			
Others	29,133	3.8			

April 8 Illinois

Taft	935,867	73.6		Kefauver	526,301	87.7
Stassen	155,041	12.2		Stevenson	54,336	9.1
Eisenhower[1]	147,518	11.6		Truman	9,024	1.5
MacArthur[1]	7,504	.6		Eisenhower	6,655	1.1
Warren	2,841	.2		Others[1]	3,798	.6
Others	23,550	1.9				

April 15 New Jersey

Eisenhower	390,591	60.7		Kefauver	154,964	100.0
Taft	228,916	35.6				
Stassen	23,559	3.7				

April 22 Pennsylvania

Eisenhower	863,785	73.6		Kefauver[1]	93,160	53.3
Taft[1]	178,629	15.2		Eisenhower[1]	28,660	16.4
Stassen	120,305	10.3		Truman[1]	26,504	15.2
MacArthur	6,028	.5		Robert A. Taft (Ohio)	8,311	4.8
Warren	3,158	.3		Averell Harriman (N.Y.)[1]	3,745	2.1
Harry S Truman (Mo.)	267	—		Stevenson[1]	3,678	2.1
Others	1,121	.1		Richard B. Russell (Ga.)[1]	1,691	1.0
				Others	9,026	5.2

April 29 Massachusetts

Eisenhower[1]	254,898	69.8		Kefauver	29,287	55.7
Taft[1]	110,188	30.2		Eisenhower	16,007	30.5
				Truman	7,256	13.8

May 5 Maryland[2]

Kefauver	137,885	74.8
Unpledged delegates	46,361	25.2

3

TABLE A.11 (continued)

Republican			Democratic		
	Votes	%		Votes	%
May 6 Florida					
[3]			Russell	367,980	54.5
			Kefauver	285,358	42.3
			Others	21,296	3.2
May 6 Ohio					
Taft[4]	663,791	78.8	Kefauver[4]	305,992	62.3
Stassen[4]	178,739	21.2	Robert J. Bulkley (Ohio)[4]	184,880	37.7
May 13 West Virginia					
Taft	139,812	78.5	Unpledged delegates at large	191,471	100.0
Stassen	38,251	21.5			
May 16 Oregon					
Eisenhower	172,486	64.6	Kefauver	142,440	72.3
Warren	44,034	16.5	William O. Douglas (Wash.)	29,532	15.0
MacArthur	18,603	7.0	Stevenson	20,353	10.3
Taft[1]	18,009	6.7	Eisenhower[1]	4,690	2.4
Wayne L. Morse (Ore.)	7,105	2.7			
Stassen	6,610	2.5			
Others	350	.1			
June 3 California					
Warren	1,029,495	66.4	Kefauver	1,155,839	70.4
Thomas H. Werdel (Calif.)	521,110	33.6	Edmund G. Brown (Calif.)	485,578	29.6

June 3 **South Dakota**

Taft	64,695	50.3	Kefauver	22,812	66.0
Eisenhower	63,879	49.7	Others[5]	11,741	34.0

TOTALS

Taft	2,794,736	35.8	Kefauver	3,166,071	64.5
Eisenhower	2,114,588	27.1	Brown	485,578	9.9
Warren	1,349,036	17.3	Russell	369,671	7.5
Stassen	881,702	11.3	Unpledged delegates	237,832	4.8
Werdel	521,110	6.7	Bulkley	184,880	3.8
MacArthur	44,209	.6	Humphrey	102,527	2.1
Morse	7,105	.1	Stevenson	78,407	1.6
Kefauver	386	—	Truman	62,345	1.3
Truman	267	—	Eisenhower	57,765	1.2
Others[6]	88,274	1.1	Kerr	42,467	.9
			Douglas	29,532	.6
			Taft	8,311	.2
			Harriman	3,745	.1
			MacArthur	151	—
			Farley	77	—
			Others[7]	79,866	1.6
	7,801,413			**4,909,225**	

1. Write-in.
2. Source: Kravitz, op. cit., p. 18, and the office of the Maryland secretary of state.
3. No primary.
4. Delegate-at-large vote.
5. These delegates ran on an uninstructed slate, according to Kravitz, op. cit., p. 19.
6. In addition to scattered votes, "others" includes Schneider who received 230 votes in the New Hampshire primary and 350 in the Oregon primary; Kenny who received 10,411 in the Nebraska primary; Ritter who received 26,208 and Stearns who received 2,925 in the Wisconsin primary; Slettendahl who received 22,712 in the Minnesota primary and Riley Bendar who received 22,321 votes in the Illinois primary.
7. In addition to scattered votes, "others" includes Fox who received 18,322 votes and Charles Broughton who received 15,683 votes in the Wisconsin primary; Compton who received 11,331 and Shaw who received 9,965 in the Florida primary.

TABLE A.12
1956 PRIMARIES

Republican

	Votes	%
March 13 New Hampshire		
Dwight D. Eisenhower (Pa.)	56,464	98.9
Others	600	1.1
March 20 Minnesota		
Eisenhower	198,111	98.4
William F. Knowland (Calif.)	3,209	1.6
Others	51	—
April 3 Wisconsin		
Eisenhower	437,089	95.9
Others	18,743	4.1
April 10 Illinois		
Eisenhower	781,710	94.9
Knowland	33,534	4.1
Others	8,455	1.0
April 17 New Jersey		
Eisenhower	357,066	100.0
Others	23	—

Democratic

	Votes	%
Estes Kefauver (Tenn.)	21,701	84.6
Others	3,945	15.4
Kefauver	245,885	56.8
Adlai E. Stevenson (III.)	186,723	43.2
Others	48	—
Kefauver	330,665[1]	100.0
Stevenson	717,742	95.3
Kefauver[2]	34,092	4.5
Others	1,640	.2
Kefauver	117,056	95.7
Others	5,230	4.3

322

April 24 **Alaska** (Territory)

Eisenhower	8,291	94.4	Stevenson	7,123	61.1
Knowland	488	5.6	Kefauver	4,536	38.9

April 24 **Massachusetts**

Eisenhower[2]	51,951	95.1	John W. McCormack (Mass.)[2]	26,128	47.9
Adlai E. Stevenson (Ill.)[2]	604	1.1	Stevenson[2]	19,024	34.9
Christian A. Herter (Mass.)[2]	550	1.0	Kefauver[2]	4,547	8.3
Richard M. Nixon (N.Y.)[2]	316	.6	Dwight D. Eisenhower (Pa.)[2]	1,850	3.4
John W. McCormack (Mass.)[2]	268	.5	John F. Kennedy (Mass.)[2]	949	1.7
Knowland[2]	250	.5	Averell Harriman (N.Y.)[2]	394	.7
Others[2]	700	1.3	Frank J. Lausche (Ohio)[2]	253	.5
			Others[2]	1,379	2.5

April 24 **Pennsylvania**

Eisenhower	951,932	95.5	Stevenson	642,172	93.6
Knowland	43,508	4.4	Kefauver[2]	36,552	5.3
Others	976	.1	Others	7,482	1.1

May 1 **District of Columbia**[3]

Eisenhower	18,101	100.0	Stevenson	17,306	66.2
			Kefauver	8,837	33.8

May 7 **Maryland**

Eisenhower	66,904	95.5	Kefauver	112,768	65.9
Unpledged delegates	3,131	4.5	Unpledged delegates	58,366	34.1

May 8 **Indiana**

Eisenhower	351,903	96.4	Kefauver	242,842[1]	100.0
Others	13,320	3.6			

TABLE A.12 (continued)

	Republican			Democratic	
	Votes	%		Votes	%
May 8 Ohio					
John W. Bricker (Ohio)	478,453[1]	100.0	Lausche	276,670[1]	100.0
May 8 West Virginia					
Unpledged delegates at large	111,883[3]	100.0	Unpledged delegates at large	112,832[3]	100.0
May 15 Nebraska					
Eisenhower	102,576	99.8	Kefauver	55,265	94.0
Others	230	.2	Others	3,556	6.0
May 18 Oregon					
Eisenhower	231,418[1]	100.0	Stevenson[2]	98,131	60.2
			Kefauver[2]	62,987	38.6
			Harriman[2]	1,887	1.2
May 29 Florida					
Eisenhower	39,690	92.0	Stevenson	230,285	51.5
Knowland	3,457	8.0	Kefauver	216,549	48.5
June 5 California					
Eisenhower	1,354,764[1]	100.0	Stevenson	1,139,964	62.6
			Kefauver	680,722	37.4

June 5 Montana

S.C. Arnold[4]	32,732	85.7	Kefauver	77,228[7]	100.0
Others	5,447	14.3			

June 5 South Dakota

Unpledged delegates[5]	59,374[7]	100.0	Kefauver	30,940[7]	100.0

TOTALS

Eisenhower	5,007,970	85.9	Stevenson	3,051,347	52.3
Bricker	478,453	8.2	Kefauver	2,278,636	39.1
Unpledged delegates	174,388	3.0	Lausche	276,923	4.7
Knowland	84,446	1.4	Unpledged delegates	171,198	2.9
S.C. Arnold	32,732	.6	McCormack	26,128	.4
Stevenson	604	—	Harriman	2,281	—
Herter	550	—	Eisenhower	1,850	—
Nixon	316	—	Kennedy	949	—
McCormack	268	—	Others	23,280	.4
Others[6]	48,545	.8			
	5,828,272			5,832,592	

1. Favorite son.
2. Write-in.
3. Democratic delegates supported Stevenson, Republican delegates supported Eisenhower.
4. Voters cast their ballots for S. C. Arnold, "Stand-in" candidate for Eisenhower.
5. Slate unofficially pledged to Eisenhower but appeared on the ballot as "No preference."
6. In addition to scattered votes, "others" includes Lar Daly who received 8,364 votes in the Illinois primary, 13,320 votes in the Indiana primary and 5,447 votes in the Montana primary, and John Bowman Chapple who received 18,743 votes in the Wisconsin primary.

TABLE A.13
1960 PRIMARIES

Republican

	Votes	%
March 8 New Hampshire		
Richard M. Nixon (N.Y.)	65,204	89.3
Nelson A. Rockefeller (N.Y.)[1]	2,745	3.8
John F. Kennedy (Mass.)[1]	2,196	3.0
Others[1]	2,886	4.0
April 5 Wisconsin		
Nixon	339,383[2]	100.0
April 12 Illinois		
Nixon	782,849[2]	99.9
Others[1]	442[2]	.1
April 19 New Jersey		
Unpledged delegates at large	304,766[2]	100.0

Democratic

	Votes	%
John F. Kennedy (Mass.)	43,372	85.2
Others	7,527	14.8
Kennedy	476,024	56.5
Hubert H. Humphrey (Minn.)	366,753	43.5
Kennedy[1]	34,332	64.6
Adlai E. Stevenson (Ill.)[1]	8,029	15.1
Stuart Symington (Mo.)[1]	5,744	10.8
Humphrey[1]	4,283	8.1
Lyndon B. Johnson (Texas)[1]	442	.8
Others[1]	337	.6
Unpledged delegates at large	217,608[2]	100.0

326

April 26 Massachusetts

Nixon[1]	53,164	86.0	Kennedy[1]	91,607	92.4
Rockefeller[1]	4,068	6.6	Stevenson[1]	4,684	4.7
Kennedy[1]	2,989	4.8	Humphrey[1]	794	.8
Henry Cabot Lodge (Mass.)[1]	373	.6	Richard M. Nixon (Calif.)[1]	646	.7
Adlai E. Stevenson (Ill.)[1]	266	.4	Symington[1]	443	.4
Barry Goldwater (Ariz.)[1]	221	.4	Johnson[1]	268	.3
Dwight D. Eisenhower (Pa.)[1]	172	.3	Others[1]	721	.7
Others[1]	592	1.0			

April 26 Pennsylvania

Nixon	968,538	98.1	Kennedy[1]	183,073	71.3
Rockefeller[1]	12,491	1.3	Stevenson[1]	29,660	11.5
Kennedy[1]	3,886	.4	Nixon[1]	15,136	5.9
Stevenson[1]	428	—	Humphrey[1]	13,860	5.4
Goldwater[1]	286	—	Symington[1]	6,791	2.6
Others[1]	1,202	.1	Johnson[1]	2,918	1.1
			Rockefeller[1]	1,078	.4
			Others[1]	4,297	1.7

May 3 District of Columbia[3]

Unpledged delegates	9,468	100.0	Humphrey	8,239	57.4
			Wayne L. Morse (Ore.)	6,127	42.6

May 3 Indiana

Nixon	408,408	95.4	Kennedy	353,832	81.0
Others	19,677	4.6	Others	82,937	19.0

May 3 Ohio

Nixon	504,072[2]	100.0	Michael V. DiSalle (Ohio)	315,312[2]	100.0

TABLE A.13 (continued)

Republican

	Votes	%
May 10 Nebraska		
Nixon[1]	74,356	93.8
Rockefeller[1]	2,028	2.6
Goldwater[1]	1,068	1.3
Others[1]	1,805	2.3
May 10 West Virginia		
Unpledged delegates at large	123,756[2]	100.0
May 17 Maryland		
May 20 Oregon		
Nixon	211,276	93.1
Rockefeller[1]	9,307	4.1
Kennedy[1]	2,864	1.3
Goldwater[1]	1,571	.7
Others[1]	2,015	.9

Democratic

	Votes	%
May 10 Nebraska		
Kennedy	80,408	88.7
Symington[1]	4,083	4.5
Humphrey[1]	3,202	3.5
Stevenson[1]	1,368	1.5
Johnson[1]	962	1.1
Others[1]	669	.7
May 10 West Virginia		
Kennedy	236,510	60.8
Humphrey	152,187	39.2
May 17 Maryland		
Kennedy	201,769	70.3
Morse	49,420	17.2
Unpledged delegates	24,350	8.5
Others	11,417	4.0
May 20 Oregon		
Kennedy	146,332	51.0
Morse	91,715	31.9
Humphrey	16,319	5.7
Symington	12,496	4.4
Johnson	11,101	3.9
Stevenson[1]	7,924	2.8
Others[1]	1,210	.4

May 24 Florida

Nixon	51,036[2]	100.0	George A. Smathers (Fla.)	322,235[2]	100.0

June 7 California

Nixon	1,517,652[2]	100.0	Edmund G. Brown (Calif.)	1,354,031	67.7
			George H. McLain (Calif.)	646,387	32.3

June 7 South Dakota

Unpledged delegates	48,461[2]	100.0	Humphrey	24,773[2]	100.0

TOTALS

Nixon	4,975,938	89.9	Kennedy	1,847,259	32.5
Unpledged delegates	486,451	8.8	Brown	1,354,031	23.8
Rockefeller	30,639	.6	McLain	646,387	11.4
Kennedy	11,935	.2	Humphrey	590,410	10.4
Goldwater	3,146	.1	Smathers	322,235	5.7
Stevenson	694	—	DiSalle	315,312	5.5
Lodge	373	—	Unpledged delegates	241,958	4.3
Eisenhower	172	—	Morse	147,262	2.6
Others[5]	28,619	.5	Stevenson	51,665	.9
			Symington	29,557	.5
			Nixon	15,782	.3
			Johnson	15,691	.3
			Others[6]	109,115	1.9
	5,537,967			5,686,664	

1. Write-in.
2. Delegate-at-Large vote.
3. Source: District of Columbia Board of Elections.
4. No primary.
5. In addition to scattered votes, "others" includes Paul C. Fisher who received 2,388 votes in the New Hampshire primary and Frank R. Beckwith who received 19,677 in the Indiana primary.

6. In addition to scattered votes, "others" includes Lar Daly who received 40,853 votes in the Indiana primary and 7,536 in the Maryland primary; Paul C. Fisher who received 6,853 votes in the New Hampshire primary; John H. Latham who received 42,084 in the Indiana primary and Andrew J. Easter who received 3,881 votes in the Maryland primary.

TABLE A.14
1964 PRIMARIES

	Republican			Democratic	
	Votes	%		Votes	%
March 10 New Hampshire					
Henry Cabot Lodge (Mass.)[1]	33,007	35.5	Lyndon B. Johnson (Texas)[1]	29,317	95.3
Barry M. Goldwater (Ariz.)	20,692	22.3	Robert F. Kennedy (N.Y.)[1]	487	1.6
Nelson A. Rockefeller (N.Y.)	19,504	21.0	Henry Cabot Lodge (Mass.)[1]	280	.9
Richard M. Nixon (Calif.)[1]	15,587	16.8	Richard M. Nixon (Calif.)[1]	232	.8
Margaret Chase Smith (Maine)	2,120	2.3	Barry M. Goldwater (Ariz.)[1]	193	.6
Harold E. Stassen (Pa.)	1,373	1.5	Nelson A. Rockefeller (N.Y.)[1]	109	.4
William W. Scranton (Pa.)[1]	105	.1	Others[1]	159	.5
Others	465	.5			
April 7 Wisconsin					
John W. Byrnes (Wis.)	299,612	99.7	John W. Reynolds (Wis.)	522,405	66.2
Unpledged delegate	816	.3	George C. Wallace (Ala.)	266,136	33.8
April 14 Illinois					
Goldwater	512,840	62.0	Johnson[1]	82,027	91.6
Smith	209,521	25.3	Wallace[1]	3,761	4.2
Henry Cabot Lodge[1]	68,122	8.2	Robert F. Kennedy[1]	2,894	3.2
Nixon[1]	30,313	3.7	Others[1]	841	.9
George C. Wallace (Ala.)[1]	2,203	.3			
Rockefeller[1]	2,048	.2			
Scranton[1]	1,842	.2			
George W. Romney (Mich.)[1]	465	.1			
Others[1]	437	.1			
April 21 New Jersey					
Henry Cabot Lodge[1]	7,896	41.7	Johnson[1]	4,863	82.3
Goldwater[1]	5,309	28.0	Wallace[1]	491	8.3
Nixon[1]	4,179	22.1	Robert F. Kennedy[1]	431	7.3
Scranton[1]	633	3.3	Others[1]	124	2.1
Rockefeller[1]	612	3.2			
Others[1]	304	1.6			

April 28 Massachusetts

Henry Cabot Lodge[1]	70,809	76.9	Johnson[1]	61,035	73.4
Goldwater[1]	9,338	10.1	Robert F. Kennedy[1]	15,870	19.1
Nixon[1]	5,460	5.9	Lodge[1]	2,269	2.7
Rockefeller[1]	2,454	2.7	Edward M. Kennedy (Mass.)[1]	1,259	1.5
Scranton[1]	1,709	1.9	Wallace[1]	565	.7
Lyndon B. Johnson (Texas)[1]	600	.7	Adlai E. Stevenson (Ill.)[1]	452	.5
Smith[1]	426	.5	H'bert H. Humphrey (Minn.)[1]	323	.4
George C. Lodge (Mass.)[1]	365	.4	Others[1]	1,436	1.7
Romney[1]	262	.3			
Others[1]	711	.8			

April 28 Pennsylvania

Scranton[1]	235,222	51.9	Johnson[1]	209,606	82.8
Henry Cabot Lodge[1]	92,712	20.5	Wallace[1]	12,104	4.8
Nixon[1]	44,396	9.8	Robert F. Kennedy[1]	12,029	4.8
Goldwater[1]	38,669	8.5	William W. Scranton (Pa.)[1]	8,156	3.2
Johnson[1]	22,372	4.9	Lodge[1]	4,895	1.9
Rockefeller[1]	9,123	2.0	Others[1]	6,438	2.5
Wallace[1]	5,105	1.1			
Others[1]	5,269	1.2			

May 2 Texas[2]

Goldwater	104,137	74.7
Henry Cabot Lodge[1]	12,324	8.8
Rockefeller	6,207	4.5
Nixon[1]	5,390	3.9
Stassen	5,273	3.8
Smith	4,816	3.5
Scranton[1]	803	.6
Others[1]	373	.3

Republican

	Votes	%
May 5 District of Columbia[3]		
3		
May 5 Indiana		
Goldwater	267,935	67.0
Stassen	107,157	26.8
Others	24,588	6.2
May 5 Ohio		
James A. Rhodes (Ohio)	615,754[4]	100.0
May 12 Nebraska		
Goldwater	68,050	49.1
Nixon[1]	43,613	31.5
Henry Cabot Lodge[1]	22,622	16.3
Rockefeller[1]	2,333	1.7
Scranton[1]	578	.4
Johnson[1]	316	.2
Others[1]	1,010	.7
May 12 West Virginia		
Rockefeller	115,680[4]	100.0

Democratic

	Votes	%
Unpledged delegates	41,095	100.0
Matthew E. Welsh (Ind.)	376,023	64.9
Wallace	172,646	29.8
Others	30,367	5.2
Albert S. Porter (Ohio)	493,619[4]	100.0
Johnson[1]	54,713	89.3
Robert F. Kennedy[1]	2,099	3.4
Wallace[1]	1,067	1.7
Lodge[1]	1,051	1.7
Nixon[1]	833	1.4
Goldwater[1]	603	1.0
Others[1]	904	1.5
Unpledged delegates at large	131,432[4]	100.0

May 15   Oregon

Rockefeller	94,190	33.0	Johnson	272,099[4]	99.5
Henry Cabot Lodge	79,169	27.7	Wallace[1]	1,365[4]	.5
Goldwater	50,105	17.6			
Nixon	48,274	16.9			
Smith	8,087	2.8			
Scranton	4,509	1.6			
Others	1,152	.4			

May 19   Maryland

Unpledged delegates	57,004	58.2	Daniel B. Brewster (Md.)	267,106	53.1
Others	40,994	41.8	Wallace	214,849	42.7
			Unpledged delegates	12,377	2.5
			Others	8,275	1.6

May 26   Florida

Unpledged delegates	58,179	57.8	Johnson	393,339[4]	100.0
Goldwater	42,525	42.2			

June 2   California

Goldwater	1,120,403	51.6	Unpledged delegates[5]	1,693,813	68.0
Rockefeller	1,052,053	48.4	Unpledged delegates[5]	798,431	32.0

June 2   South Dakota

Unpledged delegates	57,653	68.0	Unpledged delegates	28,142[4]	100.0
Goldwater	27,076	32.0			

TABLE A.14 (continued)

Republican

	Votes	%
TOTALS		
Goldwater	2,267,079	38.2
Rockefeller	1,304,204	22.0
Rhodes	615,754	10.4
Henry Cabot Lodge	386,661	6.5
Byrnes	299,612	5.0
Scranton	245,401	4.1
Smith	224,970	3.8
Nixon	197,212	3.3
Unpledged delegates	173,652	2.9
Stassen	113,803	1.9
Johnson	23,288	.4
Wallace	7,308	.1
Romney	727	—
George C. Lodge	365	—
Others[6]	75,303	1.3
	5,935,339	

Democratic

	Votes	%
Unpledged delegates	2,705,290	43.3
Johnson	1,106,999	17.7
Wallace	672,984	10.8
Reynolds	522,405	8.4
Porter	493,619	7.9
Welsh	376,023	6.0
Brewster	267,106	4.3
Robert F. Kennedy	33,810	.5
Henry Cabot Lodge	8,495	.1
Scranton	8,156	.1
Edward M. Kennedy	1,259	—
Nixon	1,065	—
Goldwater	796	—
Stevenson	452	—
Humphrey	323	—
Rockefeller	109	—
Others[7]	48,544	.8
	6,247,435	

1. Write-in.
2. No primary authorized.
3. Source: District of Columbia Board of Elections. No figures available for vote for delegates to Republican convention.
4. Delegates supported President Johnson.
5. Gov. Edmund G. Brown (D Calif.) headed the winning slate of delegates and Mayor Sam Yorty of Los Angeles headed the losing slate.
6. In addition to scattered votes, "others" includes Norman LePage who received 82 votes in the New Hampshire primary; Frank R. Beckwith who received 17,884 votes and Joseph G. Ettl who received 6,704 votes in the Indiana primary; John. W. Steffey who received 22,135 votes and Robert E. Ennis who received 18,859 votes in the Maryland primary.
7. In addition to scattered votes, "others" includes Lar Daly who received 15,160 votes, John H. Latham who received 8,067 votes and Fay T. Carpenter Swain who received 7,140 votes in the Indiana primary; and Andrew J. Easter who received 8,275 votes in the Maryland primary.

334

TABLE A.15
1968 PRIMARIES

Republican

March 12 New Hampshire

	Votes	%
Richard M. Nixon (N.Y.)	80,666	77.6
Nelson A. Rockefeller (N.Y.)[1]	11,241	10.8
Eugene J. McCarthy (Minn.)[1]	5,511	5.3
Lyndon B. Johnson (Texas)[1]	1,778	1.7
George W. Romney (Mich.)	1,743	1.7
Harold E. Stassen (Pa.)	429	.4
Others	2,570	2.5

April 2 Wisconsin

	Votes	%
Nixon	390,368	79.7
Ronald Reagan (Calif.)	50,727	10.4
Stassen	28,531	5.8
Rockefeller[1]	7,995	1.6
Unpledged delegates	6,763	1.4
Romney[1]	2,087	.4
Others	3,382	.7

April 23 Pennsylvania

	Votes	%
Nixon[1]	171,815	59.7
Rockefeller[1]	52,915	18.4
McCarthy[1]	18,800	6.5
George C. Wallace (Ala.)[1]	13,290	4.6
Robert F. Kennedy (N.Y.)[1]	10,431	3.6
Reagan[1]	7,934	2.8
Hubert H. Humphrey (Minn.)[1]	4,651	1.6
Johnson[1]	3,027	1.1
Raymond P. Shafer (Pa.)[1]	1,223	.4
Others[1]	3,487	1.2

Democratic

New Hampshire

	Votes	%
Lyndon B. Johnson (Texas)[1]	27,520	49.6
Eugene J. McCarthy (Minn.)	23,263	41.9
Richard M. Nixon (N.Y.)[1]	2,532	4.6
Others	2,149	3.9

Wisconsin

	Votes	%
McCarthy	412,160	56.2
Johnson	253,696	34.6
Robert F. Kennedy (N.Y.)[1]	46,507	6.3
Unpledged delegates	11,861	1.6
George C. Wallace (Ala.)[1]	4,031	.5
Hubert H. Humphrey (Minn.)[1]	3,605	.5
Others	1,142	.2

Pennsylvania

	Votes	%
McCarthy	428,259	71.7
Robert F. Kennedy[1]	65,430	11.0
Humphrey[1]	51,998	8.7
Wallace[1]	24,147	4.0
Johnson[1]	21,265	3.6
Nixon[1]	3,434	.6
Others[1]	2,556	.4

TABLE 15 (continued)

	Republican		Democratic	
	Votes	%	Votes	%

April 30 Massachusetts

	Republican			Democratic	
Rockefeller[1]	31,964	30.0	McCarthy	122,697	49.3
John A. Volpe (Mass.)	31,465	29.5	Robert F. Kennedy[1]	68,604	27.6
Nixon[1]	27,447	25.8	Humphrey[1]	44,156	17.7
McCarthy[1]	9,758	9.2	Johnson[1]	6,890	2.8
Reagan[1]	1,770	1.7	Nelson A. Rockefeller (N.Y.)[1]	2,275	1.0
Kennedy[1]	1,184	1.1	Wallace[1]	1,688	.7
Others[1]	2,933	2.8	Others[1]	2,593	1.0

May 7 District of Columbia

	Republican			Democratic	
Nixon-Rockefeller[2]	12,102	90.1	Robert F. Kennedy[3]	57,555	62.5
Unpledged delegates[2]	1,328	9.9	Humphrey[3]	32,309	35.1
			Humphrey[3]	2,250	2.4

May 7 Indiana

	Republican			Democratic	
Nixon	508,362[4]	100.0	Robert F. Kennedy	328,118	42.3
			Roger D. Branigin (Ind.)	236,700	30.7
			McCarthy	209,695	27.0

May 7 Ohio

	Republican			Democratic	
James A. Rhodes (Ohio)	614,492[4]	100.0	Stephen M. Young (Ohio)	549,140[4]	100.0

May 14 Nebraska[5]

Nixon	140,336	70.0	Robert F. Kennedy	84,102	51.7
Reagan	42,703	21.3	McCarthy	50,655	31.2
Rockefeller[1]	10,225	5.1	Humphrey[1]	12,087	7.4
Stassen	2,638	1.3	Johnson	9,187	5.6
McCarthy[1]	1,544	.8	Nixon[1]	2,731	1.7
Others	3,030	1.5	Ronald Reagan (Calif.)[1]	1,905	1.2
			Wallace[1]	1,298	.8
			Others	646	.4

May 14 West Virginia

Unpledged delegates at large	81,039[4]	100.0	Unpledged delegates at large	149,282[4]	100.0

May 28 Florida

Unpledged delegates	51,509[4]	100.0	George A. Smathers (Fla.)	236,242	46.1
			McCarthy	147,216	28.7
			Unpledged delegates	128,899	25.2

May 28 Oregon

Nixon	203,037	65.0	McCarthy	163,990	44.0
Reagan	63,707	20.4	Robert F. Kennedy	141,631	38.0
Rockefeller[1.]	36,305	11.6	Johnson	45,174	12.1
McCarthy[1]	7,387	2.4	Humphrey[1]	12,421	3.3
Kennedy[1]	1,723	.6	Reagan[1]	3,082	.8
			Nixon[1]	2,974	.8
			Rockefeller[1]	2,841	.8
			Wallace[1]	957	.3

June 4 California

Reagan	1,525,091[4]	100.0	Robert F. Kennedy	1,472,166	46.3
			McCarthy	1,329,301	41.8
			Unpledged delegates	380,286	12.0

Republican

	Votes	%
June 4 New Jersey		
Nixon[1]	71,809	81.1
Rockefeller[1]	11,530	13.0
Reagan[1]	2,737	3.1
McCarthy[1]	1,358	1.5
Others[1]	1,158	1.3
June 4 South Dakota		
Nixon	68,113[4]	100.0
June 11 Illinois		
Nixon[1]	17,490	78.1
Rockefeller[1]	2,165	9.7
Reagan[1]	1,601	7.1
Others[1]	1,147	5.1

Democratic

	Votes	%
McCarthy[1]	9,906	36.1
Robert F. Kennedy[1]	8,603	31.3
Humphrey[1]	5,578	20.3
Wallace[1]	1,399	5.1
Nixon[1]	1,364	5.0
Others[1]	596	2.2
Robert F. Kennedy	31,826	49.5
Johnson	19,316	30.0
McCarthy	13,145	20.4
McCarthy[1]	4,646	38.6
Edward M. Kennedy (Mass.)[1]	4,052	33.7
Humphrey[1]	2,059	17.1
Others[1]	1,281	10.6

TOTALS

Reagan	1,696,270	37.9
Nixon	1,679,443	37.5
Rhodes	614,492	13.7
Rockefeller	164,340	3.7
Unpledged delegates	140,639	3.1
McCarthy	44,358	1.0
Stassen	31,598	.7
Volpe	31,465	.7
Robert F. Kennedy	13,338	.3
Wallace	13,290	.3
Nixon-Rockefeller[2]	12,102	.3
Johnson	4,805	.1
Humphrey	4,651	.1
Romney	3,830	.1
Shafer	1,223	—
Others[6]	17,707	.4
	4,473,551	

McCarthy	2,914,933	38.7
Robert F. Kennedy	2,304,542	30.6
Unpledged delegates	670,328	8.9
Young	549,140	7.3
Johnson	383,048	5.1
Branigin	238,700	3.2
Smathers	236,242	3.1
Humphrey	166,463	2.2
Wallace	33,520	.4
Nixon	13,035	.2
Rockefeller	5,116	.1
Reagan	4,987	.1
Edward M. Kennedy	4,052	.1
Others[7]	10,963	.1
	7,535,069	

1. Write-in.
2. Prior to the primary, the District Republican organization agreed to divide the nine delegate votes, with six going to Nixon and three going to Rockefeller, according to the 1968 Congressional Quarterly Almanac, Vol. XXIV.
3. Two slates favored Humphrey; a member of an "independent" Humphrey slate received 2,250 votes.
4. Humphrey stand-in.
5. In the American Party presidential primary. Wallace received 493 of the 504 votes cast, or 97.8% of the vote, according to the office of the Nebraska secretary of state.
6. In addition to scattered votes, "others" includes Willis E. Stone who received 527 votes, Herbert F. Hoover who received 247 votes, David Watumull who received 161 votes, William W. Evans who received 151 votes, Elmer W. Coy who received 73 votes and Don DuMont who received 39 votes in the New Hampshire primary; and Americus Liberator who received 1,302 votes in the Nebraska primary.
7. In addition to scattered votes, "others" includes John G. Crommelin who received 186 votes, Richard E. Lee who received 170 votes and Jacob J. Gordon who received 77 votes in the New Hampshire primary.

Republican

Democratic

	Votes	%

	Votes	%

March 7   New Hampshire

	Votes	%
Richard M. Nixon (Calif.)	79,239	67.6
Paul N. McCloskey (Calif.)	23,190	19.8
John M. Ashbrook (Ohio)	11,362	9.7
Others	3,417	2.9

	Votes	%
Edmund S. Muskie (Maine)	41,235	46.4
George S. McGovern (S.D.)	33,007	37.1
Sam Yorty (Calif.)	5,401	6.1
Wilbur D. Mills (Ark.)[1]	3,563	4.0
Vance Hartke (Ind.)	2,417	2.7
Edward M. Kennedy (Mass.)[1]	954	1.1
Hubert H. Humphrey (Minn.)[1]	348	.4
Henry M. Jackson (Wash.)[1]	197	.2
George C. Wallace (Ala.)[1]	175	.2
Others	1,557	1.8

March 14   Florida

	Votes	%
Nixon	360,278	87.0
Ashbrook	36,617	8.8
McCloskey	17,312	4.2

	Votes	%
Wallace	526,651	41.6
Humphrey	234,658	18.6
Jackson	170,156	13.5
Muskie	112,523	8.9
John V. Lindsay (N.Y.)	82,386	6.5
McGovern	78,232	6.2
Shirley Chisholm (N.Y.)	43,989	3.5
Eugene J. McCarthy (Minn.)	5,847	.5
Mills	4,539	.4
Hartke	3,009	.2
Yorty	2,564	.2

March 21 Illinois

Nixon[1]	32,550	97.0
Ashbrook[1]	170	.5
McCloskey[1]	47	.1
Others[1]	802	2.4
Muskie	766,914	62.6
McCarthy	444,260	36.3
Wallace[1]	7,017	.6
McGovern[1]	3,687	.3
Humphrey[1]	1,476	.1
Chisholm[1]	777	.1
Jackson[1]	442	—
Kennedy[1]	242	—
Lindsay[1]	118	—
Others	211	—

April 4 Wisconsin

Nixon	277,601	96.9
McCloskey	3,651	1.3
Ashbrook	2,604	.9
None of the names shown	2,315	.8
Others	273	.1
McGovern	333,528	29.6
Wallace	248,676	22.0
Humphrey	233,748	20.7
Muskie	115,811	10.3
Jackson	88,068	7.8
Lindsay	75,579	6.7
McCarthy	15,543	1.4
Chisholm	9,198	.8
None of the names shown	2,450	.2
Yorty	2,349	.2
Patsy T. Mink (Hawaii)	1,213	.1
Mills	913	.1
Hartke	766	.1
Kennedy[1]	183	—
Others	559	—

TABLE A.16 (continued)

	Republican			Democratic	
	Votes	%		Votes	%

April 25 Massachusetts

	Votes	%		Votes	%
Nixon	99,150	81.2	McGovern	325,673	52.7
McCloskey	16,435	13.5	Muskie	131,709	21.3
Ashbrook	4,864	4.0	Humphrey	48,929	7.9
Others	1,690	1.4	Wallace	45,807	7.4
			Chisholm	22,398	3.6
			Mills	19,441	3.1
			McCarthy	8,736	1.4
			Jackson	8,499	1.4
			Kennedy[1]	2,348	.4
			Lindsay	2,107	.3
			Hartke	874	.1
			Yorty	646	.1
			Others	1,349	.2

April 25 Pennsylvania

	Votes	%		Votes	%
Nixon[1]	153,886	83.3	Humphrey	481,900	35.1
George C. Wallace (Ala.)[1]	20,472	11.1	Wallace	292,437	21.3
Others[1]	10,443	5.7	McGovern	280,861	20.4
			Muskie	279,983	20.4
			Jackson	38,767	2.8
			Chisholm[1]	306	—
			Others	585	—

342

May 2 District of Columbia

2

Walter E. Fauntroy (D.C.)	21,277	71.8
Unpledged delegates	8,381	28.2

May 2 Indiana

Nixon	417,069	100.0	Humphrey	354,244	47.1
			Wallace	309,495	41.2
			Muskie	87,719	11.7

May 2 Ohio

Nixon	692,828	100.0	Humphrey	499,680	41.2
			McGovern	480,320	39.6
			Muskie	107,806	8.9
			Jackson	98,498	8.1
			McCarthy	26,026	2.1

May 4 Tennessee

Nixon	109,696	95.8	Wallace	335,858	68.2
Ashbrook	2,419	2.1	Humphrey	78,350	15.9
McCloskey	2,370	2.1	McGovern	35,551	7.2
Others	4	—	Chisholm	18,809	3.8
			Muskie	9,634	2.0
			Jackson	5,896	1.2
			Mills	2,543	.5
			McCarthy	2,267	.5
			Hartke	1,621	.3
			Lindsay	1,476	.3
			Yorty	692	.1
			Others	24	—

Republican

	Votes	%
May 6 North Carolina		
Nixon	159,167	94.8
McCloskey	8,732	5.2
May 9 Nebraska		
Nixon	179,464	92.4
McCloskey	9,011	4.6
Ashbrook	4,996	2.6
Others	801	.4
May 9 West Virginia		
Unpledged delegates at large	95,813[3]	100.0
May 16 Maryland		
Nixon	99,308	86.2
McCloskey	9,223	8.0

Democratic

	Votes	%
North Carolina		
Wallace	413,518	50.3
Terry Sanford (N.C.)	306,014	37.3
Chisholm	61,723	7.5
Muskie	30,739	3.7
Jackson	9,416	1.1
Nebraska		
McGovern	79,309	41.3
Humphrey	65,968	34.3
Wallace	23,912	12.4
Muskie	6,886	3.6
Jackson	5,276	2.7
Yorty	3,459	1.8
McCarthy	3,194	1.7
Chisholm	1,763	.9
Lindsay	1,244	.6
Mills	377	.2
Kennedy[1]	293	.2
Hartke	249	.1
Others	207	.1
West Virginia		
Humphrey	246,596	66.9
Wallace	121,888	33.1
Maryland		
Wallace	219,687	38.7
Humphrey	151,981	26.8

May 16 **Maryland (continued)**

Ashbrook	6,718	5.8
McGovern	126,978	22.4
Jackson	17,728	3.1
Yorty	13,584	2.4
Muskie	13,363	2.4
Chisholm	12,602	2.2
Mills	4,776	.8
McCarthy	4,691	.8
Lindsay	2,168	.4
Mink	573	.1

May 16 **Michigan**

Nixon	321,652	95.5
McCloskey	9,691	2.9
Unpledged delegates	5,370	1.6
Others	30	—
Wallace	809,239	51.0
McGovern	425,694	26.8
Humphrey	249,798	15.7
Chisholm	44,090	2.8
Muskie	38,701	2.4
Unpledged delegates	10,700	.7
Jackson	6,938	.4
Hartke	2,862	.2
Others	51	—

May 23 **Oregon**

Nixon	231,151	82.0
McCloskey	29,365	10.4
Ashbrook	16,696	5.9
Others	4,798	1.7
McGovern	205,328	50.2
Wallace	81,868	20.0
Humphrey	51,163	12.5
Jackson	22,042	5.4
Kennedy	12,673	3.1
Muskie	10,244	2.5
McCarthy	8,943	2.2
Mink	6,500	1.6
Lindsay	5,082	1.2
Chisholm	2,975	.7
Mills	1,208	.3
Others	618	.2

TABLE A.16 (continued)

Republican

	Votes	%
May 23 Rhode Island		
Nixon	4,953	*88.3*
McCloskey	337	*6.0*
Ashbrook	175	*3.1*
Unpledged delegates	146	*2.6*
June 6 California		
Nixon	2,058,825	*90.1*
Ashbrook	224,922	*9.8*
Others	175	—
June 6 New Jersey		
Unpledged delegates at large	215,719[3]	*100.0*

Democratic

	Votes	%
May 23 Rhode Island		
McGovern	15,603	*41.2*
Muskie	7,838	*20.7*
Humphrey	7,701	*20.3*
Wallace	5,802	*15.3*
Unpledged delegates	490	*1.3*
McCarthy	245	*.6*
Jackson	138	*.4*
Mills	41	*.1*
Yorty	6	—
June 6 California		
McGovern	1,550,652	*43.5*
Humphrey	1,375,064	*38.6*
Wallace[1]	268,551	*7.5*
Chisholm	157,435	*4.4*
Muskie	72,701	*2.0*
Yorty	50,745	*1.4*
McCarthy	34,203	*1.0*
Jackson	28,901	*.8*
Lindsay	26,246	*.7*
Others	20	—
June 6 New Jersey		
Chisholm	51,433	*66.9*
Sanford	25,401	*33.1*

June 6 New Mexico

Nixon	49,067	88.5
McCloskey	3,367	6.1
None of the names shown	3,035	5.5
	52,820	100.0

McGovern	51,011	33.3
Wallace	44,843	29.3
Humphrey	39,768	25.9
Muskie	6,411	4.2
Jackson	4,236	2.8
None of the names shown	3,819	2.5
Chisholm	3,205	2.1
	28,017	100.0

June 6 South Dakota

Nixon	52,820	100.0
McGovern	28,017	100.0

TOTALS

Nixon	5,378,704	86.9
Unpledged delegates	317,048	5.1
Ashbrook	311,543	5.0
McCloskey	132,731	2.1
Wallace	20,472	.3
None of the names shown	5,350	.1
Others[4]	22,433	.4
	6,188,281	

Humphrey	4,121,372	35.8
McGovern	4,053,451	25.3
Wallace	3,755,424	23.5
Muskie	1,840,217	11.5
McCarthy	553,955	3.5
Jackson	505,198	3.2
Chisholm	430,703	2.7
Sanford	331,415	2.1
Lindsay	196,406	1.2
Yorty	79,446	.5
Mills	37,401	.2
Fauntroy	21,217	.1
Unpledged delegates	19,533	.1
Kennedy	16,693	.1
Hartke	11,798	.1
Mink	8,286	.1
None of the names shown	6,269	—
Others[5]	5,181	—
	15,993,965	

1. Write-In.
2. No republican primary in 1972.
3. Delegates supported Nixon.
4. In addition to scattered votes, "others" includes Patrick Paulsen who received 1,211 votes in the New Hampshire primary.
5. In addition to scattered votes, "others" includes Edward T. Coll who received 280 votes in the New Hampshire primary and 589 votes in the Massachusetts primary.

Republican

February 24 New Hampshire	Votes	%
Gerald Ford (Mich.)	55,156	49.4
Ronald Reagan (Calif.)	53,569	48.0
Others	2,949[1]	2.6

March 2 Massachusetts	Votes	%
Ford	115,375	61.2
Reagan	63,555	33.7
None of the names shown	6,000	3.2
Others	3,519[1]	1.9

Democratic

New Hampshire	Votes	%
Jimmy Carter (Geor.)	23,373	28.4
Morris Udall (Ariz.)	18,710	22.7
Birch Bayh (Ind.)	12,510	15.2
Fred Harris (Okla.)	8,863	10.8
Sargent Shriver (Md.)	6,743	8.2
Hubert Humphrey (Minn.)[1]	4,596	5.6
Henry Jackson (Wash.)[1]	1,857	2.2
George Wallace (Ala.)[1]	1,061	1.3
Ellen McCormack (N.Y.)	1,007	1.2
Others	3,661	4.4

Massachusetts	Votes	%
Jackson	164,393	22.3
Udall	130,440	17.7
Wallace	123,112	16.7
Carter	101,948	13.9
Harris	55,701	7.6
Shriver	53,252	7.2
Bayh	34,963	4.8
McCormack	25,772	3.5
Milton Shapp (Penn.)	21,693	2.9
Humphrey[1]	7,851	1.1
Edward Kennedy (Mass.)[1]	1,623	.3
Lloyd Bentsen (Tex.)	364	—
Others	14,709	1.9

March 2 Vermont

Ford	27,014	84.0	Carter	16,335	42.2
Reagan	4,892[1]	15.2	Shriver	10,699	27.6
Others	251[3]	.8	Harris	4,893	12.6
			McCormack	3,324	8.6
			Others	3,463	9.0

March 9 Florida

Ford	321,982	52.8	Carter	448,844	34.5
Reagan	287,837	47.2	Wallace	396,820	30.5
			Jackson	310,944	23.9
			Shapp	32,198	2.5
			Udall	27,235	2.1
			Bayh	8,750	.7
			McCormack	7,595	.6
			Shriver	7,084	.5
			Harris	5,397	.4
			Robert Byrd (W.V.)	5,042	.4
			Frank Church (Id.)	4,906	.4
			Others	45,515	3.5

March 16 Illinois

Ford	456,750	58.9	Carter	630,915	48.1
Reagan	311,295	40.1	Wallace	361,798	27.6
Lar Daly (Ill.)	7,582	1.0	Shriver	214,024	16.3
Others	266[1]	—	Harris	98,862	7.5
			Others	6,315[1]	.5

March 23 North Carolina

Reagan	101,468	52.4	Carter	324,437	53.6
Ford	88,897	45.9	Wallace	210,166	34.7
Others	3,362[2]	1.7	Jackson	25,749	4.3
			Udall	14,032	2.3
			Harris	5,923	1.0
			Bentsen	1,675	.3
			Others	22,850	3.8

Republican   TABLE A.17 (continued)   Democratic

	Votes	%		Votes	%
April 6 Wisconsin					
Ford	326,869	55.2	Carter	271,220	36.6
Reagan	262,126	44.3	Udall	263,771	35.6
None of the names shown	2,234[2]	.4	Wallace	92,460	12.5
Others	583[1,2]	.1	Jackson	47,605	6.4
			McCormack	26,982	3.6
			Harris	8,185	1.1
			None of the names shown	7,154	1.0
			Shriver	5,097	.7
			Bentsen	1,730	.3
			Bayh	1,255	.2
			Shapp	596	.1
			Others	14,473[1]	1.9
April 27 Pennsylvania					
Ford	733,472	92.5	Carter	511,905	37.0
Reagan	40,510[1]	5.1	Jackson	340,340	24.6
Others	22,678[1]	2.8	Udall	259,166	18.7
			Wallace	155,902	11.3
			McCormack	38,800	2.8
			Shapp	32,947	2.4
			Bayh	15,320	1.1
			Harris	13,067	.9
			Humphrey[1]	12,563	.9
			Others	5,032	.3
May 4 District of Columbia[4]					
[5]			Carter	9,759	39.7
			Udall	6,381	25.9
			Harris	392	1.6
			Uncommitted (Fauntroy Slate)	5,310	21.6
			Uncommitted (Washington Slate)	2,740	11.1

350

May 4 Georgia

Reagan	128,671	68.3	
Ford	59,801	31.7	

Carter	419,272	83.4
Wallace	57,594	11.5
Udall	9,755	1.9
Byrd	3,628	.7
Jackson	3,358	.6
Church	2,477	.5
Shriver	1,378	.3
Bayh	824	.2
Harris	699	.1
McCormack	635	.1
Bentsen	277	.1
Shapp	181	.1
Others	2,393	.5

May 4 Indiana

Reagan	323,772	51.3
Ford	307,582	48.7

Carter	417,463	68.0
Wallace	93,120	15.2
Jackson	72,070	11.7
McCormack	31,708	5.1

May 11 Nebraska

Reagan	113,493	54.5
Ford	94,542	45.4
Others	379[a]	.1

Church	67,297	38.5
Carter	65,833	37.6
Humphrey	12,685	7.2
Kennedy	7,199	4.1
McCormack	6,033	3.4
Wallace	5,567	3.2
Udall	4,688	2.7
Jackson	2,642	1.5
Harris	811	.5
Bayh	407	.2
Shriver	384	.2
Others	1,467	.9

May 11 West Virginia

Ford	88,386	56.8
Reagan	67,306	43.2

Byrd	331,639	89.0
Wallace	40,938	11.0

Republican

	Votes	%
May 18 Maryland		
Ford	96,291	58.0
Reagan	69,680	42.0
May 18 Michigan		
Ford	690,180	64.9
Reagan	364,052	34.3
Unpledged delegates	8,473[2]	.8
Others	109[1]	—
May 25 Arkansas		
Reagan	20,628	63.4
Ford	11,430	35.1
Others	483[2]	1.5

Democratic

	Votes	%
Edmund Brown, Jr. (Cal.)	286,672	48.4
Carter	219,404	37.1
Udall	32,790	5.5
Wallace	24,176	4.1
Jackson	13,956	2.4
McCormack	7,907	1.3
Harris	6,841	1.2
Carter	307,559	43.4
Udall	305,134	43.1
Wallace	49,204	6.9
Unpledged delegates	15,853	2.2
Jackson	10,332	1.5
McCormack	7,623	1.1
Shriver	5,738	.8
Harris	4,081	.6
Others	3,142	.4
Carter	314,306	62.6
Wallace	83,005	16.5
Udall	37,783	7.5
Jackson	9,554	1.9
Others[2]	57,152	11.4

May 25 Idaho

Reagan	66,743	74.3	Church	58,570	78.7
Ford	22,323	24.9	Carter	8,818	11.9
Others	727[2]	.8	Humphrey	1,700	2.3
			Brown[1]	1,453	2.0
			Wallace	1,115	1.5
			Udall	981	1.3
			Jackson	485	.7
			Harris	319	.4
			Others[2]	964	1.3

May 25 Kentucky

Ford	67,976	50.9	Carter	181,690	59.4
Reagan	62,683	46.9	Wallace	51,540	16.8
Unpledged delegates	1,781	1.3	Udall	33,262	10.9
Others	1,088	.8	McCormack	17,061	5.2
			Unpledged delegates	11,962	3.9
			Jackson	8,186	2.7
			Others	2,305	.8

May 25 Nevada

Reagan	31,637	66.2	Brown	39,671	52.8
Ford	13,737	28.8	Carter	17,567	23.3
None of the names shown	2,365[3]	5.0	Church	6,778	9.0
			Wallace	2,490	3.3
			Udall	2,237	3.0
			Jackson	1,896	2.5
			None of the names shown	4,603	6.1

May 25 Oregon

Ford	150,181	50.3	Church	145,394	33.6
Reagan	136,691	45.8	Carter	115,310	26.7
Others	11,663[1]	3.9	Brown[1]	106,812	24.7
			Humphrey	22,488	5.2
			Udall	11,747	2.7

Republican

	Votes	%

Democratic

	Votes	%
Kennedy	10,983	2.5
Wallace	5,797	1.3
Jackson	5,298	1.2
McCormack	3,753	.9
Harris	1,344	.3
Bayh	743	.2
Others[1]	2,963	.7

May 25 Tennessee

	Votes	%		Votes	%
Ford	120,685	49.8	Carter	259,243	77.6
Reagan	118,997	49.1	Wallace	36,495	10.9
Unpledged delegates	2,756	1.1	Udall	12,420	3.7
Others	97[1]	1.1	Church	8,026	2.4
			Unpledged delegates	6,148	1.8
			Jackson	5,672	1.7
			McCormack	1,782	.6
			Harris	1,628	.5
			Brown[1]	1,556	.5
			Shapp	507	.2
			Humphrey[1]	109	—
			Others[1]	492	.1

June 1 Montana

	Votes	%		Votes	%
Reagan	56,683	63.1	Church	63,448	59.4
Ford	31,100	34.6	Carter	26,329	24.6
Others	1,996[2]	2.2	Udall	6,708	6.3
			Wallace	3,680	3.4
			Jackson	2,856	2.7
			Others[2]	3,820	3.6

June 1 Rhode Island

Ford	9,365	65.3	Unpledged delegates	19,035	31.5
Reagan	4,480	31.2	Carter	18,237	30.2
Others	507[2]	3.5	Church	16,423	27.2
			Udall	2,543	4.2
			McCormack	2,468	4.1
			Jackson	756	1.3
			Wallace	507	.6
			Bayh	247	.4
			Shapp	132	.2

June 1 South Dakota

Reagan	43,068	51.2	Carter	24,186	41.2
Ford	36,976	44.0	Udall	19,510	33.3
Others	4,033[2]	4.8	McCormack	4,561	7.8
			Wallace	1,412	2.4
			Harris	573	1.0
			Jackson	558	1.0
			Others	7,871	13.4

June 7 California

Reagan	1,604,836	65.5	Brown	2,013,210	59.0
Ford	845,655	34.5	Carter	697,092	20.4
			Church	250,581	7.3
			Udall	171,501	5.0
			Wallace	102,292	3.0
			Jackson	38,634	1.1
			McCormack	29,242	.9
			Harris	16,920	.5
			Bayh	11,419	.3
			Others[2]	78,595	2.3

TABLE A.17 (continued)

Republican

	Votes	%
June 8 New Jersey		
Ford	242,122	100.0
June 8 Ohio		
Ford	516,111	55.2
Reagan	419,646	44.8
TOTALS		
Ford	5,529,968	53.3
Reagan	4,758,318	45.9
Others	74,298	.7
Daly	7,582	.1
	10,374,167	

Democratic

	Votes	%
June 8 New Jersey		
Carter	210,655	58.4
Church	49,034	13.6
Jackson	31,820	8.8
Wallace	31,183	8.6
McCormack	21,774	6.0
Others	16,373	4.5
June 8 Ohio		
Carter	593,130	52.3
Udall	240,342	21.2
Church	157,884	13.9
Wallace	63,953	5.6
Jackson	35,404	3.1
Others	43,661	3.9
TOTALS		
Carter	6,235,592	38.9
Brown	2,449,374	15.3
Wallace	1,995,387	12.4
Udall	1,611,754	10.0
Jackson	1,134,365	7.1
Church	830,818	5.3

TOTAL (continued)

Byrd	340,309	2.1
Shriver	304,399	1.9
McCormack	238,027	1.5
Harris	234,568	1.5
Shapp	88,254	.5
Bayh	86,438	.5
Humphrey	61,992	.4
Kennedy	19,805	.1
Bentsen	4,046	—
Others	410,021	2.5
	16,045,149	

Note: Delegate selection primaries were held in Alabama, New York, and Texas. Since no presidential preference primary was held in these states, figures are not recorded here.

1. Write-in.
2. No Preference/Uncommitted
3. Scattered.
4. 8,873 votes were declared invalid in District of Columbia Democratic presidential preference primary by D.C. Board of Elections.
5. Ford unopposed; no primary held.

Appendix B:
Presidential Primary Campaign Finance Data, 1976

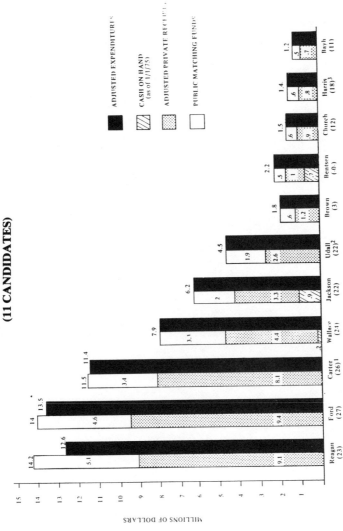

FIGURE B.1

ADJUSTED PRIMARY RECEIPTS, CASH ON HAND AND EXPENDITURES: CANDIDATES EXCEEDING $1M ADJUSTED RECEIPTS 1976 PRESIDENTIAL CAMPAIGN[1]

(11 CANDIDATES)

ADJUSTED EXPENDITURES

CASH ON HAND (as of 1/1/75)

ADJUSTED PRIVATE RECEIPTS

PUBLIC MATCHING FUNDS

Source: FEC Disclosure Series, No. 7: *1976 Presidential Campaign Receipts and Expenditures,* Washington, D.C.: Federal Election Commission, May 1977, p. 11.

Note: Figures in parentheses indicate number of primary ballots on which candidate's name appeared. These figures do not include Alabama, New York or Texas where there was no preference vote.

1. Cash on hand as of 1/1/75 was $16,377.
2. Cash on hand as of 1/1/75 was $8,472.
3. Cash on hand as of 1/1/75 was $2,230.

FIGURE B.2

LEVELS OF INDIVIDUAL PRIMARY CONTRIBUTIONS:
CANDIDATES EXCEEDING $1M ADJUSTED RECEIPTS 1976 PRESIDENTIAL CAMPAIGN
(11 CANDIDATES)

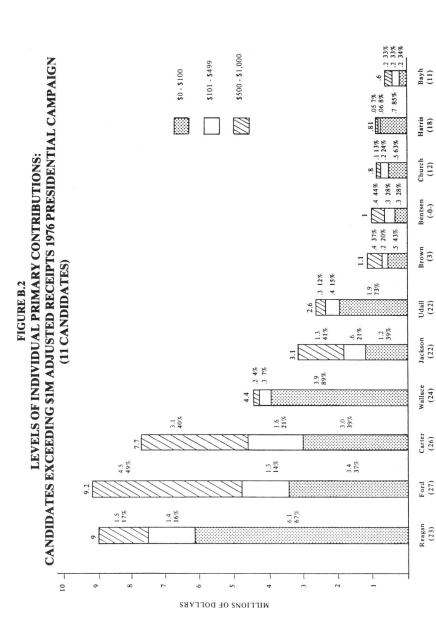

Source: FEC Disclosure Series, No. 7: *1976 Presidential Campaign Receipts and Expenditures,* Washington, D.C.: Federal Election Commission, May 1977, p. 12.

Note: Figures in parentheses indicate number of primary ballots on which candidate's name appeared. These figures do not include Alabama, New York or Texas where there was no preference vote.

TABLE B.1
PRIMARY RECEIPTS: DEMOCRATIC CANDIDATES 1976 PRESIDENTIAL CAMPAIGN
(13 CANDIDATES)

CANDIDATE	Cash on Hand 1/1/75	Individual Contributions (Number of Contributions)			Candidate Contributions	U.S. Treasury Funds	Political Committee Contributions		Outstanding Loans (Gross)	Interest, Other Income	Receipts Reported	Receipts Adjusted
		$0 - $100	$101-$499	$500-$1000			Party	Non-Party				
BAYH	$ -0-	$260,033	$256,440 (1,082)	$203,166 (289)	$ -0-	$469,200	$1,350	$50,572	$ -0- (5,096)	$750	$1,265,041	$1,232,630
BENTSEN	652,952	269,226	263,712 (1,108)	414,541 (514)	44,000[1]	511,023	65	18,259	75,500[2] (75,500)	9,521	1,676,807	1,604,846
BROWN	-0-	500,929	230,380 (1,038)	427,640 (547)	-0-	580,629	100	50,202	-0- (375,000)	-0-	2,193,321	1,783,683
CARTER	16,377	3,071,878	1,683,795 (7,370)	3,115,395 (4,073)	31,200[3]	3,465,585	10,311	300,740	2,290 (1,714,130)	-0-	14,389,505	11,560,146
CHURCH	-0-	563,821	218,073 (945)	118,089 (181)	-0-	622,747	3,242	1,000	2,399 (136,245)	-0-	1,709,634	1,505,876
HARRIS[4]	2,230	691,122	67,350 (316)	57,006 (76)	1,250	633,099[5]	-0-	6,000	-0-[6] (89,061)	-0-	1,767,841	1,472,657
JACKSON	938,982	1,232,692	656,508 (2,913)	1,312,073 (1,717)	-0-	1,980,555	-0-	107,413	-0- (42,700)	62,223	5,611,472	5,341,954
McCORMACK	116	224,486	50,263 (229)	5,421 (7)	-0-	244,125	-0-	-0-	-0-[7] (3,500)	1,285	535,137	525,580
SANFORD	11,951	79,653	160,393 (387)	77,478 (100)	-0-	246,388[12]	100	3,310	3,950[8] (13,950)	-0-	591,740	571,105
SHAPP	-0-	108,682	155,252 (649)	103,495 (152)	141,000	299,066[12]	1,800	2,225	98,961[8] (98,961)	-0-	979,368	894,232
SHRIVER[4]	-0-	174,785	115,127 (496)	114,045 (141)	58,200[9]	285,069[5]	1,120	3,625	191,975[10] (207,000)	-0-	850,549	824,432
UDALL	8,475	1,902,684	399,449 (1,871)	313,888 (425)	-0-	1,898,687	1,939	45,993	18,114[11] (218,045)	-0-	5,838,941	4,567,508
WALLACE	198,364	3,971,396	293,352 (1,367)	189,240 (278)	-0-	3,291,308	3,998	-0-	-0- (35,000)	-0-	8,006,264	7,727,715
TOTAL	$1,829,447	$13,051,387	$4,550,094 (19,771)	$6,451,477 (8,500)	$275,650	$14,527,484	$24,025	$589,339	$393,189 (3,014,188)	$73,780	$45,415,620	$39,612,365

Source: FEC Disclosure Series, No. 7: *1976 Presidential Campaign Receipts and Expenditures*, Washington, D.C.: Federal Election Commission, May 1977, p. 15.

1. Total includes $33,000 in contributions in excess of $1,000 from identifiable members of the candidate's immediate family.

2. Total loan is from the candidate.

3. Total represents $26,000 in contributions from the candidate's wife and $5,200 in-kind contributions from the candidate.

4. Accounting discrepancies may make final figures subject to amendment.

5. Figure represents amount certified by Commission.

6. Outstanding loans cannot be verified due to accounting discrepancies.

7. Gross total includes $9,200 loan from candidate.

8. Total loan is from the candidate.

9. Total includes $24,000 contribution from candidate's wife, and a $9,300 refund.

10. Total includes a $182,000 loan from the candidate, which is still outstanding.

11. Gross total includes $70,000 worth of loans from the candidate, $10,000 of which is still outstanding.

12. These figures do not reflect repayments by Sanford and Shapp.

TABLE B.2
PRIMARY EXPENDITURES: DEMOCRATIC CANDIDATES 1976 PRESIDENTIAL CAMPAIGN
(13 CANDIDATES)

Name of Candidate	Expenditures as Reported	Expenditures Adjusted	Cash on Hand 12/31/76	Those in Deficit	Those in Surplus
BAYH	$1,198,406	$1,169,030	$66,643	−$126,597	
BENTSEN	2,318,802	2,249,831	10,956	−64,544	
BROWN	2,156,562	1,746,924	36,758	−143,316	+58,194
CARTER	14,367,094	11,387,734	37,778	−25,289	
CHURCH	1,704,105	1,500,346	5,529	−32,639	
HARRIS[1]	1,751,946	1,406,741	4,259		+67,404
JACKSON	6,483,049	6,213,662	67,404	−2,897	
McCORMACK	533,390	523,833	- 0 -		
SANFORD	604,025	583,389	- 0 -	−18,374	
SHAPP	977,218	829,882	2,149	−247,475[2]	
SHRIVER[1]	678,754	640,137	3,948	−31,479[3]	
UDALL	5,850,820	4,531,888	13,204	−60,841	
WALLACE	8,177,245	7,898,695	27,383		
TOTALS	$46,801,416	$40,682,092	$276,011	−$753,451	+$125,598

Source: FEC Disclosure Series, No. 7: *1976 Presidential Campaign Receipts and Expenditures*, Washington, D.C.: Federal Election Commission, May 1977, p. 16.

1. Committee's files are incomplete. Amendments have been requested.
2. Figure is as of 6/30/76, and does not appear on Year-End 1976 Report.
3. Some authorized committees, while continuing to file separate reports, transferred debts to the candidate's principal campaign committee. Therefore, the total deficit reported may be an inflated figure.

TABLE B.3
PRIMARY RECEIPTS AND EXPENDITURES: REPUBLICAN CANDIDATES
1976 PRESIDENTIAL CAMPAIGN
(2 CANDIDATES)

RECEIPTS

Candidate	Cash on Hand 1/1/75	Individual Contributions $0-$100 (Number of Contributions)	$101-$499	$500-$1000	Candidate	U.S. Treasury Funds	Political Committee Contributions Party	Non-Party	Outstanding Loans (Gross)	Interest, Other Income	Receipts as Reported	Receipts Adjusted
FORD	$ - 0 -	$3,442,800	$1,319,705 (5,738)	$4,544,195 (5,754)	$ - 0 -	$4,657,007	$1,599	$153,215	$ - 0 -	$9,541	$14,654,943	$14,031,054
REAGAN	- 0 -	6,161,338	1,437,911 (6,252)	1,590,015 (2,155)	- 0 -	5,088,910	3,951	27,982	1,505 (3,347,226)	24,388	18,809,744	$14,224,205
TOTAL	$ - 0 -	$9,604,138	$2,757,616 (11,990)	$6,134,210 (7,909)	$ - 0 -	$9,745,917	$5,550	$181,197	$1,505 (3,347,226)	$33,929	$33,464,687	$28,255,259

EXPENDITURES

Candidate	Expenditures as Reported	Expenditures Adjusted[1]	Cash on Hand (12/31/76)	Those in Deficit	Those in Surplus
FORD	$14,349,497	$13,575,428	$305,447		+$305,447
REAGAN	17,198,960	12,610,920	1,610,784		+1,674,997
TOTAL	$31,548,457	$26,186,348	$1,916,231		+$1,980,444

[1]Includes fundraising, legal, and accounting fees which are exempt from spending limitations.

Source: FEC Disclosure Series, No. 7: *1976 Presidential Campaign Receipts and Expenditures*, Washington, D.C.: Federal Election Commission, May 1977, p. 17.

1. Includes fundraising, legal, and accounting fees which are exempt from spending limitations.

365

TABLE B.4
STATE BY STATE ALLOCATION OF PRIMARY EXPENDITURES: 1976 PRESIDENTIAL CAMPAIGNS
(15 CANDIDATES)

State Limitation	AL $425,752	AK $218,200	AZ $258,678	AR $252,937	CA $2,590,470	CO $312,338	CT $379,144	DE $218,200	DC $218,200	FL $1,050,851	GA $575,001	HI $218,200
BAYH	1	0	0	1	1,612	14	212	0	0	7	2	0
BENTSEN	356	0	100	12,286	114,738	3,167	1,142	0	0	11,517	5,497	1,621
BROWN	0	0	0	0	668,204	6,252	0	0	4,989	0	0	0
CARTER	58,648	897	8,349	42,057	654,106	26,887	76,275	7,943	135,165	567,858	116,817	721
CHURCH	0	0	3,323	0	109,234	74,766	2,561	0	0	0	0	0
HARRIS	0	0	0	0	55,250	1,914	6,664	105	131	34	0	0
JACKSON	0	757	1,200	2,500	36,731	1,903	39,331	0	0	556,708	0	0
McCORMACK	0	0	5,850	0	33,293	2,296	9,696	272	0	10,837	0	0
SANFORD	0	0	204	0	3,622	0	0	0	0	0	0	0
SHAPP	3,173	0	0	4,499	12,324	5,055	8,113	5,568	11,893	223,471	7,417	0
SHRIVER	0	579	0	0	1,500	354	2,360	0	3,000	2,879	0	0
UDALL	0	500	49,452	3,851	49,569	2,290	31,661	0	1,788	100	1,441	0
WALLACE	297,279	0	105,314	114,353	197,867	112,139	96,770	97,709	0	744,709	158,892	0
FORD	50,210	25,834	19,869	37,810	911,874	55,190	28,022	5,631	93,747	843,998	90,387	15,612
REAGAN	99,927	1,103	45,010	53,854	1,065,327	74,614	22,174	2,313	3,326	790,979	125,107	2,939
TOTAL	$509,594	$29,670	$238,671	$271,211	$3,915,251	$366,841	$324,981	$119,541	$254,039	$3,753,097	$505,560	$20,893

TABLE B.4 (continued)

State Limitation	ID $218,200	IL $1,336,082	IN $628,591	IA $345,105	KS $277,900	KY $404,281	LA $432,036	ME $218,200	MD $490,863	MA $715,172	MI $1,072,671	MN $465,028
BAYH	0	2,700	15,988	62,597	512	105	251	3,845	340	201,911	60	926
BENTSEN	0	4,637	468	373	4,137	4,064	3,088	0	2,347	11,082	6,744	1,523
BROWN	0	0	0	0	0	0	0	0	266,647	0	0	0
CARTER	2,196	127,156	75,767	87,257	13,491	79,564	36,448	31,677	211,747	157,824	169,160	5,778
CHURCH	36,748	0	0	2,251	0	0	0	0	0	0	0	0
HARRIS	0	7,228	0	48,556	0	51	445	264	6,846	158,300	4,457	10,059
JACKSON	0	2,033	7,507	13,896	3,461	540	0	0	9,838	659,343	11,912	0
McCORMACK	0	21,799	15,257	390	683	14,074	358	796	21,857	58,302	24	9,415
SANFORD	0	0	0	0	0	0	0	0	0	8,010	0	0
SHAPP	0	7,943	7	643	0	830	182	4,301	5,780	158,913	5,025	2,884
SHRIVER	0	33,788	1,000	44,592	0	2,000	1,000	1,000	8,799	199,976	1,250	250
UDALL	0	2,382	133	76,116	627	22,767	0	2,873	27,368	452,637	137,815	33
WALLACE	103,794	447,749	153,149	104,518	100,368	121,126	120,350	96,163	125,127	441,817	137,225	125,511
FORD	20,426	795,384	236,339	49,955	35,614	77,171	4,660	13,728	62,126	163,523	222,255	32,571
REAGAN	34,688	571,431	237,387	62,140	14,615	110,306	20,684	8,493	69,494	149,895	155,946	44,803
TOTAL	$197,852	$2,024,230	$743,002	$553,284	$173,508	$432,598	$187,466	$163,140	$818,316	$2,821,533	$851,873	$233,753

TABLE B.4 (continued)

State Limitation	MS $265,157	MO $580,063	MT $218,200	NE $218,200	NV $218,200	NH $218,200	NJ $890,605	NM $218,200	NY $2,231,051	NC $652,156	ND $218,200	OH $1,284,238
BAYH	265	255	0	254	7	138,630	0	0	252,024	0	0	3,588
BENTSEN	68,631	30,332	112	6,337	78	148	5,764	1,707	69,849	4,358	0	12,892
BROWN	0	0	0	0	29,279	0	20,091	0	114,014	0	0	0
CARTER	109,353	45,789	881	72,188	45,314	208,821	431,384	23,692	462,228	127,477	4,751	533,843
CHURCH	0	0	35,284	77,029	13,212	0	375	0	0	0	0	80,939
HARRIS	3,130	1,464	0	2,175	0	104,268	6,209	3,895	43,883	1,002	0	1,671
JACKSON	0	27,809	0	0	5,836	44,728	0	0	892,857	42,078	0	24,314
McCORMACK	0	0	0	10,280	0	6,301	13,123	0	17,411	0	443	18,750
SANFORD	0	0	0	0	0	11,680	0	0	157	0	0	0
SHAPP	0	3,643	0	726	6,435	937	7,895	0	32,325	4,185	2,216	4,484
SHRIVER	31,064	500	500	576	0	80,467	0	0	5,604	0	0	1,000
UDALL	0	4,386	0	313	0	209,667	83,003	8,300	174,265	389	0	256,828
WALLACE	152,588	127,550	102,943	103,169	97,576	95,854	115,433	102,490	255,626	358,005	96,222	142,229
FORD	16,201	65,840	24,639	106,542	56,311	198,679	33,400	27,816	31,601	321,211	6,253	219,676
REAGAN	17,441	84,051	13,442	91,493	63,371	219,855	38,466	15,451	85,436	560,341	4,987	284,673
TOTAL	$398,673	$391,619	$177,801	$471,082	$317,419	$1,320,035	$755,143	$183,351	$2,437,280	$1,419,046	$114,872	$1,584,887

TABLE B.4 (continued)

State Limitation	OK $330,966	OR $280,343	PA $1,459,845	RI $218,200	SC $327,125	SD $218,200	TN $505,351	TX $1,435,756	UT $218,200	VT $218,200	VA $598,566	WA $429,418
BAYH	308	377	5,653	3	50	0	18	9	0	0	53	0
BENTSEN	153,870	0	65,070	406	9,301	974	13,492	132,733	0	0	38,418	0
BROWN	0	170,332	0	65,311	0	0	0	0	742	0	0	0
CARTER	51,561	96,949	472,117	82,944	43,128	36,615	88,349	199,390	9,731	26,847	34,551	8,154
CHURCH	0	124,542	113	42,602	146	0	0	0	7,312	0	0	0
HARRIS	6,503	3,856	25,300	5,493	174	0	107	6,591	0	787	390	6,925
JACKSON	2,497	4,178	167,150	5,080	0	0	365	0	0	0	1,179	44,095
McCORMACK	68	4,800	17,733	8,152	0	7,937	0	9,625	1,539	6,285	63	0
SANFORD	0	0	0	0	0	0	0	1,673	0	0	0	0
SHAPP	0	0	366,723	1,086	1,452	0	10	4,553	0	3	4,956	0
SHRIVER	0	0	2,952	1,000	0	0	308	5,408	0	38,509	1,407	0
UDALL	0	12,737	217,368	250	117	33,975	254	178	0	100	540	1,384
WALLACE	126,833	104,751	134,677	96,669	200,764	100,552	126,451	179,088	98,861	95,711	131,330	120,999
FORD	23,641	162,952	34,885	23,242	17,392	19,153	87,306	1,048,205	15,741	2,652	13,246	20,554
REAGAN	32,366	79,407	68,712	16,838	34,881	16,994	144,612	470,927	23,262	5,019	36,180	63,053
TOTAL	$397,647	$764,881	$1,578,453	$349,076	$307,405	$216,200	$461,272	$2,058,380	$157,188	$175,913	$262,313	$265,164

TABLE B.4 (continued)

State Limitation	WV $219,073	WI $551,071	WY $218,200	PR $--	GUAM $--	VI $--	TOTAL
BAYH	0	0	0	0	0	0	$692,578
BENTSEN	71	1,696	1,735	33	0	0	$806,894
BROWN	0	0	0	0	0	0	$1,345,861
CARTER	442	197,651	30	11,525	0	0	$6,119,493
CHURCH	0	0	0	0	0	0	$610,437
HARRIS	0	13,200	0	0	0	0	$537,327
JACKSON	0	50,509	220	0	0	0	$2,660,555
McCORMACK	0	13,227	0	0	0	0	$340,936
SANFORD	0	0	0	0	0	0	$25,346
SHAPP	0	527	185	0	0	0	$910,362
SHRIVER	1,000	3,000	0	0	0	0	$477,622
UDALL	0	501,665	0	0	0	0	$2,369,122
WALLACE	113,463	199,180	98,008	0	0	0	$7,678,951
FORD	22,909	381,108	3,116	0	183	119	$6,876,509
REAGAN	43,266	148,664	5,653	8,823	255	286	$6,444,760
TOTAL	$181,151	$1,510,427	$108,947	$20,381	$438	$405	$37,896,753

Source: FEC Disclosure Series, No. 7: 1976 Presidential Campaign Receipts and Expenditures, Washington, D.C.: Federal Election Commission, May 1977, p. 19.

Appendix C: Presidential Primaries, 1980

TABLE C.1
1980 PRESIDENTIAL PRIMARIES BY STATE

| State | Date | Convention Delegate Vote | |
		Democratic	Republican
Alabama	March 11	45	27
Arkansas	May 27	33[a]	—
California	June 3	306	168
Connecticut	March 25	54	35
District of Columbia	May 6	19	14
Florida	March 11	100	51
Georgia	March 11	63	36
Idaho	May 27	17	21
Illinois	March 18	179	102
Indiana	May 6	80	54
Kansas	April 1	37	32
Kentucky	May 27	50	27
Louisiana	April 5	51	30
Maryland	May 13	59	30
Massachusetts	March 4	111	42
Michigan	May 20	141	82
Montana	June 3	19	20
Nebraska	May 13	24	25
Nevada	May 27	12	17
New Hampshire	February 26	19	22
New Jersey	June 3	113	66
New Mexico	June 3	20	22
New York	March 25	282	123
North Carolina	May 6	69	40
Ohio	June 3	161	77
Oregon	May 20	39	29
Pennsylvania	April 22	185	83
Puerto Rico	March 16	41	14
Rhode Island	June 3	23	13
South Carolina	March 8	—	25[b]
South Dakota	June 3	19	22
Tennessee	May 6	55	32
Texas	May 3[c]	152	80
Vermont	March 4	12	19
West Virginia	June 3	35	18
Wisconsin	April 1	75	34
		2,700	1,532
		(1,662 delegate votes needed to nominate)	(997 delegate votes needed to nominate)

a. Arkansas primary is for Democrats only.

b. The Republican party of South Carolina will hold a party-sponsored presidential preference primary on March 8, 1980. The South Carolina Democratic party will continue to use the caucus-convention system.

c. Texas primary may be held only by Republicans.

TABLE C.2
1980 PRESIDENTIAL PRIMARY DATES

Date	State
February 26	New Hampshire
March 4	Massachusetts
	Vermont
March 8	South Carolina[a]
March 11	Alabama
	Florida
	Georgia
March 16	Puerto Rico
March 18	Illinois
March 25	Connecticut
	New York
April 1	Kansas
	Wisconsin
April 5	Louisiana
April 22	Pennsylvania
May 3	Texas[b]
May 6	District of Columbia
	Indiana
	North Carolina
	Tennessee
May 13	Maryland
	Nebraska
May 20	Michigan
	Oregon
May 27	Arkansas[c]
	Idaho
	Kentucky
	Nevada
June 3	California
	Montana
	New Jersey
	New Mexico
	Ohio
	Rhode Island
	South Dakota
	West Virginia

a. The Republican party of South Carolina will hold a party-sponsored presidential preference primary; the South Carolina Democratic party will continue to use the caucus-convention system.

b. Texas primary may be held only by Republicans.

c. Arkansas primary is for Democrats only.

Selected Bibliography

Alexander, Herbert E. *Financing the 1972 Election*. Lexington, Mass.: D. C. Heath, 1976.

_____. *Financing the 1976 Election*. Washington, D.C.: Congressional Quarterly Press, 1979.

_____. *Money in Politics*. Washington, D.C.: Public Affairs Press, 1972.

Bagby, Wesley M. *The Road to Normalcy: The Presidential Campaign and Election of 1920*. Baltimore: The Johns Hopkins University Press, 1962.

Bain, Richard C., and Parris, Judith H. *Convention Decisions and Voting Records*. 2nd ed. Washington, D. C.: Brookings Institution, 1973.

Barber, James David, ed. *Choosing the President*. Englewood Cliffs, N.J.: Prentice-Hall, 1974.

_____, ed. *Race for the Presidency*. Englewood Cliffs, N.J.: Prentice-Hall, 1978.

Brams, Steven J. *The Presidential Election Game*. New Haven: Yale University Press, 1978.

Burns, James MacGregor. *Roosevelt: The Lion and the Fox*. New York: Harcourt, 1956.

Chester, Lewis; Hodgson, Godfrey; and Page, Bruce. *An American Melodrama: The Presidential Campaign of 1968*. New York: Viking Press, 1969.

Courtney, John C. *The Selection of National Party Leaders in Canada*. Hamden, Conn.: Shoe String Press, 1973.

Crotty, William J. *Political Reform and the American Experiment*. New York: Thomas Y. Crowell, 1977.

David, Paul T.; Goldman, Ralph M.; and Bain, Richard C. *The Politics of National Party Conventions*. Washington, D. C.: Brookings Institution, 1960.

David, Paul T.; Moos, Malcolm; and Goldman, Ralph M., eds. *Presidential Nominating Politics in 1952*. 5 vols. Baltimore: The Johns Hopkins University Press, 1954.

Dawson, Robert MacGregor. *The Government of Canada*. 5th ed. Revised by Norman Ward. Toronto: University of Toronto Press, 1970.

Dillon, Mary Earhart. *Wendell Willkie 1892-1944*. Philadelphia: Lippincott, 1952.

Farley, James A. *Behind the Ballots*. New York: Harcourt, Brace and World, 1938.

_____. *Jim Farley's Story: The Roosevelt Years*. New York: McGraw-Hill, 1948.

Fishel, Jeff, ed. *Parties and Elections in an Anti-Party Age.* Bloomington: Indiana University Press, 1978.

Hadley, Arthur T. *The Invisible Primary.* Englewood Cliffs, N.J.: Prentice-Hall, 1976.

Heard, Alexander. *The Costs of Democracy.* Chapel Hill: University of North Carolina Press, 1960.

Hofstadter, Richard. *The Age of Reform: From Bryan to F.D.R.* New York: Alfred A. Knopf, 1955.

Jacob, Herbert, and Vines, Kenneth N., eds. *Politics in the American States.* 3rd ed. Boston: Little, Brown, 1976.

Keech, William, and Matthews, Donald R. *The Party Choice.* Washington, D.C.: Brookings Institution, 1976.

Key, V. O., Jr. *American State Politics: An Introduction.* New York: Alfred A. Knopf, 1956.

King, Anthony, ed. *The New American Political System.* Washington, D.C.: American Enterprise Institute, 1978.

Kirkpatrick, Jeane J. *Dismantling the Parties: Reflections on Party Reform and Party Decomposition.* Washington, D.C.: American Enterprise Institute, 1978.

Link, Arthur S. *Wilson: The Road to the White House.* Princeton: Princeton University, 1947.

McKenzie, R. T. *British Political Parties.* 2nd ed. New York: Praeger, 1963.

Matthews, Donald R., ed. *Perspectives on Presidential Selection.* Washington, D.C.: Brookings Institution, 1973.

Michels, Robert. *Political Parties: A Sociological Study of the Oligarchical Tendencies of Modern Democracy.* Trans. by Eden and Cedar Paul. New York: Free Press, 1949.

Moore, Jonathan, and Fraser, Janet, eds. *Campaign for President.* Cambridge, Mass.: Ballinger, 1977.

Moos, Malcolm. *The Republicans.* New York: Random House, 1956.

Mowry, George E. *Theodore Roosevelt and the Progressive Movement.* Madison: University of Wisconsin Press, 1947.

Nie, Norman H.; Verba, Sidney; and Petrochik, John. *The Changing American Voter.* Cambridge: Harvard University Press, 1976.

Overacker, Louise. *The Presidential Primary.* New York: Macmillan, 1926.

Polsby, Nelson W., and Wildavsky, Aaron. *Presidential Elections.* 4th ed. New York: Charles Scribner's Sons, 1976.

Pomper, Gerald. *Nominating the President.* Evanston, Ill.: Northwestern University Press, 1963.

_____. *Nominating the President: The Politics of Convention Choice.* New York: W. W. Norton, 1966.

Ranney, Austin. *Curing the Mischiefs of Faction.* Berkeley: University of California Press, 1975.

_____. *The Federalization of Presidential Primaries.* Washington, D.C.: American Enterprise Institute, 1978.

_____. *Participation in American Presidential Nominations, 1976.* Washington, D.C.: American Enterprise Institute, 1977.

Roseboom, Eugene H. *A History of Presidential Election.* New York: Macmillan, 1957.

Rubin, Richard L. *Party Dynamics: The Democratic Coalition and the Politics of Change.* New York: Oxford University Press, 1976.

Schattschneider, E. E. *Party Government.* New York: Rinehart, 1942.

_____. *The Semi Sovereign People.* New York: Holt, Rinehart and Winston, 1960.

Schram, Martin. *Running for President: A Journal of the Carter Campaign.* New York: Pocket Books, 1976.

Shannon, Jasper. *Money and Politics.* New York: Random House, 1959.

Thomson, Charles A. H., and Shattuck, Frances M. *The 1956 Presidential Campaign.* Washington, D.C.: Brookings Institution, 1960.

White, Theodore H. *The Making of the President, 1960.* New York: Atheneum, 1961.

_____. *The Making of the President, 1964.* New York: Atheneum, 1965.

_____. *The Making of the President, 1968.* New York: Atheneum, 1969.

_____. *The Making of the President, 1972.* New York: Atheneum, 1973.

White, William Allen. *A Puritan in Babylon.* New York: Macmillan, 1938.

Witcover, Jules. *Marathon: The Pursuit of the Presidency, 1972-1976.* New York: Viking Press, 1977.

Index

About the Author

James W. Davis is Dean of the College of Arts and Sciences at Western Washington University in Bellingham, Washington. He is the author of *National Conventions: Nominations Under the Big Top* and co-author of *The President and Congress: Toward a New Power Balance.*